Ethics and economic affairs

There has been a remarkable growth of interest in the ethical dimension of economic affairs. Whilst the interest in business ethics has been long-standing, it has been given renewed emphasis by high-profile scandals in the world of business and finance. At the same time many economists – dissatisfied with the discipline's emphasis on self-interest and individualism and by the asocial nature of much economic theory – have sought to enlarge the scope of economics by looking at ethical questions.

In *Ethics and Economic Affairs* a group of interdisciplinary scholars provide contributions of international interest in this aspect of socio-economics and economic-psychology. The book is divided into four parts. The first looks at Business Ethics and Management. This includes a discussion of moral issues for multinational companies and goes on to look at the philosophical aspects of business ethics and moral development. The final chapter focuses on the wider implications of social responsibility and the firm. Part II enlivens the debate with empirical data. The four papers in this section represent differing approaches to descriptive ethics: case study, varying types of interview surveys and laboratory experiments. The third part examines the implications for economic theory and asks if the integration of ethics in the economy is possible or if they are fundamentally different systems. Finally, Part IV introduces perspectives from other disciplines, sets economics within its wider context and looks to the future. The editors have brought together a group of contributors from nine different countries and a broad range of disciplines. *Ethics and Economic Affairs* provides a comprehensive and valuable insight into a complex and increasingly important aspect of economics. As such it should be of interest to students and practising management alike.

Alan Lewis is Director of the Centre of Economic Psychology at the University of Bath. He has published a number of books on economic psychology. **Karl-Erik Wärneryd** is Professor Emeritus of Economic Psychology at the Stockholm School of Economics, Sweden. He has extensive research experience both in his native Sweden and abroad. He is the author of various publications on the subject.

Ethics and economic affairs

Edited by Alan Lewis
and Karl-Erik Wärneryd

 ROUTLEDGE

London and New York

First published 1994
by Routledge
11 New Fetter Lane, London EC4P 4EE

Simultaneously published in the USA and Canada
by Routledge
29 West 35th Street, New York, NY 10001

Typeset in Garamond by
J&L Composition Ltd, Filey, North Yorkshire
Printed and bound in Great Britain by
Biddles Ltd, Guildford and King's Lynn

British Library Cataloguing in Publication Data
A catalogue record for this book is available from the British Library

Library of Congress Cataloging in Publication Data
Ethics and economic affairs/edited by Alan Lewis and Karl-Erik Wärneryd.
    p. cm.
Includes bibliographical references and index.
ISBN 0–415–09396–1
1. Business ethics. 2. Social responsibility of business.
I. Lewis, Alan, 1952– . II. Wärneryd, Karl-Erik, 1927– .
HF5387.E826 1994   93–45693
174'.4–dc20   CIP

ISBN 0–415-09396–1

To Emma Strawford-Lewis wishing her well in her new career in business and to Karl and Jan-Erik Wärneryd wishing them continued success in developing economic theory and financial practice, respectively.

Contents

Figures, tables and exhibits

FIGURES

TABLES

EXHIBITS

About the contributors

Lars Bergkvist has a master's degree in business and economics and is a doctoral student in economic psychology at the Stockholm School of Economics. He has for the last two years been doing research on ethical issues in the Swedish world of finance in cooperation with the Center for Business and Policy Studies, Stockholm, a non-profit organization for conducting policy-oriented research on economic and social issues. His present work will result in a publication in which a group of leading persons in the field of finance will give their views on ethical issues.

Norman E. Bowie is the Elmer L. Andersen Chair of Corporate Responsibility and holds a joint appointment in the Departments of Strategic Management and Organization and Philosophy at the University of Minnesota, USA. He currently serves as chair of the Strategic Management and Organization Department. Professor Bowie is co-author of *Business Ethics* (second edition) and the co-editor of *Ethical Theory and Business* (fourth edition). He is the author or co-editor of nine other books on professional ethics and political philosophy ánd is a frequent contributor to scholarly journals and conferences. His research interests include the morality of markets, stakeholder management and international business ethics. A book on university–business partnership is in press. Professor Bowie teaches courses in corporate responsibility, theories of justice, and business, government and society. He is a frequent consultant to business schools, government agencies and corporations. He also serves on numerous editorial boards.

Monroe Burk is fully retired but continues to maintain his daily academic programme with the support of the University of Maryland (Baltimore County). Burk received his Bachelor of Social Science (BS) degree from the College of the City of New York (1938), his Masters of Business Administration (MBA) from Harvard (1940), and, after military service in the Second World War, his PhD in economics from the American University, where he also taught economics prior to and subsequent to obtaining his doctoral degree. His subsequent career as an economist combined public service and university teaching. His principal employment (1948–73) was with the US State Department, much of it abroad as a member of the Foreign Service, often as the economics theory specialist of a team. He, however, retained his university connection and taught as an adjunct professor when stationed in Washington, DC. Subsequent to retiring from the State Department, he continued as a consultant and as an adjunct professor at the University of Baltimore, Loyola (at Baltimore) and the University of Maryland. While the great bulk of his written output is in the form of government documents, he has also published one book and numerous technical articles. He has also served on many public commissions and has run for public office.

Richard H. Guerrette is principal consultant and director of the EquiPax Center for Human and Ethical Resources in Newport, Vermont. He has been a research fellow at Yale University Divinity School in Corporate Ethics and has lectured in social psychology at the University of Connecticut and in organization psychology at Vermont College of Norwich University. His research interests are in organization culture, corporate ethics and management systems. His works include two books on organization culture and human resource management in the church and numerous articles in theological and social science journals, including *Concilium* and the *Journal of Business Ethics*. He is currently conducting an applied research project at the EquiPax Gallery in Newport, Vermont on corporate value-system-building and the linkage of corporate ethics and corporate culture through corporate art.

Benedetto Gui is associate professor of economics at the University of Venice, Italy. His scientific work has mainly focused on active labour market policies and the economics of cooperative, participatory and non-profit organizations. His principal publications include: *I sussidi marginali all'occupazione* (Marginal Employment Subsidies) (1990) (Giuffrè, Milan, 1990), *The Nonprofit Sector in the Mixed Economy* (1993, co-edited with Avner Ben-Ner, forthcoming by Michigan University Press, Ann Arbor), and several articles in periodicals such as the *Journal of Comparative Economics, Advances in the Economic Analysis of Participatory and Labor-managed Firms* and *Annals of Public and Cooperative Economics*. His current research interests concern the viability of worker-managed firms and interpersonal relations as an economic good.

Claes Gustafsson is associate professor of business administration and head of the Department of Business Administration at Åbo Akademi University, Finland. His research has been aimed at questions of power and leadership, organization culture, business ethics and decision making. He has published two books: *Theories of Power* (in Swedish) and *Business, Morality and Action* (in Swedish), and co-edited one, *Accounting and Organized Action* (with Lars

Hassel). He is currently working on a study regarding the dynamics of human knowledge and conceptions of rationality.

Patrick J. Kaufmann is an associate professor of marketing at Georgia State University, Atlanta, Georgia. He is a lawyer and holds a PhD in marketing from Northwestern University. Professor Kaufmann's research focuses on franchising and public policy in marketing. He is on the editorial board of the *Journal of Retailing* and the *Journal of Marketing Channels.*

Alan Lewis is a reader in psychology and director of the Centre for Economic Psychology, School of Social Sciences, University of Bath, UK. His research interests have spanned such topics as economic socialization, 'lay' economic explanations, attitudes towards taxation and government spending and, more recently, 'ethics'/'social' investment behaviour. His principal publications are *The Psychology of Taxation* (1982) (St Martin's, New York) and with Adrian Furnham, *The Economic Mind* (1986) (Wheatsheaf, Sussex). He is currently working on *The New Economic Mind* (with Paul Webley and Adrian Furnham) to be published by Simon & Schuster, New York, in 1994.

Paul E. M. Ligthart graduated in 1988 as an experimental social and organizational psychologist and now works as a research fellow at the Interuniversity Center of Social Science Theory and Methodology (ICS), University of Groningen in the Netherlands. In his research, he is especially interested in considering both social and economic aspects of individual behaviour in the explanation of economic transactions. In his PhD thesis 'Solidarity effects on economic transactions: an experimental test of framing effects' he deals particularly with variations in gain maximization of transacting parties, the influence of relational costs as part of the overall transaction costs, and the selection of transacting parties.

Siegwart Lindenberg is professor in theoretical sociology at the University of Groningen, the Netherlands, and scientific director of the ICS. His research centres on theories of framing, contracting and institutions. His latest publications include: 'Homo-socio-oeconomicus: the emergence of a general model of man in the social sciences', *Journal of Institutional and Theoretical Economics*, 146, 727–748 (1990), 'An extended theory of institutions and contractual discipline', *Journal of Institutional and Theoretical Economics*, 148, 125–154 (1992) and 'Interdisciplinary perspectives on organizational studies' (1993, Pergamon Press: Oxford), edited with H. Schreuder.

Ralph E. Miner is associate professor of political science at Western Washington University, Bellingham, Washington, USA. His research interests include bureaucracy, organization behaviour, public policy and the socio-economic critique of public choice. He has published in *Public Choice, Policy*

Studies Journal and the *Public Finance Quarterly.* He is currently working on the role of formal organizations in individual preference formation.

Gwen Ortmeyer received her BS from the University of California at Berkeley and her PhD in management from Stanford University's Graduate School of Business. As an assistant professor at the Harvard Business School and, before that, Columbia's Graduate School of Business, she taught courses in introductory marketing, marketing strategy and market planning. She has also taught at Duke University's Fuqua School of Business, as an associate professor of business practice. Gwen has conducted management and training seminars in marketing, retailing and strategic business management for a number of companies, including American Cyanamid, Chase Securities Inc., Citibank, Northern Telecom, Nutrasweet, Ralph Lauren, Textron, Household International and Weyerhauser. Her consulting experience includes work with Ameritech, Avon, the US government, Management Analysis Center and Pacific Telephone. In her research, Gwen has focused on retailing issues including pricing strategy and channel partnerships. Her publications include 'Restoring credibility to retail pricing', with John Quelch and Walter Salmon in the *Sloan Management Review,* 'Fairness in consumer pricing', with Patrick Kaufmann and Craig Smith in the *Journal of Consumer Policy,* 'Brand experience as a moderator of the negative impact of promotions', with Joel Huber in *Marketing Letters,* and 'Individual differences in response to consumer promotions', with James Lattin and David Montgomery in the *International Journal of Research in Marketing.*

William Ossipow is an ordinary professor of political science at the University of Geneva, Switzerland. He has worked in the field of political ideologies and of political discourse analysis. He has published a book in French about the transformation of the political discourse of the Catholic Church. His present research interests are about ethics in political and social life, and about the institutional aspects of politics. He is also working on Swiss politics, particularly Swiss direct democracy.

Lynne M. H. Rosansky PhD is assistant professor of international business and business policy at Babson College, USA. She also teaches cross-cultural business and management to Japanese managers participating in the Intensive International Executive Program at the International University of Japan. Her research interests include global leadership, managing change and global forces of change. Her publications include cases, articles and simulations as well as two books: *What Managers Do* (with Natalie Taylor) and *Anthropology and Management Consulting: Forging a New Alliance* (with Maureen Givannini). Her work in progress is on forces of change in Japan.

N. Craig Smith is associate professor, Georgetown School of Business, Georgetown University, Washington DC. He is the author of *Morality and the Market: Consumer Pressure for Corporate Accountability* (1990), a co-author of

Ethics in Marketing (1993), the co-author of a book on research, and has contributed journal articles on a variety of marketing management and business ethics topics. He consults with firms on problems of good marketing practice, including marketing ethics.

Peter Söderbaum is associate professor (docent) in environmental economics at the Department of Economics, Swedish University of Agricultural Sciences, Uppsala. He sees institutional economics as a promising paradigm and argues that our views of economics, human beings as actors, decision making, progress in society and environmental policy have to be reconsidered in relation to environmental and other societal problems. His most recent book in Swedish is called *Ekologisk ekonomi* (1993). Internationally he contributes to journals such as *Ecological Economics* and the *Journal of Economic Issues.*

Robert Stallaerts is a researcher at the Centre for Ethics of UFSIA (University of Antwerp), Belgium. He is a member of a team working on a project 'Ethics and economics'. His main research interests include the interaction of economics and ethics in economic doctrines and the economics of self-management and participation. His principal contributions are on the economics and politics of former Yugoslavia, for example in *Economic Analysis and Workers' Management* (Beograd) and *Afscheid van Joegoslavië. Achtergronden van de crisis* (1992, Garant, Leuven). He is currently working on a *Historical Dictionary of Croatia* to be published by the Scarecrow Press, Methuen in 1994.

Philip J. Stone is a professor of psychology at Harvard where he teaches social psychology and participates in a joint doctoral programme in organizational behaviour with the Harvard Business School. His books, mostly co-authored or co-edited with graduate students and colleagues, include *Experiments in Induction* (Academic Press), *The General Inquirer: A Computer Approach to Content Analysis* (MIT Press), *The Analysis of Communication Content* (Wiley), *Computer Recognition of English Word Senses* (North-Holland), *The Use of Time* (Mouton) and *The SYMLOG Practitioner* (Praeger). In addition, he has published in the *Harvard Business Review* and trade journals on the application of environmental psychology to creating offices that support collaboration. He is currently co-editing a book on organizational psychology for Dartmouth Press International Library of Management series.

John F. Tomer is associate professor of economics and finance at Manhattan College, Riverdale, New York, USA. His research is on the socio-economic aspects of business behaviour including such topics as social responsibility, strategy and structure, rational decision making, organizational learning, worker participation and organizational capital. His articles have appeared in the *Journal of Economic Issues*, the *Journal of Post-Keynesian Economics*, the *Journal of Behavioral Economics*, the *Journal of Socio-Economics, Technovation* and the

International Review of Applied Economics as well as several edited books. His principal publication is *Organizational Capital* (1987) (Praeger). He is currently working on a book entitled *The Human Firm: A Socio-Economic Analysis of its Behavior and Potential.*

Karl-Erik Wärneryd is Professor Emeritus of economic psychology at the Stockholm School of Economics and is currently fellow at the Centre for Economic Research, Tilburg University, the Netherlands. He holds a PhD in psychology from the University of Chicago and an honorary doctor's degree in economics from the Helsinki Swedish School of Economics and Business Administration. His research interest has during the last decade focused on the psychology of saving, fiscal psychology and behavioural aspects of business ethics. He is co-editor of the *Handbook of Economic Psychology* (together with W. F. van Raaij and G. M. van Veldhoven).

Paul Webley obtained both his undergraduate and postgraduate degrees from the London School of Economics. Although originally an economics student, he switched after a year and a half to the study of social psychology and has been interested in the psychology of economic behaviour ever since. He is the joint author of three books in this area: *The Individual in the Economy, Tax Evasion: An Experimental Approach* and *Children's Saving.* He is currently a senior lecturer and head of the department of psychology, University of Exeter, UK. For the last two years most of his research has been concerned with personal finance, particularly debt, saving and investment.

Kristin Westlund holds a master's degree in business and economics from the Stockholm School of Economics. She earlier was a research assistant at the school before joining the Ministry of Foreign Affairs.

Josef Wieland studied economics and philosophy and is director of the Centre for Business and Economic Ethics at the University of Münster, Germany. His research interests have spanned such topics as history of economic thought, new institutional economics, organizational economics, business and economic ethics and empirical studies about forms and contents of institutionalizing moral communication in a business enterprise. His principal publications are *Die Entdeckung der Ökonomie* (The Discovery of Economics, 1989, Bern/Stuttgart: Haupt), *Sozialphilosophische Grundlagen Ökonomischen Handelns* (Social-Philosophical Foundations of Economical Action, 1990, Frankfurt: Suhrkamp), *Formen der Institutionalisierung von Moral in der Unternehmung* (Forms of Institutionalizing Morality in Business Enterprises, 1993, Bern/Stuttgart: Haupt) and *Wirtschaftsethik und Theorie der Gesellschaft* (Business Ethics and Theory of Society, 1993, Frankfurt: Suhrkamp).

The contents of the book

*Philip Stone's chapter refers to South Africa before the May 1994 election.

The book is organized in four parts, namely 'Business Ethics and Management'; 'Case, Questionnaire and Experimental Studies'; 'A New Economics?' and finally 'Interdisciplinary Perspectives'. Most of the papers first saw the light of day in earlier versions presented at the joint International Association of Researchers in Economic Psychology (IAREP) and the Society for the Advancement of Socio-economics (SASE) conference at the Stockholm School of Economics in June 1991.

PART I: BUSINESS ETHICS AND MANAGEMENT

The first part is of particular interest to students, researchers and teachers of business administration and management. The questions posed are also relevant to practising managers faced with ethical dilemmas and decisions. Philip Stone starts the ball rolling in 'Exit or Voice? Lessons from Companies in South Africa'.* Using Hirschman's tripartite litany Stone enquires what multinational companies should have done in South Africa. Should they have ceased trading in South Africa: 'exited?' Should they have 'voiced' their disapproval? Or continued their 'loyalty' to the company and hoped things would improve? Lynne Rosansky deals with similar issues in her contribution 'Moral and Ethical Dimensions of Managing a Multinational Business'. Should multinationals adapt themselves to the culture they are dealing with or impose their own? When is a bribe not a bribe? Gifts after all may be a cultural expectation. At the extremes it is a choice between moral relativism and moral imperialism. Richard Guerrette in his paper 'Management by Ethics: A New Paradigm and Model for Corporate Ethics' provides some specific advice for managers. How, Guerrette asks, can a 'corporate conscience' be brought about? Guerrette's answer relies heavily on social and developmental psychology, especially the insights of Lawrence Kohlberg. The next paper by Claes Gustafsson entitled 'Moralization as a Link between Idealism and Naturalism in the Ethical Discourse' adds a more philosophical flavour to the continuing study of business ethics and moral development. One of the most interesting questions is, are business managers less scrupulous than the rest of us or do they have multiple selves, an ability to find the most appropriate script for a given play? (Some more direct empirical evidence on the differences among business managers and other representatives of the world of finance (plus potential managers) can be found in the paper by Wärneryd, Bergkvist and Westlund in Part II). Part I is rounded off by the ambitious paper by John Tomer, 'Social Responsibility in the Human Firm: Towards a New Theory of the Firm's External Relationships'. Tomer not only considers the appropriate role companies should have in terms of their social responsibilities but also the wider implications for economic theory if it is accepted that firms are motivated by some kind of pragmatic mixture of self-interest and socially responsible behaviour.

PART II: CASE, QUESTIONNAIRE AND EXPERIMENTAL STUDIES

For those readers who may have had enough of talk, the papers in this section all attempt to generate some empirical data to fuel the debate. The four papers represent differing approaches to descriptive ethics: case study, varying types of interview surveys and laboratory experiments. The paper by Patrick Kaufmann, Gwen Ortmeyer and N. Craig Smith 'Fairness in Consumer Pricing', presents two case studies with legal and ethical implications. When is a department store sale not a sale? (The subject of the first case.) The second: what constitutes a fair price in the housing and real estate market? To what extent should the law legislate for fair play in the relationship between buyer and seller: *caveat emptor* or *caveat venditor*? Next comes Alan Lewis and Paul Webley, 'Social and Ethical Investing: Beliefs, Preferences and the Willingness to Sacrifice Financial Return'. A small questionnaire study and some experiments using information displayed on personal computer screens are employed to investigate what price people put on their moral values. When individual economic actors make investment decisions the decisions may be in two parts: the first is economic, how safe is my investment? What kind of interest can I expect?; while the second may be ethical, am I prepared to invest in companies which manufacture military weapons, in companies with poor pollution records and so forth? If the answer is 'no', what happens when the return on investment is less favourable as a consequence? There are people whose principles are strong enough to counter economic losses, but surely we would not count on those active in financial markets (and those training to join them) to be too bothered by moral scruples – but is this true? Karl-Erik Wärneryd, Lars Bergkvist and Kristin Westlund in 'Ethical Issues in the World of Finance: Two Empirical Studies' put this to the test. In a cross-sectional study of economic and moral socialization, questionnaires asking for judgments of actual unethical behaviours are used to compare the views of financial analysts, economic journalists and financial managers of the largest companies listed on the Stockholm Stock Exchange with undergraduates studying economics and business at the Stockholm School of Economics. The final paper by Paul Ligthart and Siegwart Lindenberg, 'Ethical Regulation of Economic Transactions: Solidarity Frame versus Gain-maximization Frame', reports on an experiment where 'sellers' are required to set prices as a function of their social role and the form of their relationship with potential buyers. Should you charge a stranger more than a friend?

PART III: A NEW ECONOMICS?

Tomer, in Part I, has already discussed the possibility of a socio-economics incorporating individuals with mixed motives: the contributions to Part III also display a willingness to develop a more imaginative economics incorporating ethical concerns which make this section most accessible to those with some knowledge of economic theory.

The collection kicks off with Peter Söderbaum's 'Ethics, Ideological Commitment and Social Change: Institutionalism as an Alternative to Neoclassical Theory'. Söderbaum speculates on whether orthodox economics, in the guise of neoclassical environmental economics, is really up to the task of dealing with contemporary problems and suggests that a more holistic economics would be more informative and successful. Benedetto Gui in 'Interpersonal Relations: A Disregarded Theme in the Debate on Ethics and Economics' enlarges on the theme raised earlier by Ligthart and Lindenberg. Gui proposes that economists should take interpersonal relations more seriously and outlines some of the paradoxical and ideologically unacceptable consequences of treating interactions between doctors and patients, between marriage partners, purely in a reductionist manner. Josef Wieland in 'Economy and Ethics in Functionally Differentiated Societies: History and Present Problems' partly redresses the balance by illustrating that the study of ethics needs some economics – just as the discussion of economics without recourse to moral concerns makes little sense it also follows that ethics without the deductive logic and methods of economic theory is utopian. Finally in a concise piece Robert Stallaerts's 'Social Ownership: A Comparison of the Property Rights, Social Choice and Economic Justice Approaches' waves the flag for a continued use of axiomatic assumptions and analytic rigour in an economics that *does* include ethics – the inclusion of ethical concerns *does not* mean that economics needs to be fashionably holistic.

PART IV: INTERDISCIPLINARY PERSPECTIVES

The last part of our anthology deals with the grandest themes of all, starting with William Ossipow's 'Niklas Luhmann's Sociology of the Economic

System: Some Moral Implications'. Ossipow's brief is broad: can the specialized position of economics, as separate from other disciplines, be maintained? Is this desirable? Is economics and the profession 'economist' an exclusive gentlemen's club with initiation ceremonies, rules to be obeyed before one can become a respected member? Following Ossipow is Monroe Burk, 'Ideology and Morality in Economics Theory'. Burk is not optimistic about the utilitarianism of economics and favours instead communitarianism allied with a deontological (Kantian) ethics – economics and politics are inseparable. Ralph Miner takes a similar line in 'Politics, Public Choice and Ethical Progress'. Self-interest assumptions should not drown 'public-spiritedness', the 'market spirit' should not dominate 'moral sentiments' Miner argues. In contrast to some of the other contributions the finale strikes a note of optimism about the future; Norman Bowie in his 'Economics and the Enlightenment: Then and Now' proposes that market economies develop in a way that seems to fulfil some of the utopian ideas of the Enlightenment: improved ethics, world peace and communication among peoples! The end of the world is not nigh, markets are liberating, markets encourage civilized and ethical behaviour.

Finally, an 'Endpiece' is presented by the editors, Alan Lewis and Karl-Erik Wärneryd, which draws together some of the main themes of the book and begs the question 'Whither now?'

The papers . . .

Preface

This very important and timely collection of essays speaks to the central issue of our times. As the recent events in the former Soviet Union underscore, attempts to have economic competition without strong moral, social and legal rules, leads to corruption, crime, and endangers the legitimacy and viability of the economic system itself. It further highlights how incomplete, to put it moderately, is any theory of economics that either does not encompass moral factors or treats them as a separate arena.

Essays in this book show that there is no dimension of economic activities that are not deeply affected by the moral dimension. Should we test drugs in other countries? Ship cigarettes? Exploit cheap labour? Child labour? Bribe government officials to land contracts? Exploit the environment? Burden future generations? These are all economic questions deeply affected by moral considerations – or their absence.

Most essays in this fine volume approach these questions the way scholars do. They apply concepts, provide evidence, contain learned discussion. There is less passion here than preachers may reveal but no less conviction, as carefully modulated this sometimes is.

The more people will engage in studying these matters, explore their ramifications, and dialogue about them with their students, policy makers and those directly affected, the more we shall be able to understand the ethical factors, and the complex ways they are intertwined with economic ones. The book takes us a long way down this road. The next step is, appropriate social action.

Professor Amitai Etzioni
The George Washington University

Acknowledgements

The editors acknowledge the permission of the publisher Kluwer to reprint the article by Kaufmann, Ortmeyer and Smith; Cambridge University Press and Harper and Row for the reproduction of tables in Chapter 4; Harper Collins for excerpts reproduced in Chapter 17. John Cullis, Adrian Winnett, David Collard and Helen Haste of the Bath University Centre for Economic Psychology have all made useful comments on the text.

The editors wish to thank Ms Birgitta Lorenius and Ms Malin Jacobsson for secretarial assistance at the Stockholm School of Economics, especially in the early part of the project.

Special thanks go to Jo Schol from Bath who prepared the manuscript with efficiency and good humour.

Chapter 1

The longstanding interest in business ethics

An introduction

Karl-Erik Wärneryd and Alan Lewis

Since the beginning of philosophy in ancient Greece, ethics has been a fundamental part, often subsumed under the concept of moral philosophy. Many philosophical debates have concerned ethical issues and opposing views have often been ventilated with apparently little agreement about whether some action is ethical or not.

> It appears to me that in Ethics, as in all other philosophical studies, the difficulties and disagreements, of which its history is full, are mainly due to a very simple cause: namely to the attempt to answer questions, without first discovering precisely what question it is which you desire to answer.
>
> (Moore, 1903/1960: VII)

Moore formulates two questions which in his view have occupied moral philosophers over the centuries: 'What kind of things ought to exist for their own sakes?' 'What kind of actions ought we to perform?' When there is agreement about the questions to ask, the answers will (according to Moore) be more convergent.

Ethics is not the exclusive concern of moral philosophers. Ethical issues have (for reasons which will become clear from the contents of this book) given rise to heated debates in the social and behavioural sciences. Defined simply, ethics deals with what is good and what is bad and more particularly with judgments of actions as good or bad. This simple definition does not exhaust what is meant by ethical issues and is not accepted by all who have dealings with ethics, but it will serve our purposes here: this book focuses on judgments of what are good and bad actions in economic affairs.

What is good or bad behaviour in business? Questions about the role of ethics in business are longstanding. The Roman orator Cicero (106–43 BC) used to tell stories from his own experience to stimulate ethical thinking from among his audience. Here is one of his cases which deals with the use of what is now called asymmetrical information.

Suppose that there is a food-shortage and famine at Rhodes, and the price of corn is extremely high. An honest man has brought Rhodes a large stock of corn from Alexandria. He is aware that a number of other traders are on their way from Alexandria – he has seen their ships making for Rhodes, with substantial cargoes of grain. Ought he to tell the Rhodians? Or is he to say nothing and sell his stock at the best price he can get? I am assuming that he is an enlightened, honest person. What I am imagining are the deliberations and self-searchings of a man who would not keep the Rhodians in ignorance if he thought it dishonest to do so, but who is not certain that it would be dishonest.'

(Cicero, pp. 37–39; quoted from the back cover of the *Journal of Political Economy*, 1988, 96, no. 4)

Cicero raised an ethical question that is still of pertinence and great interest. He did not stop with presenting the problem, he also provided a solution: 'But I must record my opinion about these cases, for I did not write them down merely to raise problems, but to solve them. I believe, then, that the corn-merchant ought not to have concealed the facts from the Rhodians.' Cicero (undated/1991, p. 121) further notes: 'For it is not concealment to be silent about anything, but when you want those in whose interest it would be to know something that you know to remain ignorant of it, so that you may profit.'

When the use of asymmetrical information is judged as unethical, the following case must be judged even more unethical.

Suppose that a good man is selling his house because of certain faults that he knows and that others do not know, say, that it is unsanitary but thought to be salubrious, or that it is not generally known that vermin can be found in all the bedrooms, or that it is structurally unsound and crumbling, but no one except the owner knows this. My question is this: if the seller does not tell the buyers these things, but sells the house at a higher price than that at which he thought he would sell it, will he not have acted unjustly or dishonestly?

(Cicero, undated/1991, p. 120)

Cicero added a third case where actual lying was involved. In this case a seller of some land provides fraudulent information and thus inveigles the buyer to buy. He asks a rhetorical question: 'Furthermore, if those who kept quiet are to be denounced, what are we to think of those who actually told lies as well?' He concludes:

Therefore all untruthfulness must be removed from our dealings. The seller will not employ an artificial bidder, nor the buyer someone to bid low against him. If one of the two has come to declare a price, he should not do so more than once.

(Cicero, undated/1991, p. 123)

These statements could have been taken from a discussion of recent ethical problems in the world of finance. The US Treasury Bond Market was a few years ago shaken by a scandal which was evidently caused by the neglect of rules similar to those pronounced by Cicero. Through unethical manipulations a single firm had gained almost a monopoly in some auctions of Treasury bonds, allowing it to set its own prices.

Cases similar to those presented by Cicero have been used in many normative discussions of ethics, i.e. discussions trying to answer the type of questions raised by Moore, about what ought to be. Recent research in behavioural economics has employed similar descriptions, albeit much shorter, to investigate the general public's ideas about fairness – one dimension of business ethics – in economic transactions. Here is an example:

> A hardware store has been selling snow shovels for $15. The morning after a large snowstorm, the store raises the price to $20. Please rate this action as: Completely fair, Fair, Acceptable, Unfair, Very Unfair.
>
> (Kahneman *et al.*, 1986, p. 729)

In a survey with residents in some Canadian metropolitan areas as respondents, 82 per cent rated this action as unfair. A recent replication with businessmen as respondents found similar, though less clear results (Gorman and Kehr, 1992).

There are many indicators of an upsurge in interest in ethical questions. Courses dealing with ethics are introduced in the business school curricula, professional associations adopt codes of conduct and there are new associations for stimulating debate and research on ethical issues among business representatives and business educators. An example of the latter is the recently formed European Business Ethics Network (EBEN) which has the explicit purpose of bringing together academicians and business executives who are concerned about ethical conduct. The *Journal of Business Ethics* was founded in 1981 and, more recently, *Business Ethics* appeared. *Economics and Philosophy*, which is less than a decade old, devotes part of its contents to ethics with an emphasis on the relations between economics and ethics.

There are two major reasons for the currently increased interest in ethics and economic affairs. One reason is the disclosure of unethical conduct in important branches of business and industry. Trusted brokers have made immense profits from using confidential, thus asymmetric information, to make investments in shares or to get rid of such investments. Some empire builders have based their success on the systematic use of fraudulent information. Many such cases have got publicity all over the world. The second reason is the discussion of the relationships between economics and ethics. Economics is accused of leaving out ethical considerations and focusing on pure technology at the expense of human values. Economic theory is, correctly or incorrectly, blamed for influencing business to focus on profit maximization in a narrow sense.

The fact that ethical issues have become a concern within the social and behavioural sciences has led to empirical research on ethical issues. It can now be said that there is *descriptive ethics* as well as the traditional *normative ethics*. While normative ethics is focused on what ought to be, descriptive ethics is aimed at finding out what people think in ethical matters, how they act and what influences ethical stances (cf. Fritsche and Becker, 1984). Case studies can serve the dual purposes of describing attitudes and behaviour and at the same time giving food for normative considerations when used in teaching courses in ethics. Survey research, working with samples of selected groups of professionals, can give insights into prevalent ethical norms among professionals. While this no doubt is a valuable enlargement of the field of business ethics, it nevertheless gives rise to new problems: what, for example, are the most appropriate research methods for studying these highly sensitive issues? (See, for example, Randall and Gibson, 1990, and Gustafsson's contribution to this book.) Debates about methods can hopefully lead to more sophisticated use of methods in future research.

THE UNETHICAL CONDUCT ISSUE

Deception in advertising is a well-known phenomenon and both voluntary and legislative measures have been introduced to ensure truth in advertising. Much attention has been given to the marketing of defective products, and manufacturers of such products have been accused of unethical conduct when they have marketed their products despite knowledge of deficiencies. In the 1960s, General Motors was accused by Ralph Nader of selling a car which was unsafe at any speed. In the 1970s, Ford launched the Pinto which had a fuel tank that could catch fire even after minor accidents. A recent analysis of the Pinto case by one of those involved in the early stages of the developments provides an interesting illustration (Gioia, 1992).

The Pinto was launched by Ford after an unusually short design and development period. Routine crash tests indicated that the position of the fuel tank was dangerous if the car was hit from behind. Pressure to keep the price competitively low and a tight time schedule led to a decision to go on rather than change, despite the fact that the cost of the least expensive alternative was only $11. Gioia, who was Coordinator of Recall at the time, describes how it came that he and others did not react to the early signs of hazard. He suggests that 'script schemas' guided the cognition and action at the time which precluded consideration of issues in ethical terms: the scripts did not include ethical dimensions.

When safety is involved, product recalls and free exchanges or repairs are today common, not only in the automobile industry, but also in many other industries. Partly this is a result of legislation, partly it is a sign that manufacturers want to avoid trouble with customers which can give bad publicity. It is a moot question to what extent this development is due to higher ethical standards in an absolute sense or whether the new policies are motivated by a wish to avoid certain undesired consequences. The latter interpretation reflects the reasons given in marketing textbooks.

More recent cases are the disclosures of malpractices in the world of finance which have in some cases led to prison sentences for perpetrators. The business firms concerned by the events have usually been eager to reshuffle their organization and get rid of the perpetrators so as to preclude further unethical conduct. In the case of the US Treasury Bond Market scandal, this involved changing chairman and chief executive officer in the offending firm. Disclosures of such unethical behaviours have placed ethical issues higher on the agenda and have contributed to creating new awareness of ethical issues. The mass media often report on instances of deficiencies in business ethics. The frequency of such reports gives an impression of an increasing number of occurrences in the Western world over the last decade or so. Scanning an issue of a newspaper leads to the discovery of a surprisingly large number of events recognized as examples where ethical and legal norms have somehow been violated. Has business behaviour become more unethical or is it only a sign that there is an increased awareness of ethical issues?

No unambiguous answer to this question can be found, but it is certain that there is an increased awareness of the relevance and significance of ethical issues. There are presumably many reasons behind this development, one of these being an assumed or real increase in perpetrated violations of ethical norms. A second reason is the raised vigilance of the mass media, especially after the Watergate affair which was not really an affair of business ethics, but encouraged journalists to question the ethics of actions in many other contexts. A further reason for the new emphasis on ethical issues is the fact that improved morality is seen as a possible and desirable consequence of creating increased attention to the problems. There seems to be little agreement about ways of improving the fulfilment of ethical norms, except that discussion of ethical issues is valuable in itself. Some advocates ask for more regulation by law and stricter enforcement of the law while others claim that generated rules, accepted as codes by professional associations, are the way forward. A third type of argument draws attention to the influence of education and special training, sometimes going so far as to include the whole process of socialization.

Whereas the discussion of business ethics is not a recent phenomenon, the intensity of the discussion has increased. When the so-called leftist movement started in May 1968 in France and spread to many countries, there was a tendency to regard business as immoral and wicked in itself. Subsequent ideological changes have meant that business is now viewed as necessary and integral to progressive economies: businessmen and women are even perceived by some as minor heroes, essential for improving standards of living. Economies without entrepreneurs and possibilities of exercising economic entrepreneurship are seen as doomed to fail. However, the liberalization of capital markets has involved financial operations that have ultimately led to turbulence in the markets and many frauds have in the end been discovered. Latterly, the conduct of important persons in the financial world has aroused suspicion and those people have become targets of ethical critique. It is of course in the interest of business that attitudes do not run full circle.

Business firms face decisions with important ethical dimensions in many different areas:

- Product design, product functions and safety
- Pollution of the environment
- Employee relations
- Marketing and distribution policies
- Gifts and bribery
- Taxes and charges
- Accounting practices
- Financial operations.

In market economies, most, if not all firms, work for profit. In economics, the assumption is that firms try to maximize profit. If they do not try to maximize profit, the efficiency of the economy is reduced. Baumol (1961) has, for example, shown that firms which strive for a satisfactory rather than a maximal profit tend to spend more on advertising and other marketing costs than profit-maximizing firms. His reasoning is, of course, based on some assumptions whose realism can be questioned, but it illustrates the importance of the assumption of profit maximization for market efficiency in the thinking of economists.

If firms are profit maximizers, how can they reconcile ethical considerations, that may entail costs, with the profit motive? It could be that ethical considerations are necessary for long-run profits; if a firm behaves unethically, it may gain something in the short run, but it will lose in the long run. The reason for this difference is said to be damage to the reputation or image of the firm which may involve loss of customer, supplier and financier confidence. Another reason given is that business firms are run by people who are driven by feelings of what they think is right or wrong. It is conceivable that there are situations in which a business decision maker acts more in accordance with her/his own personal beliefs than with profit considerations. It is probably correct to say that most business firms feel that damage to their long-term image must be avoided and that ethical considerations are a part of this. To a varying degree, the personal conviction of the chief executive officer and of other leading incumbents of offices plays an additional role. The private interests of the latter may, however, work in the opposite direction, judging from many recent cases of violations of ethics. Whereas the long-term (and sometimes also the short-term) interest of the firm involves ethical deliberations, the more or less private interests of a decision maker can lead her/him astray and cause unethical actions.

The ethical affairs that have most shocked the business world and shaken the trust of the general public have taken place in the world of finance. Insider trading, the issuance of junk bonds, fraudulent information are all examples where unethical practices have occurred. This should not conceal the fact that there are plenty of examples in other business areas: deceptive practices in marketing, hostile takeovers, failure to protect the environment or irregular actions towards employees among them. In the early 1970s an interest in the *social responsibility* of business emerged, possibly as a consequence of many attacks on business, although the concept of social responsibility was a self-selected response on the part of business firms rather than one directly imposed on them by outside forces. Part of the message was that the responsibility taken should be made visible, for example, through social accounting: the latter was seen as complementary to regular accounting and should, according to some promoters of the idea, show up in the annual statements. The social responsibility of business and industry now seems quite well established and accepted by most members of the business community in Western industrialized countries. There are still of course disagreements about what social responsibility actually involves.

It is said that business firms do not decide or act: it is individuals who make the decisions and see to it that the decided actions are carried out. Thus individuals are responsible for unethical acts and should be taught how to behave in advance of facing the problems. Some critics focus the attention on the role of the educational system. The business schools in particular have been accused of neglecting ethical issues in their training programmes. In the critique of business school programmes it is often maintained that the training is essentially based on an ideology that derives from economic theory which is said to prescribe maximization of profit for business firms and maximization of individual utility for consumers. This is then interpreted as promoting egoism as a guideline for business behaviour as well as for individual behaviour. Does the teaching in schools of business entail a technological slant at the expense of ethical considerations? If so, is this a consequence of economic theory's emphasis on maximization of utility/ profit? The causal relationships are by no means simple. Even though the profit motive dominates economic theory, the teaching in schools of business may be independent of this thinking. Business schools that favour the case-study method and devote little time and interest to the study of abstract theory are hardly less intent on profit maximization than others with a more theoretical orientation. The solutions of practical problems presented to students may enhance the short-term profit at the expense of other indicators of success and long-term profit. Many schools of business have taken the question of improved ethics very seriously and introduced mandatory courses and research programmes on ethics.

ECONOMIC THEORY AND ETHICS

The present discussion of economics and ethics seems to be informed by a growing discontent with a prevailing tendency to focus on technological and economic aspects of economic and social development at the expense of human and social benefits. Both business and societal decisions are made under the influence of production and cost considerations which at least up to a point are a necessity. It becomes questionable if incorrect assumptions are made about human and social effects. The tendency towards a narrow focus may be due to the fact that there are theoretical and practical models for handling economic and technological problems whereas human and ethical aspects somehow are hard to make precise and tractable. In this context the role of economic theory which is usually represented by neoclassical economic theory has been subjected to many discussions and exposed to criticism. Over the years, the neoclassical theory has been the object of many attacks, both from economists and from other social scientists, for not being realistic and for being too narrow in its assumptions about human behaviour. In the field of economic psychology, this has been a constant bone of contention with economists ever since, in 1881, the French social psychologist Gabriel Tarde wrote his first allegations against the psychological foundations of Adam Smith's economic theory: Smith disregarded the important interactions between people. The study of fairness mentioned above is an indication of some of the questions asked: can the fairness in dealing with other people that is apparently demanded by consumers be made consonant with economic theory's tenet of rationality? Critics contend that the theory is led astray by the strict adherence to the rationality concept.

Etzioni (1988) rejects the neoclassical concept of utility as maximization of self-interest or pleasure and proposes two kinds of utility, one having to do with the pursuit of pleasure, the other with moral considerations. Human actions and behaviour are a continuous conflict between pleasure seeking and moral constraints. In his treatment of moral reasoning Etzioni draws on the *deontological* view of ethics: the idea that there should be absolute ethical values to be upheld independent of consequences. Kant talked about 'The Categorical Imperative' and claimed that ethical values could be tested through the question of what happened if the behaviour was practised by everyone. Etzioni adopts what he calls 'a moderate deontology (with consequences as second consideration)'. He denounces the neoclassical theory's single, isolated decision maker and suggests instead individuals with emotional and causal relations to collectivities. The latter involve shared identities and commitments to values. He maintains that adherence to shared values is often a matter not of expedient conformity but of internalization of moral values. The socio-economic theory that Etzioni launches is, according to him, not the opposite of the neoclassical or public choice positions.

The position is (1) that individuals are, simultaneously, under the influence of two major sets of factors – their pleasure, and their moral duty (although both reflect socialization); (2) that there are important differences in the extent each of these sets of factors is operative under different historical and societal conditions, and within different personalities under the same conditions. Hence, a study of the dynamics of the forces that shape both kinds of factors and their relative strengths is an essential foundation for a valid theory of behavior and society, including economic behavior, a theory referred to as socio-economics.

(Etzioni, 1988, p. 63)

Amitai Etzioni's book *The Moral Dimension* has given a new angle to the debate about the deficiencies of economic theory. Etzioni cites empirical evidence to show that men and women are affected by moral considerations when they make their economic decisions. Such considerations lead to decisions and actions that are not economically optimal. Etzioni questions the foundations of the market economy to the extent that the latter depends on the pursuit of self-interest in the sense used by many economists. In his book *The Market Experience* Lane (1991) also questions the functions of the market economy. Relying on an impressive array of findings in the behavioural sciences, he proposes that the market would serve better if two maximizers were pursued: Happiness which is related to utility, but not equivalent to it, and human development which involves, among other things, self-esteem. Lane points out that need satisfaction has often been stated as the goal for economics and that the market as it now functions does not serve this goal in any complete way because of the narrow focus on profit and utility maximization.

Consequentialism such as utilitarianism has, rather than deontology, dominated economic thinking. Adam Smith brought together ideas about the pursuit of self-interest (self-love) which had been proposed by earlier thinkers like Bernard Mandeville and added some highly original thinking of his own to lay a foundation for economic theory. Smith's work *The Wealth of Nations* is in a way the bible of economics. Seventeen years before Smith published this work, he had written a book on morality, *The Theory of Moral Sentiments*. Ever since the publication of *The Wealth of Nations* writers have commented on Smith's presumed change of mind from the former book to the latter. In the 1759 book, Smith discussed the importance of virtue in which he included benevolence and justice. In the 1776 book, he advocated pursuance of self-interest. Some writers have found the messages in the two books perfectly compatible: one line of argument is that self-interest like the preference scale or utility notion used in economic theory can comprise benevolence (Sen, 1979). Conceivably, good relations to at least some other people are within the boundaries of self-interest. Another line of reasoning is that in his later book Smith devoted himself to the problem of how the market could become maximally effective and found that the pursuance of self-interest led to optimal market behaviour (cf. Hayek, 1985/1978). The social or national product is thereby maximized. A much-quoted passage from Smith (1982/1776) is the following:

> It is not from the benevolence of the butcher, the brewer, or the baker, that we expect our dinner, but from their regard to their own interest. We address ourselves, not to their humanity but to their self-love, and never talk to them of our own necessities but of their advantages.

Sen (1987, p. 23) comments:

> While many admirers of Smith do not seem to have gone beyond this bit about the butcher and the brewer, a reading of even this passage would indicate that what Smith is doing here is to specify why and how normal transactions in the market are carried out, and why and how division of labour works, which is the subject of the chapter in which the quoted passage occurs. But the fact that Smith noted that mutually advantageous trades are very common does not indicate at all that he thought self-love alone, or indeed prudence broadly construed, could be adequate for a good society. Indeed, he maintained precisely the opposite.

Sen (1987, pp. 27–28) summarizes:

> The misinterpretation of Smith's complex attitude to motivation and markets, and the neglect of his ethical analysis of sentiments and behaviour, fits well into the distancing of economics from ethics that has occurred with the development of modern economics.

Utilitarianism as proposed by Bentham tried to reconcile private interest and the benefit of the nation. Like Smith, Bentham saw little conflict between individual happiness pushed by self-interest and societal welfare (Sen, 1979). Utilitarianism focused on the duty of governments to create maximum happiness for the greatest number. Somehow it was expected that humans when pursuing their hedonistic self-interest would observe the happiness of others and consider it as a means contributing to their own happiness. Interestingly, hedonism and utilitarianism became the main ingredients in nineteenth-century economics. Jevons (1911/1871) who formulated marginal utility theory in mathematical terms, for example, defined economics as the study of pleasure and pain.

More recently, there has been a focus on a presumed lack of a moral dimension in economic theory. This is an idea that is rejected by many mainstream economists. Economic theory is held to be compatible with moral values provided that the individual makes moral considerations when forming her/his utility function. An important influence was Robbins's (1935/1979) work on the nature of economics. He rejected the idea that economics and ethics were closely related and asserted that it was not logically possible to associate economics and ethics except as mere juxtaposition. He wrote:

> So far as we [the economists] are concerned, our economic subjects can be pure egoists, pure altruists, pure ascetics, pure sensualists, or – what is much more likely – mixed bundles of all these impulses. The scales of relative valuation are merely a convenient formal way of exhibiting certain permanent characteristics of man as he actually is.
>
> (Robbins, 1935/1979, p. 44)

The view that economics is neutral with respect to ethics seems to be the preference of mainstream economists. Some excerpts from Stigler's (1982) lectures on economics and ethics, published under the suggestive title *The Economist as Preacher* will mirror some of this thinking, spiced with the witticisms that are characteristic of this economist. 'An economist is a person who, reading of the confinement of Edmond Dantès in a small cell, laments his lost alternative product' (Stigler, 1982, p. 7). The fact that economists use the rationality concept unflinchingly and do not consider ethical aspects may, according to Stigler, lead to the discovery of unexpected consequences.

> Members of other social sciences often remark, in fact I must say complain, at the peculiar fascination that the logic of rational decision-making exerts upon economists. It is such an interesting logic: it has answers to so many and varied questions, often answers that are simultaneously reasonable to economists and absurd to others. The paradoxes are not diminished by the delight with which economists present them. How pleased Longfeld must have been when he showed that if, in periods of acute shortage, the rich bought grain and sold it at half price to the poor, the poor were not helped. How annoyed the ecclesiastical readers of Smith must have been to learn that the heavy subsidization of clerical training served only to lower the income of curates. How outraged even some economists are with Becker's 'rotten kid theorem,' which demonstrates that altruistic treatment of a selfish person forces him to behave as an unselfish person would.
>
> (Stigler, 1982, p. 21)

The assumption that human motivation is equal to self-interest and remains the same over time in its essentials is held to lead to many applications which are approached with consistent methods:

> They [the economists] have sought persistently to employ prices to abate pollution or to ration energy or to incite safety conditions. They have been at the forefront of what presently appears to be a modest policy of deregulation of certain areas of economic behaviour.
>
> (Stigler, 1982, p. 22)

Stigler (1982, p. 26) concludes by suggesting a test in which self-interest competes with ethical values: 'Much of the time, most of the time in fact, the self-interest theory (as I interpreted it on Smithian lines) will win.' He makes the final point that most ethical values do not conflict with individual utility-maximizing behaviour. Ordinary economic analysis is applicable to crime as well as to other areas of human behaviour.

> Fraudulent securities will be supplied in such quantity that their marginal costs, including selling costs, equal their marginal revenue. One would not expect criminals to earn more than they could obtain in legitimate callings, proper allowance being made for all costs of doing business. The ordinary propositions of economics hold for crime.
>
> (Stigler, 1982, p. 24)

Sen (1979, 1987) has in several contexts pleaded for a very different treatment of ethical dimensions in economics. After noting that for many years economics had been considered more or less a branch of ethics, Sen (1987) proposes that economics has had two rather different origins. Both of them were in Aristotle's philosophy related to politics, but could be distinguished as 'ethics' and 'engineering'. Aristotle demarcated politics as the science that studied the supreme good for man. According to Sen this involved two ethical issues that were particularly foundational for economics. First, there is the problem of human motivation related to the broadly ethical question 'How should one live?' Sen calls this 'the ethics-related view of motivation'. The second issue is the judgment of social achievement. While the end was to achieve the good for man, it was finer and more god-like to attain it for a nation or for city-states than for oneself.

The engineering approach originated in practical demands in the management of household and property. It developed as 'cameralistics' and was at the end of the Middle Ages busy with bookkeeping, accounting and finance. In the late nineteenth century, economic theory was elaborated by engineers such as Léon Walras who combined the philosophical thinking with what had turned out to be practical in the natural sciences. Sen argues that economics has embodied both approaches though in different proportions for different economic writers. The ethical approach has rather substantially weakened as modern economics has evolved. Sen (1987) argues that welfare economics can be substantially enriched by paying more attention to ethics and that the study of ethics can also learn something from economics with its technological orientation.

For the purpose here, an important question is whether there is an influence of economic theory on practical economic affairs. In his contribution to this volume, Söderbaum claims this and cites Keynes as a support. Keynes (1936, pp. 383–384) notes the importance to practical men of what economists say:

> At the present moment people are unusually expectant of a more

fundamental diagnosis; more particularly ready to receive it; eager to try it out, if it should be even plausible. But apart from this contemporary mood, the ideas of economists and political philosophers, both when they are right and when they are wrong, are more powerful than is commonly understood. Indeed the world is ruled by little else. Practical men, who believe themselves to be quite exempt from any intellectual influences, are usually the slaves of some defunct economist . . . for in the field of economic and political philosophy there are not many who are influenced by new theories after they are twenty-five or thirty years of age, so that the ideas which civil servants and politicians and even agitators apply to current events are not likely to be the newest.

Keynes talked about the influence of defunct economists on business practice. Etzioni (1988) implies that business decisions are influenced by the theories that are espoused by businessmen. Lane (1991) criticizes the theory of the market and suggests that in the long run the market will change if a better theory, consonant with behavioural findings, is adopted. What he proposes is a return to ethics by means of the concept of happiness and human development which, rather than a narrowly defined profit, should be maximized by the market economy. Following up on Lane's thinking, an enriched theory of the market would tend to give ideas about new ways to judge the functions and utility of the market and this would lead to devising new indicators of success, somewhat differently conceived than mere profit.

REFERENCES

Aristotle (undated/1976) *The Ethics of Aristotle, the Nicomachean Ethics*, Harmondsworth: Penguin.

Baumol, W. J. (1961) *Economic Theory and Operations Analysis*, Englewood Cliffs, NJ: Prentice-Hall.

Cicero (undated/1988) 'How to make the right decisions', in M. Grant (ed.), *Latin Literature. An Anthology*, Harmondsworth: Penguin, pp. 37–39. (Quoted from the back cover of the *Journal of Political Economy*, 1988, 96, no. 4.)

Cicero (undated/1991) *On duties*, M. T. Griffin and E. M. Atkins (eds), Cambridge: Cambridge University Press.

Edgeworth, F. Y. (1881/1967) *Mathematical Psychics*. An essay on the application of mathematics to the moral sciences. New York: Augustus M. Kelley. Reprints of economic classics.

Etzioni, A. (1988) *The Moral Dimension. Toward a New Economics*, New York: Free Press.

Fritsche, D. J. and Becker, H. (1984) 'Linking management behaviour to ethical philosophy: an empirical investigation', *Academy of Management Journal*, 27, 166–175.

Gioia, D. A. (1992) 'Pinto fires and personal ethics: a script analysis of missed opportunities', *Journal of Business Ethics*, 11, 379–389.

Gorman, R. F. and Kehr, J. B. (1992) 'Fairness as a constraint on profit-seeking: comment', *American Economic Review*, 82, 353–358.

Hayek, F. A. (1985/1978) *New Studies in Philosophy, Politics, Economics and the History of*

Ideas, Chicago, IL: University of Chicago Press and London: Routledge & Kegan Paul.

Jevons, W. S. (1911/1871) *The Theory of Political Economy*, 4th edn. London: Macmillan (first published in 1871).

Kahneman, D., Knetsch, J. L. and Thaler, R. (1986) 'Fairness as a constraint on profit seeking', *American Economic Review*, 76, 728–741.

Keynes, J. M. (1936) *The General Theory of Employment, Interest and Money*, Cambridge: Cambridge University Press.

Lane, R. (1991) *The Market Experience*, Cambridge: Cambridge University Press.

Mandeville, B. (1924/1732) *The Fable of the Bees: or, Private Vices, Publick Benefits. With a Commentary Critical, Historical, and Explanatory by F. B. Kaye*, vols 1 and 2, London: Oxford University Press (first published 1712 to 1732).

Moore, G. E. (1903/1960) *Principia Ethica*, Cambridge: Cambridge University Press.

Randall, D. M. and Gibson, A. M. (1990) 'Methodology in business ethics research: a review and critical assessment', *Journal of Business Ethics*, 9, 457–471.

Robbins, L. (1935/1979) 'The nature of economic generalizations', in F. Hahn and M. Hollis (eds), *Philosophy and Economic Theory*, Oxford: Oxford University Press, pp. 36–46 (first published in 1935).

Sen, A. (1979) 'Rational fools: a critique of the behavioural foundations of economic theory', in F. Hahn and M. Hollis (eds), *Philosophy and Economic Theory*, Oxford: Oxford University Press, pp. 87–109.

Sen, A. (1987) *On Ethics and Economics*, Oxford: Blackwell.

Smith, A. (1982/1759) *The Theory of Moral Sentiments*, in D. D. Raphael and A. L. Macfie (eds), Liberty Classics, Indianapolis.

Smith, A. (1982/1776) *An Inquiry into the Nature and Causes of the Wealth of Nations*, Harmondsworth: Penguin (first published in 1776).

Stigler, G. J. (1982) *The Economist as Preacher*, Oxford: Blackwell.

Tarde, G. (1902) *La Psychologie Économique*, Paris: Alcan (2 vols).

Part I

Business ethics
and management

Chapter 2

Exit or voice? Lessons from companies in South Africa

Philip J. Stone[1]

During their customary lunch together at the town's best table-cloth restaurant, Mr Sundra Naidoo describes to Dr Coetzee several pharmaceuticals that his company recently brought to market. As is obvious to leading local citizens who lunch there, Mr Naidoo provides valuable information and advice to their highly respected physician.

Place: A rural, Afrikaans-speaking region of South Africa.

Time: The mid-1970s, when South Africans with Indian origins as Mr Naidoo were not customarily served at this restaurant or received by conservative Afrikaners such as Dr Coetzee.

Company: South African Cyanamid Ltd, a subsidiary of American Cyanamid.

*　　　*　　　*

After disastrous regional floods swept away black farmers' rice paddies, Dennis Cochius consults with participants in this innovative agricultural project, advised by Taiwanese agrarianists, to help black farmers increase their income by growing medium-grain rice used in breakfast cereals. Couchius's company bought the entire 274-tonne crop at a premium over market prices.

Place: The Makatini region of Kwa Zulu, Natal, South Africa.

Time: 1987.

Company: Kellogg Company of South Africa, Ltd, a subsidiary of the Kellogg Company of Michigan.

*　　　*　　　*

Lavishly illustrated with historic photographs, a new South African history book spares no politically sensitive issues in vividly recounting what it calls 'the real story'. The book, which cost several million rand to produce, reflects the work of an outstanding editorial board, well chosen to garner respect from all South African communities. The publisher wants black and white

South African readers to identify with the book's compelling story of their ancestors and utilizes its huge mailing lists to market the book extensively.

Place: Cape Town, South Africa.

Time: Late 1988.

Company: The Reader's Digest Association South Africa, Ltd, a subsidary of Reader's Digest of New York.

*   *   *

These experiences of American companies in South Africa illustrate taking initiative to demonstrate standards of responsible civil behaviour. For many multinational companies in South Africa, taking such initiatives was a new venture in social responsibility. Their experiences provide lessons about how organizations can exercise social influence wherever they encounter discriminative traditions or policies, whether they be against races, ethnic groups, tribes, castes or women, and wherever norms of civil society commonly assumed for conducting business prove shaky.

Drawing out lessons from these pioneering South African experiences in social responsibility requires a theory of social influence that clearly contrasts strategies available to companies and compares their costs and benefits. Evaluating each strategy requires ascertaining various ways it is likely to be perceived.

Although analysts have examined how multinational organizations create forces for social change (Apter and Goodman, 1976) and have drawn analogies between South Africa and situations elsewhere (Berger and Godsell, 1989), little attention has been given to the mechanisms available to them for exercising social influence. As will be shown, examining the alternatives that were available to multinational companies in South Africa can inform strategic thinking about their options elsewhere as new parts of the world open up to business.

THREE BASIC OPTIONS

During the late 1960s, when university students were protesting both in America and Europe, Albert Hirschman, an economist, proposed a theory of social influence based on 'exit', 'voice' and 'loyalty' (Hirschman, 1970, 1981, 1986). Those dissatisfied with a performance of others, according to Hirschman, have three options:

1 They can 'send a message' by exiting, whether by quietly switching from brand X to brand Y or by noisily 'voting with their feet', as many of those against apartheid – South African citizens as well as multinational organizations – have done by leaving. Hirschman reaffirmed Tocqueville's

observation that Americans have been exceptionally prone to pack up and move out when dissatisfied, making exit for them a natural first choice.

2 They can voice dissatisfaction through petitions, strikes, newspaper advertisements or other forms of protest. Voice can be outspoken confrontation, as in student demonstrations, or take place quietly, as in some types of lobbying. Hirschman pointed out that opportunities to exercise voice – and usually voice's credibility as well – greatly diminish once exit is completed.

3 They can remain steadfastly loyal in hopes that improvements will be forthcoming. Hirschman argues that some loyal customer support is usually necessary to provide adequate time for a supplier to make improvements, for if everyone immediately exits when performance declines, a company will be bankrupt before it can remedy its behaviour. Loyalty also allows an organization to concentrate on remedying the problem rather than have to divert their attention to respond to voice.

Most companies count on the continuing loyalties of employees, suppliers and customers to survive. Inasmuch as they expect some loyalty from others, many companies in turn are accustomed to remain loyal in many situations if there are indications that the situation may improve. Loyalty also may be the only reasonable course for a company when exit or voice are inappropriate. A company may consider India, for example, with its immense market of 850 million people, as an 'economic miracle waiting to happen' (*Economist*, 1991) should it become another rapidly developing Asian economy, but because Indian bureaucratic policies can frustrate voice and make exit – if one closes an operation down – often costly, loyalty in the form of compliance and maintaining a routine presence may be the best alternative.

Quiet loyalty also may be the best choice when more visible actions could endanger others or lead to repression. For example, companies doing business within China's Guangdong province in the 1980s could engage in economic endeavours unheard of in northern China (Vogel, 1989). Little social influence would have been achieved by these companies from voice or exit.

Loyalty, however, is easily interpreted as approval, especially when it has involved – as with companies in South Africa – compliant behaviours such as paying taxes or conforming to reprehensible laws. Loyalty then becomes difficult to justify, especially inasmuch as it can be understood to signal that a continuation of the status quo is considered inevitable. To distinguish loyalty from approval, further loyalty may be made contingent on changes being implemented. In the case of South Africa, for example, both Reverend Sullivan and Bishop Tutu made this contingency clear by announcing dates after which – if apartheid continued – they would recommend that foreign companies leave the country. Each was then obliged to keep his word when his date passed and apartheid still prevailed.

Inasmuch as multinational companies could not realistically just remain in business in South Africa and expect the government to discontinue apartheid policies, the choices available to these companies reduced to two: exit or voice. Companies unwilling to exercise voice, with its risks, stresses and other costs, clearly should have exited. However, evaluating the trade-offs between the exit and voice options available to companies in South Africa necessitates going beyond Hirschman's theory to distinguish two kinds of voice as well as several functions of exit.

TWO TYPES OF VOICE

Hirschman's theory compares exit as a concept in economics with voice as a concept in political science. By considering voice from the perspective of political science, Hirschman and others naturally focus on confrontation as its main form of expression. For example, Freeman and Medoff's *What Do Unions Do?* (1984) applies Hirschman's theory to compare the effectiveness in reducing wage inequality of American unions' confrontational voice with exit in the form of labour turnover.

Confrontation may be the only appropriate kind of voice when only the other party can instigate a desired change – such as paying higher wages – or when a joint action is necessary for a desired change to occur. However, in situations where unilateral action can demonstrate a desired change, the dissatisfied party can take the initiative and show that this action effectively produces intended results without creating dire consequences. Parents, for example, often instil new behaviours in their children by modelling them.

This second form of voice – which I call 'enacted', 'modelled' or 'demonstrated' voice – originates not from political science, but from organizational behaviour, a field that assigns considerable importance to demonstrating the workability of new agendas. Organizational theorist Karl Weick (1969) points out that diverse initiatives within organizations provide the 'requisite variety' organizations need to stay competitive. Innovation, according to Weick, requires not only making suggestions, but also demonstrating that they work. Peters and Waterman's *In Search of Excellence* (1982) supported Weick's claims by their finding that highly successful companies value such initiatives as part of their 'bias for action'.

Successful initiatives can be more persuasive than confrontations simply because they convincingly demonstrate to all who observe it that the behaviour works. Those who would resent a confrontation have to acknowledge an initiative's success. Moreover, such enactments also demonstrate the style and spirit in which an activity is to be carried out and not just the rules that should govern behaviour.

Many companies model behaviour in order to exercise social influence when they set up a programme in one department in order to demonstrate to other departments its advantages, thereby short circuiting much unnecessary conjecture, debate and second guessing. Some companies have management trainees 'shadow' experienced managers to learn how they manage. One consulting company even designed its offices so that each beginning consultant shares a workspace with a veteran consultant and can learn by observing.

Many companies also are familiar with television's advantages, compared to other media, as a modelling tool, for it allows them to show how their products and services are used. South Africa resisted introducing television for years, but South Africans now regularly view television shows that model American black middle-class life styles as well as local commercials that show blacks engaged in middle-class consumerism.

PUTTING ENACTED VOICE TO WORK

Modelled behaviour, when successful, can demonstrate agendas that are hard to ignore. After companies in South Africa successfully integrated their workplaces and set up multi-racial schools, it became difficult to claim that integrated workplaces and schools are not viable in that society. When companies purchased homes in upscale white suburbs and their black managers who live in them were accepted by the community, it became difficult to claim that black middle-class residents will destabilize these suburbs. As many countries privatize their commerce, initiatives taken by multinational companies in modelling desirable behaviour could similarly contribute to setting ethical standards of civil society.

Modelled behaviour becomes especially significant in situations where confrontation is likely to fail. For example, petitioning South Africa's government to supply more books to black schools would have had little effect, therefore American companies went ahead and gave books to schools as part of an adopt-a-school programme. Its purpose was not to do someone else's job for them, but to demonstrate acceptable standards.

Modelled behaviour, as a form of social influence, does not require that others take immediate interest in the actions being undertaken. It may be adequate at first if others tolerate the behaviour as not creating undue problems. To press for this, the party modelling the behaviour should make clear that its actions are an integral aspect of how it will operate, whatever others may think of them.

Inasmuch as the modelled behaviour represents taking a stand, it should not be compromised. A company programme in South Africa to support housing for black employees, for example, should not be limited to providing housing in black townships. Otherwise, such behaviour encourages what Bloom (1986) calls 'acceptance of the second best' – in this case behaviour that assumes the separatism of apartheid.

Multinational companies may have a considerable advantage over local companies in modelling behaviour because of a hesitation to interfere with international business practices. South Africa did not want to be considered as redneck by the international business community any more than communities in the American South have wanted to antagonize large companies that located there. Multinational companies in South Africa could therefore 'fly closer to the wall' – as one South African businessman put it – than local companies without getting into serious trouble. Once they model new agendas, it becomes less risky for local companies to copy their examples.

Modelled behaviour can be particularly relevant in situations where confrontation is considered to be in bad taste. This was true in South Africa, where American-style lobbying by organizations infringed on a well-established separation of business from government. American companies that subscribed to the Sullivan Principles[2] were instructed to engage in confrontational lobbying, but they soon learned their lobbying efforts were not well received. Some South Africans complained of American confrontations as 'government bashing', forcing the government into responses that would appease its hardline constituency. In such situations where confrontation proves ineffective, modelling behaviour becomes the main remaining way of exercising voice.

Outside companies may be in an especially good position to demonstrate civil rights, as has been illustrated even in America. Those who focus on dramatic confrontations at Selma, Montgomery, Little Rock and the University of Mississippi overlook the significance of behaviour modelled by businesses. It happened that these events occurred about the time that new national franchise operations were being installed along highway 'strips' outside American cities, and some of these new chains implemented the same policies at each local site that they had in effect nationally. Those who wanted their fast foods and other services had to queue up with everyone else. These policies helped further civil rights by demonstrating that treating each other as equals works just fine, and by providing a model of equal practices – in spirit as well as technically conforming to the law – for local businesses and other organizations.

The American South differed from South Africa, of course, in that discrimination was not supported by the national government. Putting civil rights into practice might result in one's business being torched, but federal arrest was not a problem. Modelling some behaviours in South Africa risked arrest, but this risk diminished as various integrated activities became common in South African life. Many new shopping malls that became as much part of South Africa as America's metropolitan life served their numerous black customers without discrimination. Non-discrimination became common among restaurants and hotels, with many frequented by middle-class blacks. A growing number of urban residential districts – including one of the interesting, dynamic sections of Johannesburg – became racially mixed. Integrated beaches and the removal of intermarriage prohibitions also became signs of an increasing tendency to avoid confrontation. As we know, it becomes easier to press the speed limit when almost everyone around is doing it too.

Modelled behaviour may be especially useful in situations where traditions instead of reprehensible laws are the problem. Companies could confront government about traditions that discriminate against women or an ethnic group and insist on the government's responsibility to legislate equal treatment. But often they may exercise greater impact by modelling well-chosen behaviours that can help empower those who are disadvantaged.

Modelled behaviour, as a form of voice, sends signals in two directions, and it is helpful to note their difference. People usually think of voice in terms of what O'Donnell (1986) and Hirschman (1986) call 'vertical voice', such as that from employees to their boss or from an organization to a government. The second – and often just as important – direction is 'horizontal voice' that sends a message to individuals or organizations like themselves. This was illustrated when American companies in South Africa set examples for South African companies in desegregating workplaces, taking a lead in providing higher minimum wages, and installing training programmes to further black advancement. It is also illustrated when a large American accounting firm in Japan vigorously moves well-trained Japanese women up to positions of responsibility. And it was illustrated when Sony, Honda and Nissan successfully implemented Japanese management techniques in their American factories, prompting American companies to reconsider some of their management practices.

Those who initiate new practices may not intend to generate horizontal voice, but if their actions are successful and not secret, they are likely to have this effect. An American private school, for example, may be primarily concerned with improving its own educational programme, but its successful innovations are likely to set an agenda for private and public schools alike. Indeed, one justification for maintaining private education in the United States is its agenda-setting influence on public schools. Similarly, the many South African multi-racial private schools supported by companies have set significant examples for public schools. One American company there further amplified this influence by organizing cooperative activities between its multi-racial private school and a black township public school – an example of horizontal voice that some American private schools might do well to consider.

Because modelled behaviour demonstrates the style and spirit in which an activity is to be carried out, it can be used to address aspects of civil behaviour that would be difficult to make a target of negotiations, thus providing an important avenue of international influence quite apart from what can be achieved through diplomatic channels in shaping civil society. People have become more aware that economic participation is as essential as political participation in bringing about social improvement, with some South

African blacks arguing that American blacks have bought into an unfortunate package of political enfranchisement without economic enfranchisement, a mistake they do not want to repeat in South Africa (Mathabane, 1989). Many South African blacks have looked to progressive multinational companies as important resources for furthering economic enfranchisement, and many people in countries recently opened to multinational business are likely to share this expectation.

WHY SHOULD COMPANIES ENACT VOICE?

American companies differ greatly in their commitment to social responsibility programmes. Many businesses do not consider social responsibility to be their concern. Some justify this by citing Milton Friedman's oft-quoted conclusion that 'few trends could so thoroughly undermine the very foundations of our free society as the acceptance by corporate offices of a social responsibility other than to make as much money for their stockholders as possible,' (Friedman, 1962, p. 133). They anticipate that their stockholders would rightly complain if they engaged in more social responsibility than the law requires.

In contrast, American companies like Johnson & Johnson have a corporate credo that includes responsibilities to clients, employees and the communities in which they live and work, as well as to their stockholders. Those who purchase Johnson & Johnson stock accept this published business philosophy as part of the deal.

Johnson & Johnson, with its one-page credo hanging in every executive office of its worldwide operation, has been in South Africa since 1930 and is committed to help bring South Africa 'beyond apartheid'. Johnson & Johnson has considered itself to have a covenant with its 1,600 employees there – 60 per cent of whom are black – and with the South African medical profession to strive towards creating a post-apartheid society. It has shown a strong sense of purpose in carrying out a programme of initiatives that was widely endorsed by its employees.

As companies move into new parts of the world, they often find that they have to create conditions they would normally take for granted. Most companies operating in South Africa have been less committed to social responsibility than Johnson & Johnson, but nevertheless consider it sound business to make sure their employees have decent benefits, reasonable living standards and opportunities for advancement, for such actions help assure the company of a capable, dedicated workforce. Because of blacks' living conditions, this translates not only into pensions, training programmes, medical care and other benefits, but also helping employees obtain decent housing and adequate schools in safe communities.

Some companies in South Africa also consider it sound business to participate in programmes that increase black purchasing power and to educate blacks so they can assume management positions. For example, National Beverage Service – Coca-Cola's successor in South Africa, except for its syrup manufacture relocated to Swaziland – recognizes that well-educated black managers are essential to Coke's future, especially inasmuch as 70 per cent of its market is black. With many black managers on its staff and a Coca-Cola bottling plant black-owned by the late 1980s, NBS has looked to the future by supporting over a dozen multi-racial schools.

On the other hand, companies that struggle to survive in today's fiercely competitive global economy by providing lower-cost products rather than innovative products – what has been called 'defender' companies in contrast to 'prospector' companies (Miles and Snow, 1978) – are more concerned about reducing immediate costs than creating long-range opportunities. Like some *maquiladoras* south of the Rio Grande, they instead are likely to exploit labour as well as the environment. John Price, a manager in *The Gamesman*, expresses this perspective when he bluntly concludes: 'Maybe if we were more affluent, we could worry about the social costs of the products we are making. Today we live in a competitive world' (Maccoby, 1976).

Unfortunately, multinational companies that have an advantage in initiating social responsibility also have leverage to exploit developing countries, especially countries desperate for foreign exchange. For example, if a multinational has its production distributed across several countries, it can selectively exploit each country's union policies, environmental regulations, exchange rates and tax codes, using transfer pricing that favours its profits and puts domestic companies at a disadvantage. Because developing countries can do so little about this, codes of conduct for multinational corporations, including those of the International Chamber of Commerce, the OECD, the ILO and the UN Commission on Transnational Corporations[3] need to be expanded in setting and monitoring standards.

Some companies may hesitate to take action in situations that cry out for social responsibility because it would raise questions about a company's social responsibility elsewhere. Very few multinationals would qualify for membership in the Minneapolis association of businesses that give 5 per cent of their *profits* to community programmes, much less the tenth of their *payroll* that companies subscribing to the Sullivan Principles in South Africa were asked to provide. The South African press questioned the ethical consistency of companies that spent a tenth of their South African payroll on social responsibility – apart from whether their operations there made any profit – when these companies, like most American businesses, spent less than 0.5 per cent of their profits on social responsibility back home. Similar questions were raised in South Africa about multinationals that vigorously moved blacks into management positions in South Africa when their affirmative-action track records at the management level back home were less than stellar. One South African black manager was not impressed when he addressed 300 managers in the United States and saw only six blacks.

'American civil rights and management affirmative action!' he exclaimed to me. 'Tell me about it!'

Ethical consistency is likely to loom as a larger issue for multinational companies because people are becoming more cynical about companies using ethics as a public relations tool. Many regard companies as only being ethical when forced into such behaviours, such as those demanded by the Sullivan Principles or the ecology movement. Students point out, for example, that the self-proclaimed ecology-conscious McDonald's continues to use non-degradable containers in countries where ecology is less of an issue. Many take the view that Ben and Jerry's is only into programmes that support family farmers or rainforest products because appearing ethical makes money.

In addition to a consistent corporate commitment, companies also must have dedicated employees willing to face immense social pressures and outright hostility that new initiatives can generate. Sundra Naidoo, in the example at the beginning of this article, risked physical attack. Michele Laxalt, when representing her American client at a Japanese shareholders' meeting, endured stockholders calling her a 'stripper' (Boone Pickens, 1991). Many people understandably prefer to opt out of such encounters. Taking these kinds of initiatives clearly is not for everyone.

MAKING ENACTED VOICE MORE EFFECTIVE

The size of many multinational companies gives them a significant presence, whether they seek the responsibilities that go with it or not. For these companies and others, the experiences of companies operating in South Africa suggest several ways to make modelling behaviour a more effective as well as less risky form of social influence.

Take advantage of the company's resources and talents. The three examples at the beginning of this article describe ways that American companies were able to take advantage of the kind of business they were in to bring about change. Each company should contribute those skills and resources where its impact is greatest, whether their expertise be in publishing, pharmaceuticals, agricultural machinery, breakfast cereals, or whatever. Companies that market consumer goods, for example, can engage in more visible initiatives than companies that only produce for export or have have a limited set of customers. Initiatives by one company can complement those of another, so as to address a social problem on many fronts.

Unfortunately, the programme that was set up to guide the behaviour of American companies in South Africa did not encourage companies to emphasize their unique strengths. Companies that 'volunteered' to be monitored (usually under pressure from their large pension-fund share-holders) were called 'signatories' to the programme and were assigned annual ratings by Arthur D. Little, a consulting company, as to how well they were performing. However, Reverend Sullivan, the Baptist minister who started the programme, seems to have been especially concerned that the annual rating reflect a company's demonstrated stand on the side of righteousness. Rather than give unfair advantage to companies like the Reader's Digest that are in a unique position to have a considerable impact against apartheid, the ratings have emphasized actions that all companies can take, like affirmative internal promotion practices and adopting a school.

Although this rating process motivated inactive companies to initiate social responsibility programmes, one consequence was a uniformity, rather than complementarity, among the programmes of different signatories. Companies were informed that all companies could receive high ratings, but executives realized that the credibility of the ratings would be questioned if this happened. With annual bonuses tied to achieving satisfactory annual ratings, managers were hardly willing to take risks that might not be fully credited. Even if they achieved a comfortably high rating one year, the fact that the rating standards were raised each year – with new standards often not announced until mid-year – left little room to take risks.

The result was that signatory companies often competed with one another. Although they did pool their efforts – especially in regards to education – in order to be more effective in some areas, one executive confided: 'If I had a good idea, I usually did not share it with others because they could make points from it too.' Many executives resented competing for good ratings, or as one executive put it, 'being treated like schoolchildren'.

In contrast, privately-held companies were in a better position to take initiatives that might not earn high ratings because they were under less public scrutiny. For example, Reader's Digest risked losing subscriptions to the South African edition of its *Digest* by regularly including articles exposing apartheid's futility and the misery it creates, even though these actions might earn it few points towards a high signatory rating. But it also limited social responsibility activities in areas where it felt it had little to offer.

Address a problem's many faces. Many countries have deep-rooted problems that make themselves manifest in many ways and create numerous fronts where change is needed. In South Africa, Pulitzer Prize journalist Joseph Lelyveld argued that by 1985 the objectives of legislated apartheid – to create separateness within the society – were mostly achieved and that apartheid's legacy will continue to manifest itself after blacks are enfranchised, just as residential segregation and inferior black education remain decades after American civil rights legislation and Supreme Court decisions (Lelyveld, 1985). In Eastern Europe, countries face the many consequences of ethnic tensions that go back for generations. In addition, decades of socialism have etched deeply into the work ethic, creating problems that will not be easily remedied.

Although some companies are advantageously positioned to make significant contributions, every company probably has unique contributions it could make. For example, the FMC Corporation once made fire engines in a Cape Town suburb. Inasmuch as its sales were primarily to South African towns, it had to be cautious about anti-apartheid actions, even though it had a vigorous programme of moving blacks up its manufacturing ranks. Nevertheless, it was in a unique position to help black communities such as Soweto – whose three million residents had a score of police stations, but only one fire station – exercise better efficacy in fire prevention. Even though such programmes could provide training in mobilizing community resources, few would question such a programme dedicated to saving lives. And the enhanced fire-consciousness it engendered could only in the long run help boost FMC sales.

Get good local advice. Companies from overseas need good local advice so they can implement effective initiatives. To achieve this, some companies in South Africa created advisory boards of leading blacks and South African academics known for their stance against apartheid and authorized them to allocate funds as they deemed best, even if it were in ways contrary to the company's preferences. Mobil's board, for example, decided to downplay black enterprise programmes based on individual initiative that Mobil executives favoured and instead gave several million dollars to cooperatives and other group-centred black enterprises.

Care also is needed to ensure that a particular programme fits into the needs of the recipient community. Sundra Naidoo, who became head of South African Cyanamid's social responsibility programmes, created committees of local community leaders to work with him in targeting and administering programmes. The committees' members were given considerable training to help them serve their community effectively – including training in how to obtain funds from sources other than South African Cyanamid.

Rating standards devised overseas may not consider special local circumstances. For example, signatory companies in South Africa had to show that their lowest-paid worker received a wage 30 per cent above the minimum necessary to support a family. As is common practice in many African and Asian countries, many organizations in South Africa have elderly tea ladies who do light housekeeping chores and prepare tea. Some executives were deeply annoyed that their companies chose to dismiss tea ladies who had been loyal employees for decades in order to improve their annual ratings. These women were secondary wage earners who were not supporting a family, they argued. They could not handle a job that justified a family-supporting wage, and there were few other jobs in the community they could do.

Valuable local advice may come from managers with unique experiences. For example, South African Albert Koopman – a former manager of Cashbuild retailers – proposed strategies to enhance black participation that included sharing managerial power and profits (Koopman *et al.*, 1987).

Because of South Africa's inadequate education system, Koopman found, however, that many black employees lacked an understanding of how businesses function. Training on the basics of 'how and why profits are made' – topics that an American employer might take for granted – proved a necessary first step.

Avoid initiatives that entail too much confrontation. Any initiative taken because of disagreement with current practices is likely to involve some confrontation. Care should be taken that the amount of confrontation involved in taking an initiative would not subvert the effectiveness of the initiative. Too much confrontation drains energies better spent elsewhere. Roger Fisher (1978) also points out that confrontation often reduces receptivity to other kinds of influence.

For example, one of the first projects American companies sponsored in South Africa was to create a black college and vocational school in Soweto. The project was selected partly because of its high visibility, but this also then entailed considerable confrontation, including a year of negotiations with the Pretoria government. Attending to all this confrontation resulted in less attention being given to other decisions, including staffing and community relations. As a result, the project at best was a mixed success with but modest impact.

By comparison, many companies – South African as well as American – have successfully engaged in various initiatives without getting involved in long-term confrontation. For example, when the faculty of a major Cape Town university decided to admit blacks and the government attempted to block them by refusing to allow blacks in its dormitories, businesses supported the faculty by funding the acquisition of integrated dormitories.

Start initiatives where they will have a good chance of success. Multinational businesses can exercise considerable influence at a local level, for the desire to have businesses locate within the region often provides communities with a compelling reason to shape up. The threat of a company scaling down local operations or moving elsewhere is also likely to induce a host community to attend closely to what standards the company considers acceptable.

To the extent that modelled behaviour that is shown to work in one community is likely to spread to others, companies can simplify their task by starting first in favourable settings. In South Africa, communities have varied widely in their attitudes, offering businesses a diverse spread of target communities. For example, when the national government first proposed to allow local governments to decide whether residential areas would be restricted, Cape Town announced its districts would be open to all. But when a conservative east Johannesburg suburb announced it would reinstate park segregation, businesses located there could exercise considerable leverage by threatening to leave.

Frustrated with the power of South Africa's conservative regions at the time to block progressive national legislation, two South Africans, Kendall and Louw (1986), garnered considerable attention several years ago by proposing that the country decentralize into something like Swiss cantons. They predicted that progressive communities would soon move so far ahead economically that all but the most diehard segregationist regions would soon strive to catch up. To speed this process, they proposed a national constitution that guaranteed universal enfranchisement, freedom of movement between cantons and no laws – restrictive or affirmative – that referred to race.

Take initiatives that will be considered credible. People will not interpret an initiative at face value if they consider the company to be corrupt, for the initiative is likely to be regarded as part of a cover-up, a distraction from unsavoury activities, or part of a complicity. In South Africa, the social responsibility programmes of oil companies were especially suspect because the government obtained bulk oil imports for the companies and provided military security for refineries. In countries where bribery is common, many initiatives are likely to be suspect.

Credible initiatives may also be especially hard to establish where people have become cynical and the economy is chaotic. Where topdown directives have prevailed, any initiatives designed to help empower people may be wasted effort. In such cases, companies may do better to target their initiatives to communities where their practices have more credibility.

Taken together, these recommendations should help make enacted voice a more effective vehicle of social influence. But before drawing conclusions about the utility of this type of voice, compare what several kinds of exit offer.

A CLOSER LOOK AT EXIT

Hirschman's rule that exit usually diminishes opportunities for voice especially applies to taking initiatives, for complete exit removes any opportunity to model behaviour. Given the valuable contributions that taking initiative can make, does the value of exit as a one-time signal usually outweigh the value of being able to continue to make such enactments?

Exit, like voice, turns out to be somewhat more complicated than Hirschman described. Voice was found to have roots in organizational behaviour as well as political science. Similarly, exit has roots stemming from several disciplines and takes several forms, including one that complements rather than excludes taking initiative. A comparison of exit with enacted voice therefore depends on which type of exit is being considered.

Exit that is a market signal. Economics – the origins of Hirschman's concept of exit – treats exit as an important signal in a market economy. A business must be responsive to this signal to survive. Yet exit can be a difficult signal to read. When a store loses its customers, it may be because they have shifted to the store across the street, have moved out of town, or are currently short on money and trying to avoid making purchases. Far from providing a clear signal by itself, the store owner may have to read local financial reports for baseline information to interpret the store's declining sales. Even if the proprietor learns that customers' allegiances have shifted to another store, is it because of better products, better service, or what?

Hirschman complains that people often are not forthright in giving their real reasons for exit, thereby making exit an ambiguous signal. He notes, for example, that government officials who resigned because they strongly disagreed with America's Vietnam policy nevertheless said they resigned for 'personal reasons'. Similarly, companies that exited South Africa partly because of poor economic performance have made face-saving claims of leaving for 'moral reasons'. Indeed, once poor performance and reduced market share was rumoured as the real reason for exit – as it was for Eastman Kodak, a early departure from South Africa – the exits of other companies became more suspect.

Exit therefore is often accompanied by inadequate contextual information for people to interpret what motivates it. This is likely to be especially true when the exit decision is made by those far away. Many South Africans wondered about Kodak's sudden exit, with long-term employees dismissed and social responsibility programmes abandoned with very little notice. Few seemed aware that Kodak also had endured extensive confrontation about its lack of social responsibility in its headquarters city of Rochester, New York.

Exit's significance as a signal was also greatly weakened when some executives made it known that their companies were departing because their South African operations took up too much corporate attention, given their minor revenue significance. Even more cynical was the South African response to reports that some American companies had yielded to certain large pension funds, regarding South Africa as an expedient way to silence them for a while on ecology and other issues.

Exit that deprives. Many advocates of exit assumed that the departure of American companies would not only send a signal, but also create serious deprivation, especially of consumer goods. Exit becomes a punishment by denying goods that make life pleasant, removing jobs and weakening the economy.

Economic sanctions created considerable deprivation when used against what was then Southern Rhodesia, but since then secondary markets have become much more developed. For example, the South Africa government demonstrated that it can resist oil sanctions by negotiating crude-oil supplies from spot markets and undisclosed sources, even though this is an industry that has relatively few producers.

The notion that the exit of American companies by themselves would have created serious consumer-goods deprivation in South Africa ignores today's global markets. South African shopping malls resemble European and Australian shopping centres in being stocked from goods around the world, with American goods having no more predominance there than they do in these other places. Moreover, American companies did not constitute an essential or large enough portion of employment or invested capital in South Africa to cause a significant economic deprivation by exit (Bloom, 1986). South Africa adjusted to the exit of much larger operations, like Barclays Bank, compared to American companies there. Instead of having secure South African markets, American businesses were under siege from competitors in such areas as automobiles, photocopiers, cameras and film. Those sectors where an American exit could have caused significant deprivation – proprietary drugs, for example – would have deprived blacks as well.

Coca-Cola, which by far outsells other soft drinks in South Africa, is undoubtedly the most salient American consumer product in South Africa, for many South Africans, including blacks, find Coke irresistible. When Cuba was deprived of American goods, Cubans replicated Coca-Cola – which they did quite successfully – and then brought the product back to market, even in its traditional green bottle. South Africa could have handled its Coke dependency similarly.

Because company takeovers are now commonplace, customers have learned to pay more attention to sales and service continuity than who owns the company. Not surprisingly then, when IBM sold its South African operations to its South African management, the new company – named ISM – widely advertised assurances of improved service continuity. ISM entered into a backup supply arrangement with Hitachi – an arrangement IBM would not have made – should the US Congress block IBM from selling parts. It also entered into a joint venture with Barlow Rand, a large South African conglomerate, for manufacturing key parts locally. Instead of divestiture signalling a strong stance against apartheid, it opened up hedging opportunities within a business where assured continuity is essential.

One sanction, however, that did deprive many South Africans stemmed from a British actors' guild requirement that BBC and ITV should not distribute their videos to South Africa. South African television could not by itself replicate British talent and programming volume. To the consternation of many South Africans, they were left with American sitcoms and 'soaps' to watch.

Instead of fostering economic deprivation, the exit of some American companies – especially after a devaluation of the South African rand – provided bargains for South African purchasers. Xerox, for example, was bought at an attractive price by a conservative South African electronics company which dropped Xerox's social responsibility programmes and soon had blacks removed from managerial positions.

Some South Africans who were accustomed to participating in their international professional communities also have experienced the deprivation of being barred from meetings or no longer invited to speak. This type of deprivation, however, assumes that people should be judged on their nationality rather than their character and personal values, a stance that many view as crude because it shares assumptions about treating people with apartheid itself.

Even when exit successfully deprives, it may foster a siege mentality that delays social change rather than hastens it. It surely is not coincidental that Cuba, a target of extensive economic sanctions, remains one of the last communist societies. Visitors to Cuba have witnessed the defiance with which Cuba, with its lack of spare parts and consumer goods for many years, nevertheless keeps itself band-aided together and determined to resist at any cost.

Exit that stigmatizes. Exit may be a market signal for economists, but for other social scientists separation has other meanings. Anthropologists Mary Douglas (1966) and F. Steiner (1956) have described how cultures isolate – using taboos – as a way of handling danger. Menstruating women, for example, were confined to certain places because their blood was considered dangerous. The quarantine – which derives from the forty days a suspected ship had to remain isolated from shore – is still used to control certain dangers. As Erving Goffman (1963) notes, isolating or avoiding association with someone often stigmatizes, especially if it connotes that those targeted are polluted or have, as he calls it, 'a spoiled identity'. Stigmatizing is an unfortunate human tendency that children sometimes cruelly exhibit towards the handicapped or deformed.

Hirschman correctly notes that America is a country where exit has predominated, but he also claims that the people who left Europe for America or who moved out West rarely wished a pox on those they left behind. However, America has also been the country of the scarlet letter, the pillory, tar-and-feathers and ostracism that included being banished to the wilderness. It is the country that isolated its Japanese citizens at a time of war and used congressional investigations and 'blacklisting' to root out 'communist pollution' at the cost of ruined careers. It is perhaps not surprising then that Americans took a lead in using exit to exert influence on South Africa.

Imprecatory exit becomes especially evident when basic values are compromised in order to be vindictive. The Pittsburgh School Board, for example, threatened publishers to ban from its schools the books of publishers who sold books to South Africans. Because American public school textbook sales are much larger than the entire South African market, some publishers had to reject South Africans' orders for books. Not only did this compromise American and United Nations principles of freedom of the press, but it could also do harm. For example, a surgeon who operates mostly on blacks in South Africa's largest hospital said it became difficult to obtain new American medical books.

Stigmatizing generally is a poor way to go about changing the behaviour of others. Roger Fisher and William Ury (Fisher and Ury, 1981) argue that influencing others is best accomplished by being hard on the problem, soft on the people. At a minimum, stigmatizing others diverts attention from the problem and makes people defensive. Although it can be argued that stigmatizing a country – as when a country is excluded from the Olympic Games – is a useful diplomatic strategy that is different from stigmatizing a person, the propensity to stigmatize should be handled with insight and caution.

Partial exit. The social psychologists Rusbult *et al.* (1982) who have utilized Hirschman's concepts of exit, voice and loyalty to analyse how people handle unsatisfactory marital relations add a fourth category called 'neglect'. Those dissatisfied with their marriage can just neglect it rather than voice complaints or seek divorce. Similarly, many people who are dissatisfied with their job have been found to put in minimal effort rather than complain or quit (Withy and Cooper, 1989). In both cases, the relationship continues, but the commitment goes.

Neglect, however, is but a form of partial exit in which the dissatisfied party no longer invests in a relationship. Although it is associated with irresponsibility in living up to commitments, a more meritorious form of partial exit occurs when an organization is explicit about honouring past commitments, but is also explicit that it does not consider it sensible to make further investments under current conditions. Banks, for example, have on occasion honoured past agreements, but been open in announcing that no new investments will be made until changes are forthcoming. A manufacturing company might similarly announce that it will continue to operate its current equipment and keep its employees on the payroll so long as the operation at least breaks even, but that it is not going to invest in new equipment as long as the current situation continues.

Partial exit has different implications for voice than full exit because enough presence is maintained to continue a vigorous programme of taking initiatives as well as provide frequent reminders of the partial exit. Moreover, a continued presence – as some married people know well – is likely to block opportunities for the other party to form substitute relations. As long as a company continues to serve its markets – even if with antiquated equipment – it will be more difficult for competitors to enter. When a company's equipment has already been fully depreciated and there are major first-mover advantages to already being in the market, a company may be able to hold this position for some time, especially in small and potentially risky markets.

Companies that choose to continue their operations but make clear that they are not going to modernize or expand until certain changes are made, may exercise more influence in the long run than those companies that make a one-time exit. Such announced intentions will drive home the point that reprehensible policies are likely to drive the economy downwards, plagued with obsolete equipment. Just as American towns and states with poor bond ratings are highly motivated to merit lower interest rates, South Africa seeks to be well-rated in financial markets. Any signs of being non-competitive or any extra premium that South Africa has had to pay because of the risks that apartheid has created have made its costs loud and clear, without being vindictive. Partial exit, by raising the fear of being left behind and neglected, is likely to be more effective than one-time exit in creating a continuing sense of being deprived.

Some of South Africa's largest companies were quite open in acknowledging that apartheid policies made South Africa a dubious place for long-term investment if apartheid should continue in any form. South Africa's demographics show a growing black population, so that in a few decades the current ratio of more than four to one is likely to be ten to one, especially should more whites leave. Much of South Africa's best and brightest managerial and professional talent – including graduates of major South African universities – have been leaving South Africa for what they perceive to be more promising futures elsewhere. Attracting talented managers from overseas to go to South Africa – especially for long-term assignments – became difficult. Faced with such stark demographic trends and dubious future human-capital resources, intelligent investors rightly looked elsewhere.

Clem Sunter (1987, p. 94) a prominent planner at Anglo-American, South Africa's largest conglomerate, sounded this alarm by arguing that 'statutory apartheid will have to go, because it is being overtaken by demands of an increasingly integrated and complex economy'. He considered it 'an ever greater stumbling block to being a "winning nation"'. South Africa, in his view, had to choose between the high road of an integrated economy with a heavy emphasis on developing small businesses, or a low road that maintained some form of apartheid and relies on mineral exports to sustain it as long as possible. Sunter pointed out that mining cannot continue to substitute for other forms of economic development that should be occurring. For example, by the mid-1980s, Spain had developed its tourist industry to produce as much income as South Africa was earning from gold. If South Africa reverts to the low road, Sunter predicted it 'will gradually vanish off the world radar screen' (1987, p. 99).

South Africa's own conglomerates in fact offer a greater threat to the South African economy by taking partial exit. Because a few domestic conglomerates with extensive international ties control a large amount of the South African economy, any shift they make of capital, resources and personnel to other countries makes the message of partial exit loud and clear. Not surprisingly, the South African financial press monitors their overseas activities closely.

A remaining advantage of partial exit over one-time exit is that it increases the likelihood that a company will participate in the later development of the economy. Companies that completely exit – if generalizations can be drawn from the numerous companies that left Zimbabwe – are unlikely to return to help reconstruct a new economy. Partial exit shares with loyalty the advantage of maintaining enough presence to participate in a country's future.

Exit that clears the stage for a showdown. Those who believe in revolt as a way to achieve social change have argued that foreign businesses should not be in the way when a showdown occurs. South Africans are well aware today of the struggles neighbouring countries are having in starting with next to nothing, and few, of any race, are interested in a showdown that reduces their country to similar circumstances. Complete exit risks signalling that the time for a showdown is at hand, but partial exit avoids sending this message.

CONCLUSIONS

As new parts of the world open up to business, multinational companies have an opportunity to exercise influence as they never had before. The competition between communities around the world to host multinational businesses can serve to multiply a company's leverage in exercising social influence, for a decision to locate in one community is likely to be perceived as a rejection of communities not chosen. Those communities that seek to attract international business will imitate the standards of successful communities, thereby furthering a more rapid diffusion of these standards than would otherwise occur.

An analysis of social-influence mechanisms that were available to multinational companies in South Africa has identified more alternatives than just a choice between confrontational voice and complete exit. In some situations, modelled behaviour is more likely to be successful than confrontational voice, especially in the long run. Partial exit may have significant advantages over complete exit, including more opportunities to model voice. Companies may often find that their best social influence strategy, especially for influencing behaviour at a community level, is to model desired behaviours and to at least point to some form of partial exit – such as making no further investments – if change is not forthcoming.

The strategic question of *how* to best exert social influence differs, of course, from the question of *what* goals to support. The answer to the first question, as this article has shown, draws upon concepts in economics, political science, organizational psychology and anthropology. The answer to the second question is a matter of ethics and depends on what kind of a community a company needs to function successfully, as well as a company's moral standards and sense of social responsibility. Here, the social sciences prove less useful, for the answer to the second question is primarily a matter of business policy and philosophy (Donaldson, 1989).

Social responsibility through modelled behaviour and/or partial exit, therefore, may not be appropriate for every company or for every situation:

1 A company may not want to commit the time and energy necessary to carry out initiatives effectively and clearly communicate its intentions. Some companies may not consider such actions to be part of their business policy or are too besotted with survival. Others may be unsure of their commitments in a country.
2 The heritages of some societies may make them unreceptive to some behaviours, no matter how well they are modelled (Seligman, 1992).
3 In any situation in which people have obfuscated their intentions through ambiguity, concealment and deception – indeed, in 1985 South Africa's press reported a consultant advising this to Pretoria – a policy other than straightforward confrontation may be perceived as more of the same.
4 Inasmuch as action other than complete exit may be interpreted as loyalty or even complicity, companies may prefer not to truck with such reprehensible situations in any way.
5 A company's staff in some countries may not have an interest or the courage to carry out bold initiatives.
6 Although it is better to light a candle than curse the darkness, there is a limited amount of change that any one organization can accomplish.

Nevertheless, to the extent that a new world order cannot be shaped by politics and diplomacy alone, multinational companies can exert significant social influence by modelling behaviours – in both spirit and style – that extend economic enfranchisement and provide a civil context for conducting business. In the process, organizations may also learn useful information about themselves as change agents.

NOTES

1 Harvard University's Program in Ethics and the Professions and its American Express Fund for Curricular Development supported interviewing in South Africa and the United States. Albert Hirschman and Susan Helper provided helpful advice.
2 The Sullivan Principles were drafted by American minister Leon Sullivan to cover non-racist practices for companies operating in South Africa; see 'The [Sullivan] Statement of Principles', International Council for Equality of Opportunity Principles Inc., Philadelphia, PA, 1984.
3 *The Tripartite Declaration of Principles Concerning Multinational Enterprise Social Policy*, Geneva: ILO, 1977; *The OECD Guidelines for Multinational Enterprises*, Paris: OECD, 1986; Werner Feld, *Multinational Corporations and UN Politics: The Quest for Codes of Conduct*, New York: Pergamon Press, 1980.

REFERENCES

Apter, D. E. and Goodman, L. W. (eds) (1976) *The Multinational Corporation and Social Change*, New York: Praeger.
Berger, P. L. and Godsell, B. (eds) (1989) *A Future South Africa: Visions, Strategies and Realities*, Boulder: Westview Press.

Bloom, J. (1986) *Black South Africa and the Disinvestment Dilemma*, Johannesburg: Jonathan Ball.

Boone Pickens, T. (1991) *Seattle Times*, 9 June, E9.

Donaldson, T. (1989) *The Ethics of International Business*, Oxford: Oxford University Press.

Douglas, M. (1966) *Purity and Danger: An Analysis of the Concepts of Pollution and Taboo*, London: Routledge & Kegan Paul.

Economist (1991) 'A survey of India', 4 May, 5.

Fisher, R. (1978) *Points of Choice: International Crises and the Role of Law*, New York: Oxford University Press.

Fisher, R. and Ury, W. (1981) *Getting to Yes: Negotiating Agreement without Giving*, Boston: Houghton Mifflin.

Freeman, R. and Medoff, J. (1984) *What Do Unions Do?* New York: Basic Books.

Friedman, M. (1962) *Capitalism and Freedom*, Chicago: University of Chicago Press.

Goffman, E. (1963) *Stigma: Notes on the Management of Spoiled Identity*, New York: Simon & Schuster.

Hirschman, A. (1970) *Exit, Voice and Loyalty: Responses to Decline in Firms, Organizations and States*, Cambridge, MA: Harvard University Press.

Hirschman, A. (1981) *Essays in Trespassing: Economics to Politics and Beyond*, Cambridge: Cambridge University Press.

Hirschman, A. (1986) 'Exit and voice: an expanded sphere of influence', in A. Hirschman (ed.), *Rival Views of Market Society and Other Recent Essays*, New York: Viking Penguin.

Kendall, F. and Louw, L. (1986) *South Africa: The Solution*, Bisho, Ciskei: Amagi Publications.

Koopman, A. D., Nasser, M. E. and Nel, J. (1987) *The Corporate Crusaders*, Johannesburg: Lexicon Publishers.

Lelyveld, J. (1985) *Move Your Shadow: South Africa, Black and White*, New York: Viking Penguin.

Maccoby, M. (1976) *The Gamesman: Winning and Losing the Career Game*, New York: Simon & Schuster, Bantam edition, p. 114.

Mathabane, M. (1989) *Kaffir Boy in America*, New York: Collier Press.

Miles, R. E. and Snow, C. C. (1978) *Organizational Strategy, Structure and Process*, New York: McGraw-Hill.

O'Donnell, G. (1986) 'On the fruitful convergencies of Hirschman's exit, voice and loyalty and shifting involvements: reflections from the recent Argentine experience', in A. Foxley, M. S. McPherson and G. O'Donnell (eds), *Development, Democracy and the Art of Trespassing: Essays in Honor of A. O. Hirschman*, Notre Dame, IN: University of Notre Dame Press.

Peters, T. and Waterman, R. (1982) *In Search of Excellence: Lessons from America's Best-run Companies*, New York: Harper & Row.

Rusbult, C., Zembrodt, I. and Gunn, L. (1982) 'Exit, voice, loyalty, and neglect: responses to dissatisfaction in romantic involvements', *Journal of Personality and Social Psychology*, 43, 1230–1242.

Seligman, A. (1992) *The Idea of Civil Society*, New York: Free Press.

Steiner, F. (1956) *Taboo*, London: Penguin.

Sunter, C. (1987) *The World and South Africa in the 1990s*, Cape Town: Tafelberg Publishers.

Vogel, E. (1989) *One Step Ahead in China: Guangdong under Reform*, Cambridge, MA: Harvard University Press.

Weick, K. (1969) *The Social Psychology of Organizing*, Reading, MA: Addison-Wesley.

Withy, M. and Cooper, W. (1989) 'Predicting exit, voice, loyalty, and neglect', *Administrative Science Quarterly*, 34, 521–539.

Chapter 3

Moral and ethical dimensions of managing a multinational business

Lynne M. H. Rosansky[1]

INTRODUCTION

This paper seeks to develop a model for understanding the moral and ethical dimensions of the decision-making process as it occurs in multinational and global businesses. These decisions are not made by 'the company' but by people who are managing the enterprise. Thus the managerial process and the role of individual managers is the focus here.

The social context of action which drives managerial decision making creates dilemmas due to conflicting moral and ethical systems. These are exaggerated in the global context of a transnational business. A manager's success depends upon an ability to sort through the challenges posed by the tension between an extreme relativism and moral imperialism. The moral dimension, although conditioned by the social context of action, is an individualist dimension of the managerial process. The conclusion suggests ways to better prepare managers to meet the moral challenges of working in the global economy.

THE MANAGEMENT PROCESS

Whatever the question, management is the right answer these days, be it a question of the problem or the solution. If it is a question of what a company needs to turn it around – management. If it is a question of what brought the company to its knees – management. And increasingly, if it is a question of why a company's employees behaved unethically – management is still the answer. It was a 'management decision' to launch the Challenger; to market infant formula in Africa; as well as to take Tylenol off the market and to limit production of harmful pesticides. What is this all-powerful 'management'?

Managers are charged to 'get results'. They organize, direct, plan and control. They motivate, influence, communicate, lead and negotiate. Most competent managers are 'proactive' and 'spontaneous' in initiating action to get results (Boyatzis, 1982). Individually, competent managers identify ways to improve customer service before the complaints begin. In a fast-food business, a proactive manager will notice when a line seems to be forming and she will open another cash register or direct customers to a different counter. In cases of a delivery problem, competent managers will get on the telephone to discover what the causes of the hold-up are and find another way to get the goods delivered.

Managers are also connected to the larger organizational context. They respond and react to organizational reward and incentive systems so that if their success is measured by unit profitability, they are likely to initiate action to improve the bottom line such as stimulating more sales or cutting costs.

Managers are both actors in and agents of the culture of their organizations. They reflect and react to the shared-value system of organizational culture. Many organizational theorists have adopted the perspective that culture is a managerial tool. Deal and Kennedy (1982) first popularized this notion and it has persisted. Others have argued that culture is not a 'control device' but rather 'a set of social constructs negotiated between organizational members to anticipate and control the motivational and cognitive diversity in the organization. These shared constructs allow organizational members to make sense of ongoing organizational activities' (Krackhardt and Kilduff, 1990, p. 143).

Organizational reward and incentive systems are based upon the neoclassical assumption that rational self-interest is the fundamental motivating force in human decision making, but every managerial decision and action has a moral and ethical dimension inherent in the act. As Etzioni (1988) and other socio-economists have shown, the neoclassical assumption of 'economic' man (or woman) leaves out the moral dimension which is what drives people to make moral choices despite incentives to cheat. Etzioni's 'moral dimension' is grounded in the assumption that individuals are motivated by normative/affective (N/A) factors which are not necessarily constrained by the principle of rational self-interest. Other theories of human motivation such as sociological (role, status and hierarchy as prime motivator), political (power as the motivator) or psychological (hierarchy of need) also omit the moral dimension. (See Maccoby, 1989, pp. 31–32.)

In the end, 'what we choose to do depends more on our ethics than on satisfying needs' (Maccoby, 1989, p. 32). There is no such thing as a 'value-free' decision. Even the most 'objective' assessment rests on a value system; frequently this is the rationalist tradition of Western cultures.

The managerial process is the pattern of decisions which managers make in the organizational context. These decisions are influenced by reward systems and the organizational culture but they are also moral choices made by individuals.

THE QUESTION OF AGENCY

What is this 'management' which is the problem as well as the solution? Does management refer to individual managers? Organizational systems and structures? The corporate leaders? All of the above? If we accept that N/A factors are significant motivating factors, they are the basis for managerial action and decision making. Where do they come from? Normative/affective factors emerge largely from the social context of action. Therefore the social context of action is a large part of 'management'.

Many have argued that corporations qualify as moral agents (Donaldson, 1982, 1989; Goodpaster and Matthews, 1982). According to this argument, just as corporate 'rights' are legally recognized in the same way that individual 'rights' are, corporate 'responsibility' should also be acknowledged. Others (notably Velasquez, 1988) have argued that it is dangerous to attribute characteristics of agency to a corporate entity. In fact, 'the corporation itself (as lawyers are fond of reminding one another) is a *persona ficta*, a legal fiction with "no pants to kick or soul to damn"' (Stone, 1975, p. 3). Likewise, society has neither pants to kick nor soul to damn. Yet we all recognize the powerful influence of society and the corporation on individual behaviour.

Western intellectual debate has tended to assume that the individual should be the principal unit of analysis (see Etzioni, 1988, p. 4). Neoclassical theory rests on the assumption that maximizing utility is the basic behavioural motivator. This is consistent with the tradition of individualism and self-determination so characteristic of Western culture (Bellah *et al.*, 1985). Even the legal notion of corporate 'agency' has its roots in the tradition of individualism (Stone, 1975).

Perhaps one of the difficulties in operationalizing the notion of corporate responsibility lies in the analogy between corporate and individual. The analogy attributes motive to corporations which cannot have self-conscious 'motives' to the same extent that individuals can.

The control mechanisms which effect individual behaviour cannot have the same result on corporate entities because of the unique institutional nature of corporations. Sanctions such as death or imprisonment which work for individuals cannot work for corporations. Likewise, incentives such as 'duty', 'honour' and 'integrity' which work for individuals do not carry the same clout for a corporation. This is because the essence of a corporation is that it has no 'soul', it is fundamentally a network of social relationships.

Organizational culture is often cited as the culprit when unethical (and often illegal) practices are discovered in a company. This attribution suggests that 'culture' is somehow an agent but culture is not so unidimensional. Krackhardt and Kilduff's (1990) research shows the power of friendship networks in creating multidimensional aspects of organizational culture. They suggest that friendship networks are the vehicles through which individuals interpret cultural values. This means that an organization which values honesty and initiative could spawn a subculture which interprets the action of insider trading as demonstrating great initiative and another subculture which interprets the same action as dishonest. Accordingly, 'within any organizational culture the same set of cultural values can lead to discrepant attributions about the same people' (1990, p. 151).

Goodpaster (1991) refers to 'business ethics' as having three levels: individual, organization and systemic. This suggests that the individual is in a central position interacting with the organization (and its levels) and this whole is contained by the social system. While this scheme is a useful descriptive model, it does not answer the question of causation or agency – who/what is responsible?

The question of moral agency seeks the source of moral reasoning in the organization. Jones argues that 'moral reasoning patterns not only vary from issue to issue but also may vary in rough proportion to moral intensity' (1991, p. 385). If characteristics of the moral issue in part determine appropriate decision and behaviours, then how are these decisions made when the perception of the very definition of 'moral issue' varies as it does in cross-cultural interaction? A senior manager of a large multinational company described his shock and dismay when he discovered that his Asian business partners discussed price structures with each other. (Interview with the author, June 1991.) He and his American colleagues felt that this kind of collaboration was wrong and amounted to collusion, while the Asians felt that 'we all agree on what will be and a few months later, we let the market know'. A significant moral issue for the American was a non-issue for his Asian partners.

Jones ascribes variation in moral reasoning to the intensity of the issue but this in turn derives from the meaning imbued to the event. The meaning ascribed to particular behaviour is largely a product of the context in which the event occurs.

If it is true that 'meaning and value' emerge from any interaction, then the 'unit' of analysis should be the entire interrelated network, which I call the social context of action. This includes individuals with all the various intersecting collectivities that influence behaviour, beliefs and values. By using the social context of action as the unit of analysis, causality (and hence agency) is two-way: individuals both affect and are affected by the contexts in which they are operating. They are both agents and recipients of action.

The social context of action is especially difficult to use as a unit of analysis because it is never static (and may lead to criticisms of extreme relativism as discussed below). The ethno-methodologists such as Garfinkel (1967) have suggested that roles are defined in the process of interaction in a social context. This perspective suggests that the social process is an important determinant of outcome.

MANAGEMENT DILEMMAS

Multiple roles and social contexts are increasingly the normal reality. In any given day, individuals move between contexts and each context creates pressures for a response that is consistent with the norms and ethic of the particular group. For a manager, this means a workday peppered with contextual shifts as the requirements of peers, boss, subordinates, suppliers and customers require different responses. For example, a manager (call her Carol) of network services of a large company was in the process of upgrading the equipment (from the author's research). Carol's boss had made this upgrade a priority in order for the company to be better connected. She had finally decided upon a vendor (having spent weeks learning about products and vendors). No sooner had she announced her decision than she received a phone call from a peer on the salesforce suggesting that an alternate vendor would be a better choice because the alternate was a very large high-profile potential customer. The next phone call was from a peer in the marketing department suggesting that her choice of vendor was not a good one because the company she had chosen was competing with Carol's company on a bid in Venezuela. Her subordinates were complaining that the connection with existing hardware would be difficult and next to impossible and hoped that she did not expect that they would be responsible for the connection.

The manager's dilemma is trying to sort out these multiple interests. Each interest is often grounded in strongly held beliefs and values so that below the surface of this situation rests a potential question of Carol's 'ethics'. Should she give the business to a competitor company or would that raise questions of 'conflict of interest'? Will the increased workload on subordinates raise a cry of 'unfair'? The corporation does not have an answer to these kinds of dilemmas. It is up to the individual manager, in this case Carol, to decide what is right and best for the situation and Carol will be influenced by her understanding of the core values of her company. These she will decipher from observing the pattern of rewards and punishments which the company metes out and from the interpretations of her friendship network. The complexity of Carol's situation is magnified in the global economy.

As globalization progresses, all businesses are being forced to participate. Business organizations are no longer merely local interests serving local customers but must respond to multiple stakeholders from many nations. The world of the future is here. On any given day companies may have customers in Poland, suppliers in Taiwan, employees from the Dominican Republic and distributors in Sweden. The result is an increasingly complex web of interconnected interactions and relationships.

The networks are expanding, and as they expand there are increased differences in beliefs and values among the pieces. Nepotism is an accepted way of doing business in India, and an Indian manager may be pulled very strongly by his loyalty to kin relations. Nepotism is frowned upon in US firms and an Indian manager working in a US company could easily find a situation in which traditional kinship loyalties require doing business with a particular supplier while the rules of the firm require open bidding. These kinds of managerial dilemmas are becoming more common as the world shrinks and our social networks expand to include more diverse cultural systems. Here is the cause of many moral and ethical dilemmas of managing multinational businesses.

DIMENSIONS OF MANAGING MULTINATIONALS: STRATEGY, STRUCTURE AND MORAL

There has been much debate about terminology. Multinational, international, global and transnational have each been used to refer to slightly different organizational realities. I use multinational according to Bartlett and Ghoshal (1989, p. 15). They suggest a distinction between international, multinational and global on the basis of strategic capability, in which international is primarily focused on diffusing and adapting parent company advantage; global is focused on building efficiency through central, global-scale operations; and multinationals respond to national differences and build local organizations.

Without accepting the causality implied in Chandler's (1962) suggestion that form follows function, strategy and structure are two important dimensions of managerial decision making. They are related, and there are tensions along each dimension.

The tension along the strategic dimension is between a global orientation in which the business attempts to add value by building economies of scale and leveraging operations around the globe, and a multinational approach which requires building strong local operations to respond more directly and quickly to local customer needs.

The strategic choice a business makes depends largely on the industry (see Chandler, 1986). Consumer product businesses require more local adaptability than commodity businesses such as oil or rubber or industrial equipment businesses. It is difficult to sell exactly the same hair products, cosmetics or food around the world in the same way. Consumer preferences for food products are very locally specific. The number of regional cuisines is testimony to the incredible diversity of taste and habit. Food companies must take into account local preferences in the preparation, packaging, advertising and distribution of their product.

Oil is a global commodity and can be refined anywhere in the world and shipped for use. The requirement for oil does not depend upon local tastes. Likewise, many industrial products in which economies of scale decrease the delivered cost can be manufactured centrally and shipped around the world.

Strategic choices about market targets tend to favour particular organizational structures to most effectively implement the strategy. Accordingly, the multinational consumer products companies tend to be more decentralized, putting more of their resources close to their customers, while commodity businesses tend to be more centralized to obtain economies of scale and control costs. Strategy and structure are interdependent. Strategic changes often require concomitant structural changes. For example, in 1983 Johnson & Johnson, the medical products company, had a very big commitment to a decentralized organization. (See Harvard Business School case no. 384–053.) It consisted of 150 companies each focused on a particular product line and market segment. In the early 1980s, the pressures for cost control in healthcare began to rise. Hospitals centralized their purchasing decisions in order to negotiate volume discounts with their suppliers.

American Hospital Supply seized the opportunity of this trend by creating a one-stop shop for hospital purchases. They computerized order forms and served as a distributor for many different manufacturers. Johnson & Johnson was a major supplier to hospitals and found that American Hospital Supply was cutting them out of the market. Johnson & Johnson had to rethink their strategy of very decentralized and market-focused units. In order to offer competitive prices, they had to leverage more cost savings from economies of scale so they created a centralized distribution service organization to serve a more broadly defined customer base and meet the challenge of American Hospital Supply.

Multinational strategies tend to favour more decentralized structures and global strategies tend to favour more central structures. Nestlé or Procter & Gamble, which pay attention to local differences and respond with variation in product, promotion and service, are multinational in strategic orientation and tend to operate more decentralized structures. Likewise, Johnson & Johnson had operated in this mode. Companies such as IBM and NEC which market more complicated technical products tend to be more global in their strategy because they can achieve advantage through economies of scale and their structures tend to be more centralized.

Honda has a global strategy and has decentralized nearly all the functions except research and development (R&D). A senior Honda executive envisioned a day when the company would essentially become a global holding company because each national unit would be entirely self-sufficient with its own marketing, production, finance and R&D. (Interview with the author, January 1992.)

In addition to business determinants of a company's structural and strategic tendency, the contextual cultural circumstances are a factor. The role of national ideologies may lead to a propensity to select either one or the other strategy. Honda, like most Japanese companies, tends towards global strategy and centralized structure. Lodge and Vogel (1987, p. 317) suggest that the value attributed to communitarianism evident in many East Asian nations leads to a propensity towards the global and centralized strategy. They conclude by suggesting that the success of these firms may lead other firms to become more integrated and global in their strategies.

According to Donaldson (1989, p. 41), 'the strategic status of the multinational . . . will affect the character of organizational decision making, including decision making with a moral component'. Thus the ethical dimension must be added to the model of managerial decision making.

At the organizational level, the ethical dimension is an ethic reflecting the system which determines the value decisions of the organizational culture. Different organizations have different priorities. These are the foundation of the organization ethic.

I call this an ethical dimension rather than a moral dimension because it represents the principle of organizational reality rather than individual behaviour. William Graham Sumner stated the issue well when he said ethics 'is an attempt to systematize the current notions of right and wrong upon some basic principle' (in Donaldson and Werhane, 1988, p. 22). Business organizations in their substitute roles as organizers of social relations and mores, often make deliberate attempts to 'systematize current notions of right and wrong' through the use of corporate codes of conduct.

The extreme poles of the ethical dimension are extreme relativism and a dogmatic universalistic position. Neither extreme alone is acceptable but each moderates the opposite in a dynamic state.

The tension of the opposing forces in this model suggests that managing multinationals puts the manager and the organization at the outer limits of this model, i.e. tending towards decentralized structures and relativistic ethics. This raises the danger of extreme ethical relativism.

EXTREME RELATIVISM VERSUS MORAL DOGMATISM

The tension between an extreme relativism and a universalistic moral dogmatism creates the moral dilemma for individual managers. Extreme relativism within a local orientation and a decentralized organization will produce 'when in Rome, live as the Romans do'. The implication of extreme relativism is that a manager working in Nigeria operates according to a different set of rules, code of conduct and ethical standards than a manager working in Britain. What is considered the right thing to do and a good job in Nigeria is wrong and a bad job in Britain. Can a company really demand that its managers become moral chameleons?

At the other extreme, a dogmatic position is likely to breed imperialistic actions such as imposing a worldwide ban on all pesticides or some other technology which less-developed nations depend upon for their food supply and increased standard of living. It could also reinforce discriminatory practices by dogmatically asserting the primacy of one value system. For example, company X has determined that it will not tolerate bribery, despite the fact that it is common practice in country Y. Natives of country Y may be discriminated against because it is assumed by management that they will engage in practices common to their native background and will not uphold the values of company X.

Matthews *et al.* (1985) advocate a meta-ethical relativism which accords a local validity to ethical relativism while acknowledging a universal ethical standard. This approach assumes that careful description and analysis of cultural belief systems will reveal that the ethical premises are in close conformity with a universal standard. For example, the rituals of self-mutilation and fire walking practised among some north African tribes may appear to be torturous and callous acts, but when analysed in context they serve as cathartic treatment and re-entry rituals for deviants who otherwise might be unable to re-establish functional social relationships in the close-knit society.

The ultimate dilemma is the nature of human beings. To what degree do we diverge, and what is common to us all? Can it be argued that there is such a 'saint' that we would all recognize across all social and cultural boundaries?

At a meeting of the Babson College International Advisory Board in April 1991, a group of chief executive officers from eleven different global companies suggested that one of the great challenges in managing multinationals is how to maintain a single ethical standard in a diverse world. The managerial challenge was one of the ethics of choices. Given that managers must make choices about their behaviour, what kind of principles and guidance should they have? The moral dimension for managers is the ability to make judgments and mediate the untenable extremes of relativism or dogmatism. Ultimately this is an individual act but to the extent that individual acts are part of social contexts, there will be effects on the context.

PREPARING FUTURE MANAGERS

The dynamic and complex nature of the global economy is likely to bring increasing complexity to the network of relationships, and it is also likely to increase the pace of change. This complexity will further stretch the moral dimension of managerial decision making. How can managers be prepared to meet the challenges of the constantly shifting contexts?

Shifting contexts as a pattern for society driven by a capitalism founded on individual self-interest is likely to produce the primacy of 'the survival ethic, i.e. everyone for him- or herself for the sake of survival' (Nash, 1990, p. 17). Without a greater good to work towards, what will prevent the world from becoming the eighth level of Dante's Hell populated with 'fellows who'd swear black's white for half-a-crown' (XXI, p. 42) doing 'subsurface deals and secret money-grabbing' (XXI, p. 53).

While individuals are products of their respective social contexts of action, they are also agents in those contexts. Managers are characters, agents and moral actors who adapt and react to the multiple contexts in which they live.

Michael Maccoby (1989, p. 8) suggests 'the larger society, of which business is but a subsystem, depends for its greatness not only on the head but on the heart – the qualities of courage, compassion, generosity, idealism. If the most dynamic sector of society continues to select out these qualities, where will we find future leaders who possess the moral strength to know right from wrong and the courage to act on those convictions?'

It is incumbent upon educators to teach students moral strength and to provide opportunities for students to learn how to act with conviction. We need leaders, not lemmings. It takes practice articulating one's own commitment to a set of values, testing and refining those values in order to be able to act with conviction.

A pressing question is how to do this. At some point institutions of higher learning have to be accountable for the products they produce. The classroom is the context and students do learn meaning and value in the context of the classroom. They learn to dismiss such things if a dismissive attitude is modelled. They learn to ignore the questions about responsibility and accountability in favour of questions about how to beat the competition.

Classroom dynamics communicate values – intended or not – because the classroom is the social context of action much as the business organization is the social context of action. The ideal academic ivory tower in which truth and learning emerge from careful 'value-free' objective analysis is a myth.

Using the entire context as the unit of analysis, the messages and meanings of the classroom emerge from the dynamic exchanges which occur among students and teachers. A nod of the head indicating approval, a quick rebuttal, a dismissive wave, all these contain messages and values.

The greater good is escaping much of modern society in the whirl of fast-paced change and the pressure to consume and spend. What institutions are there which can maintain and reinforce the greater good? The Church has lost much of its former power to do this. Community meetings and gatherings rarely occur. Schools, colleges and universities maintain some credibility and must meet the challenge. In these institutions, in the context of the classrooms, the debate must be engaged. What is the greater good? Students must be prodded, cajoled, pushed and enticed to develop the sensitivity and awareness which is so important in finding the path through the jungle to a better world.

CONCLUSION

This paper has argued that the ethical dimension of managing multinational businesses lies in the social context of action. It was suggested that the social context of action be considered the appropriate unit for analysis because this is more appropriately the agent of moral decision and action. It includes both the individual and the elements of the social group which affect individual choice and action. Analysis is made more complicated because the social context of action is primarily a process rather than a unidimensional agent.

The moral dimension of managing multinationals lies in the tension between extreme relativism and moral dogmatism. This is conditioned by the context in which the manager works. The social context of action is determined by the organizational culture and the immediate social network in which the manager operates. Controlling the social network is a difficult challenge. Organizational reward and incentive systems which reinforce ethical behaviour are a beginning, but ultimately the manager depends upon the moral choices of the individuals working in the company.

It will be important to find ways to develop the kind of strong moral character required to negotiate the complexity of the multinational business world. This is a challenge for educational institutions and for the society and businesses they serve.

NOTE

1 Thanks to the Babson Board of Research for providing support for this paper and to the Babson International Advisory Board for their comments on the subject.

REFERENCES

Alighieri, D. (1949) *The Comedy of Dante Alighieri the Florentine: Cantica I. Hell*, Trans. by D. L. Sayers, Harmondsworth: Penguin.

Bartlett, C. and Ghoshal, S. (1989) *Managing Across Borders*, Boston, MA: Havana Business School Press.

Bellah, R. N. *et al.* (1985) *Habits of the Heart*, New York: Harper & Row.

Boyatzis, R. E. (1982) *The Competent Manager*, New York: Wiley.

Chandler, A. D. Jr (1962) *Strategy and Structure*, Cambridge, MA: MIT Press.

Chandler, A. D. Jr (1986) 'The evolution of modern global competition', in M. Porter (ed.), *Competition in Global Industries*, Boston, MA: Harvard Business School Press.

Deal, T. and Kennedy, A. A. (1982) *Corporate Cultures*, Reading, MA: Addison-Wesley.

Donaldson, T. (1982) *Corporations and Morality*, Englewood Cliffs, NJ: Prentice-Hall.

Donaldson, T. (1989) *The Ethics of International Business*, New York: Oxford University Press.

Donaldson, T. and Werhane, P. H. (1988) *Ethical Issues in Business*, Englewood Cliffs, NJ: Prentice-Hall.

Etzioni, A. (1988) *The Moral Dimension*, New York: Free Press.

Garfinkel, H. (1967) *Studies in Ethnomethodology*, Englewood Cliffs, NJ: Prentice-Hall.

Goodpaster, K. E. (1991) Presentation on 'The manager: character, agent and moral actor', given at the James E. Waters Colloquium on Ethics in Practice, Boston College, 24 April.

Goodpaster, K. E. and Matthews, J. B. Jr (1982) 'Can a corporation have a conscience?', *Harvard Business Review*, January–February, 132–141.

Handy, C. (1989) *The Age of Unreason*, Boston, MA: Harvard Business School Press.

Hoffman, M. W., Lange, A. E. and Fedo, D. A. (eds) (1986) *Ethics and the Multinational Enterprise*, Lanhyam, MD: University Press of America.

Jones, T. M. (1991) 'Ethical decision making by individuals in organizations: an issue-contingent model', *Academy of Management Review*, vol. 16, no. 2, 366–395.

Krackhardt, D. and Kilduff, M. (1990) 'Friendship patterns and culture: the control of organizational diversity', *American Anthropologist*, vol. 92, no. 1, March, 142–154.

Lodge, G. C. and Vogel, E. F. (1987) *Ideology and National Competitiveness*, Boston, MA: Harvard Business School Press.

Maccoby, M. (1989) 'The corporate climber has to find his heart', in Kenneth E. Goodpaster and Thomas Piper (eds), *Managerial Decision Making and Ethical Values*, Boston, MA: Harvard Business School Press.

Matthews, J. B., Goodpaster, K. and Nash, L. (1985) *Note: Relativism in Ethics. Supplement to Policies and Persons: A Casebook in Business Ethics*, New York: McGraw-Hill.

Nash, L. L. (1990) *Good Intentions Aside*, Boston, MA: Harvard Business School Press.

Stone, C. D. (1975) *Where the Law Ends*, New York: Harper & Row.

Velasquez, M. G. (1988) 'Why corporations are not morally responsible for anything they do', in T. L. Beauchamp and N. E. Bowie (eds), *Ethical Theory and Business*, Englewood Cliffs, NJ: Prentice-Hall, pp. 69–75.

Chapter 4

Management by ethics
A new paradigm and model for corporate ethics

Richard H. Guerrette

When reputable business firms and conscientious executives see their companies exposed in ethical scandals, they soon discover the costly consequences to the corporate image and often pay the heavy price of moral bankruptcy. They then realize that corporate ethics cannot be left to uninformed individual consciences nor to corrective strategies. When the verdicts are in and the culprits are out, they face the moral mandate that management ethics must be formative of a corporate conscience and corporate behaviour reflective of an ethical image.

It is thus time that these hard lessons from the business and political 'scandalgates' of this era be systematized into a management paradigm for corporate ethics that opens directives for value-system-building in corporations and ethical performance in operations.

Management by ethics (MBE) is such a paradigm and its corresponding model for management practice offers a new design and programme for executives and managers in moral education through corporate ethical socialization. This new paradigm is drawn from the social and behavioural sciences with interdisciplinary linkage to philosophy and economics. As such, it is grounded in social psychological theory within which the corporate conscience can be traced through social processes. It is also anchored in sociology and organization studies from which value-system-building can be planned through management processes. Finally, upon this inter-theoretical base, MBE opens into an applied management model for corporate conscience formation at executive levels of management, ethical consciousness development through the workforce, and moral incentive building for optimal performance efficiency in the workplace. In summary, the paradigm is instrumental for locating the corporate conscience in the 'organization self' of the corporation; and the model, for forming this conscience through the moral education of its human resources.

THE MBE PARADIGM

Since corporate ethics arise out of the social organization context of corporate culture and management interaction processes, the practical application of its philosophical principles in the day-to-day business operations of a company require more strategic clarification for executives and managers in organization scientific terms. More attention is due to the 'critical practical understanding'[1] of corporate ethics as social psychological processes emanating from the 'complex organization environment' of a company. It is in this domain that corporate ethical behaviour is managed as a complexity of a company's interrelationships both in its internal departmental structures, including individual and collective units of production, and in its external environmental structures encompassing interorganizational networks of operation. From this multi-level spectrum of interorganizational relationships, new methodological directions have opened research perspectives to the organization itself as the unit of analysis (see Brinkerhoff and Kunz, 1972; Brinkerhoff, 1984; Perrow, 1972; Levine and White, 1972; Etzioni, 1960). It is thus critical to note that these wider research perspectives have expanded the focus of corporate ethical analysis from individuals and their isolated occupational/professional performances to the corporate entity itself and its corporate moral performance. In effect, this change of focus has set the interdisciplinary stage not only for the philosophical and social psychological analysis of the corporate conscience but also for the moral responsibility and legal accountability of corporate behaviour (see Goodpaster, 1983; Goodpaster and Matthews, 1982).

Ethical principles and social processes

The MBE paradigm will attempt to trace the social psychological dimensions of the corporate conscience and to explore a moral developmental course for its formation. With these new directions, it will offer a 'critical practical' model for the ethical management of corporate behaviour through the organization reconstruction of a moral climate. The paradigm represents change, not only in the way moral performance is analysed in a company but in the way it is measured in research. Social scientific studies need to analyse a company's culture, its value-system and its moral performance in the interorganizational environment of its investors, suppliers and clientele. Studies of this kind could not only help to clarify the organizational processes for applying abstract ethical principles to concrete corporate practices but would specify the data-gathering methods for reviewing corporate ethical performance (see Blasi, 1980). Etzioni (1988) affirms this need to move the study of corporate ethics beyond the deductive margins of philosophical categories to the inductive methods of socio-economic realities. This more objective approach to corporate ethics could open more socialization and training benefits to companies for moral performance development and more effective management planning for moral performance consistency (Blasi, 1980). It could also open more ethically reconstructive discourse among organization analysts and economists, and moral educators beyond philosophical ethics to moral economics (Hausman and McPherson, 1993).

Philosophical ethics – a fixed paradigm

Whereas ethics have been traditionally studied in the domain of philosophy, moral behaviour among individuals and moral performance in corporations are actually in the domain of social psychology. Philosophers reason about principles that guide behaviour. Their philosophical thought patterns have been shaped by methods of deductive reasoning and have produced important theories, such as utilitarian, contractarian and deontological theories (see Beauchamp, 1988), that have for so long constituted the paradigm for business ethics. But it is people who act and corporations who perform and their behaviour and direction do not always reflect ethical principles. One reason for this is that human behaviour and corporate performance are outcomes of social processes.

Social psychology – an open paradigm

It is therefore plausible to expect that the practical improvement of ethics in the workplace should arise out of a social psychology of ethics (Baum, 1974). Researchers and managers must begin to pay attention to the socio-economic context of ethics and to the complex organization environment within which corporate performance is conducted. The new studies need to go beyond the philosophical analysis of what happens in Washington loops and Wall Street firms. The new paradigm needs to *open* a view to the social reconstruction of ethics beyond the corporate ruins of insider-trading and junk-bond-dealing. Philosophical theories and ethical principles will not stop 'lieutenant-colonels' who salute unethical commanders, but development of corporate conscience and value-system-building by corporate executives may.

The new paradigm here being proposed for the social psychology of corporate ethics is based on symbolic interaction and role theory in sociology (Cooley, 1902; Mead, 1934; Blumer, 1969), open system theory in the social psychology of complex organizations (Allport, 1962; Katz and Kahn, 1972) and moral development theory in psychology (Kohlberg, 1981, 1984; Gilligan, 1982). Out of this inter-theory link, one can begin to understand the social psychology of the corporate conscience and, therefore, how it might be cultivated in the organizational context of management interaction and corporate culture.

A similar interdisciplinary approach linking psycho-social role theory to moral development studies has opened wider research perspectives for analysing the social contextual variables that influence moral decision-making and moral behaviour (Kurtines, 1984). This approach likewise draws on open system theory in organization studies (Allport, 1962; Katz and Kahn, 1978) and views human behaviour as governed by rules in situation-specific activity within larger social systems. As in complex organization research methodologies, it expands the units of analyses in moral development studies to rules, roles and systems. These perspectives led Kurtines to suggest the importance of considering particular situational factors and social system contingencies as influencing moral conduct. Kurtines's psycho-social approach, however, appears to be laden with structuralist influence from sociology. He follows Parsons's (1956) functional imperatives and views morality in terms of 'system maintenance and integration' (Kurtines, 1984, p. 305). In the end, his focus is less projective than his approach, as he continues to maintain the individual as the immediate focus of analysis and the ultimate agent of responsibility.

It is at these points where the social psychological paradigm moves on. It opens a vision to explore moral responsibility beyond the person and the situation to wider interactive levels of the complex organization environment where moral reasoning and socio-cultural meanings shape the understanding of morality in the individual and collectivities (Weinreich-Haste, 1984). Its focus expands, therefore, beyond the individual, broadening the scope of corporate ethics to internal organizational collectivities, such as departmental divisions and work-teams and their situation-specific vulnerabilities; and to the corporation itself with its open system environments, such as culturally specific industry domains and rule-governing agencies. Corporate morality, in this paradigm, is not conceived as system maintenance or even integration but as *dynamic interactional development* for 'the preservation of the character of the system' (Katz and Kahn, 1972, p. 42). More immediately, this dual focus on the individual and the corporation will open symbolic interactionist perspectives from sociology to trace the origins of the corporate conscience and to identify the 'corporate mind' and the 'corporate self' as collective units of analyses. In the end, the dual focus will propose new symbolic organization constructs in the moral atmosphere of a company to analyse and evaluate these units and to preserve the 'corporate character' through the co-responsibility of the individual and the corporation.

Corporate conscience and social process

To understand how the corporate conscience works, it may be helpful to compare its social processes and organizational dimensions with the individual conscience and its interactional dimensions. If the individual mind and the self develop out of the social context of self–other role interaction processes, it could be postulated that the development of the 'corporate mind' and the 'corporate self' would follow the same social psychological processes. George Herbert Mead (1934) demonstrated that the individual mind and the self develop out of what others say about that individual. He explained these processes through role theory. The self interacts with others, dramatizes its image by taking the role of others and applies symbols to that role which formulate impressions for its identity. The individual's self-image thus forms out of the feedback from the perceived impressions of others. This self-image contains two internal dialectical dimensions: the assertive self, the 'I', and the reflexive self, the 'Me'. As their interactional dialectic becomes conducive to self-knowledge and self-reflection, reflexivity actually becomes constitutive of the individual conscience.

Charles Horton Cooley (1902) typified these identity-making attributes as the 'looking-glass self'. Projecting his analogy from the individual to the collective unit of analysis helps to trace the social psychological processes of corporate conscience formation. Thus, when the 'corporate mind' sees itself in the internal organizational mirror of its own workforce and hears about its management behaviour from its employees, it knows in truth how it looks. When it sees itself in the 'looking-glass' reflectors of its complex organizational environment and hears about its own corporate behaviour from its suppliers, clients and public, it begins to face its inner conscience. It would appear plausible to suggest this as a model for the development of the organization self and the corporate conscience. Notice, for example, the 'corporate mind' of Campeau's Federated Stores, as it saw itself in the complex organizational 'looking-glass' of the retail environment, the stock market and the consumer world. It knew in truth how it looked in the corporate dress of leveraged buy-outs but left serious doubt about its striving for moral redevelopment through its calculating postures for bankruptcy redemption (Quint, 1990).

Such truth-facing dilemmas constitute a challenge for companies seeking to create an ethical image. The internal struggle for the corporate mind is one between its assertive organization self and its reflexive organization self. The social psychological processes are the same. That is, both self-images derive from the perceived impressions of others; the difference between the formations, however, arises from the respective culturally specific meanings (Weinreich-Haste, 1984) in the corporate mind as it perceives itself in the different organizational 'looking-glasses' in its complex organization environment. Thus, when a Savings and Loan CEO uses his executive office, and dramatizes his transactions to his directors and management staff through scheming investment symbols, his asserted executive self-image becomes dependent on his perceived impressions of admiring colleagues and compliant subordinates. This image can be quite different from how his reflexive self-image appears when he perceives the responses of the investigating media, complaining investors, punitive courts and a distrustful nation. Rediscovering a company's ethical image then is a matter of exposing executives and managers to knowledge of the reflexive processes of self-image formation and how these are dependent upon organizational reference group perception. Executives and directors have to pay attention to the differences in how and why the company is being perceived by its networking reference groups. It is through these comparisons that organizational reflexivity becomes plausible and ethical image reconstruction possible. Such reconstructive work demands the application of reality construction theory (Berger and Luckman, 1967) to the ethos of corporate culture and to the ethics of management process (Guerrette, 1988).

Inasmuch as this theory explains reality as shaped by the social interactional symbols of an organization as constituted on the values of its culture, executives can change an established organization by rebuilding the interactional value symbols of its business enterprises and managerial processes. Not only can they so change the reality of its organization culture and reorder its value system but they can also manage its corporate ethical image to preserve the 'character' of the system. And because every organizational image needs flexibility for adjusting to the various reference groups in its interorganizational environment, executives have to direct the reflexive processes of the company conscience in order to coordinate necessary corporate image variations in its multiple organizational self-images. Such reflexive organizational direction manages a critical ethical consistency in the overall corporate image and establishes the social psychological groundwork in the company for ethical plausibility in its corporate structure and value-system-building in its management process.

Value-system-building and management process

Building values in a company is not particularly difficult. It is a basic social organization process that more often than not just happens in any business enterprise or economic venture. Since values are really nothing more than priorities, any company that sets policy goals and has a strategy for attaining these goals, obviously has its priorities in place and thus can be said to have values. The reflexive questions are however – are these values good, honourable or ethical? Are they based on universal principles? Only with these kinds of values and the moral performance they would generate in a company can a corporate ethical image be created. The task in value-system-building is to synchronize company priorities with values grounded in the universal ethical principles of justice and reciprocity (Kohlberg *et al.*, 1990) and the human resource concerns of interactional caring and sensitivity (Gilligan, 1982).

William Weiss, chairman and CEO of Ameritech Corporation, has demonstrated a facility for synchronizing these reflexive management processes with principled value-system-building. Perceiving his leadership role as the principal architect for establishing the corporate culture and for defining the character of its business, he anchors his value-system-building in *three basic operational principles* that signify universal morality: first, moral consistency with the corporate conscience; second, moral efficiency with ambiguous reality; and third, moral governance with interdependent benefits (1986). In observance of these principles, he builds the company's value system on *seven fundamental value cornerstones* that establish the corporate culture in a caring service-reciprocity: (1) *the dignity of the individual,* by which he means 'leading people to self-realization and giving them the freedom to achieve it'; (2) *openness to people and to ideas* - to 'allow us to do the job, not just well, but better'; (3) *optimum standards of service* in preservation of the company's historical tradition of contractual excellence; (4) *entrepreneurship* for attitudinal creativity and latitudinal responsibility; (5) *synergism* as a corporate motivating force for shaping a social and global environment; (6) *leadership through competence,* analogizing from academic freedom to managerial freedom to promote initiative; (7) *behaviour based on values* to preserve organization consistency. On these value cornerstones, Weiss has shaped a social character for Ameritech with his own morally stimulating mandate:

> I want everyone in Ameritech to have respect for one another, respect for their co-workers and for their ideas and aspirations . . . respect for our customers and their needs and expectations. Respect for others, in my book, is an essential characteristic. Without it, you cannot have self-respect.
>   Finally, I want us to trust ourselves and to trust one another, so that together we can achieve more than we ever thought possible [p. 247].

Reflecting 'an ethic of care' (Gilligan, 1982), he has set this deontological mandate as the moral charter of the company value system. As moral leader, he has made it expressively clear that his executive mission is to expect no less from his workforce than moral consistency with this value-system:

> Our task is to discuss and crystallize issues of a corporate value system – values that have meaning and are useful in reality, as well as in the forum that created them. In short, we should be able not just to *define* a value system – we must be able to *live* by it! [p. 243].

By discussing and crystallizing issues of the company value system, executives enable management to be in touch with the corporate conscience. It is through these discussions that executives can direct organizational reflexivity and assess ethical image consistency in the company in accordance with its value-system and its own operational versions of universal ethical principles.[2] With this reflexive awareness in place, management can pay attention to corporate ethical image-projection, keeping the company on a moral course by managing the appropriate symbolic imagery for achieving this critical ethical consistency.

Ethical image-projection and impression management

Erving Goffman demonstrated how one can take charge of one's own self-image formation through 'techniques of impression management' (1959). He showed that individuals deliberately select an array of symbols in the orders of dress, fashion, style, etc., to manage a distinct impression on others. Analogously, corporate planners need to select the appropriate ethical symbols of policy formulations and company operations that render corporate ethical behaviour and the organizational image plausible (Guerrette, 1988). This can be accomplished by dramatizing, *with authenticity*, such symbols as: ethical policy and value statements; ethical guidelines for business practice and management process; interactive 'face-work' (Goffman, 1955) that pays attention to company history, seniority and service, performance management and employee development planning, employee assistance programming, organization ritual and ceremony, art and architecture in the workplace, occupational health and safety for the workforce; etc. In this symbolic corporate cultural context, the dramatization of interactional encounters among personnel in companies can be creatively managed for intentional and planned outcomes through organization rituals. These kinds of ritualized impression management techniques can thus serve as an embodiment of social order (Goffman, 1963, 1971) and function as constitutive of a corporate value-system

Per-Olof Berg of the Copenhagen School of Economy and Business Administration identifies such impression management techniques as 'framing the context' for company-image-building (1986). In such a frame, the corporate planner fashions the kind of organizational image he or she wants projected and presents the company through, what he calls, 'symbolic fields of action' or 'shared frames of meanings' (p. 559). A successful company that understands the analogous interplay of the individual and the corporate conscience with dramatized symbolic management impression strategies and by framing a local context for the interactional caring of its workforce, clients and even the community is Ben and Jerry's Ice Cream. Ben Cohen, CEO, and Jerry Greenfield, president of the corporation, have consistently fashioned a corporate ethical image for their company through shared frames of cultural meanings in the workplace and have projected this image to the community through symbolic festival activities in the marketplace. By means of these organizational ethical strategies and interactional festive rituals, they have shown how a corporate conscience is an effective managerial instrument for economic planning and development and market profitability (see Lawson, 1988).

According to Berg, framing the corporate image through such shared interactive symbols and organization rituals, structures the priorities of a company, generates a common purpose for its workforce and provides direction for its business mission. A symbolic field of reference creates a common reality perspective in an organization and a value orientation for its members to follow. Berg further contends that this kind of strategic planning of corporate image-projection not only creates the desired company identity but its reflection in the 'reference group mirrors' of its interorganizational environment feeds back into the company and impels the workforce to live up to the projected image. If ethics are a constitutive part of that framed context, the company value-system will be in place and its ethical image secured.

THE MBE MODEL

Corporate conscience formation and management by ethics (MBE)

Such value-system-building may be relatively simple to plan but a further challenge is the socialization of corporate conscience formation. A corporate ethical image, framed to manage an impression, may be the product of planned social psychological processes but these are not enough. The corporate ethical image needs validity. Impression management and contextual framing may project a desired corporate face but such strategies do not automatically deliver the corporate ethical image, especially when there may be covert flaws in the image (see Lutz, 1983; Olasky, 1985).[3] These very phrases have a hollow sound. An image needs more than an impression, more than a frame. It needs, above all, *authenticity.* The image needs an identity; and its representation, a reality. A corporate ethical image needs the reality of a corporate ethical identity and it is the corporate conscience that gives this identity and establishes its ethical reality. Not only must corporate planners understand this but also corporate advertisers as well. The public knows a fraud and the organizational other can see through any hollow frame.

Corporate planners can meet the challenge of cultivating the corporate conscience by recognizing their roles as company socialization agents. The literature of social psychology characterizes parents and teachers as '*caretakers*' (Lindesmith *et al.*, 1975, p. 300 – emphasis added) and 'socialization agents' (Sewell, 1970) for the cultivation of the individual conscience in the child. In this sense, senior management and especially corporate executives can fulfil this role for the cultivation of the corporate conscience, as expressed above by the Ameritech CEO (Weiss, 1986). Executive development seminars and management training workshops can provide an effective communication forum for enacting these socialization roles. These seminars and workshops can demonstrate how moral development theory and its practical application in company operations can shape worker attitudes and contribute to their ethical performance (Guerrette, 1986, 1988).

The shaping of worker attitudes in company operations as a socialization effect of the interactional authority styles of management has been a subject of analysis with some moral significance in critical sociology (see Mills, 1948/ 1970; Rioux, 1970). Mills defined how the 'power factor' in authority systems conditions response levels of workers and thus shapes workforce morale. His critical thought challenged earlier attempts in applied industrial sociology and humanistic management models (Mayo, 1945; Roethlisberger and Dickson, 1946) to a more practical/political approach to morale-building and the social reconstruction of industrial relations. Blumer (1947) also promoted the need for the *moral* and political critique of industrial relations. Based on his development of Mead's (1934) theories into symbolic interactionism in sociology (Blumer, 1969), MBE represents a 'critical practical' model designed to reshape workforce morale through the application of moral development theory and the organizational reconstruction of authority systems.

Ethical consciousness development and moral development theory

Moral development theory was developed by Lawrence Kohlberg (1981) to explain how moral reasoning functions within the cognitive structures of individuals and how it progresses through time to higher stages of moral judgments and responsibility awareness. It was derived by him from a series of longitudinal and cross-cultural studies of 'the child as a moral philosopher'. The studies were designed to trace the moral reasoning of his subjects, in a sample of ten- to sixteen-year-old boys, from their responses to hypothetical moral dilemmas (1984).

Historical overview of the research

In the first period of his research, he observed that these responses revealed six stages of moral reasoning which his subjects invoked to support their moral judgments: (1) a fear of punishment stage; (2) an instrumental exchange stage; (3) an interpersonal conformity stage; (4) a social system stage; (5) a social contract stage; and (6) a universal ethical principle stage. He also noticed that these stages were divided into three larger categories of moral reasoning, reflecting developing levels of socio-cultural conventions: I, pre-conventional; II, conventional; and III, post-conventional.

By repeating the studies every four years with his original sample, Kohlberg noticed that his subjects progressed through the sequence of these stages without skipping a stage, though not all reached the higher stages. He subsequently introduced these studies into other cultures in addition to the United States, including Mexico, Taiwan, Israel and Turkey. In this work, not only did he discover these same sample patterns and progressions; but he also learned that they manifested no significant variance with reference to social class, religious or non-religious affiliation, or cultural conditions. Finally, Kohlberg found that progression through these stages reflected learning patterns of cognitive organization with increasing differentiation of stage meanings and incremental integration of stage reasoning (Power *et al.*, 1989).

In later periods of his research, Kohlberg initiated experiments in moral education in schools and in prisons, studying pedagogical methods and organizational climates that were conducive to the moral development of his subjects through these stages (Kohlberg *et al.*, 1975; Kohlberg, 1986). By developing measurement instruments for assessing populations, he subsequently found that very few reach stage 6; that only about 15 per cent reach stage 5; and that most attain a 3- and 4-stage conventional level (Colby and Kohlberg, 1987). He also found that, in the American study, increased role-taking opportunities for middle-class children allowed experiences of societal integration and thus facilitated social system reasoning. In this study, he likewise noticed that formal education was a facilitating factor in development to this stage (Colby and Kohlberg, 1987).

These critical findings challenged Kohlberg to redefine his stages and to reformulate his descriptions of their sequences (see Table 4.1). In this work, he addressed the problems of subjectivity and relativity in the conscience decisions of some stage 6 adolescents. In turn, these practical complications forced him to redefine this stage in terms of the psychological components and philosophical principles that open a consistent 'moral point of view' (Kohlberg *et al.*, 1990). By this he meant a 'moral method' for arriving at moral judgments. He saw this method as a way of reasoning to right judgments that are *prescriptive*, i.e. duty-bound; *reversible*, i.e. applicable equally to one as well as to another in all situations; and *universal*, i.e. consistent 'to any life and to anyone's point of view' (Kohlberg, 1973; Kohlberg and Candee, 1984, p. 61). Responding to the lack of evidence from his empirical findings regarding the plausibility of such an ideal development of moral reasoning at this level, Kohlberg concluded that 'stage 6 may perhaps be viewed as part of a broader level of "ethical and religious philosophy" supporting moral action' (Kohlberg, 1984, p. 35).

MBE and moral development theory application

Inasmuch as MBE is a social psychological model to support and improve moral action in the workplace, the application of Kohlberg's moral development theory and its redefined scale, with the six stages, will be pursued to advance the workforce through the scale and even to the higher stages. Retaining stage 6 in this use of the scale is not a matter of an idealistic value bias, either in religion or philosophy. It is rather supported by a certain 'psychological attractiveness' that bears 'empirical significance' from 'a verified line of development' (Kung, 1985). It is, moreover, grounded in a critical sociological perspective from symbolic interaction theory and dialectical conflict theory (Guerrette, 1981; Heydebrand, 1977), suggesting

Table 4.1 The six stages of moral judgment

Level and Stage	What is right	Reasons for doing right	Social perspective of stage
		Content of Stage	
LEVEL I. Pre-conventional	Avoiding breaking rules backed by punishment; obedience for its own sake; to avoid physical damage to persons and property	Avoidance of punishment, and the superior power of authorities.	*Egocentric point of view.* Doesn't consider the interests of others or recognize that they differ from the actor's; doesn't relate two points of view. Actions are considered physically rather than in terms of psychological interests of others. Confusion of authority's perspective with one's own.
Stage 1: Heteronomous morality			
Stage 2: Individualism, instrumental purpose and exchange	Following rules only when it is to someone's immediate interest; acting to meet your own interests and needs and letting others do the same. Right is also what's fair, an equal exchange, a deal, an agreement	To serve your own needs or interests in a world where you have to recognize that other people have their interests too.	*Concrete individualistic perspective.* Aware that everybody has his own interest to pursue and these conflict, so that right is relative (in the concrete individualistic sense).
LEVEL II. Conventional	Living up to what is expected by people close to you or what people generally expect of people in your role as son, brother, friend, etc. 'Being good' is important and means having good motives, showing concern about others. It also means keeping mutual relationships, such as trust, loyalty, respect and gratitude.	The need to be a good person in your own eyes and those of others. Your caring for others. Belief in the Golden Rule. Desire to maintain rules and authority which support stereotypically good behaviour.	*Perspective of the individual in relationships with other individuals.* Aware of shared feelings, agreements and expectations which take primacy over individual interests. Relates points of view through the concrete Golden Rule, putting yourself in the other guy's shoes. Does not yet consider generalized system perspective.
Stage 3: Mutual Interpersonal expectations, relationships and interpersonal conformity			

Stage 4: Social system and conscience	Fulfilling the actual duties to which you have agreed. Laws are to be upheld except in extreme cases where they conflict with other fixed social duties. Right is also contributing to society, the group or institution.	To keep the institution going as a whole, to avoid the breakdown in the system 'if everyone did it', or the imperative of conscience to meet your defined obligations (easily confused with Stage 3 belief in rules and authority).	*Differentiation of societal points of view from interpersonal agreement or motives.* Takes the point of view of the system that defines roles and rules. Considers individual relations in terms of place in the system.
LEVEL III. Post-conventional or principled			
Stage 5: Social contract or utility and individual rights	Being aware that people hold a variety of values and opinions, that most values and rules are relative to your group. These relative rules should usually be upheld, however, in the interest of impartiality and because they are the social contract. Some non-relative values and rights like *life* and *liberty*, however, must be upheld in any society and regardless of majority opinion.	A sense of obligation to law because of your social contract to make and abide by laws for the welfare of all and for the protection of all people's rights. A feeling of contractual commitment, freely entered upon, to family, friendship, trust and work obligation. Concern that laws and duties be based on rational calculation of overall utility, 'the greatest good for the greatest number'.	*Prior-to-society perspective.* Perspective of a rational individual aware of values and rights prior to social attachments and contracts. Integrates perspectives by formal mechanisms of agreements, contract, objective impartiality and due process. Considers moral and legal points of view; recognizes that they sometimes conflict and finds it difficult to integrate them.
Stage 6: Universal ethical principles	Following self-chosen ethical principles. Particular laws or social agreements are usually valid because they rest on such principles. When laws violate these principles, one acts in accordance with the principle. Principles are universal principles of justice: the equality of human rights and respect for the dignity of human beings as individual persons.	The belief as a rational person in the validity of universal moral principles, and a sense of personal commitment to them.	*Perspective of a moral point of view* from which social arrangements derive. Perspective is that of any rational individual recognizing the nature of morality or the fact that persons are ends in themselves and must be treated as such.

Source: Kohlberg (1984, pp.174-176).

that the lack of empirical verification of stage 6 may be attributable to social system problems and organization contradictions. The fact that few can be documented in his research as having attained sixth-stage moral conscious-ness is not a reflection on the validity of the stage but is likely evidence of the futility of hegemonic, conventional hierarchical systems in social structures to allow and support fuller moral development of people. Etzioni (1988) alludes to the 'Moral Implications' of socio-economic hegemony as a determinant to moral behavioural outcomes: '. . . preferences are to a significant extent socially formed and hence reflect the society's values, culture, and power structure' (pp. 246–247). He also recognizes the natural moral development capacity of people for making right moral choices:

> In short, it seems quite clear that neo-classical economics, and its 'consumer sovereignty' assumptions, in effect reflect a value system and a social, economic, and political structure – that of mature capitalism [Hirsch, 1976] – rather than *human nature* [emphasis added]. To maintain otherwise, leads those who internalize such a theory to assume that their buying preferences reveal normatively correct choices, because they made them, presumably on their own, while in effect they are largely culturally bound and conformist [p. 247].

In short, it seems quite clear, from a socio-economic perspective and the latent philosophical assumptions in moral development theory, that workers can function as 'natural philosophers' at least through stage 4 (Gibbs, 1977; Habermas, 1990a), if not through stage 5 (Colby and Kohlberg, 1987). It would also seem that if few can reach stage 5 in hegemonic conventional systems, moral development capacity might be more fully realized in reformed moral structures and open organization systems.

Finally, inasmuch as opening systems for moral structural reform is radically dependent on a communication ethic, MBE application of moral development theory is consistent with the approach of the works of Jurgen Habermas (1979, 1984, 1990a, b; see also Forester, 1985). Sharing the critical reconstructive perspectives of this approach, the applied MBE model represents an attempt to build the social psychological constructs in organization planning and reform that can facilitate a communication ethic in workplace structures and lead to both an individual and corporate 'moral point of view'.

MBE as a moral education model

MBE, therefore, presents a moral education model for corporate executives and managers with a six-step plan to recreate a moral climate in the company and to open its system to organization and governance change. As such, the MBE model is a critical reconstructive intervention plan to cultivate the corporate conscience and educate the workforce. Although it relies on

Kohlberg's development theories and dilemma methods for moral education advancement, MBE is not merely an intervention plan for ethical problem resolution in the workplace. The model will subsequently discuss the techniques and skills required to recognize such problems and to resolve them. Its overall purpose, rather, is to raise an ethical consciousness in the workforce that develops moral reasoning skills towards a 'moral point of view' in work performance. It is thus a moral education programme for stimulating moral responsibility and facilitating advanced moral performance.

To this end, the pedagogical dynamic for MBE moral education intervention is ethical communication. With an interactional medium for communicative ethics (Habermas, 1990b), MBE offers an informing socialization design for managers to supportively interact with workers. Through this medium and by a practical and ideal typical use of the Kohlberg scale, it reconstructs a forum for managers to coach workers towards higher moral performance outcomes (Baxter and Rarick, 1987; Harding and Snyder, 1991). In this reconstructed moral climate, designed to gradually open a 'moral point of view' among executives, managers and workers, it is reasonable to expect that worker performance preferences can reflect the higher post-conventional stages in more significant numbers at stage 5, and with some, possibly, at stage 6.

Similar conclusions were reached by Oser and Schlafli (1985) whose moral education interventions with banking apprentices in Switzerland were posited on the higher expectations of the moral development capacity:

> And it is especially apprentices, whose training is above all geared to production, who should have a right to acquire a higher socio-moral competence and thereby a greater social identity. . . . What we have striven for, and achieved, must however be judged by the general human goal of education toward social autonomy and competence. This means that higher socio-moral development enables an individual who has the requisite thinking ability to attain the highest universal principles of justice and of society with which he can understand and tackle what he encounters in his dealings with others in his work [p. 294].

Moral education and intervention paths. The six-step MBE plan for raising ethical consciousness in the workforce can be facilitated by following the intervention strategies of the Oser and Schlafli experiment. Their study stressed that moral learning stimulation by the socializing supervisors requires defined intervention paths to higher-level development. These paths need to follow *four phases of a subject's transition* towards higher development: first, the phase of *disequilibrium*, through which a worker is stimulated to realize that there is a moral problem or conflict; second, the phase of *dissatisfaction* which emanates from the worker's disturbance that his or her solutions are inconsistent or inadequate; third, the phase of *integration* that evolves out of discourse with others, directing previous insights towards new visions for better or more just solutions; and fourth, the *reinforcement* phase, during which the integrated vision is confirmed by practice or performance.

Moral education and intermediary goals. Along these transitional paths to higher development, it is imperative, according to Oser and Schlafli, that the supervising leaders understand the social and interactional processes of the moral development transformation in terms of *six intermediary goals*: (1) moral stage theory understanding; (2) moral sensitization; (3) moral problem-solving engagement; (4) moral climate conduciveness; (5) discourse empathy and frankness; and (6) value hierarchy upgrading. Understanding the socialization processes of these intermediary goals allows supervisors or managers to collectively and individually organize their own teaching plans for stimulating moral development. For example, managers need to understand the theory themselves as they launch moral education intervention in their companies. The theory, as supplemented by the MBE social psychological paradigm explained above, frames the moral learning and guides the interactional processes through the transitional phases, indicating to managers how to improve the moral sensitivity of the workers. It also lays out pedagogical methods for evoking moral awareness through comparative analytical discussions of hypothetical and actual moral dilemmas in the workplace. As these social and interactive processes develop through the four phases, the managers draw on the social psychological and organization theories within the paradigm to reconstruct the appropriate moral climate for value hierarchy upgrading through frank, empathic communication. *By understanding these socialization processes, managers enjoy a framework and a direction for their interventions*, allowing them to coach workers through their transitional phases towards the ultimate goals of higher development transformation. The intervention paths through these transitional phases and the socialization processes of their intermediary goals will open more clearly and concretely through the unfolding of the six-step MBE plan.

The Kohlberg scale in the workplace

The *first step* in utilizing MBE as a model for ethical consciousness development *is to show managers how a worker's moral awareness and ethical stance might be plotted on the Kohlberg scale.* (See Exhibit 4.A – this is a descriptive table aligning the moral stages with a worker's occupational perspectives in terms of work, work performance and work relationships, as interpreted by the author.)

Measuring individuals. In becoming familiar with the Kohlberg scale, executives and managers should recall the measurement findings that Kohlberg and his associates report; namely, that most subjects' scores were at the conventional levels of stages 3 and 4; and that only about 15 per cent reached stage 5, with very few reaching stage 6. They should also know that, as this research finds its way into corporate culture and management studies,

Exhibit 4.A Kohlberg's moral development scale (commentary by Richard H. Guerrette, PhD)

Stages	Worker occupational perspectives
1. Punishment avoidance	*Egocentric point of view* Considers work as imperative for personal goals and engages in work performance with purely functional efforts to complete orders. Considers authority relations to be avoided for fear of punishment.
2. Instrumental exchange	*Individual expediency perspective* Considers work as instrumental for personal goals and engages in work performance for functionally expedient self-interest gain. Considers work relationships as relative to vested-interest and need exchange.
3. Interpersonal conformity	*Interpersonal concordance perspective* Considers work as expressive for personal accomplishments and engages in work performance with self-affirming dependability incentives. Considers work relationships as opportunities for interpersonal caring reciprocities.
4. Social system	*Generalized system perspective* Considers work as good for the company and as functional for the system and engages in work performance as a moral obligation to the company and to society. Considers work relationships with caring reciprocity as integral to operations and as profitable for the company.
5. Social contractual	*Individual rational perspective* (Utilitarian perspective with a social justice point of view) Considers work as beneficial for the company and the overall good of society and engages in work performance with moral consistency as a legal obligation to the company and society. Considers work relationships as egalitarian with a contractual commitment to fairness, according to the principle of social justice for all.
6. Universal ethical principles	*Individual universal perspective* (Deontological perspective with a 'moral point of view') Considers work in its own integrity, i.e., in an overall ecology and engages in performance with an ideal value latency in positive or negative conditions (e.g., working in a company with congruent or contrary values). Considers work relationships in terms of ideal role-taking and caring reciprocities according to the universal ethical principles of justice, equality of human rights and respect for the dignity of persons.

later findings tend to confirm these averages. Higgins and Gordon (1985), for example, found that in two worker-owned companies, in Northern and Southern regions of the United States, both management and worker averages in the Northern company were at stage 4. With ownership restructuring and increased democracy, the new president, one board member and two other executives, who stayed on, used stage 4/5 reasoning. All other board members and two executives, who stayed on, used stage 4/5 reasoning. All other board members and two executives from the past were at stage 4 and another at stage 3. In the Southern company, they found that the moral reasoning of managers was at stages 3 and 3/4, and the workers were at stages 2/3 to 3/4.

In a more recent and more representative sample of seventy-four managers from different sized corporations with thirty-seven interviewed respondents, Weber (1990) found that 86.4 per cent were at the conventional level of the scale, with 45.9 per cent at stage 3 and 40.5 per cent at stage 4. As these scores tend to reflect averages among adults (Blasi, 1980) and other business professionals (Wood *et al.*, 1988), it should also be remembered that the research has only just begun to be applied in the corporate domain and that newer interdisciplinary theoretical paradigms and management models, such as MBE, may significantly influence future measurements and their methodologies (see below and also Payne and Giacalone, 1990).

Measuring collectivities. In this regard, it is important to single out the interdisciplinary approach and methodological advancement of the Higgins and Gordon study (1985). This work has not only opened new interlinking tracks between moral psychology and sociology, but has created new measuring instruments, similar to those used in complex organization studies (see above), shifting the unit of analysis in corporate ethics from the individual to the organization. By measuring, for example, work-related norms in their two sample organizations, in terms of (1) their legitimacy of origin, i.e., authority imposed or collectively decided; (2) their regulative power, i.e., its commitment and institutional holding power; and (3) their 'moral stage' of articulation, i.e., the reasoning level of their social understanding, individual or collective, the study has introduced a method to begin ways of measuring the collective dimensions of the corporate conscience. 'The stage of representation of a truly collective norm, therefore, is the shared meaning a norm has for the functioning of the group and not the average stage of the individuals within it' (p. 250).

It is in this sense that executives should approach the *second step* of MBE ethical consciousness development: *plotting their company's moral reasoning and ethical norms on the Kohlberg scale.* (See Exhibit 4.B – this exhibit is likewise the author's descriptive table aligning the moral stages with a company's operational perspectives in terms of corporate interests and production, as articulated in its policy norms and production strategies.) The exhibit reflects organizational comparisons between the functional norms of production, as

Exhibit 4.B Kohlberg's moral development scale (commentary by Richard H. Guerrette, PhD)

Stages	Corporate operational perspectives
1. Punishment avoidance	*Corporate-centric point of view* Doesn't consider the interests or well-being of workers or consumers or other corporations in its organization-set or domain. Considers production in exacting operational terms for optimal efficiency and in functional economic terms for profit maximization. Stay out of court.
2. Instrumental exchange	*Corporate expediency perspective* Considers the interests of workers and others in its organization-set or domain in exchange for the company good or for operational advantages. Considers production in expedient instrumental terms relative to company goals and purposes and in exchange-economic terms by bargain-dealing calculations.
3. Interpersonal conformity	*Corporate relations perspective* Considers the interests of workers and others in its organization-set or domain for company-affirming corporate responsibility. Considers production in conventional operational terms and conforming to normative interorganizational expectations and government regulations and in traditional economic terms of what's profitable for the company is good for workers.
4. Social system	*Corporate system perspective* Considers the interests of others in its organization-set relative to the functional social and economic good. Considers corporate relations in terms of the company's place in the socio-economic system. Considers production from functional imperatives of integration and latency of values in terms of 'pattern maintenance' and 'system management'.
5. Social contractual	*Corporate rational perspective* Considers the interests of others relative to individual and corporate rights through social justice and legal contractual processes. Considers production contractually with organization consistency in the workforce and corporate responsibility in the marketplace according to the overall good of society from a corporate rational point of view.
6. Universal ethical principles	*Corporate universal perspective* Considers the interests of others with respect for the dignity of all persons and beings and especially with care for its human and natural resources. Considers production from the interactional imperatives of integrity and ideal role-taking reciprocity from a corporate 'moral point of view'.

grounded in the functional imperatives of Talcott Parsons (1956) and the interactional norms of production, as interpreted by the author for moral development process.

In becoming familiar with the use of the Kohlberg scale at this corporate or collective unit of analysis, it might help executives to compare their own company estimates with the results of the Higgins and Gordon (1985) study. The normative structure in the Northern company in this work was articulated in terms of four work-related norms: (1) working hard; (2) work quality by professional standards; (3) productivity; and (4) responsibility to complete work. As these norms were tested for their legitimacy, regulative power, and moral reasoning and social understanding, as explained above, the first norm scored at stage 4; the other three scored at stages 3/4. The normative structure in the Southern company was articulated in terms of three similar norms: (1) working hard; (2) maintaining productivity; and (3) caring and cooperation. According to the same testing criteria, the first norm scored at stages 2–2/3; the second scored at stage 3; and the third scored at stages 3–3/4. Since the executives' estimates are only suggested with reference to Exhibit 4.B and because the normative structures in their companies may differ substantially in their articulation, general comparisons from the descriptions in the exhibit are obviously sufficient for assessment learning familiarity.

Authoritative styles and moral development

Individual management domain and workforce morality. The *third step* of MBE ethical consciousness development is *to communicate to managers how their authority styles might be influencing the compliance postures and attitudinal dispositions of their subjects.* This is to suggest that if we conceptualize workplace relationships, recalling Kurtines's (1984) psycho-social role-theoretical approach to behaviour as rule-governed, it is plausible to expect the authority–subordinate correlations in Exhibit 4.C. This approach '. . . views moral development as the outcome of an interaction between the individual rule user, follower, or maker and the network of rules that constitutes the essence of morality [Piaget, 1965] and focuses on the attitudes, affects, and cognitions of the individual toward those rules' (p. 306). The interactional correlations, therefore, between the individual employee and the rule-governing manager can be assessed on this scale according to their respective levels of reasoning about the rules, their authority style enforcement, and their compliant postures and attitudinal effects. For these assessments, it should be noted that the correlations in the exhibit are plausible when one recalls the research of Hertzberg (1968) who found that 60–75 per cent of workers reported that their immediate supervisor was the most stressful aspect of their job. Moreover, it should be remembered that socialization and selection processes for leadership in corporations are not known to have moral criteria as significant for

Exhibit 4.C Moral development scaling and authority–subordinate interaction

Stages	Authority style	Compliance pattern	Worker attitude
1. Punishment avoidance	Coercive	Alienative	Avoidant
2. Instrumental exchange	Remunerative	Calculative	Vested-interest
3. Interpersonal conformity	Normative	Moral	Caring
4. Social system	Systemic	Social	Conscientious
5. Social contractual	Rational	Committed	Trustworthy
6. Universal ethical principles	Collegial	Cooperative	Ideal caring

hierarchical promotion, in spite of widespread public opinion among employees that honesty and ethics are very important qualities for management (Emler and Hogan, 1991). With such discrepancy between leadership selection significance and employee preference insignificance, it is no small wonder that Emler and Hogan conclude: 'Almost all employed adults report that they had to spend some considerable time during the course of their career working for an *intolerable* boss' (p. 87). Neither is it any wonder that Hogan *et al.* (1988) report exactly the same results of 60–75 per cent as a base-rate for 'flawed leadership' in corporate America, further suggesting the plausibility of the correlations in Exhibit 4.C. Furthermore, it should be noted that the correlations in the exhibit are supported, in part, by Etzioni's (1961/1975) studies of authority–subordinate relations in terms of authority styles and compliance patterns. These studies found that coercive authority types provoke alienative compliance among their subjects; that remunerative (exchange) types evoke calculative compliance; and that normative types receive moral compliance. While these findings represent correlations through the first three stages of the scale, they would suggest that similar correlations, as those speculated in the exhibit, are likely to be found at the remaining stages, along with the worker attitude speculations for all corresponding stages. Finally, it should be noted that the authority styles, compliance patterns and worker attitudes speculated for stages 5 and 6 could also be found at stages 3 and 4, respectively. The differences between these categories are that, at the post-conventional levels of 5 and 6, the reasoning prompting the attitudes and behaviour would be emanating from principles with universal application, beyond an individual company or manager.

Corporate power domains and organization morality. The reason why it is so important for executives and managers to pay attention to their authority styles is not just because they may be influencing compliance patterns and attitudinal dispositions among workers but even more critically because the overall authority culture in a company may be actually controlling the way its executives and managers think and the way its workers perform relative to moral issues (Emler and Hogan, 1991). This critical practical matter is only to recognize the complex multidimensional and cross-cultural influences that bear upon moral reasoning and moral action discrepancy both at individual personal and collective organizational levels (Turiel and Smetana, 1984). For instance, at the individual level, workers, managers and even some executives may reflect high-stage moral reasoning and behaviour in other cultural domains of life and activity, but display serious discrepancies of high moral performance in the workplace because of persistent conflicts between personal performance goals and the organization production goals of senior company executives and policy makers (see Gellerman, 1986; see also note 2 below). Again, at the collective level, a company may be striving to live up to the corporate responsibility norms in production and marketing in its industrial sector; but, because of unyielding competition forces and less responsible normative policies or operational strategies among other collectivities within this sector, its corporate performance record may fall well short of its ethical codes and environmental goals.

Inasmuch as these multidimensional influences can factor into moral performance consistency problems in the workplace, it may help to identify their domain orientations in the company's 'organization-set'. This term represents the interacting network of a company's reference organizations within its wider interorganizational environment (Evan, 1972). In organization studies it locates the 'organizational domain' of companies (Levine and White, 1972) in the 'task environment' of its production sectors, e.g., suppliers, competitors, customers, regulatory groups, etc. (Dill, 1958). Since companies cannot arbitrarily set their own domain, an exchange agreement among their reference organizations is generally reached within the organization-set (Thompson, 1967). This agreement is referred to as the 'domain consensus' and is critical for the power relationships that form between an organization and its task environment (Braito et al., 1972). These structural organization terms suggest multiple-level interorganizational units of analysis to 'critical' moral development studies in the workplace (see note 1 below). Such analysis would address moral reasoning and moral performance inconsistency problems for the moral atmospheric reconstruction of the organization-set and the moral coordination of its domains (see Turiel and Smetana, 1984). More practically, these terms suggest to executives and managers wider interorganizational areas for knowing where to look when they assess authority-style stages and for knowing what to target to convert power relationships into moral collectivities. In sum, this 'critical practical understanding' is to suggest that authority-style adjustments may not be enough to reconcile moral reasoning and performance inconsistencies in a company, but that the political and economic power structures of its corporate culture and its organization domain may themselves require extensive MBE reform. If improved moral performance is to be an attainable and permanent goal for any company, executives must be prepared to identify performance inconsistencies throughout its corporate cultural domains and use MBE strategies and programming to coordinate moral reasoning among all levels of its organization-set.

Moral reasoning in the workplace

The *fourth step* of MBE ethical consciousness development *is to train managers how to use the Kohlberg scale for advancing a worker's moral performance through moral reasoning*. While advanced ethical consciousness does not necessarily translate into higher moral action, it can serve as a reasonable predictor of this desired outcome and help managers to attain the attractive goals of superior moral performance.

Moral reasoning and moral action. Kohlberg himself recognized the relationship between moral awareness and moral behaviour through the teaching of virtue. His understanding of virtue was immune to the cultural problems of moral relativism. He appears to have understood virtue as the *courage* (in Latin, *virtus*) emanating *from a knowledge conviction* which engenders effective incentives for action: '. . . true knowledge, knowledge of principles of justice does predict virtuous action' (1971, p. 305). In later empirical studies, he confirmed his predictive understanding by testing for ego control factors, analysing IQ and attention variables as moral reasoning determinants to cheating resistance. He suggested that '. . . *ego strength* [emphasis added] helps to carry out whatever decisions are derived from one's moral outlook, whether it is high or low' (Blasi, 1980, p. 25). This finding would appear to isolate the moral reason–moral action link to the problems of moral consistency and personal integrity, i.e., '. . . to act in ways that are consistent with one's normal insights' (pp. 40–41). Finally, he found that moral reasoning and moral action consistency can be cognitively traced through knowledge of what is right to knowledge of what is responsible. His testing here revealed that moral consistency increased not only at the higher stages of moral reasoning but even at lower stages with subjects who tended to bear an aptitude for autonomous judgments. This finding led him to '. . . give credibility to the notion that moral action is responsible choice guided by intuitions of moral values not dependent on stage sophistication' (Kohlberg and Candee, 1984, p. 63).

In more recent case-study work, Haste (1990) not only gives credibility to this notion but confirms its plausibility through a wider level of developmental analysis. She expands insight into the moral reasoning– moral action continuum by tracing an affective linkage through moral responsibility and moral commitment. She identifies three paths to moral commitment: *cognitive, affective* and *associative*, the latter two of which converge into generating an experiential response to moral engagement. The *cognitive* path opens a commitment consciousness through the understanding of moral issues in a social justice reference; the *affective* part leads to a commitment disposition form experiencing these issues in a political context; and the *associative* path derives from an historical background of exposure associations with other committed role models in a politically aware environment. Haste suggests that moral commitment can open from any of these three paths. Her explanations thus allow for responsibility as emanating *from an affective conviction* integrated with some degree of moral issue awareness, either suddenly by a conversional experience or gradually by associative exposure, compelling a moral agent to a moral action. Her conclusions are convincing because they account for the experiential realities of moral commitment in various sectors of society, particularly in social movement behaviour (see Guerrette, 1981) prior to the development of higher-stage reasoning; and because they allow for the structural plausibility of moral commitment and moral responsibility at the conventional levels of workplace behaviour and management performance.

The moral reasoning training challenge, therefore, is not only to open communication structures with workers about understanding the corporation's value-system and normative policies, but also to create an organization climate that allows workers *to experience the moral commitment of its managers to company values and norms.* The socialization imperative, in such a discursive experiential learning climate, is the moral consistency on the part of executives and managers to live up to company values and norms; and the corporate responsibility on the part of the company to live up to its policies (Weiss, 1986). This kind of affective communication is what delivers a company–management ethic for organizational consistency that creates a corporate cultural background of associative exposure for workers and fosters performance responsibility through their individual moral commitment to company values and workplace norms.

Moral reasoning and learning structure. Inasmuch as Kohlberg left a body of research on the communication structures of moral reasoning, it might be helpful for executives and managers to draw from this legacy to plan an efficient and conducive learning structure for moral development in the workplace. The value of this legacy is that it demonstrates how to provide a structured learning context for interactive ethical discourse as a forum for moral reasoning. The studies show that moral development awareness occurs over relatively long periods of time in the interactional processes of role-taking[4] and within communal arrangements of shared learning through moral dilemma resolution. Kohlberg found that when his subjects were exposed to one another in meetings, classrooms or learning groups, they engaged in open discussions, learned the viewpoints of others by taking their roles and were stimulated to higher moral reasoning manifested by others. By using the participatory structures of Socratic discourse in such peer groupings, he evoked reasoning differentiation through discussions of hypothetical moral dilemmas, allowing participants' comparisons of moral judgments between two adjacent stages. He found that when students perceived the differences of moral judgment at one stage higher than their own, they became dissatisfied with their own perceptions, integrated their learning into their own moral reasoning and tended to advance to that next higher stage. He summed up his findings this way:

> knowledge of the good is always within but needs to be drawn out . . . we have found that children and adolescents prefer the highest level of thought they can comprehend. Children comprehend all lower stages than their own, often comprehend the stage one higher, and occasionally two stages higher, although they cannot actively express these higher stages of thought. If they comprehend the stage one higher than their own, they

tend to prefer it to their own. This is basic to moral leadership in our society.

(1971, p. 307)

Moral reasoning and moral leadership. This research offers executives and managers a structured method for moral leadership in their companies. Through executive development and management-training seminars at different hierarchical levels of a company, MBE programming can be initiated with an introduction to moral development theory and practice. In the initial stages of the programming, management trainers may need more consultation resources for planning and implementing these moral reasoning learning methods, as explained here. But, subsequently, by their familiarity with the scale and their facility with Kohlberg's Socratic methods of discourse, they could easily disseminate the learning through the company, even to the levels of engaging workers in peer groups with their line managers, discussing ethical workplace dilemmas and moral performance problems (Payne, 1991).[5]

This kind of programming was utilized by a refrigeration contractors' company in the Northeast for whom the author served as management consultant. Through periodic executive development seminars, this small family-owned business firm became familiar with moral development theory in a practical experimental manner by their personal readings of the Kohlberg scale, as illustrated in Exhibit 4.A, and their company level assessments from Exhibit 4.B. Their interests grew rapidly by their authority-style reflections in Exhibit 4.C, as they faced the actual organizational moral dilemmas of internal executive peer rivalry, which was demoralizing the workforce. They discussed their interpersonal rivalries with frankness and admitted that their instrumental authority posturing was causing significant degrees of calculative compliance and scheming behaviour among the workforce and even their line managers. They also agreed that their own divisive and vested-interest exchanges were causing interdepartmental allegiance rivalries and promoting self-interested shirking behaviour on the part of service crew individuals. Continuing these seminars, weekly over several months, they argued through these organization moral dilemmas, analysing and comparing both management and workforce performance levels according to the Kohlberg scale. The executives began to perceive the higher stage attractions of rational and collegial authority styles. They then pulled together as a team and invited their line managers into the seminars. By sharing a basic and simple theoretical orientation to moral development with them, they engaged their reasoning on the relevant workforce problems at actual job sites, including abuse of company privileges and the labour cost of unapplied time. Assessing their own authority styles and matching these with the compliance patterns and attitudes of their workers in their respective departments, the line managers reasoned to their own performance dissatisfaction. They reflected a certain motivation responsibility for having been invited into collective authority deliberations, which, in turn, appeared to generate incentives for their own authority-style adjustments and moral performance advancement. By so utilizing Kohlberg's scale and integrating his moral reasoning methods with their actual experiences, the executives awakened to *courageous convictions* for personal change and to an *affective engagement* for restructuring the moral atmosphere of their small company. From their *exposure to the moral commitment of their superiors*, the line managers, in turn, effectively assumed their own individual moral responsibility for changing their departmental climates and resolving the allegiances and abuses of their subordinates.

Moral leadership and unethical scandals. Moral leadership reasoning of this kind that engages executives, line managers and workers in ongoing participatory learning structures can be much more effective in raising ethical consciousness and moral commitment than costly episodic consulting programmes. These latter programmes are usually packaged to address ethical problems, especially those that are exposed in the aftermath of public, media-ridden scandals. The company motivation, in these crisis-driven eruptions, is forced into frantic corporate face-saving tactics to restore an already ruined company image. The packages themselves are correctively framed to reverse scandals. Approaches of these kinds are limited, short-range and, however necessary, quite ineffective in forming an enduring ethical consciousness. Compare, for example, the long-term MBE structured learning approach to the scandal-solving approach of a major defence contractor, whose moral reasoning conclusion, after expensive workshop consultations with a prestigious ethical institute, was to establish an ethical ombudsman office within the company to investigate unethical production complaints.[6] MBE is an internally managed programme not just to prevent scandals and protect images but to raise ethical consciousness through moral reasoning development and to foster moral commitment through courageous and affective convictions. In short, it is a programme that is designed to create a moral atmosphere for moral responsibility, not an ethical office for unethical complaints.

Moral education and moral problems. While preventive moral education may be an attractive reason for avoiding ethical scandals, its ethical consciousness-raising benefits are not always sufficient to deal with moral problems in the workplace. These actual problems can develop in any company or industry over complicated moral issues that require practical procedures for analysis and resolution. Candee (1985) has developed systematic intervention methodologies for addressing and resolving these kinds of moral problems. Though his work was conducted in the healthcare sector and addressed moral problems in medical ethics confronted by practising professionals, his analytical methods and measuring instruments can be applied to moral problems in any workplace situation. He offers an eight-step plan that guides healthcare workers through a moral reasoning process for analysing a problem and clarifying the choices for its moral resolution. *The first step is to identify the moral dilemma.* Since not every workplace problem is a moral one in the strict sense of justice and rights and of fairness and integrity (honesty, consistency, equality, reciprocity, etc.) and since moral problems in this strict sense have multiple non-moral dimensions within their dilemmas, it is necessary to screen problems for their moral issues. *The second step is to gather and elicit claims.* This is done by defining a moral claim in terms of what a claimant wants or feels entitled to. *The third step is to establish bases for the claims.* This is accomplished by evaluating the rights or entitlements in terms of the moral language that establishes a moral argument. *The fourth and fifth steps are to determine the validity of the claim.* The criteria for these assessments are either to determine utilities or overall consequences of the claims (utilitarianism) or to determine entities as beings, i.e., people, collectivities, natural and environmental resources in their overall ecologies (deontological – see Guerrette, 1988). The *sixth, seventh and eighth steps are the problem resolution steps, involving communicating, negotiating and implementing the moral decision.* These systematic steps provide a framework within which executives, directors, managers and even workers, especially professionals in medical, legal, technological and scientific workplaces, can open a discursive ethical climate for collaborative moral reasoning and moral problem resolution (see Bowen and Power, 1993).

Moral atmosphere in the workplace

Reconstructive change in moral atmosphere does not always follow so easily from moral reasoning and its structured learning methods. Moral reasoning, with courageous and affective convictions, may induce moral commitment to moral action; but these paths to organization change do not in themselves create moral atmosphere. And so, a *fifth step* to consider for MBE ethical consciousness development through the workforce *is the systematic creation of a positive moral atmosphere in the workplace.*

Moral climate and work democracies. Again, Kohlberg's research has much to offer executives and managers for such a reconstructive mandate. He realized that for individual moral development to be an attainable goal in education, a conducive moral atmosphere would be required in schools that encompassed systematic organization change and governance reconstruction. With his colleagues, he thus developed the 'just community' model as a cluster design in participatory democracy (Power, 1988). Through this democratic approach to organization management, he created a moral atmosphere in selected secondary school environments that engaged students with an equal voice in organization deliberations and rule-making. Accordingly, his experiments allowed students to experience meaningful justice in communal structures that naturally evoked their emotional sensitivities to role-taking interaction.

Through active participation in assemblies and meeting and classroom discussions, students were led to take the role of the other, feeling the anxieties of another classmate and understanding the dilemmas of the principal or teacher. As these communal experiences awakened their consciousness to moral reasoning in group life situations, moral responsibility opened into collective awareness, establishing an organizational climate for individual and collective reciprocity.[7] As one of Kohlberg's colleagues described: 'This shared consciousness represents the authority of the group and is the real agency of moralization' (Power, 1988, p. 203). Thus, a 'just community' approach to MBE ethical consciousness development, as a participatory democratic model for sharing responsibilities as well as meanings, can open a more comprehensive, interactional strategy for organizational reframing in companies and moral atmosphere reforming in the workplace.

A similar democratic approach to moral atmosphere reform from the Kohlberg research legacy can be derived from the workplace democracy studies of his colleagues (see Higgins and Gordon, 1985). This research has opened a socio-moral perspective on the workplace and has developed methods to measure the moral levels of a work climate. By analysing the normative culture of a company and comparing its work-related norms to the individual values of its workers, these studies can assess the various role-taking opportunities of workers in the organization and within its subgroups. They can also determine the motivational dispositions of workers by comparing their moral judgment stages to the moral reasoning stages of the norms. Opening these analytical dimensions into workplace operations, the studies can predict organizational efficiency and corporate stability. In two worker-owned companies studied, Higgins and Gordon found that when the norm stages of the companies were lower than or congruent to the worker stages, the work climate was not conducive to the moral development of the workers. They therefore concluded:

> Theoretically, a company and workforce that are able to create norms understood at a stage higher than the mean individual stage should create a work climate that is seen as challenging and exciting and, thus, would lead to the moral development of individuals within it [p. 265].

They also found that when organizational diversity became manifest through value subgrouping exclusivities, role-taking opportunities among workers diminished and polarized the organizational climate. They suggest that role-taking impairment is a sign of a low moral climate and a predictor of organization instability. More positively, they conclude that caring and helping norms, democratically formulated by collaborative subgroupings in a company, enjoy more workforce legitimacy than authority-imposed norms. As such, these democratic norms create a discursive learning climate in the company, facilitate role-taking reciprocity and strengthen organization stability.

Although these studies of moral climate were conducted in two democratically organized worksites, they have particular relevance for MBE implementation and significance for the corporate re-organization planning of executives.

First, regarding MBE implementation, it needs to be acknowledged that studies like those of Higgins and Gordon are moral development research approaches. They are conducted to advance the theory and/or to intervene in organization development strategies designed to reconstruct a moral climate. Their legacy represents a resource wealth in the theory and its application in different organization settings that can guide parents, teachers, prison officials, and now executives and managers towards implementing moral development programming. While MBE implementation does require some working knowledge of the theories, it does not require formal research studies of these kinds, unless particular re-organization problems are encountered that demand scientifically reliable data for their resolution.

Second, to the extent that corporate re-organization planning may develop in a company where democratizing strategies are being seriously considered, pursuance of these research and consulting interventions, as described in Higgins and Gordon (1985), is strongly recommended:

> The ability to recognize the fragility of organizations and whether they represent environments conducive to socio-moral development is a critical aspect of our work climate research.
>
> . . . The use of the research to identify organizational stress and environments of manageable diversity is only one way that research can aid the democratization process. It can also explain the ways that workers understand democracy and the democratization process, . . . Knowing this is critical for determining how to intervene [p. 266].

In democratizing deliberations, such interventions can spare executives the stressful concerns about organization instabilities and hierarchical defences (see Argyris, 1990).

Moral climate and organization hierarchies. While this research legacy from Kohlberg offers executives and managers several approaches to moral atmosphere reconstruction in the workplace, the participatory democratic forms discussed here and in the research may not offer them impelling incentives for engaging in reconstructive organizational change. Corporations are obviously not schools or prisons. For the most part, they are organizations in the private sector and are thus governed by private ownership structures. Most of these structures are hierarchically arranged in established corporate cultures that may not be readily receptive to 'work democracy' and 'just community' governance. However, in deciding what structures might be appropriate for their companies, it may help executives in their planning to recall Kohlberg's own critique of organizational hierarchies:

> For various reasons, 'cooperative' structures go with democracy; competitive ones with autocracy. In an authoritarian system, all members are competing for rewards from an authority, in a democratic system they are exchanging rewards with each other.
>
> (Kohlberg *et al.*, 1975, p. 60)

It might also be helpful for executives to recall that research on workplace democracy has consistently demonstrated positive results regarding job dissatisfaction and work productivity measures (Blumberg, 1973) and social reasoning development about work (Hamilton *et al.*, 1985).

If, however, corporate governance is firmly established in an authoritarian system, executives may be able to assess the structural plausibility for MBE programming and moral atmosphere reforming within their own organizational realities. In many traditional hierarchies, for example, it may be possible to integrate MBE programming, on a microorganization scale, into existing corporate structures and organizational divisions, such as offices of corporate responsibility or corporate communications. Simply setting up a corporate ethical discussion group within such units could begin to open and expand moral awareness at executive and managerial levels of hierarchy (Payne, 1991): '. . . through this dialogue ethical sensitivities and creative visions should occur that otherwise would not be recognized' (p. 75). Following Habermas (1984, 1990b) on communication ethics in organizations, Payne outlines actual content issues and process recommendations for starting such groups and for directing their influence to decision-making power centres in corporations (see pp. 75–77; see also Deetz, 1983; Trevino, 1986; Rusk, 1993).

From such seminal reform proposals, more organization development strategies could plan for the wider macro-organizational introduction of MBE with the gradual implementation of its moral atmosphere reform programme. In hierarchical cultures that are not so resistant to governance change, newer innovative management models, that are more conducive to collegial forms of work performance and company production, can serve as re-organization compromises towards wider MBE horizontal implementation. The growing wave of work-team structures within traditional organization hierarchies (Orsburn *et al.*, 1990; Stewart, 1991; Miller, 1990; Miller, 1992; Walker and Hanson, 1992; Schweiger *et al.*, 1992), for example, can open a conveniently conducive path for introducing 'just community' and 'work democracy' strategies to the workplace. These structures are ready-made organizational units for MBE. As collaborative work-management forms in a company, they offer an ongoing structured learning context for moral reasoning discourse and a social interactional climate for peer group role-taking and collective responsibility building.

Moral climate reform and moral type reformer. Whatever form of corporate restructuring is pursued to reform the moral atmosphere of a company, executives would be wise to carefully consider the strategic implications that become salient from other findings in Kohlberg's research on heteronomous and autonomous moral reasoning (Colby and Kohlberg, 1987). These studies indicate that moral reasoning, at its different incremental levels, reflects two development types: 'A', the *heteronomous* type, whose authority judgments tend to be dependent on others, like superiors; and 'B', the *autonomous* type, whose authority judgments tend to be independent, as self-formulated (see Table 4.2 for a comparative descriptive analysis of the types according to personal, social and organizational criteria, which have operational relevance to management types in corporations). Colby and Kohlberg explain that while these types are found at most stages, a stage 1 person could not logically make type 'B' judgments and a stage 5 person would not very likely render type 'A' judgments. They found that these types are age-related and developmental. In this regard, they explain that subjects who initially rely on heteronomous judgments tend to shift at some particular developmental awareness point to autonomous judgments; and that reversals to heteronomous judgments are not likely. As an effect of this awareness growth, they claim that autonomous-type individuals are more likely to translate their judgments into moral action than the heteronomous type. They also stress that both developmental types are related to socio-cultural environments and social relations. The relevance of these findings and analyses for executives, who may be deliberating on organization restructuring plans for moral climate reform, is salient from the predictions of Colby and Kohlberg themselves:

> we expect socio-cultural environments and social relations that stress democracy, equality, cooperation, and mutuality of relationships to be likely to exert a positive influence on the development of autonomous moral judgment. In contrast, we expect environments that are authoritarian, where a strict traditional social hierarchy is followed, and where obedience and generational respect are stressed, to be less likely to facilitate the development of autonomy [p. 351].

While this second hypothesis was only partially supported in their samples, which included strongly established cultural variables in Turkish and Taiwanese gerontocratic societies, it still warrants the consideration of executives in corporations where strict social hierarchies and ranking seniority status arrangements persist.

Inasmuch as there is likely to be in any given company, hierarchical or democratic, a significant number of both moral types at different stage levels among its management staff and within its workforce, the following practical considerations become relevant matters for executives in their deliberations and planning for change: (1) calculating what receptivity levels are viable in their respective corporations for introducing type 'B' managers; (2) balancing efficient manager–worker combinations and integrations of types 'A' and 'B'; and (3) assessing what effects these introductions and balancing strategies would have on the organization and on the individual managers. For example, what would be the effects of introducing stage 5 type 'B' autonomous manager(s) into the company at large or into any particular department or team in its current hierarchical alignments and moral type postures/attitudes? And, what would be the effects of such an introduction on the manager him/herself? The admonishing predictions of Colby and Kohlberg might influence these assessments:

> we expect that a change in social environment from one that is supportive of moral autonomy to one that is not may cause an individual to change from making autonomous to making heteronomous moral judgments [p. 350].

A more encouraging prediction for guiding these assessments, however, in terms of reform planning and reformer action, is the following conclusion from Kohlberg and Candee (1984):

> if we are going to look for a relationship between moral thought and moral action, we should look to those persons who judge that it is right to perform the more moral behavior either by virtue or their Stage 5 reasoning or the type B intuitions [p. 64].

Because of actual moral dilemmas that these kinds of assessments may generate for executives in their deliberations, one last consideration would seem to be in place, namely, that they consider engaging other colleagues from their senior and junior level staffs in the deliberations. This kind of a discursive climate could itself serve as a barometer of what moral reasoning stages and types prevail in the company and what appropriate governance structures are plausible for reforming its moral atmosphere.

Gender in the workplace. Any deliberations about moral atmosphere reform and hierarchical governance arrangements need to include gender issues relative to moral reasoning in the workplace. Inasmuch as the Colby and Kohlberg (1987) research did not find moral-type differences to be gender specific, the relevant issues about this subject should focus on the interactional arrangements and organization structures of a corporate care ethic. This specific focus is not intended to ignore the controversies in the moral development field regarding Gilligan's (1982) contention that an 'ethic of care' is gender related (see Tronto, 1987). It is rather intended to explore what her theories imply for executive deliberations over moral atmosphere reform and caring in the workplace. Her findings suggest that men and women generally develop along different cultural tracks which tend to shape their identity impressions and reasoning perspectives with alternate views of social realities and moral priorities. For example, women are usually

Table 4.2 Criteria upon which heteronomy–autonomy distinction is based

1. *Freedom*: Autonomous judgments are made without reference to external parameters, such as authority, tradition or law, for justification or validation. Heteronomous judgments fall under the constraint of external parameters for justification and validation

2. *Mutual respect*: Autonomous judgments reflect an awareness of the importance of cooperation among equals in coming to just and fair moral decisions. Mutual respect also entails treating others as one would like to be treated. Heteronomous judgments exhibit unilateral respect towards authority, law, tradition or power - whether in the form of persons or institutions.

3. *Reversibility*: Autonomous judgments are reversible or equilibrated because they explicitly involve some form of (at least rudimentary) mutual and reciprocal role taking. Thus all the actors in a particular situation are understood to consider each other's interests, claims and points of view before a just or fair solution to the problem can be reached. Heteronomous judgments do not involve explicit role taking to this degree, and tend to focus on a particular moral problem from only one perspective.

4. *Constructivism*: Autonomous judgments reflect an awareness that rules and laws used to guide and frame moral decisions are actively formulated by the human mind, in the context of a social group ideally based in cooperation among equals. Thus rules and laws are understood to be flexible and able to adapt to special situations and circumstances. Heteronomous judgments reflect a sacred, rigid and inflexible view of rules and laws.

5. *Hierarchy*: Autonomous judgments reflect a clear hierarchy of values that places moral values and prescriptive duties above pragmatic, descriptive, consequentialist or aesthetic considerations in the resolution of a moral dilemma. Heteronomous judgments do not reflect a clear moral hierarchy. Instead non-moral and pragmatic considerations are weighed heavily in the resolution of a moral dilemma.

6. *Intrinsicalness*: Autonomous judgments are based on a fundamental valuing of persons as ends in themselves, tied to a basic respect for moral personality, personal autonomy and human dignity. Heteronomous judgments are based on a much more pragmatic and instrumental view of persons. Consequently, heteronomous judgments are much more likely to advocate treating persons as means to another end than are autonomous judgments.

7. *Perscriptivity*: Autonomous judgments reflect a view of moral duty that prescribes a certain set of moral obligations and actions regardless of the inclination of the actor, or various pragmatic considerations. Moral duty is based on inner compulsion, moral necessity or conscience. Heteronomous judgments reflect an instrumental or hypothetical view of moral duty.

8. *Universality*: Autonomous judgments reflect the willingness to generalize and universalize moral judgments in order that they apply to anyone and everyone in the same or relevantly similar circumstances. Heteronomous judgments are not explicitly universalized or generalized. Instead, heteronomous moral judgments or values are either uncritically assumed to be held by everyone, or understood to be relative to instrumental self-interest.

9. *Choice*: In response to a particular moral dilemma, the individual who makes autonomous moral judgments is much more likely to choose and justify the solution to the dilemma that is generally seen as *just and fair* from the standpoint of the post-conventional stages of moral judgment than is the individual who makes heteronomous judgments.

Source: Colby and Kohlberg (1987, p. 349).

acculturated into stronger and more enduring intimacy attachments than men, especially in early adolescence, whereas men, in this same period, tend to be socially and culturally encouraged to separation and independence. Their developmental life experiences thus lead them to different moral awareness and moral value viewpoints, with women more focused on responsibilities and caring relationships, and men on reciprocities and just partnerships. These different viewpoints do not reflect on the moral character or moral type of men or women but they do reflect on the cultural mores of society and on the economic and organizational arrangements of the workplace. What is at issue is that if executive deliberations are really as serious about a respect and caring ethic for their companies, as is Weiss (1986) for Ameritech, they need to address the problems of organizational moral consistency not just in 'glass ceiling' boardrooms but in sexually harassing cloakrooms (Davidson, 1992; Morrison, 1992). Critical, reflexive ethical discourse is needed in executive deliberations to confront the moral inconsistencies on gender discrimination in the workplace in areas of economic opportunities and occupational and managerial equalities (see Martin, 1989). A corporate ethic of care must not be gender biased, lest the alarming words of Gilligan for the research patriarchy come to haunt the corporate hierarchy:

> But while women have thus taken care of men, men have, in their theories of psychological development, as in their economic arrangements, tended to assume or devalue that care.
>
> (1982 p. 17)

MBE is a corrective and preventive interactional plan to create a moral atmosphere that addresses the problems of moral inconsistencies in the workplace. It can make a *difference* in clearing the 'corporate voice' towards restoring the value of *equal care*.

Moral performance in the workplace

If structured learning in a morally conducive atmosphere is so critical to moral reasoning advancement, and ultimate moral performance improvement, then it would seem logical that a *sixth final step* of an implemented MBE programme would have *to include some form of structured performance evaluation*. Since many companies already have their particular forms of performance evaluation instruments in place, this step should not be that difficult to implement, especially if the forms and procedures are based on recent recommendations in the organization management literature (Boyett and Conn, 1988; Vroom *et al.*, 1990, Orsburn *et al.*, 1990; Willis and Dubin, 1990).

MBE and performance evaluation instruments. Inasmuch as most of these instruments do not contain any moral evaluation component in their systems, however, it may be necessary to revise or adapt their forms and procedures to coordinate with the MBE programme. Any revisions or adaptations of these instruments should be composed not just to reflect value-system symbolization in the company, as discussed earlier, but to detect value-system inconsistencies in its operations. Revisions may also be needed to incorporate MBE governance strategies, socialization and learning pedagogies, and open system organization processes. The easiest and most comprehensive method for revising performance evaluation instruments for these MBE purposes is to incorporate or append appropriate forms of the Kohlberg scale into the evaluation manual. The basic form of the scale and its six-stage categories can be composed for the manual or its appendix with industry-specific language that respects the particularities of company, profession or occupation. In the refrigeration company, mentioned above, the revision was integrated into the Performance Evaluation Manual of the Employee Handbook with language appropriate for its industrial sector, its organization-set, and for its service and contracting divisions.

In any case, this revised instrument should be careful to focus exclusively on productive reasoning and work performance. The Kohlberg scale was not designed to be utilized as an instrument of moral inquisition. It is a fascinating and extremely useful instrument for moral education in any domain, including corporations. It contains, moreover, an untapped assessment and critically reconstructive review potential for restoring the credibility of many traditional performance evaluation systems. Kurtines *et al.* (1991), for instance, have utilized the basic Kohlberg development categories to construct their own socio-moral performance instruments for measuring a respondent's basic orientation to moral understanding. Their instruments can allow preliminary assessments of how workers view morality along five comparative dimensional lines of application, i.e., (1) by *relative or universal* standards; (2) according to *utilitarian* (consequential) *or deontological* (dutiful) purposes; (3) as emphasizing *individual or social* aspects; (4) as emanating from *religious or secular* incentives; and (5) by *intuitive or rational* processes. They suggest that these simple categories allow a researcher or reviewer preliminary evaluative knowledge of how one approaches socio-moral performance. In further work, Pollard *et al.* (1991) move beyond moral learning categories to the critically reconstructive review potential that MBE programming requires. In this regard, their evaluation instruments are readily compatible for the social and organization reconstruction of performance evaluation systems and processes. They have developed moral-issue and moral-dilemma competence scales for facilitating the use of critical discursive thinking and the social evolutionary development of co-constructive performance planning. Their studies stress the importance of these kinds of moral evaluation instruments as institutionalizing the democratic and participatory processes of competency development through critical reconstructive performance education.

Inasmuch as the procedures of traditional performance appraisal systems are so often conducted perfunctorily for regulated compensation ends and calculated promotion purposes (Hackman, 1986), the evaluation usually suffers from a lack of learning and has become symbolic of pre-conventional moral reasoning processes. Argyris (1991) claims that these processes are counter-productive and 'locked in defensive reasoning.' He proposes that workers can be taught how to reason productively and to identify performance inconsistencies by reflecting on the discrepancies 'between their espoused and actual theories of action' (p. 106). While he offers no social psychological formulas for individual or corporate conscience arousal about these discrepancies nor moral climate restructuring plans for reasoning development, he does suggest an important self-evaluation learning method through the composition of situational case-study write-ups by executives and managers. He illustrates a reflexive format for these case studies, through which the individual executive can reflect on his or her own leadership reasoning skills utilized in communicating an actual company business problem to the management staff. He suggests how the case-study write-up should have a simulated meeting column, describing the imaginary authority–subordinate communication flow; and a corresponding self-reflexive column, describing predictive suppressions of self-generated thoughts and feelings provoked by the imagined responses of subordinates.

> The case became the catalyst for a discussion in which the CEO learned several things about the way he acted with his management team.
>
> He discovered . . . his conversations as counter-productive. In the guise of being 'diplomatic,' he would pretend that a consensus about the problem existed, when in fact none existed. The unintended result: instead of feeling reassured, his subordinates felt wary and tried to figure out 'what is he *really* getting at?'
>
> The CEO also realized that the way he dealt with the competitiveness among department heads was completely contradictory. On the one hand, he kept urging them to 'think of the organization as a whole.' On the other, he kept calling for actions – department budget cuts, for example – that placed them directly in competition with each other [p. 107].

Argyris concludes that by so role-playing the case-study privately and subsequently sharing its unmasked write-up with the staff, comparative role-taking reasoning is evoked and authentic performance evaluation occurs:

> In effect, the case study exercise legitimizes talking about issues that people have never been able to address before. Such a discussion can be emotional – even painful. But for managers with the courage to persist, the payoff is great: management teams and entire organizations work

more openly and more effectively and have greater options for behaving flexibly and adapting to particular situations.

(1991, p. 107)

By utilizing the revised performance evaluation instrument in concert with such reflexive models of case-study simulations, MBE performance evaluation can create the intermediary goal of an empathic and frank moral evaluation climate (Oser and Schlafi, 1985) and engage participants in cooperative moral learning 'loops' (Argyris, 1991; see also 1990).

Finally, whatever forms or procedures that may be chosen as appropriate for performance evaluation in a company, their instruments should be applied as consistent with the implementation of the first four steps of the MBE programme, in such a way as to maintain an organizational unity and a managerial integration.

Performance evaluation and organization unity. With regard to organizational unity, it is imperative that performance evaluation takes place in the reconstructed moral atmosphere already in place. This social psychological imperative is based on the interactional dynamics of open system theory. Accordingly, it stresses the importance of achieving a cyclical flow of activities and events in an organization which feeds back into its system, strengthening its processes and structures (Allport, 1962). The performance evaluation, as a periodic activity and a cyclical event, can be an effective developmental experience that not only opens performance morality to individuals and collectivities but also feeds ethical principles and moral reasoning back into the system. It is in this sense that the evaluation needs to respect the climate. Its assessment and reviewing processes need to replicate the intervention paths and to reinforce the intermediary goals of the whole moral education endeavour, which were described above. By means of the revised instruments, the evaluation needs to monitor the ongoing progress of individuals and collectivities through the four phases of transformation to higher-stage development. It also needs to reassess critically the intermediary goals within the moral climate that constitute the conducive factors for moral development. Such application of open system theory in the performance evaluation process will preserve the overall organizational unity of the moral education intervention.

Performance evaluation and managerial integration. With regard to managerial integration, it is imperative that executives or managers entrusted with the performance evaluation process understand that its implementation is a moral education intervention and not just a ritual convention. They should, therefore, keep in mind the organizational unity of the whole MBE programme, as they intervene with its evaluation instruments and procedures. With this unified focus that encompasses understanding of their own place as moral leaders on these intervention paths, they will be prepared to use these instruments and procedures as integrated into the

MBE system. This implies moral leadership by stimulating the moral consciousness raising processes that these instruments and procedures should be designed to promote. Thus, as they assess and review worker performance measures, they need to get 'inside' of the reasoning and consistency tracks that lead to moral performance (Oser and Schlafli, 1985, p. 276). They also need to assess the four phases of transformation to higher moral performance among individual workers and their collectivities. In addition, they need to reassess critically the moral climate conditions in the company or in their respective divisions, evaluating the six intermediary goals as the conduciveness factors for performance growth or inconsistency failures (see above). And finally, they need to understand this integrating role of moral leadership as one that takes time and patience and that moral performance growth is not always visible even with the instruments. If, however, they persist in their leadership and coaching roles, progress will move:

> For these six measurements are movements without which there can be no transformation in stage. It could, therefore, be said that achieving positive changes in these six fields does actually signify development, provided that the basis is a stimulation of moral conflict. For this reason, we can make the assumption that development also takes place if prerequisites are first stimulated by pushing them along [p. 277].

It should thus be clear that the administration of performance evaluation requires the executive or manager to perceive their leadership roles in terms of moral stimulation and 'pushing' their subordinate colleagues along. This can be done privately with the worker in a hierarchical setting; or collectively and privately in both collegial work-team and participatory democratic settings. Whatever setting seems appropriate, the executive or manager needs to integrate role-taking interaction in the evaluation that fosters both hierarchical and peer reciprocity for performance management and collegial information flow. This implies the need to integrate the evaluation process into a non-threatening organizational climate within the moral atmosphere of the company that allows frank and interactive constructive feedback. By so integrating performance evaluation into a morally discursive learning forum, workers should feel safe to discuss their performance with their superiors and their peers from the job-role standpoint of their position, the departmental needs of the collectivity, the managerial standpoint of the hierarchy and the organization responsibilities of the company (see Turner, 1956). Through this integrating role, as sensitive moral leaders, executives and managers should be ready for inviting workers and/or teams to engage in self-appraisal strategies, for drawing out and coordinating their own moral reasoning to higher moral performance outcomes (Kohlberg, 1971).[8]

Personal consistency and moral responsibility. Since the coordination of moral reasoning and moral action is ultimately a matter of self-consistency through the personal domain of one's moral identity (Blasi, 1984), it would be appropriate that this phase of performance evaluation be self-conducted. And since self-evaluation in the workplace is a complex process overlapping personal and intra-organizational domains, these self-appraisal strategies may need to be redesigned to respect the internal private zones of moral conscience and the external collective norms of moral performance. Moreover, these strategies need to reflect interactive self-appraisal processes that achieve a balance between the subjective personal judgments of the worker and the objective company norms of work performance. These interaction appraisals are the reflexive processes of conscience, as described earlier, and should take place in the two noted domains. First, in the *personal domain*, the individual worker will usually take care of the reflexive processes regarding personal consistency and moral responsibility over work performance within his or her own conscience. Second, in the *intra-organizational domain*, the individual worker needs to present his or her self-appraisal judgments to the superior and/or collectivity in professional/ occupational ethical discourse covering moral-norm and moral-performance consistencies. In some cases of moral inconsistency problems, especially those dealing with serious unethical performance complications that might be overspilling into individual compensation responsibilities, the worker may be disposed, or might even need counselling, to open ethical communication with the superior or the collective leadership about personal consistency and moral responsibility redevelopment strategies.

Organizational consistency and corporate responsibility. The performance evaluation challenge here is to implement the same interactive self-appraisal processes, just described, at the collective and corporate levels of the company. Coordination at these levels can become much more complex, particularly when the evaluation focus relates to other interorganizational units or entities within the company's organization-set. Whatever the scene, these interactive appraisals need to follow the same reflexive processes of the collective or the corporate conscience, also as described earlier, and should take place both in the corporate and interorganization domains. First, in the *corporate domain*, the company and/or its lower-level intra-organizational collectivities need to reflect over organizational consistency and collective or corporate responsibility matters regarding its moral norms and its corporate performance. Second, in the *interorganization domain*, the company needs to evaluate organization consistency and corporate performance in the wider sectors of its organization-set. These two domain evaluations may require extensive revisions of the performance evaluation instruments so that effective communication feedback can be drawn from within the company and from other organization-set units, such as from its suppliers, clientele and industry-sector organizations. If the company has redesigned appropriate governance structures in its reconstructed moral climate, it should have competent review boards representing higher-stage and autonomous type 'B' moral leadership from every level of management, workforce and its organization-set in open critical ethical discourse of this feedback. These boards need to deal with company policy, corporate responsibility and corporate ethical performance consistency at all levels of both domains (see Hausman and McPherson, 1993, on policy evaluations and the moral appraisals of economic arrangements). They need to review from the evaluation feedback data whether company business and operational decisions reflect moral consistency in performance behaviour.

Bowen and Power (1993) emphasize the importance of such an ethical forum for corporate evaluation processes and interorganizational consistencies. Drawing from contemporary decision theorists regarding uncertainty contingencies in decision-making processes that were encountered in the Exxon Valdez disaster, they offer a set of decision criteria that adds to the organization consistency moral imperative. They suggest that in addition to consistency monitoring, decision makers should explore different situational perceptions and resource availabilities for implementing solutions to all expected and assessed possible outcomes (see also Trevino, 1986). They therefore stress the need for corporate decision makers faced with the uncertainties of unexpected outcomes to an least strive in a co-responsible forum for the possible realities of reasonable judgments rather than the 'impossible dream' of infallible strategies.

> Our approach to moral management is thus grounded in, and builds upon, this approach to making *reasonable* decisions; an approach that emphasizes dialogical decision making procedures. It follows then that the requirements for managing ethically are consistent with those for managing effectively, and we suggest . . . that a sensible approach to evaluating the performance of managers facing dilemmas (moral and other) must deal directly with the uncertainty that exists at the level of policy making [p. 104].

Continuous learning discourse in these performance evaluation review boards allows not only for provident decision-making strategies for dealing with uncertainty contingencies but for an ethical way of bearing organizational co-responsibilities. Organizational and moral inconsistencies not only reflect lower-stage performance in a company but, even more seriously, demoralize its workforce and impair its own corporate ethical development. The Kohlberg research legacy clearly shows the critical importance of moral consistency in moral development. Every phase of performance evaluation and all instrument forms should not only be monitoring for its individual and organizational manifestation in the workplace, but for its open system promotion in company structures. It can thus be concluded that organization consistency and corporate responsibility, as its moral development link, are the ethical keystones for MBE programming. Without these correlated open system 'fronts', the moral atmosphere of the company will remain a vulnerable organizational climate not only for unethical management 'storms' but for unproductive workplace inefficiencies.

MBE and economic incentive system models

With this six-step moral education programme as the ethical archway of a company's reformed moral climate, it can be argued that MBE also represents an economic investment model for addressing the perennial problems of short-range incentive systems and persistent organizational inefficiencies. As a socio-economic moral incentive system, MBE can offer long-term dividends for developing personal consistency and individual responsibility in the workforce along with organizational consistency and collective responsibility in the company. Its ethical management strategies and moral socialization processes can also create economic benefits for the company by strengthening the incentive linkage between consistency and responsibility for enduring organizational efficiencies.

The problem of 'persistent organization inefficiencies' remains controversial for numbers of organization behaviourists and some organization economists (see Miller, 1992). Much of the controversy centres around the role of leadership. While the literature in the field of organizational economics tends to de-emphasize the role of leadership in incentive system models, other schools of thought from political science and organizational psychology stress the role of leadership for creating workplace incentives (ibid.). Briefly, the debate follows this argument. Traditional economists propose that no matter what incentive system models are used in the workplace, there remains a latent self-interest drive within individuals that determines a certain 'moral hazard' towards shirking behaviour, causing performance inefficiency (Holmstrom, 1979, p. 74, 1982). Acknowledging this hazard, Miller (1992) presents arguments from political science and organization psychology, contending that incentive-building leadership in the workplace can, nevertheless, make a difference: 'Those organizations whose managers can inspire members to transcend short-term self-interest will always have a competitive advantage' (p. 3).

With some linkage to classical organizational economics, Miller stakes his position in modern game theory and provides a theoretical structure for building an incentive system by achieving work-team cooperation through political leadership in organizational hierarchies. In contrast, with inter-theory linkage to economic psychology and socio-economics, MBE provides a moral development structure for achieving more enduring individual and collective work performance through moral leadership in workplace democracies as well as organizational hierarchies.

A moral critique of the political economic incentive model

Whereas Miller's innovative economic and behavioural incentive system attempts to address the problems of persistent organizational inefficiency, his design focuses on organization and human resource development strategies. He attempts to resolve the complicated managerial dilemmas between authoritarian hierarchy and incentive system inadequacy by proposing rational behavioural models for intrafirm cooperation. His analyses describe the inverse complexity of self-interest preference problems as potentially dysfunctional in all traditional economic incentive systems. Consistently enough, he starts his incentive-building by acknowledging the 'moral hazard' problem: 'While a great many contractual forms and incentive systems have been proposed, the best economic analysis argues that in every such system there must remain incentives for at least one individual to persist in behaviour that leads to organizational inefficiency' (Miller, 1992, p. 12).

Accordingly, the best inter-theoretical explanation from philosophical ethics for addressing this traditional economic rationale in Miller's incentive-system-rebuilding is 'psychological egoism' (see Beauchamp, 1988). While this theory may realistically explain why people behave the way they do in workplace environments in terms of ulterior motivation drives, it tends to fix some executives and economists into low expectation postures regarding the persistence of organizational efficiency. And, what is worse, it shapes their reasoning negatively and defensively (Argyris, 1991) into low expectation attitudes regarding moral development potential. The theory of psychological egoism does not deny this potential but it certainly is not heuristic of any moral pedagogies for its attainment.

Miller's attempt, however, is courageous. He offers organization hierarchies a high-involvement management model for building worker trust, job commitment, company loyalty, social reciprocity and self-responsibility, that form the irreducible elements of intrafirm cooperation. His model projects a rational behavioural incentive track beyond the managerial dilemmas of efficiency losses and personal preference gains by structuring work-team designs for intrafirm cooperation. His approach is surprisingly close to that of Piaget (1965) who studied the moral judgments of children in games and to that of Kohlberg et al. (1975) who traced their moral development paths through hypothetical dilemma activation. Miller suggests the use of 'repeated game theory' to indicate how adults arrive at cooperative behaviour through cyclical game conventions in social interaction (the so-called 'games that people play'). He thus demonstrates how workers can rationally 'play' their way to 'cooperative solutions to social dilemmas' in long-term work-group structures (1992, p. 180). But inasmuch as Miller's behavioural incentive track is only rationally grounded in the organizational realities of corporate culture and vested interests, he himself admits that his work-team designs and cooperation equilibria are flawed with fragile endurance spans.

However, individuals in social settings constrained by social norms still have important choices to make. The choices they make help to determine the expectations that others have about how the game is to be played and help to shape and alter the conventions that govern the outcome of coordination games . . .

The folk (game) theorem suggests that the beliefs of the various players about the likely responses of other players are all-important: It is this psychological network of mutually reinforcing expectations that makes one perfectly feasible outcome (e.g., cooperation) occur instead of another perfectly feasible outcome (e.g., noncooperation).

This suggests a certain fragility in cooperative equilibria. While it is rational for an employee to cooperate under the perception that others are cooperating and that one's own noncooperation would be sanctioned and/or reciprocated, a relatively few examples of nonsanctioned noncooperation could change these expectations drastically.

(1992, pp. 206–207)

This fragile flaw in Miller's cooperative equilibria is due precisely to the fact that his incentive system model does not deal with the moral developmental limitations of 'psychological egoism' and self-interested behaviour. His model is thus determined to level somewhere within the pre-conventional and conventional stages of two and three, as constrained by the social and economic conventions of corporate cultural externalities. This critique is evident from his analytical perceptions of the norm of reciprocity. In his game-theory analyses of work-team cooperation, it is to be noted that his explanations of reciprocity are not formulated at the levels of moral reasoning from which higher conventional and even post-conventional trust, role-taking initiatives and other-caring dispositions can be expected:

reciprocity will be a strong norm in successful small work groups. It is worth repeating that cooperation in a repeated game need not be based on mutual altruism; it is based on the shared knowledge that each of us can punish the other (by future noncooperation) if either of us fails to cooperate in this period.

(1992, p. 187)

It is evident that this explanation is only explicative of a second-stage *instrumental reciprocity* and vested interest exchange. The external inducements that he proposes like the 'property rights' of employment security, team production compensation, profit-sharing and ownership equities, may indeed be incentives for intrafirm cooperation; but they do not by themselves generate higher-stage trust and commitment nor automatically set a moral climate for workplace justice and *caring reciprocity*. A socially just and interactionally reciprocal moral climate needs more than rationally induced incentives. Its organization atmosphere does not need the structural flaws of 'moral hazards'; it rather needs the interactional strength of contractarian reciprocity.

> Formal models of rationality and game theoretic studies of incentives hold out the hope of superseding the ancient puzzles concerning the relations between morality, rationality, and self-interest. . . . Solution concepts in game theory may enrich the contractarian perspective that morality arises from or can be justified in terms of agreement.
>
> (Hausman and McPherson, 1993, p. 712)

Miller's instrumental reciprocity closes his incentive perceptions to worker occupational and corporate operational expediency perspectives. From these second-stage points of view, his game theories do not open his model to morally developed contractarian perspectives. In the end, his incentive-building methods do not hold any hope for resolving the moral hazard 'puzzles' with which he starts and certainly, by his own admission, do not generate the strengths of caring reciprocity.

A socio-economic moral incentive model

As a higher stage contractarian norm, caring reciprocity is fundamental to a moral incentive system model. It is the critical cognitive-emotive 'solution' that turns productive reasoning into moral reasoning and impels individuals to translate philosophical principles into moral action (Kurtines, 1984; Boyd, 1984). Caring reciprocity is what generates internal incentives for altruistic cooperation and moral leadership (Higgins and Gordon, 1985; see also Gouldner, 1970, and note 7 below).

In their study, Higgins and Gordon did find that, in the Northern worker-owned company, the intrinsic motivation values of work quality, affiliations, and democracy as an ideological governance form, constituted the stronger incentives than the external instrumental motivations of money and workplace convenience. They also found, however, that in the Southern company, the external instrumental motivations of making money outranked the more intrinsic motivations of democracy as a shared ethnic ownership form, work quality and affiliations. While they account for this reversal of incentive preference by reason of the company's location in a poor and rural high unemployment region and because of depressed economic conditions within the company's industry, they hasten to add that the strong normative caring climate within the organization and the internal ethnic incentives for moral role-taking, manifested by trust in management, ensured worker cooperation and company survival.

In this regard, Sethia and Von Glinow (1985) demonstrated the positive co-relation between caring human resource cultures and intrafirm cooperation in high-tech companies. They found that when organization cultures integrate high concern for people with strong performance expectations, successful performance results for individuals, groups and even firms were long term (see also Von Glinow, 1988).

In a broader context, both Kohlberg *et al.* (1990) and Habermas (1990a) claim that caring reciprocity is plausible in a moral atmosphere, wherein participants are not constrained by normative procedural agreements but are allowed to interact and communicate to a 'moral point of view' through 'ideal role-taking' interaction. This means that when people are coached to universal reasoning to take the role of others by means of imaginative role-playing (as in Argyris's case-study write-ups, 1991) of ideal caring reciprocity, they can come to realization of a sixth-stage 'moral point of view', valuing universal care for everyone. This also means that when organization hierarchies show concern for people and systematically encourage all their workers, even poorer performers, to reflect on their performance through private or collective discursive performance evaluation, as discussed above, they are actually cultivating a moral incentive climate and validating their policies on human resource care (as in Wiess's, 1986, validating management policies).

> Because discourses are a reflective form of understanding-orientated action . . . , their central perspective on moral compensation for the deep-seated weakness of vulnerable individuals can be derived from the very medium of linguistically mediated interactions to which socialized individuals owe that vulnerability. The pragmatic features of discourse make possible a discerning will formation whereby the interests of each individual can be taken into account without destroying the social bonds that link each individual with all others.
>
> (Habermas, 1990a, pp. 245–246)

These interlinking social bonds that morally compensate for the vulnerabilities of certain individuals in groups are what constitute the role-taking architecture of work-teams. Through discursive work information flow, they open communication lines for shared knowledge and create a moral atmosphere for mutual altruism. This moral climate is what provides the kind of incentives that impel every work-team 'player' to take the initiative to back up the 'plays' of the other for performance consistency and work integrity. Hackman's (1986) airline case study of the behavioural signs of self-management performance in the realistic contexts of worker vulnerabilities and organizational inconsistencies places initiative-taking responsibility at the highest levels of work-team maturity development. His conclusions go beyond Miller's (1992) instrumental reciprocity, confirming the value of workplace altruism as an interactional strategy to maintain performance consistency. 'People take initiatives to *help people in other areas* improve their performance, thereby strengthening the policies and performance of the organization as a whole' (1992, p. 97; see also Etzioni, 1988, for a review of empirical evidence on altruistic behaviour, ch. 4).

Such a moral climate that offers the caring reciprocity of workplace altruism to strengthen corporate policy and organizational performance is one where deeper moral incentives can germinate. Since there is clear and relatively strong confirmation of the relationship between moral reasoning and altruistic behaviour (Blasi, 1980), a lot of promise awaits the corporate ethical consciousness challenge to rebuild this kind of moral climate. The higher the moral cognition for helping other more vulnerable workers in an organizational climate of caring relationships, the deeper the incentives for collaboration persistence to compensate for work-team vulnerabilities and ultimately to promote enduring cooperation in the workplace. Emanating from the social system perspective of the company good and, gradually as the moral climate develops, from the universal principle perspective of the cosmic and global social good, these internalized inducements are more likely to motivate personal preferences for cooperation (Etzioni, 1988). 'In short *moral internalization turns constraints into preferences*' (p. 46). Etzioni typifies this preference conversion process as 'the power of internalized values' that can generate the deontological conviction for action-value consistency from a sense of duty, reflecting 'the strength of moral commitment' (pp. 47–48).

It is worth stressing in this context that moral commitment is much more than job commitment which is based on external workplace inducements and dependent on moral reasoning climate fluctuations. In any case, job commitment is as strong and as enduring as the credibility of specific managerial strategies that control incentive inducements (Miller, 1992). As such its value is *particularized*; and, moreover, its endurance span is fragile and can likewise be easily flawed by pre-conventional authority styles or management defection contingencies. As a *universalized* cognitive 'meta-preference' (Etzioni, 1988, pp. 45–48) for the integrity of work itself and an internalized affective conviction (Haste, 1990) for the quality of its performance, moral commitment is an enduring dispositional virtue that can be expected in post-conventional work climates that are striving to open a corporate 'moral point of view'.[9]

. . . internalized values have a significant impact on behavior.

As to the suggestion that internalization is merely the result of conditioning, the findings suggest that once individuals internalize guides to behavior these become *generalized* to a variety of situations beyond those in which the individual was conditioned, and are not merely a reflection of prior rewards/punishments. Further, they *last* [emphasis added] well beyond what one would expect from prior conditioning.

(Etzioni, 1988, pp. 47–48)

Incentive depth, moral breadth and cooperation persistence

As a political economic incentive system model, interlinking neoclassical economic and organizational behaviour theories, Miller's design provides the appropriate socialization techniques and organization strategies for high-involvement management and work-team interdependencies, as discussed in Walton (1990) and Lawler (1986). But it is not the kind of model that will facilitate reciprocal role-taking cooperation in a decentralized hierarchical learning atmosphere where idea communication is shared and entrepreneurial leadership is encouraged (Maremont, 1993).

In contrast, MBE, as a moral behavioural incentive system model, engenders motivation anchored in internal ethical awareness dispositions rather than in external economic posturing calculations. As seen, it is an incentive system design that can inherently broaden the morality scope of corporate governance and advance the ethical levels of enduring intrafirm cooperation. 'Organizations endure . . . in proportion to the breadth of the morality by which they are governed' (Barnard, 1938, p. 282).

In addition, as a cognitive model for human resource development in moral reasoning, its collegial learning designs can easily be integrated into other company incentive-building programmes that pursue continuing professional management and competence education (Willis and Tosti-Vasey, 1990; Farr and Middlebrooks, 1990; Miller, 1990). Moreover, it would seem that some of these incentive programmes could derive some practical benefit from MBE socialization methods. Farr and Middlebrooks (1990), for example, stress the need for intrinsic motivation in their use of expectancy theory to enhance and maintain competence. From this perspective, their approach to competence development, falling somewhat short of incentive internalization, could itself be enhanced within an MBE climate, where intrinsic motivation can secure anchorage to internal self-expectancy and collective responsibility incentives.

Similarly, as Von Glinow (1988) suggests the need for more meaningful and relevant incentives for high-tech professionals than traditional economic inducements, MBE can offer significant levels of meaning and purpose. Her studies of this group conclude: 'It is fascinating to note, from a behavioral perspective, that no single stock incentive was ranked in the upper quarter by any age group in either my research or that of others [Griggs and Manring, 1986, for example] interested in determining reward salience' (pp. 78–79). She thus argues for new incentive schemes that relate to individual values and beliefs, such as ethical, collegial and autonomous work climates which value performance commitment. It would seem that MBE, in its reliance on moral reasoning for performance and on communication ethics for learning, could effectively contribute to the rebuilding of the suitable work incentive climate for this group. '. . . once they [managers] grasp the powerful impact that productive reasoning can have on actual performance, they will have a *strong incentive* [emphasis added] to reason productively not just in a training session but in all their work relationships' (Argyris, 1991, p. 107).

Within this reforming moral scope of corporate governance, as broadened by the practical long-term planning for ethical consciousness development and by the ideal typical use of the Kohlberg scale, MBE can provide the appropriate internalized moral incentives for individual and collective competence and enduring optimal efficiency. 'This is only to say that foresight, long purposes, high ideals, are the basis for the persistence of cooperation' (Barnard, 1938, p. 282).

SUMMARY

'Foresight, long purposes, high ideals' are all germane to paradigm conception, model designing and value-system-building. The inter-theoretical conceptions in MBE have been perceived by critical analytical insights into corporate ethics as a cross-disciplinary field linking social psychology to philosophy and moral psychology, and sociology to organization-management studies and economics.

From these conceptions, new interactional dimensions have been drawn to trace the innovative social psychological constructs of the 'corporate mind, the corporate self and the corporate conscience'. Within these constructs, some insight has been opened to analyse the morally reflexive processes within the 'corporate self' that help to locate the social psychological centres of corporate image-making and the management processes of value-system-building. With reconstructive focus on these centres and processes, some critical understanding has been perceived by the practical reflections of a CEO on managing human resources for organizational consistency in company value-system-building. By further expanding this critical analytical focus to the symbolic management of human resources, some practical techniques were discussed for managing the authenticity of company-image-projection through corporate responsibility.

From these inter-theoretical conceptions and their insights into paradigm planning, the MBE management model was designed to raise ethical consciousness in the workplace. Based on the social psychology of management interaction processes and open system arrangements of organization governance, MBE was presented through a six-step implementation plan that builds company ethical consciousness through moral development of the workforce. This plan is grounded in the theories of Lawrence Kohlberg whose research legacy has left a resource bank of empirical studies on moral atmosphere building and organizational climate rebuilding. With moral development planning and 'long purpose' implementation, heuristic 'foresight' suggests the plausibility of MBE as a morally internalized incentive system in the workplace for managing the attainment of the corporate-economic 'high ideals' of persistent optimal efficiency.

CONCLUSION

Research implications: hegemony and consistency

From the critical sociological perspectives of symbolic interaction theory previously developed into research methodologies for symbolic dialectical analysis (Guerrette, 1981), the research challenge for this new interdisciplinary paradigm is to address problems left unanswered in the Kohlberg empirical legacy. Two research problems are particularly significant not just for MBE but for any moral education intervention: the problem of cultural hegemony in moral development and the problem of personal and organizational consistency in moral performance.

The hegemonic problem in moral development. This problem is provoked by practical 'hidden curricular' determinants both in the research subjects and the research processes. Kohlberg himself recognized these determinants in the subjects, acknowledging the latent ideological power bases within educational systems (Power *et al.*, 1989). But his own persistence for justice, education and democratic governance in schools is not enough to convert the macro-sociological power fortresses in wider global cultures, especially in political and economic domains that ultimately shape the curricula of corporations as well as schools. From this critical perspective, Kohlberg's justice education model may begin to stimulate post-conventional moral development in classrooms; but these higher stages may be quickly undermined when students graduate to the governance world of political economic power and experience the hegemonic cultural causes of value-norm incongruences (see Emler and Hogan, 1991).

Some of Kohlberg's associates recognized these hegemonic determinants in the research processes themselves. Their critical insights, however, were more disciplinary than reparatory. Blasi (1980), Haste (1990) and Levine (1976) began to question the limitations of cognitive developmental theory and opened broader empirical questions from related psychological traditions. Weinreich-Haste (1984) pursued the questioning beyond psychology, demonstrating how interaction processes shape the socio-cultural determinants of moral reasoning. She even pushed the limits of this expansive approach, explaining how symbolic interaction processes can lead to social change and negotiated moral meanings. But the hegemony, nevertheless, prevails. And would it matter that much, if research processes open wider disciplinary and cross-disciplinary pursuits in moral development testing for post-conventional scoring?

Moral development outcomes may indeed be related to 'domain-specific' cultures and socially interactive contexts (Turiel *et al.*, 1991); but political economic power and its value-shaping industrial constructs do have hegemonic inroads into macro- and micro-level socio-cultural institutions (Dahrendorf, 1959, pp. 243, 293; Goldman and Van Houten, 1977). Misgeld (1991) rephrases the hegemonic problem, contrasting the 'logics' of socio-moral and economic-technological development:

> Moral/intellectual and social/political development, on the one hand, economic/technological development on the other hand neither match each other nor does one support the other. . . . Can modern societies develop a rational identity?
>
> At issue is the possibility of transcending the coercive limits of hitherto existing societies. It is only in addressing this theme that critical theorists continue to think in conformity with a core idea of socialism [pp. 167–168].

From the 'critical practical' perspective, the research processes need to address the latent socio-cultural and the social system blockages that impair the full moral development of populations. The new social psychological paradigm and its 'revolutionary scientific' perceptions for socio-moral development demand critically reconstructive sets of questions (Kuhn, 1970), such as: What symbolic constructs within cultures and, especially subcultural entities, like corporations, co-exist with governance structures that might be influencing value-norm incongruences and moral inconsistencies and thus skewing moral development ratings? Might the economic arrangements of the corporate power structure of companies in some dependent local communities be determining the moral consciousness of citizens, the healthy quality of their lives and the social inequalities of their class (Krause, 1977; Walzer, 1983)? Might company policies and operational strategies, especially those shaped in traditional organization hierarchies by the functional imperatives of resource adaptation, goal attainment, integrated operations and value latency, be binding decision-makers 'to change the environment to meet the needs of the system' (Parsons, 1967, p. 493)? In effect, have not the functional imperatives 'maintained the patterns' of system 'agility' at the expense of natural and organizational environmental morality? Are they not 'systematically' impairing individual and corporate performance from developing beyond the conventional moral stages? In short, is there a 'hegemonic lid' on moral development? 'Yet on this most crucial of all questions for moral psychology – who commands and what are their moral credentials - research has thus far shed almost no direct light at all' (Emler and Hogan, 1991, p. 84).

In dialectical contrast, the *interactional imperative of ethical integrity* is the ultimate credential of unflawed leadership. As the latent value in the new paradigm, it opens cultures and systems towards developmental governance and allows the freedom of ethical discourse and the *interactional integration* of *value negotiation*. Ethical integrity, interactional integration and value negotiation require new symbolic interactional constructs, such as ethical discourse forums, to allow management decision-makers to reverse corporate priorities *to change the system to meet the needs of the environment*. From these interactional imperatives and their symbolic constructs, executives and managers would have a social psychological rationale and an organizational medium for reformulating company norms, reordering its value-system, and renegotiating corporate moral meanings. It is only from these new meanings that individuals and corporations can be stimulated to higher post-conventional moral performance. Value-free research must admit that populations will never transcend conventional boundaries, if they are not socialized beyond conventions and their institutionalized symbolic constructs (Lifton, 1970).

From this dialectical research perspective, it would appear that empirical testing of individuals in culturally bound social and organizational systems is doomed to yield 'stable' scores with unimpressive stage 5 and unverifiable stage 6 post-conventional results.

> The most fundamental control device of any *stable* social system is not its use of crude force, or even of other, nonviolent forms of punishment, but its continuing distribution of mundane rewards. It is not simply power that an hegemonic elite seeks and uses, but an authority that is rooted in the readiness of others to credit its good intentions, to cease contention when it has rendered its decision, to accept its conception of social reality, and to reflect alternatives at variance with the status quo.
>
> (Gouldner, 1970, p. 498)

The empirical challenge needs to move forward with critical reconstructive vision to identify the 'mundane rewards' and their double-edged symbols of hegemonic leadership inconsistencies that cut deeply into the social and moral fabric of organizations from Wall Street to Washington and now even to the church. It is these symbolic inconsistencies that are not only shaping the organizational realities and moral meanings of institutions but are determining the moral stages of its managers and members (see Emler and Hogan, 1991).

The problem of personal and organizational moral consistency. As Blasi (1980) and Haste (1990) have exposed some of the research limitations of the cognitive structural approach to moral development testing in terms of its failure to account for affective domain determinants, it would seem timely to consider other influences on moral reasoning and moral performance outcomes in terms of organization domain determinants. For example, research questions must begin to address judgment-action consistency problems at organizational levels of analysis in addition to individual management and worker levels. By opening methodology to collective units of focus, only initially begun by Higgins and Gordon (1985), as seen above, questions such as these need to be probed: What moral choices are available to corporations in culturally bound and morally undeveloped complex organization environments where a company's organization-set may bear differing economic determinants that influence production outcomes or restrict business options? And likewise, what moral choices are available to individual executives, managers and workers in culturally bound and morally undeveloped companies where the management power structure may bear differing economic determinants that influence performance outcomes or restrict career advancement options? And finally, if 'domain consensus' is critical for the power relationships that form between an organization and its task environment, as seen above, what is the relationship between domain and moral consensus in the overall context of company or departmental ethical discourse and interorganizational political process? These kinds of questions on personal and organizational consistency matters could open more incisive 'critical practical understanding' of actual organization–management moral, gender and power dilemmas that not only impair moral stage development but threaten organization stability and career survival.

This interactionist *praxis* approach to moral development studies is another social psychological imperative to the atmospheric reconstruction of both corporate and economic system sectors for personal and organizational moral consistency development. From its critical perspective, further moral consistency research might consider the rather cognitively structured 'role' that role-taking analysis has played in moral development studies. While this concept has been a central element in moral development theory building by Kohlberg and his followers in terms of the interactional analysis associated with social conformity and rule-governed behaviour, the full social psychological implications of role-taking processes need to be explored in terms of post-conventional stage development. Critical reconstructive research needs to explore what these wider implications mean for personal and organizational moral consistency. Role-taking is not simply a structured cognitive process for rule-conformity and institutionalized conventions. It is rather a dynamic interactional process that allows individuals and collectivities to plan for change (Turner, 1962; see also Yussen, 1976). Through symbolic coordination and the sharing of reconstructed meanings, these individuals and groups can change the established conventions of structures and systems and facilitate their own consistency development to new post-conventional moralities towards the 'moral point of view'.

Practical implications: realities and possibilities

Realities. As this study presents the 'high ideals' of moral development for both corporate organization structures and economic incentive systems, it acknowledges the arresting evidence from research on the lower-level realities of morality in the workplace. It also acknowledges the real problems of individual and organizational consistency in value-system choices and moral performance records. But it does conclude from its critical analysis of the research legacy that the lower the stage, the higher the inconsistency problem for individuals and organizations. Executives and economists, therefore, need a certain philosophical realism to address these moral problems rather than an experimental cynicism about ethical complications. Alfred North Whitehead (1938) suggested that the problems of inconsistency in social organization are inherently related to the natural order of finiteness and the natural dialectical processes of order versus disorder. Without leaving his readers to the boredom of abstract thinking and to the frustrations of concrete planning, he adds: 'Our task is to evolve a general concept which allows room for both' (p. 50). As one who considers 'process and reality' (1964), Whitehead defines inconsistency as '. . . the fact that the two states of things which constitute the respective meanings of a pair of propositions cannot exist together' (1938, p. 53). His practical approach to addressing these realistic incompatibilities is to offer an understanding of process that not only explains its relationships to inconsistencies but suggests a way of dealing with them. This is the *philosophical relationship* that helps the executive's mind to accept the reality of dealing with inconsistencies in the workplace:

> . . . process, . . . is a fundamental fact in our experience. We are in the present; the present is always shifting; it is derived from the past; it is shaping the future; it is passing into the future. This is process [pp. 52–53].

And this is the *organizational relationship* that helps the executive manage his or her expectations of attaining consistent quality performance with caring role-taking reciprocity:

> Again the attainment of that last perfection of any finite realization depends on freshness. Freshness provides the supreme intimacy of contrast, the new with the old. A type of order arises, develops its variety of possibilities, culminates, and passes into the decay of repetition without freshness. That type of order decays; not into disorder, but by passing into a new type of order.
>
> (1964, p. 126)

This philosophy of managing organizational inconsistencies in the workplace is what is behind Weiss's (1986) second operational principle of value-system-building for Ameritech, namely, the principle of ambiguous reality. It is also what directs Bowen and Power's (1993) admonitions for the 'moral manager' to strive for reasonable judgments rather than insisting on correct judgments in dealing with ethical inconsistencies from managerial decision-making uncertainties.

Possibilities. If realities persist within the old order, executives and managers need to pass over to realistic possibilities. With the old order fairly well entrenched in the preconventional and conventional ways of doing business and running operations, according to the early workplace studies cited above, it would appear that moral development intervention, especially in organization hierarchies, might not be a high priority in corporate planning. The realistic possibilities for a new moral order in the workplace, therefore, might be few. But, in social movement organization process, new order change starts with social unrest (Guerrette, 1981). And there is no question, at least, in the media, that socio-moral unrest pervades through society and deeply within the corporate sector. If the culture has been searching for its 'moral bearings' through this decade, executives, managers and workers might be more ready than planners.[10] And again, in social movement process to new order change, mobilization needs to follow unrest (ibid.). The strategic task to new moral order for corporate culture, therefore, is to mobilize and that demands ethical discourse.

Initiating ethical discourse is a real possibility for any executive in any company. If the internal climate is not actively disposed, it may be passively receptive to literature, lectures and consults. As in the case of the small family-owned refrigeration business above, interest, even from passive receptive levels, builds rapidly when ethics make sense and morals earn profit. When the interest builds to active dispositions and the time to seize the new order arrives, the executive needs to act and that is when to begin the MBE process for 'passing into the future'.

A more active, unobtrusive way to initiate ethical discourse in a company, with the rational advantage of making corporate ethical sense out of strategic profit planning, is to utilize the advances of technology and interactive media in management communication processes. These modern training tools are new symbols of management interaction processes, whose socialization potential has yet to be tapped as far as ethical consciousness-raising techniques are concerned. The 'Evolution Management' series of van der Erve (1992, 1993, 1994), for example, are interactive computer programs designed to critically awaken the culture consciousness of managers through management perception analyses for the purpose of revitalizing companies and re-creating business enterprises. Van der Erve has constructed four graphic and animated software design modules that *identify prevailing dominant attitudes* in a company; *evaluate operational strategies* to uncover counter-productive behaviour; *define* strategic directions from task-oriented enterprises to *culture-specific missions*; and *integrate* these analytical *perceptions into corporate cultural reformation and organization-set transformation.*

The Evolution Management System is driven by perception knowledge . . . , leading to increased and sustainable asset utilization, revenue growth and profit. . . . In summary, [it is] a total management approach which covers economic relationships, investments, alliances and location strategies [1992].

Although there is not much formal ethical programming within van der Erve's modules, they provide a compatible technological communication medium for dialectical system analysis and corporate reconstructive planning (see 1994, ch. 9, on 'Reconstructing business'). As instruments for the new ethical imperatives of interactional integration and value renegotiation, they constitute new-order graphic symbols for 're-animating' functional systems into interactive programmes. Through coordinated usage with value-system-rebuilding and ethical discourse management, these modules can help executives to actively seize the time for MBE initiation and for mobilizing their companies into an ethical and profitable future.

Finally and perhaps the most important realistic possibility for the executive is self-mobilization. One cannot mobilize others to pass into the future, if one is not ready one's self. Ethical discourse must really start at home. It has to begin from within. Dialogue is needed between the assertive self and the reflexive self. One cannot hope to manage and direct a corporate conscience, if one is not in touch with one's own. Executives need to develop a facility for comfort with reflexivity (see Griffin, 1993). They need to consider the importance of solitude for contemplating creative paths towards personal and professional change and for planning reconstructive tracks for organization and corporate change. It might make sense in their busy lives and demanding schedules to slip away, from time to time, for private retreats where a conducive professional ethical atmosphere can help to expand their ethical consciousness. In such a centre that offers the privacy of reading, thinking, planning and discourse with a consultant, at one's own pace in re-creational leisure, 'critical practical understanding' can open to a 'moral point of view'.

This chapter itself has been a retreat into reflexive sociology as a 'moral sociology' (Gouldner, 1970, p. 491). To invite executives, moral education researchers, and organizational analysts and economists to such a retreat is reflective of a moral sociology for the self and the corporation. It is only to share a reflexive ethical awareness that can enable them 'to know those social [moral] worlds that are and those that might be' (p. 498).

ACKNOWLEDGEMENT

The author is deeply grateful to Helen Haste for her commentary on current moral development research and her suggestions for revisions of this chapter.

NOTES

1 This phrase from the literature of critical philosophy and reflexive sociology implies planning for change in an established order through practical strategies activated for the social reconstruction of a new order. (On 'critical theory' in

philosophy, see Bernstein, 1971, and McCarthy, 1978; on reflexive sociology and its affinity to the practical reconstructive aspects of critical thought, see Gouldner, 1970; see also the section on 'Critical sociology and human potential' in the *Berkeley Journal of Sociology*, vol. XV, 1970.)

2 For empirical evidence on the importance of consistency in value-system-building in the workplace, see Posner *et al.* (1985). This study demonstrates that value articulation in the workplace and value congruence in the workforce, regarding personal and organizational values, make a significant positive difference in individual and organization performance. It also suggests programmes and measures for human resource managers to facilitate ongoing value-consistency-building between the company and its workers through training, reward systems and counselling support. On value-system-measuring and training, see also Payne (1988).

3 On the individual's use of impression management techniques to project a favourable work image as a means for escaping moral accountability in performance flaws, see Goffman (1971), Wood and Mitchell (1981) and Payne and Giacalone (1990).

4 Role-taking is a social psychological concept synthesized by Mead (1934) from the works of James, Cooley and Dewey. It involves an internalized self–other interaction process whereby individuals 'imaginatively rehearse' the anticipated action lines of others, allowing them to coordinate their own responses towards socially organized and cooperative behaviour (Turner, 1978).

5 For some relevant literary resources on ethical issues and dilemmas in the workplace, see Richardson (1989–1990); and for management dilemmas, see Goodpaster (1984). Richardson offers annual editions of business ethics articles collated from public press sources for study and discussion purposes. Goodpaster offers a series of case studies along with a set of corresponding videotapes for management training seminars.

6 For further comparisons of moral adequacy in dealing with corporate ethical scandals, see Guerrette (1988) who critically analyses the prescriptive moral climate of the defence industry's responses to unethical complaints; see also Bowen and Power (1993) who propose a more communicative moral climate for dealing with corporate ethical scandals.

7 On reciprocity and its relationship to moral development and social system process, see Gouldner (1970). Gouldner claims that reciprocity generates interactional inducements within individuals that awaken their consciousness to higher-stage generalized system perspectives. Reciprocity thus strengthens organizational system collectivity and promotes social system stability. 'For reciprocity, unlike complimentarity, actually mobilizes egoistic motivations and channels them into the maintenance of the social system' (p. 242).

8 For assessing the kinds of organizational conditions and operational skills that would guide the executive or manager in the implementation of self-appraisal systems towards achieving individual and collective responsibility, see Hackman (1986).

9 See Walton (1990) for a discussion of managerial strategies, job design principles and human resource benefits in re-organizing hierarchies for commitment building and organizational competence.

10 See *Time* (25 May 1987). This issue, written in the aftermath of the Wall Street and Contragate scandals, manifests the magnitude of socio-moral unrest. Its front cover poses the national moral dilemma and defines the need for a cultural moral compass: 'What Ever Happened to ETHICS? Assaulted by sleaze, scandals and hypocrisy, America searches for its moral bearings' (coverpiece).

REFERENCES

Allport, F. H. (1962) 'A structuronomic conception of behaviour: individual and collective. I. Structural theory and the master problem of social psychology', *Journal of Abnormal and Social Psychology*, vol. 64, 3–30.

Argyris, Chris (1990) *Overcoming Organizational Defenses: Facilitating Organizational Learning*, Boston: Allyn & Bacon.

Argyris, Chris (1991) 'Teaching smart people how to learn', *Harvard Business Review*, May-June, 99–109.

Barnard, Chester (1938) *The Functions of the Executive*, Cambridge, Harvard University Press. MA.

Baum, V. (1974) *Ethics as a Behavioral Science*, Springfield, IL. Charles C. Thomas.

Baxter, G. D. and Rarick, C. A. (1987) 'Education for the moral development of managers: Kohlberg's stages of moral development and integrative education', *Journal of Business Ethics*, vol. 6, 243–248.

Beauchamp, Tom L. (1988) 'Ethical theory and its application to business', in Tom L. Beauchamp and Norman E. Bowie (eds), *Ethical Theory and Business*, 3rd edn, Englewood Cliffs, NJ: Prentice-Hall.

Berg, Per-Olof (1986) 'Symbolic management of human resources', *Human Resource Management*, vol. 25, no. 4, 557–579.

Berger, Peter L. and Luckman, Thomas (1967) *The Social Construction of Reality: A Treatise in the Sociology of Knowledge*, New York: Doubleday.

Bernstein, Richard J. (1971) *Praxis and Action: Contemporary Philosophies of Human Activity*, Philadelphia: University of Pennsylvania Press.

Blasi, Augusto (1980) 'Bridging moral cognition and moral action: a critical review of the literature', *Psychological Bulletin*, vol. 88, 1–45.

Blasi, Augusto (1984) 'Moral identity: its role in moral functioning', in W. M. Kurtines and J. L. Gewirtz (eds), *Morality, Moral Behavior, and Moral Development*, New York: Wiley.

Blumberg, P. (1973) Industrial Democracy: The Sociology of Participation, New York: Schocken Books.

Blumer, Herbert (1947) 'Sociological theory in industrial relations', *American Sociological Review*, June, 271–278.

Blumer, Herbert (1969) *Symbolic Interactionism: Perspective and Method*, Englewood Cliffs, NJ: Prentice-Hall.

Bowen, Michael G. and Power, F. Clark (1993) 'The moral manager: communicative ethics and the *Exxon Valdez* disaster', *Business Ethics Quarterly*, vol. 3, no. 2, 97–115.

Boyd, Dwight R. (1984) 'The principle of principles', in W. M. Kurtines and J. L. Gewirtz (eds), *Morality, Moral Behavior, and Moral Development*, New York: Wiley.

Boyett, Joseph H. and Conn, Henry P. (1988) *Maximum Performance Management: How to Manage and Compensate People to Meet World Competition*, Macomb, IL: Glenbridge.

Braito, Rita, Paulson, Steve and Klonglan, Gerald (1972) 'Domain consensus: a key variable in interorganizational analysis', in M. B. Brinkerhoff and P. R. Kunz (eds), *Complex Organizations and Their Environments*, Dubuque, IA: Brown.

Brinkerhoff, Merlin B. (ed.) (1984) *Work Organizations and Society: Comparative Convergences*, Westport, CT: Greenwood Press.

Brinkerhoff, Merlin B. and Kunz, P. R. (eds) (1972) *Complex Organizations and Their Environments*, Dubuque, IA: Brown.

Candee, Daniel (1985) 'Classical ethics and live patient simulations in the moral education of health care professionals', in, M. W. Berkowitz and F. Oser (eds) *Moral Education: Theory and Application*, Hillsdale, NJ: Lawrence Erlbaum.

Colby, Anne and Kohlberg, Lawrence (1987) *The Measurement of Moral Judgment*, vol. I, Cambridge: Cambridge University Press.

Cooley, Charles Horton (1902) *Human Nature and the Social Order*, New York: Charles Scribner's Sons.

Dahrendorf, Ralph (1959) *Class and Class Conflict in Industrial Society*, Stanford, CA: Stanford University Press.

Davidson, Marilyn (1992) *Shattering the 'Glass Ceiling': The Woman Manager*, London: Chapman.

Deetz, S. A. (1983) 'Keeping the conversation going: the principle of dialectic ethics', *Communications*, vol. 7.

Dill, William R. (1958) 'Environment as an influence on managerial autonomy', *Administrative Science Quarterly*, vol. 2 (March), 409–443.

Emler, Nicholas and Hogan, Robert (1991) 'Moral psychology and public policy', in W. Kurtines and J. L. Gewirtz (eds), *Handbook of Moral Behavior and Development, Volume 3: Application*, Hillsdale, NJ: Lawrence Erlbaum.

Etzioni, Amitai (1960) 'New directions in the study of organizations and society', *Social Research*, vol. 27, 223–228.

Etzioni, Amitai (1961/1975) *A Comparative Analysis of Complex Organizations*, New York: Free Press.

Etzioni, Amitai (1988) *The Moral Dimension: Toward a New Economics*, New York: Free Press.

Evan, William M. (1972) 'The organization set: toward a theory of interorganizational relations', in M. B. Brinkerhoff and P. R. Kunz (eds), *Complex Organizations and Their Environments*, Dubuque, IA: Brown.

Farr, James L. and Middlebrooks, Carolyn L. (1990) 'Enhancing motivation to participate in professional development', in S. L. Willis and S. S. Dubin (eds), *Maintaining Professional Competence*, San Francisco: Jossey-Bass.

Forester, J. (1985) 'The applied turn in contemporary critical theory', in J. Forester (ed.), *Critical Theory and Public Life*, Cambridge, MA: MIT Press.

Gellerman, Saul W. (1986) 'Why 'good' managers make bad ethical choices', *Harvard Business Review*, July–August, 85–90.

Gibbs, J. C. (1977) 'Kohlberg's stages of moral judgment: a constructive critique', *Harvard Educational Review*, vol. 47, 43–61.

Gilligan, Carol (1982) *In a Different Voice: Psychological Theory and Women's Development*, Cambridge, MA: Harvard University Press.

Goffman, Erving (1955) 'On face-work: an analysis of ritual elements in social interaction', *Psychiatry*, vol. 18, 213–231.

Goffman, Erving (1959) *The Presentation of Self in Everyday Life*, New York: Doubleday.

Goffman, Erving (1963) *Behavior in Public Places*, New York: Free Press.

Goffman, Erving (1971) *Relations in Public*, New York: Basic Books.

Goldman, Paul and Van Houten, Donald R. (1977) 'Managerial strategies and the worker: a Marxist analysis of bureaucracy', in J. K. Benson (ed.), *Organizational Analysis: Critique and Innovation*, Sage Contemporary Social Science Issues 37, Beverly Hills, CA: Sage.

Goodpaster, Kenneth E. (1983) 'The concept of corporate responsibility', *Journal of Business Ethics*, vol. 2, 1–22.

Goodpaster, Kenneth E. (1984) *Ethics in Management* (Course Module Series), Division of Research, Harvard Business School, Boston.

Goodpaster, Kenneth E. and Matthews, John B., Jr. (1982) 'Can a corporation have a conscience?' *Harvard Business Review*, January–February, 132.

Goulder, Alvin W. (1970) *The Coming Crisis of Western Sociology*, New York: Basic Books.

Griffin, Emile (1993) *The Reflective Executive: a Spirituality of Business and Enterprise*, New York: Crossroad.

Griggs, Walter H. and Manring, Susan (1986) 'Increasing the effectiveness of technical professionals', *Management Review* (May) 62–64.

Guerrette, Richard H. (1981) *The Emmanuel Servant Community: A Case Study of a Social Movement Organization*, unpublished doctoral dissertation, University Microfilm International, London, Ann Arbor, MI.

Guerrette, Richard H. (1986) 'Environmental integrity and corporate responsibility', *Journal of Business Ethics*, vol. 5, 409–415.

Guerrette, Richard H. (1988) 'Corporate ethical consulting: developing management strategies for corporate ethics', *Journal of Business Ethics*, vol. 7, 373–380.

Habermas, Jurgen (1979) *Communication and the Evolution of Society*, Boston: Beacon Press.

Habermass, Jurgen (1984) *The Theory of Communicative Action: Reason and the Rationalization of Society*, Boston: Beacon Press.

Habermas, Jurgen (1990a) 'Justice and solidarity: on the discussion concerning stage 6', in T. E. Wren (ed.), *The Moral Domain: Essays in the Ongoing Discussion between Philosophy and the Social Sciences*, Cambridge, MA: MIT Press.

Habermas, Jurgen (1990b) *Moral Consciousness and Communicative Action*, Cambridge, MA: MIT Press.

Hackman, J. Richard (1986) 'The psychology of self-management in organizations', in M. S. Pallak and R. Perloff (eds), *Psychology and Work: Productivity, Change and Employment*, Washington, DC: American Psychological Association.

Hamilton, Stephen F., Basseches, Michael and Richards, Francis A. (1985) 'Participatory-democratic work and adolescents' mental health', *American Journal of Community Psychology*, vol. 13, no. 4, 467–486.

Harding, Carol Gibb and Snyder, Kenneth (1991) 'Tom, Huck, and Oliver Stone as advocates in Kohlberg's just community: theory-based strategies for moral education', *Adolescence*, vol. 26, no. 102, 319–329.

Haste, Helen (1990) 'Moral responsibility and moral commitment: the integration of affect and cognition', in T. E. Wren (ed.), *The Moral Domain: Essays in the Ongoing Discussion between Philosophy and the Social Sciences*, Cambridge, MA: MIT Press.

Hausman, Daniel M. and McPherson, Michael S. (1993) 'Taking ethics seriously: economics and contemporary moral philosophy', *Journal of Economic Literature*, vol. XXXI, no. 2, 671–731.

Hertzberg, F. (1968) 'One more time: how do you motivate employees? *Harvard Business Review*, vol. 46, 53–62.

Heydebrand, Wolf (1977) 'Organizational contradictions in public bureaucracies: toward a Marxian theory of organizations', in J. K. Benson (ed.), *Organizational Analysis: Critique and Innovation*, Sage Contemporary Social Science Issue 37, Beverly Hills, CA: Sage.

Higgins, Ann and Gordon, Frederick (1985) 'Work climate and socio-moral development in two worker-owned companies', in M. W. Berkowitz and F. Oser (eds), *Moral Education: Theory and Application*, Hillsdale, NJ: Lawrence Erlbaum.

Hirsch, Fred (1976) *Social Limits to Growth*, Cambridge MA: Harvard University Press.

Hogan, Robert, Raskin, R. and Fazzini, D. (1988) *The Dark Side of Charisma*, unpublished manuscript, Tulsa Institute of Behavioral Sciences.

Holmstrom, Bengt (1979) 'Moral hazards and observability', *Bell Journal of Economics*, vol. 10, no. 1, 74–91.

Holmstrom, Bengt (1982) 'Moral hazard in teams', *Bell Journal of Economics*, vol. 13, 324–340.

Johannesen, Richard L. (1983) *Ethics in Human Communication*, 2nd edn, Prospect Heights, IL: Waveland Press.

Katz, Daniel and Kahn, Robert L. (1972) 'Organizations and the system concept', in M. B. Brinkerhoff and P. R. Kunz (eds), *Complex Organizations and Their Environments*, Dubuque, IA: Brown.

Katz, Daniel and Kahn, Robert L. (1978) *The Social Psychology of Organizations*, 2nd edn, New York: Wiley.

Kohlberg, Lawrence (1971) 'Indoctrination versus relativity in value education', *Zygon*, vol. 6, 285–310.

Kohlberg, Lawrence (1973) 'The claim to moral adequacy of a highest stage of moral judgment', *Journal of Philosophy*, vol. 70, 630–646.

Kohlberg, Lawrence (1981, 1984) *Essays on Moral Development*, Vol. I: *The Philosophy of Moral Development*, Vol. II: *The Psychology of Moral Development*, New York: Harper & Row.

Kohlberg, Lawrence (1986) 'The just community approach to corrections', *Journal of Correctional Education*, vol. 37, no. 2, 54–58.

Kohlberg, Lawrence and Candee, Daniel (1984) 'The relationship of moral judgment to moral action', in W. M. Kurtines and J. L. Gewirtz (eds), *Morality, Moral Behavior, and Moral Development*, New York: Wiley.

Kohlberg, Lawrence, Boyd, Dwight R. and Levine, Charles (1990) 'The return of stage 6: its principle and moral point of view', in T. E. Wren (ed.), *The Moral Domain: Essays in the Ongoing Discussion between Philosophy and the Social Sciences*, Cambridge, MA: MIT Press.

Kohlberg, Lawrence *et al.* (1975) *The Just Community School: The Theory and the Cambridge Cluster School Experiment*, Harvard University Graduate School of Education (ERIC Doc. Reproduction Services, ED 223 511), Cambridge, MA.

Krause, Elliot (1977) *Power and Illness*, New York: Elsevier.

Kuhn, Thomas S. (1970) *The Structure of Scientific Revolutions*, 2nd edn, enlarged, Chicago: University of Chicago Press.

Kung, Guido, (1985) 'The postconventional level of moral development: psychology or philosophy?' in M. W. Berkowitz and F. Oser (eds), *Moral Education: Theory and Application*, Hillsdale, NJ: Lawrence Erlbaum.

Kurtines, William M. (1984) 'Moral behavior as rule-governed behavior: a psychosocial role-theoretical approach to moral behavior and development', in W. M. Kurtines and J. L. Gewirtz (eds.), *Morality, Moral Behavior, and Moral Development*, New York: Wiley.

Kurtines, William M., Mayock, Ellen, Pollard, Steven R., Lanza, Teresita and Carlo, Gustavo (1991) 'Social and moral development from the perspective of psychosocial theory', in W. Kurtines and J. L. Gewirtz (eds), *Handbook of Moral Behavior and Development, Volume 1: Theory*, Hillsdale, NJ: Lawrence Erlbaum.

Lawler, Edward (1986) *High Involvement Management*, San Francisco: Jossey-Bass.

Lawson, Robert W. (1988) 'Two men with a corporate conscience', *Vermont Business Magazine*, May, 16–18.

Levine, Charles (1976) 'Role taking standpoint and adolescent usage of Kohlberg's conventional stages of moral reasoning', *Journal of Personality and Social Psychology*, vol. 34, 41–46.

Levine, Sol and White, Paul E. (1972) 'Exchange as a conceptual framework for the study of interorganizational relationships', in M. B. Brinkerhoff and P. R. Kunz (eds), *Complex Organizations and Their Environments*, Dubuque, IA: Brown.

Lifton, Robert Jay (1970) *Boundaries: Psychological Man in Revolution*, New York: Vintage Books.

Lindesmith, Alfred R., Strauss, Anselm L. and Denzin, Normal K. (1975) *Social Psychology*, 4th edn, Hinsdale, IL. Dryden Press.

Lutz, W. D. (1983) 'Corporate doublespeak: making bad news look good', *Business and Society Review*, vol. 44, 19–22.

McCarthy, Thomas (1978) *The Critical Theory of Jurgen Habermas*, Cambridge, MA: MIT Press.

Maremont, Mark (1993) 'Summing up: has your company unleashed the spirit of enterprise? Or is it too bureaucratic? Here's how to tell', *Business Week – Enterprise*, New York: McGraw-Hill.

Martin, Patricia Yancey (1989) 'The moral politics of organizations: reflections of an unlikely feminist', *Journal of Applied Behavioral Science*, vol. 25, no. 4, 451–470.

Mayo, E. (1945) *The Social Problems of an Industrial Civilization*, Harvard Business School, Division of Research, Cambridge, MA.

Mead, George Herbert (1934) *Mind, Self, and Society*, Chicago: University of Chicago Press.

Miller, Donald Britton (1990) 'Organizational, environmental, and work design strategies that foster competence', in S. L. Willis and S. S. Dubin (eds), *Managing Professional Competence: Approaches to Career Enhancement, Vitality, and Success Throughout a Work Life*, San Francisco: Jossey-Bass.

Miller, Gary J. (1992) *Managerial Dilemmas: The Political Economy of Hierarchy*, Cambridge: Cambridge University Press.

Mills, C. Wright (1948/1970) 'The contribution of sociology to the studies of industrial relations', *Berkeley Journal of Sociology*, vol. XV, 11–32.

Misgeld, Dieter (1991) 'Moral education and critical social theory: from the "First World" to the "Third World"', in W. Kurtines and J. L. Gewirtz (eds), *Handbook of Moral Behavior and Development, Volume 3: Application*, Hillsdale, NJ: Lawrence Erlbaum.

Morrison, Ann M. (1992) *Breaking the 'Glass Ceiling': Can Women Reach the Top of America's Largest Corporations?*, Reading, MA: Addison-Wesley.

Olasky, M. N. (1985) 'Inside the amoral world of public relations', *Business and Society Review*, vol. 52, 41–44.

Orsburn, Jack D., Moran, Linda, Musselwhite, Ed and Zenger, John H. (1990) *Self-Directed Work Teams: The New American Challenge*, Homewood, IL: Business One Irwin.

Oser, Fritz and Schlafli, Andre (1985) 'But does it move? the difficulty of gradual change in moral development', in M. W. Berkowitz and F. Oser (eds), *Moral Education: Theory and Application*, Hillsdale, NJ: Lawrence Erlbaum.

Parsons, Talcott (1956) *Economy and Society*, Glencoe, IL: Free Press.

Parsons, Talcott (1967) *Sociological Theory and Modern Society*, New York: Free Press.

Payne, Stephen L. (1988) 'Values and ethics-related measures for management education', *Journal of Business Ethics*, vol. 7, 273–277.

Payne, Stephen L. (1991) 'A proposal for corporate ethical reform: the ethical dialogue group', *Business and Professional Ethics Journal*, vol. 10, no. 1, 67–88.

Payne, Stephen L. and Giacalone, Robert A. (1990) 'Social psychological approaches to the perception of ethical dilemmas', *Human Relations*, vol. 43, no. 7, 649–665.

Perrow, Charles (1972) 'A framework for the comparative analysis of organizations', in M. B. Brinkerhoff and P. R. Kunz (eds), *Complex Organizations and Their Environments*, Dubuque, IA: Brown.

Piaget, Jean (1965) *The Moral Judgment of the Child*, trans. Marjorie Gabain, New York: Free Press.

Pollard, Steven R., Kurtines, William M., Carlo, Gustavo, Dancs, Mary and Mayock, Ellen (1991) 'Moral education from the perspective of psychosocial theory', in W.

Kurtines and J. L. Gewirtz, (eds), *Handbook of Moral Behaviour and Development, Volume 3: Application*, Hillsdale, NJ: Lawrence Erlbaum.

Posner, Barry Z., Kouzes, James M. and Schmidt, Warren H. (1985) 'Shared values make a difference: an empirical test of corporate culture', *Human Resource Management*, vol. 24, no. 3, 293–309.

Power, Clark (1988) 'The just community approach to moral education', *Journal of Moral Education*, vol. 17, no. 3, 195–208.

Power, Clark F., Higgins, Ann and Kohlberg, Lawrence (1989) *Lawrence Kohlberg's Approach to Moral Education*, New York: Columbia University Press.

Quint, Michael (1990) 'Campeau bankers are posing some $2.3 billion questions', *The New York Times*, Business (Section 3), 14 January.

Richardson, John E. (ed.) (1989–1990) *Annual Editions: Business Ethics 89/90*, Guilford, CT: Dushkin.

Rioux, Marcel (1970) 'Critical versus aseptic sociology', *Berkeley Journal of Sociology*, vol. XV, 33–47.

Roethlisberger, F. J. and Dickson, W. J. (1946) *Management and the Worker*, Cambridge, MA: Harvard University Press.

Rusk, Tom M. D. (1993) *The Power of Ethical Persuasion: From Conflict to Partnership at Work and in Private Life*, New York: Viking Penguin.

Schweiger, David M., Ridley, R. Russell, Jr and Marini, Dennis M. (1992) 'Creating one from two: the merger between Harris Semiconductor and General Electric Solid State', Susan E. Jackson (ed.), *Diversity in the Workplace: Human Resources Initiatives*, Society for Industrial and Organizational Psychology Publication, New York: Guildford Press.

Sethia, Nirmal and Von Glinow, Mary Ann (1985) 'Arriving at four cultures by managing the reward system', in Kilmann, Saxton, Serpa and Associates (eds), *Gaining Control of the Corporate Culture*, San Francisco: Jossey-Bass.

Sewell, William H. (1970) 'Some recent developments in socialization theory and research', in G. P. Stone and H. A. Farberman (eds), *Social Psychology Through Symbolic Interaction*, Waltham, MA: Xerox College Publishing.

Stewart, Jim (1991) *Managing Change Through Training and Development*, Amsterdam: Pfeiffer & Co.

Thompson, James D. (1967) *Organizations in Action*, New York: McGraw-Hill.

Tevino, L. K. (1986) 'Ethical decision-making in organizations: a person-situation interactionist model', *Academy of Management Review*, vol. 11, no. 3, 601–617.

Tronto, Joan C. (1987) 'Beyond gender difference to a theory of care', *Signs Journal of Women in Culture and Society*, vol. 12, no. 4, 644–663.

Turiel, Elliot and Smetana, Judith G. (1984) 'Social knowledge and action: the coordination of domains', in W. M. Kurtines and J. L. Gewirtz (eds), *Mortality, Moral Behavior, and Moral Development*, New York: Wiley.

Turiel, Elliot, Smetana, Judith G and Killen, Melanie (1991) 'Social contexts in social cognitive development', in W. Kurtines and J. L. Gewirtz (eds), *Handbook of Moral Behavior and Development, Volume 2: Research*, Hillsdale, NJ: Lawrence Erlbaum.

Turner, Jonathan H. (1978) *The Structure of Sociological Theory* (revised edn), Homewood, IL: Dorsey Press.

Turner, Ralph H. (1956) 'Role-taking, role standpoint, and reference group behavior', *American Journal of Sociology*, vol. 61, 316–328.

Turner, Ralph H. (1962) 'Role-taking: process versus conformity', in A. M. Rose (ed.), *Human Behavior and Social Processes*, Boston: Houghton Mifflin.

Van der Erve, Marc (1992) *Evolution Management: Winning in Tomorrow's Marketplace* (Software Program, EM Corporation), Geneva: KPMG Fides.

Van der Erve, Marc (1993) *The Power of Tomorrow's Management: Using the Vision-Culture*

Balance in Organizations, 2nd edn, enlarged, Stoneham, MA: Butterworth-Heinemann.

Van der Erve, Marc (1994) *Evolution Management: Winning in Tomorrow's Marketplace*, Stoneham, MA: Butterworth-Heinemann.

Von Glinow, Mary Ann (1988) *The New Professionals: Managing Today's High-Tech Employees*, New York: Ballinger.

Vroom, Victor H. *et al.* (1990) *Manage People, Not Personnel: Motivation and Performance Appraisal*, The Harvard Business Review Book Series, Boston, MA: Harvard Business School Publishing.

Walker, Barbara A. and Hanson, William C. (1992) 'Valuing differences at Digital equipment corporation', in Susan E. Jackson (ed.), *Diversity in the Workplace: Human Resources Initiatives*, Society for Industrial and Organizational Psychology, New York: Guilford Press.

Walton, Richard E. (1990) 'From control to commitment in the workplace', in V. H. Vroom (Pref.), *Manage People, Not Personnel; Motivation and Performance Appraisal*, The Harvard Business Review Book Series, Boston, MA: Harvard Business School Publishing.

Walzer, Michael (1983) *Spheres of Justice*, New York: Basic Books.

Weber, James (1990) 'Managers' moral reasoning: assessing their responses to three moral dilemmas', *Human Relations*, vol. 43, no. 7, 687–702.

Weinreich-Haste, Helen (1984) 'Morality, social meaning, and rhetoric: the social context of moral reasoning', in W. M. Kurtines and J. L. Gewirtz (eds), *Morality, Moral Behavior, and Moral Development*, New York: Wiley.

Weiss, William L. (1986) 'Minerva's owl: building a corporate value system', *Journal of Business Ethics*, vol. 5, 243–247.

Whitehead, Alfred North (1938) *Modes of Thought*, New York: Free Press.

Whitehead, Alfred North (1964) *Science and Philosophy*, Paterson, NJ: Littlefield, Adams & Co.

Willis, Sherry L. and Dubin, Samuel S. (1990) 'Maintaining professional competence: directions and possibilities', in *Maintaining Professional Competence: Approaches to Career Enhancement, Vitality, and Success Throughout a Work Life*, San Francisco: Jossey-Bass.

Willis, Sherry L. and Tosti-Vasey, Joanne L. (1990) 'How adult development, intelligence, and motivation affect competence', in *Maintaining Professional Competence: Approaches to Career Enhancement, Vitality, and Success Throughout a Work Life*, San Francisco: Jossey-Bass.

Wood, John A., Longenecker, Justin C., McKinney, Joseph A. and Moore, Carlos W. (1988) 'Ethical attitudes of students and business professionals: a study of moral reasoning', *Journal of Business Ethics*, vol. 7, 249–257.

Wood, Robert E. and Mitchell, Terrance R. (1981) 'Manager behavior in a social context: the impact of impression management on attributions and disciplinary actions', *Organizational Behavior and Human Performance*, vol. 28, 356–378.

Yussen, Steven R. (1976) 'Moral reasoning from the perspective of others', *Child Development*, vol. 47, 551–555.

Chapter 5

Moralization as a link between idealism and naturalism in the ethical discourse

Claes Gustafsson

THE CONCERN ABOUT MORALS

In order to understand the discourse of business ethics – or ethics as a whole – it is important to recognize that, in a way, it is always built on the possibility of moral criticism or moral praise: some act being 'wrong' or its leading to a state which is 'bad' (or, on the contrary, 'right' and 'good') discussed in relation to somebody having committed that act, thereby being responsible for the outcome, gives much of the driving force to the interest in ethics.

The apparent explanation for the current interest in business ethics, accordingly, lies in the suspicion that the activities of business firms and their managers are open to criticism, either in the sense that business as such leads to immoral behaviour, or in the way that managers more or less intentionally engage in unethical behaviour. There seem to be good grounds for both suspicions. On the other hand, it is not clear that managers do differ from the rest of the population.

There may be other reasons for being interested in business ethics, of course. Common managerial theory has been built on an assumption – a belief – that economies, in some way, are morally neutral. The socially and politically chosen economic system might be open to moral criticism. Private ownership, interest and profit, commercialism and consumerism, are questions having moral aspects often discussed on an ideological level. Leaving these aside the general assumption has been that the instrumental organization we call a 'firm' is a kind of techno-economic problem, and that the work of managers is only to manage that problem in a morality-free, rational way. This has been not only a hypothetical idea, it seems, but also an empirical assumption about managerial action. Managers, it is often said, make rational calculations about economic facts and expectations, they do not let themselves be influenced by moral considerations. And if they do, they exceed the limits of their legitimate right (Friedman, 1962).

During the last few decades this position of conventional managerial theorizing has been somewhat weakened. For anybody meeting a living manager it is easy to see that managers, like anybody else, are full of moral feelings and ethical arguments. In fact, Friedman's tenet that managers should only take care of the owners' interests presupposes strong moral feelings of responsibility – otherwise the only strictly economic urge for them would be to pocket the money themselves. Within the studies of organization culture, too, it has become clear that any working instrumental organization is full of moral feelings mixed into the background of almost any activity. Studies of the phenomena of ethics and morality in relation to economic activities also show that morality constitutes an integral part of economic reasoning. There is also reason to believe that moral feelings or moral considerations do not always function in the same way as traditional conceptions of utility assume (Etzioni, 1986, 1988; Gustafsson, 1988). To this might be added, that in studying the history of managerial theorizing we find a strong moral interest not only in Adam Smith, professor of moral philosophy, but also in some of the founding fathers of practical managerial reasoning: Benjamin Franklin (1968) is one worth mentioning, Frederick Winslow Taylor is another (Merkle, 1980; Westerlind, 1983). There might, accordingly, be reasons for studying the interface between ethics and economic action regardless of the perspective of moral criticism.

A look at what has been written on business ethics during the last decade, when the topic has made a comeback, growing almost into a fad, reveals that moral concerns dominate the discussion. On the one hand, there is the discussion regarding what is right and what is wrong in business, and about how to evade all the moral pitfalls of managerial life. This discussion seems to be motivated by a feeling that everything would work better, if only we showed people the right way to act. Partly it is also an answer to an explicit need. Many managers earnestly ask for advice. On the other hand, the suspicion that 'something is wrong' is aimed directly at managers and other actors in the economic field. Are managers really different, we ask? Are they morally deficient, in some way; are they, perhaps, more egoistic, greedy and ruthless than 'we' are? Is economic education corrupting young people? And so on.

IDEALIST ETHICS

The quest for a definite answer to the question of good and bad has followed man through history: ethics is one of the foundation stones of philosophy, and the preaching of good morals has gone on for millenniums. If there were an easy solution at hand, there would conceivably be no need for the study of business ethics any more. This simple fact sometimes gives the reader of treatises of moral philosophy a feeling of *déjà vu*, and gives rise to the thought that maybe we should try something else.

It is sometimes said that Kant's categorical imperative – in its short form telling you that you should treat others as you expect them to treat you – gives a definite and uncontestable rule, from which we might deduce all other ethical norms. Maybe so, maybe not. Try to tell that story to a cruel oppressor, or to a ruthless capitalist exploiting workers as well as consumers. They will not understand the argument but, on the contrary, ask why on earth somebody would think that such an idea should sound reasonable for them. Why would somebody, living securely in an uncontested position of power and riches, willingly choose to give all that away, when there is no practical need for it? 'On the contrary', the oppressor will reply, turning around the probabilistic point of Kant and Rawls, 'just by treating everybody else as cruelly as I do, I can keep them from doing the same to me'. The categorical imperative makes sense only if you are poor and otherwise less well off than other people are, or if you adhere to the highly abstract and clearly unprovable belief – common in the arguments of moral philosophy – that man is living in a completely probabilistic world, where everybody, at any moment, has the same chance of 'happening to be' either poor or rich. So, to answer that question, you are forced to invent some other 'higher' moral principle that he might accept – equality, fairness, legitimate rights – and then the search goes on and on again. (This points to a rather general problem in normative ethical argumentation: it is easy to persuade somebody who is already of the same opinion as you are, but almost impossible to persuade anybody who initially – morally, emotionally, logically – is of another opinion. For rational moral argumentation to be more than trivial, however, it should be able 'logically' to persuade those wanting to oppose its argument, maybe even those not able or willing to understand it.)

If so much effort has been put into this search, without any satisfactory solution, the whole question might be wrongly stated. What if there is no ultimate answer? One possible reply to this might be that even if there is no answer, one ought to be developed. Philosophers should go on refining the language of moral argumentation until, finally, they reach a system of clear and 'rational' ethical discourse, which in an unequivocal way states what is right and what is wrong. This, however, is exactly what has been tried for several thousands of years – with no clear positive result. The problem seems to be such that rational moral argumentation is possible within strictly limited perspectives, as long as we do not question our more or less intuitive axiomatic assumptions regarding right and wrong. However, as soon as the discussion turns to more generalized systems of argumentation, it either falls into the trap of practically irrelevant truisms or gets tangled in fuzzy webs of contradictions. Thus, it would seem, moral discourse is only partly open to rational argumentation.

The problem of the mainstream of moral philosophy, then, might be that it is *inherently idealist*. It rests on the implicit assumption that there exists, somewhere and somehow, an ideal set of ethical norms, hidden from us mortals by a veil of ignorance, confusion and misunderstanding.

MORALITY

'Morality' (unlike idealist ethics) can be seen as a genuinely human, social and cultural fact. There are reasons to seriously consider the socio-biological argument that some moral 'tendencies' – usually called altruistic feelings – may be advantageous to the survival of the species (Wilson, 1975, 1978; Dawkins, 1983), on a more complex level morality is probably culturally induced: the occurrence of 'instinctive' altruism hardly explains the phenomenon of complex moral argumentation (Etzioni, 1986, 1988).

When somebody is said to be a moral person or, even better, a highly moral person, or when instead somebody is called 'immoral', the existence of some invisible and intangible characteristic – a personality trait – is implied. These traits are often given other names, such as 'goodness', 'honesty', 'courage', 'loyalty', 'truthfulness' – or the antonyms 'badness', 'dishonesty', 'cowardice', 'disloyalty', 'deceitfulness', and so on. There is a strong correspondence between classical 'virtues' and 'moral characteristics', as Alastair MacIntyre (1987) shows. Virtues, as they are described in common language, are semi-stable. Being honest does not imply acting honestly in some specific situation only, rather 'honesty' is a kind of continuing behavioural pattern: if somebody is said to be 'honest', this means that she is expected to act honestly in the future, too. Accordingly, because of what she has done to help the poor in India, many people see Mother Teresa as a 'good' person. This 'goodness' implies an understanding that she will go on being good, helping the poor and the weak.

Morality, in this way, can be seen as a factual phenomenon, produced mainly by human use of language and by patterns of reasoning. It exists and is real in the same way as 'culture', and can be looked at as a culturally produced fact – a semi-stable pattern of inter-individual actions and habits.

As noted earlier, the phenomenon of morality is closely connected with the possibility of moral criticism. Unethical or immoral acts are often seen as implying some kind of inherent moral badness or weakness in the actor. People involved in criminal acts, thus, *are* criminal, and people doing immoral things *are* immoral. The fact that managers and companies are involved in immoral and/or criminal activities, then, once more reinforces the ancient conviction that doing business is a bad, or at least a questionable, activity. Business, in other words, is inherently morally suspect – and so, by association, is the manager and the firm. This can, however, be interpreted in different ways. Firms and managers in this respect seem not to deviate much from the rest of society. There is no need to argue much in favour of the notion that (almost) everyone sometimes commits 'immoral acts', and that about the same number also sometimes breaks a law. Even when talking about economic crime, there is reason to remember that firms, like individuals, seldom engage in murder, armed robbery, theft, and so on. Both, however, rather frequently engage in minor lawbreaking – mainly breaking administrative rules in society. If this is so, then the conception of absolute moral blamelessness loses some of its credibility. If everybody has moral faults, this becomes a genuine human characteristic, and being genuinely human cannot (easily be shown to) be wrong *per se*.

The same goes for companies. So far as we accept a social system, depending on semi-autonomous instrumental organizations to take care of central processes of social life, we may have to accept that they cannot all act in an ethically blameless way.

Trying to understand the moral behaviour of firms and managers, starting with the assumption that they are inherently immoral, in this way seems to be an approach leading nowhere; rather, it would seem, managers are 'normal' people, and the quintessence of the modern instrumental business organization closely mirrors that of practical life and of the surrounding culture. There is, of course, always the possibility that our culture as a whole is morally deficient. This, however, raises the question whether something that a whole culture accepts as morally good can be thought to be bad *within that culture*. Or, to put the question more sharply: can something which is felt to be morally good by the whole of humanity, every human being included, be shown to be bad – without appealing to extra-human rules?

Numerous studies, trying to find differences in moral argumentation or in moral 'traits' or in levels of moral development between managers – or students of business administration – and other people, have failed to show more than marginal differences between these and the 'general population'. At best they may be able to show some small – statistically significant – differences. Students of business administration may be somewhat more 'immoral' than managers, and than other students, in some dimension. Younger students may be somewhat more 'machiavellian' than older ones. Women are usually somewhat more 'ethically conscious' than men are, and so on. The greatest differences seem to be found between respondents from different cultures – the old truth pops up, once again, that 'foreigners' are less moral than 'we' are.

The effort to unveil the moral characteristics of managers, or of any other group of people, is, I shall argue, a case of misdirected naturalism in the field of the human sciences. 'Marginal' and 'trivial' but statistically reliable differences become non-marginal and non-trivial as soon as there is reason to believe that they are stable, and thereby generalizable outside their own context. If they can be assumed to be 'natural', they can be added to the steady growth of scientific knowledge. The dominating instability and the context-bound variability of these kinds of results, however, do not seem to warrant such an assumption. Moreover, the belief in the aggregability of scientific knowledge as a whole, not to speak of that of social science, has lost much of its credibility in the post-modern perspective. Morality is not a natural phenomenon. There is no genetically inherited 'moral gland', determining stable moral traits. Instead it is a cultural product, evolving, changing and oscillating as a part of human culture.

So, instead of all this effort put into more or less futile attempts to find marginal and mostly trivial differences between groups of people that on the whole are identical, the interest of the researcher should be aimed at studying moral and ethical differences between groups which, in a relevant way, are known to manifest clearly different moral behaviour. Then, of course, it is not interesting to ask *if* they are different, but *how* and *why* and *in what way.*

There is also another problem hidden in the belief in naturally positive moral characteristics: most managers are rather competent at using higher levels of moral argumentation, in the Kohlbergian sense (Kohlberg, 1981; Bergling, 1981). Especially in situations actualized as 'moral discourse' – e.g., when agreeing to give an interview 'concerning business ethics', or in a seminar on that topic – they tend to use arguments mostly belonging to the higher levels of morally reciprocal thought. (Not, however, always. Some managers, on the contrary, choose to take an almost theatrical hedonistic and egoistic stand – clearly belonging to Kohlberg's lower levels of moral development.)

There is, however, good reason to interpret hypothetical moralizing activities – experiments, interviews and other cases of ethical discussion – with some caution. In all these situations people can be expected to act *sub specie ludi* – as Johan Asplund (1987) notes – arguing within the frame of intellectual play and not as an act within the concrete seriousness of reality. With a given conception of the kind of play best received by the audience, the logic of the play takes form in the mind. The interesting point is that the same persons, when discussing their daily activities in a 'non-moralizing' perspective, i.e. when nobody has indicated the ethical perspective or otherwise hinted at the moral dimension of the question, often tend to use arguments related to other, usually 'lower', levels of moral development. This can be seen as a case of the problem of 'social desirability', but it is also an interesting phenomenon *per se*. Any respondent, it seems, has at his or her disposal a set of alternative 'moral logics', structures of moral argumentation or 'ethical discourses', and is perfectly able to shift from the one to the other when the situational frame changes. One way of interpreting Kohlberg's six stages of moral development, thus, could be that they do not depict any kind of development in 'goodness', but rather a transformation and restructuring of the intellectual ability to handle very simple structures of moral discourse in order to arrive at alternative, more abstract, reciprocal ones. At an intuitive level there is nothing strange in this; it only shows that man is not a one-dimensional moral automaton, and that the search for a true and stable human trait, an 'absolute degree of morality', misses the point.

The search for positive 'natural' moral characteristics is largely analogous to the long and futile search for an exhaustive unique set of 'leadership traits'. It might be a result of an objectivistic and naturalistic mistake. Thus, a property of everyday language, connected with the tendency to evaluate individuals and acts, is interpreted as indicating a truly existing natural fact. As in Plato's cave metaphor, people implicitly assume that the shadows and patterns on the wall of the cave must be only weak images of the 'real' phenomenon. If somebody is (said or thought to be) a 'good leader', then, accordingly, they try to find the property giving rise to this 'goodness'. Following this naturalistic interpretation, if somebody is morally good, then it is because he or she really *is* good; has a property called goodness. Then we might go on looking for this property, maybe in the head or the heart or some hitherto undetected moral gland or gene.

The assumption of moral badness easily leads to another kind of blindness. Most managers involved in unethical activities do not really feel that they are doing anything bad. On the contrary, they feel that 'in this situation' their choice was the right thing to do. The 'situation', namely, is usually not ethically one-dimensional. Most ethically relevant practical decision situations embrace a whole set of conflicting, or at least partly contradictory, ethical principles. The reason for this may be found not so much in the corruption of man, as in the endless complexity of practical life, and in the ensuing moral dilemmas – ethical paradoxes. The problems of business ethics are usually not caused by some wish to be bad or to act immorally. Instead, it would seem, managers are rather 'normal', and unethical activities are usually connected with efforts to 'do it right' in some way.

What I am trying to put forward is the almost trivial truth that managers seldom behave 'unethically' out of a wish to do something bad or evil. They do not, for example, decide to release wastes into rivers and lakes out of some evil desire to pollute the waters, or because they want to defile the beautiful surroundings. Unethical acts, or acts leading to outcomes deemed as unethical in some perspective, can be explained in different ways. The rare case where somebody behaves unethically out of a wish to do something bad or evil – really wanting to pollute watercourses, for example, to hurt somebody or to destroy somebody's life – seems to be a poor explanation for immoral business behaviour. Other, and more plausible, explanations might be found in variants of bounded rationality. The situation may, for example, be so unclear, that the decision maker cannot predict the outcomes of his or her activities. This might be a result of incomplete information, or, on the other hand, of too much information, of too complex cause–effect relationships.

Summarizing the arguments above, I propose that 'ethics', as a kind of 'theory of good and bad', easily leads to an inherently idealistic search for supposedly existing eternal rules, and that this search may be doomed to failure, because such rules may not exist. The idea of evolving an ultimate consistent network of ethical rules is doomed to failure, because the whole set of rules is genuinely inconsistent. The phenomenon of 'moral feelings' and 'moral behaviour', on the other hand, easily leads to a naturalistic conception of morality, leading to the search for assumedly stable 'moral characteristics'. This search has been more or less futile. The reason for this may be that morality as a whole is a cultural product, resulting from an inborn tendency to moral feelings, interacting with cultural facts like language and argumentative style.

MORALIZING

This interaction takes the form of moralizing, of day-to-day moral talk, aiming at moral criticism and moral praise. Moralizing is 'moral talk'; there is a constant moral discourse going on, where people use their more or less articulated moral feelings and ethical conceptions, in order to criticize the activities of some specific individual in a specific situation. This discussion may be seen as a process of applied ethics. When moralizing, people use the structure of the practical syllogism, assuming some intent, some knowledge regarding the consequences of action, and a conscious choice of action, trying to form a reasonable chain of hypothetical moral argumentation.

Moralizing, thus, is always a form of criticism – or praise – *in particular*, it is bound to a specific context. Ethics, again, is always a theory *in general*. We can see moralizing as a link between the clear and pure theory of morality in general, and practical moral action in particular. On the one hand, the ongoing process of moral talk clearly influences whatever we might call 'moral feelings', thus slowly changing people's morality. On the other hand, both the changes in moral feelings and the moralizing talk can be expected to influence moral theorizing, to change the structure of ethical argumentation. In this way moralization is not only a link; it functions as the pumping heart of the whole system.

Moralization, as the central part of the complex of ethics and morality, may be seen as a constantly ongoing socio-genetic process (Elias, 1978), forming and changing particular moral feelings and actions, as well as ethical theorizing, and thereby, in the long run, also the particular conceptions of good and bad in a given culture. Moralization, thus, can be seen as one of the central parts of the 'machine' driving cultural change processes – the results of which we, elements of the process, are doomed always to see as 'development'.

CONCLUDING REMARKS

Alastair MacIntyre (1987, p. 69), discussing the belief in the existence of 'natural human rights', notes that

> The best reason for asserting so bluntly that there are no such rights is indeed of precisely the same type as the best reason which we possess for asserting that there are no witches and the best reason which we possess

for asserting that there are no unicorns: every attempt to give good reasons for believing that there are such rights has failed.

In the same way, it seems, the effort to find a unique and truly rational system of moral reasoning has failed, and so has the effort to find natural moral traits in any socially relevant dimension. The failure of moral philosophy, of ethics as a theory of good and bad, despite the efforts of millenniums, might be explained by the inescapable gap between idealized general arguments and the problems of particular action in day-to-day life. The failure of naturalism, of the search for 'real' moral traits, on the other hand, might be explained if we accept that moral feelings and moral actions are not natural phenomena, but instead formed and re-formed by the ongoing process of moral talk, of moralizing.

Even if the quality of moral action may be the main reason for the interest in business ethics, deriving from the general tendency to moral criticism, it may be seen rather as a mirror image or resultant of the process of moralizing. Even if the challenge to find eternally valid moral rules is enchanting, normative ethics in general may be rather irrelevant, and even misleading, to somebody who wants to understand the phenomenon of moral reasoning and action.

Moreover, it may be fruitful to assume that moralizing, as well as ethics, can function as alternative parallel sets of moral argumentation, or ethical discourses, and that any moralizer is readily able to change instantly from one set of moral argument to another, without even noting it. These sudden changes may be caused, actualized, by the situation at hand, by practical considerations, for example, a sudden chance to make a big profit; or by another person, for example, somebody asking for an interview regarding business ethics.

The most promising field of the study of ethics, therefore, is probably to be found in *living morality* – in common moralizing discourse. What we ought to study, then, are the patterns of moralizing and the structuralistic characteristics of the process of moralizing – intellectual, emotional, logical, cultural. Morality is also never a stable and static personal or social characteristic; rather it has to be seen as a process, an ever-changing stream of moral feelings and ideas. The characteristics and development of this stream are interesting as an individual phenomenon, but also – maybe even more – as a process of reciprocal interaction, where the characteristics of *interactive moralizing* determine the patterns of moral change.

If morality and moralizing – and, of course, ethics – are seen as products of cultural socio-genetic processes, moreover, there is no strong reason to expect that these phenomena might be handled in the inherently naturalistic and idealistic way proposed by neoclassical theory. Instead of obeying the logic of the utilitarian approach, moral feelings and moral argumentation seem to be idiosyncratic, often discrete and without alternatives, sometimes non-reversible. There is little reason therefore to expect that it can encompass the mainly naturalistic energy metaphors of utilitarianism.

REFERENCES

Asplund, J. (1987) *Det Sociala Livets Elementära Former* ('The Elementary Forms of Social Life'), Göteborg: Bokförlaget Korpen.

Bergling, K. (1981) *Moral Development: The Validity of Kohlberg's Theory*, Stockholm: Almqvist & Wicksell.

Dawkins, R. (1983) *The Selfish Gene* (Swedish translation: 'Den Själviska Genen'), Stockholm: Tidens förlag.

Elias, N. (1978) *The History of Manners: The Civilizing Process*, New York: Pantheon Books, vol. I.

Etzioni, A. (1986) 'The case for a multiple-utility conception', *Economics and Philosophy*, 2, 159–183.

Etzioni, A. (1988) *The Moral Dimension: Toward a New Economics*, New York: Free Press.

Franklin, B. (1968) *Autobiography* (Swedish translation: 'Självbiografi'), Uddevalla: Forum.

Friedman, M. (1962) *Capitalism and Freedom*, Chicago: University of Chicago Press.

Gustafsson, C. (1988) *Om Företag, Moral Och Handling* ('Business, Morality and Action'), Lund: Studentlitteratur.

Kohlberg, L. (1981) *Essay on Moral Development*, San Francisco: Harper & Row.

MacIntyre, A. (1987) *After Virtue: A Study in Moral Theory*, 2nd edn, London: Duckworth.

Merkle, J. A. (1980) *Management and Ideology*, Berkeley, CA: University of California Press.

Westerlind, S. (1983) Frederick W. Taylor och Scientific Management. En vetenskapsteoretisk studie, Inst. för Vetenskapsteori, Göteborgs Universitet, Göteborg.

Wilson, E. O. (1975) *Sociobiology: The New Synthesis*, Cambridge, MA.: Harvard University Press.

Wilson, E. O. (1978) *On Human Nature*, Cambridge, MA and London: Harvard University Press.

Chapter 6

Social responsibility in the human firm
Towards a new theory of the firm's external relationships

John F. Tomer

In orthodox economics, two kinds of theory depict the firm's external relationships, its relationships with stockholders, customers, employees, suppliers, creditors and the community. First, there is the theory about how markets function, and second, is the theory about how markets fail to perform optimally. The latter, market failure theory, emphasizes positive and negative externalities. These economic literatures are almost entirely unrelated to another body of thinking concerning the external relationships of firms. That is the large and growing, non-economic literature on the ethical obligations and social responsibilities of businesses. Because the latter is very different from the economic literature, economists well-trained in orthodox economics, by virtue of that training, seem unable to appreciate the arguments concerning the social responsibilities of firms. Thus, the purpose of this article is to develop a theory of the firm's external relationships that integrates economic theory, especially theory concerning negative externalities, with non-economic insights concerning the social responsibilities of businesses. The challenge is to develop a theory that, while appreciative of the broader non-economic concerns, will allow economists to overcome the blinkers imposed by their training.

Section one of the paper outlines the orthodox economic viewpoint on the firm's motivation, the nature of externalities and the firm's social responsibilities. Section two summarizes the non-economic literature on the concept of social responsibility and the doctrine of corporate social responsibility. Section three develops a socio-economic theory of the firm's behaviour that integrates theory regarding externalities and the concept of social responsibility. Using water pollution as an example, this section indicates how the firm's behaviour is expected to vary widely depending on factors internal and external to the firm. Section four develops a number of issues related to the firm's socially responsible behaviour. Section five outlines the normative implications of the theory, and the final section provides a brief conclusion.

THE ORTHODOX VIEWPOINT

The firm's motivation

Although there are some well-known dissenting views, the modern orthodox microeconomic view is that the firm's motivation is to maximize short-run profit. For particular purposes such as investment decision making, orthodox microeconomists following finance theory may assume the firm's motivation to be maximizing the value of stockholders' wealth, which is generally taken to be the discounted sum of the stream of future profit. However, for most purposes, including externality theory, orthodox microeconomists continue to assume short-run profit maximization.

One reason for this is that the modern approach to economics prefers to characterize human behaviour 'as being based on simple and easily characterizable motives' (Sen, 1987, pp. 2–7). Thus, orthodox economics in discussing motivation ignores complex ethical considerations that earlier traditions of thinking (for example, Aristotle, Adam Smith, Karl Marx, John Stuart Mill) took more seriously. According to Sen (p. 7), 'it is hard not to notice [in economic publications today] . . . the neglect of the influence of ethical considerations in the characterization of actual human behaviour'. It is not that unethical behaviour is assumed; the self-interested behaviour assumed is simply devoid of ethical content. As Sen admits, for some purposes this approach has been productive, but in other instances this excessively narrow characterization of human motivation has not served well.

Externalities

Positive (and negative) externalities, also known as external economies (and diseconomies), are 'events which confer an appreciable benefit (inflict an appreciable damage) on some person(s) who were not fully consenting parties in reaching the decision which led directly or indirectly to the event in question' (Meade, 1973, p. 15). The emphasis in this article is on negative externalities such as when firm A harms B (the victim) as a result of its water pollution, which is a by-product of its production activity.

In this typically abstract, orthodox analysis of the negative externality, A and B have no previous relationship with each other, nor are they part of any larger collectivity or web of relationships through which they might incur social or ethical obligations. Despite the fact that harm occurs and the result is socially inoptimal, the action of firm A is not considered immoral or unethical; A experiences no obligation of any kind to stop the pollution. Firm A, an amoral entity, is simply doing what follows from profit maximization.

Normative views

The classical creed

Milton Friedman has been the most prominent defender of the classical creed regarding business's role in society. According to Friedman (1962, p. 133), the corporation has no responsibility beyond serving the interests of its stockholders. Its only responsibility is 'to use its resources and engage in activities designed to increase its profits so long as it stays within the rules of the game, which is to say, engages in open and free competition, without deception or fraud'. Moreover, Friedman (1970) argues that corporations that take on other responsibilities are pursuing public purposes, and their executives in effect become public employees, without having been selected through a political process (see also Baumol, 1974).

Another argument for the proposition that firms should simply maximize their profits is the following empirical one. This view, cited by Howard Bowen (1953, p. 115), states that

> businessmen . . . are so fully imbued with a spirit of profit-making and with pecuniary standards of value that they are unable to see the social implications of their tasks – much less to follow policies directed toward the social interest.

Perhaps this is why most economists believe that negative externalities such as pollution cannot be corrected by businesses or market forces alone and that it is futile to expect more ethical or responsible behaviour from businesses (see, for example, Blinder, 1987, pp. 139–140).

Adam Smith

Milton Friedman believes his position is consistent with Adam Smith (1776/ 1937, p. 423), who sees businesspeople to be

> led by an invisible hand to promote an end which was no part of his intention. Nor is it always the worse for the society that it was no part of it. By pursuing his own interest, he frequently promotes that of the society more effectually than when he really intends to promote it. I have never known much good done by those who affected to trade for the public good.

But Sen (1987, pp. 22–23), contrary to the conventional wisdom, points out that Adam Smith's normative view of human motivation is much broader than self-interest. Sen quotes Smith:

> 'Man . . . ought to regard himself . . . as a citizen of the world, . . . and to the interest of this great community, he ought at all times to be willing that his own little interest should be sacrificed' [pp. 22–23].

The managerial creed

In contrast to the classical creed of economic self-interest seeking is the managerial creed espoused by many corporate executives.

> In this view the actions of individual enterprises are and should be dominated by considerations of the public interest; profit-seeking takes a lesser place. If enterprises act directly in the public interest, there is much less need to rely on the competitive mechanism to demonstrate that individual actions which appear to be self-seeking are socially beneficial in the System as a whole.
>
> (Sutton *et al.*, 1956, p. 57)

The managerial creed recognizes the responsibility of the firm not only to stockholders but to employees, customers and the general public, and advocates that executives' decision making should balance the often competing claims of these groups (Silk and Vogel, 1976, pp. 134–136). While the managerial creed calls for corporations to accept broader responsibilities than advocated by the classical creed, it does not expect as much from businesses as those who are calling for businesses to be socially responsible.

THE SOCIALLY RESPONSIBLE FIRM

The doctrine of corporate social responsibility

Although individual writers differ on specific points, there is wide agreement around the central features of what is most commonly called the doctrine (or creed) of corporate social responsibility. This doctrine, as the word corporate suggests, was developed particularly with big businesses in mind. Corporate social responsibility (CSR) may be thought of as a form of control of businesses, an alternative to the control by markets or government. CSR is by nature voluntary, i.e. it is self-regulation or self-control in the social interest. This means that enterprises choose it without the compulsion of laws, contracts, governmental intervention or active community pressure (Bowen, 1978, pp. 116–117).

According to the CSR doctrine, corporations are social institutions, creatures of society that in effect have been chartered by society to perform certain purposes. These corporations must adopt policies and actions that are in conformity to the norms and goals of society. If not, the society that granted the charter can revoke it. In this view, businesses have a moral obligation to use their resources for the common good as well as obligations to particular groups such as stockholders, consumers, employees and creditors.

To behave in a socially responsible way, firms' decision-making processes must reflect broad societal concerns. For example, 'corporations need to analyze the social consequences of their decisions before they make them and take steps to minimize the social costs of these decisions when appropriate' (Jones, 1980, p. 65). CSR, thus, requires an extra degree of discipline on the part of businesses, the discipline of figuring out what it takes to align the firm's efforts with the common good in the long term.

CSR also implies accountability, the willingness of companies to be held accountable for their actions that have negative effects on others or are not aligned with the common good. Further, it implies a willingness to adjust or correct the behaviour that has been found to be wanting. In sum, corporations that behave in accord with the CSR doctrine are harmonizing their behaviour with the rest of society.

Changing the social contract

The doctrine of corporate social responsibility implies the existence of a 'social contract' between the corporation and society. This contract

> acknowledges the public's right to impose its preferences upon business, it also acknowledges the corporation's participation in shaping those preferences in accordance with management's judgment of its own . . . best interests.
>
> (Silk and Vogel, 1976, p. 158)

As society's preferences change, this means a redefining and, thus, a renegotiating of the social contract, which corporations have a right to participate in as long as they do so honestly and openly (p. 158).

The dramatic changes in social values beginning in the 1960s led to significant new public demands on businesses to be socially responsible, and accordingly to much effort to redefine the social contract. These continuing efforts and changing values are part of what defines the 'new age' we live in.

The *legitimacy* of the corporation rests on the public's perception of an identity between the goals of the corporation and the goals of society (Sethi, 1975, p. 60; Silk and Vogel, 1976, ch. 5). If corporations resist public pressures on them to alter their behaviour such as occurred in the US during the 1970s, this produces the kind of crisis in which the very legitimacy of the corporation is questioned. One result of this kind of crisis is corporate efforts to legitimize their activities. Corporations in the 1990s are still experiencing significant challenges, and thus continue to be very concerned about their legitimacy.

Sethi (1975, pp. 62–64) and others have argued that corporations in addition to becoming socially responsible should develop the capacity of social responsiveness. This means developing corporate capacity (1) to anticipate social issues and problems before they reach crisis proportions, and

(2) to adapt their policies and programmes in such a way as to minimize the disruptive conflicts that the firm might otherwise experience.

CSR as business philosophy

Although there is no uniformity of opinion among business leaders, an increasing number of them espouse a philosophy that is the same as the CSR doctrine. For example, Irving S. Shapiro (1984, p. ix), former chief executive officer of Du Pont, states

> Leaders in the private sector have quasi-public status and must accept the public responsibilities that go with this. Private gain remains a necessary condition of commerce, but it is no longer a sufficient one. The objective now should be not just to make individual companies perform better but also to make the whole system work better.

Economists and CSR

Corporate social responsibility and ethics are generally not appreciated by economists because these concepts do not have a place in the orthodox economic theory of the firm. Socially responsible motivation does not jibe with profit maximizing motivation, and the economic theory of externalities has a much more limited view of the firm's external relationships than the doctrine of CSR. Thus, it is not surprising that a leading economist, Alan Blinder (1987, ch. 5) for example, would argue that the environmentalists who believe pollution is a moral issue are simply wrong. Environmentalists, in contrast to most economists, are, according to Kelman (1981, p. 113), concerned with societal attitudes towards pollution and the motivations of businesses with respect to pollution. He explains that 'the thinking of economists allows little place for these concerns, and the case for [governmental] economic incentives ignores them'. This strongly suggests the need for an economic theory of the firm's external relationships that is integrated with corporate social responsibility considerations.

A SOCIO-ECONOMIC THEORY OF FIRM BEHAVIOUR: EXTERNALITIES AND SOCIAL RESPONSIBILITY

The purpose of this section is to develop a model of firm behaviour that integrates economic externality theory with the view that firms have social responsibilities that go far beyond making a profit. The focus of the model is a firm's decision making with respect to a negative externality, namely, water pollution. The firm in question has decided to produce a new product, and it has discovered that a by-product will be a harmful liquid requiring disposal. Will it dump the liquid in the adjacent river?

Essence of the model

The dependent variable of the model is the extent to which the firm behaves in a socially responsible way with respect to a particular sphere of activity, for example, water pollution. The firm's socially responsible behaviour (SRB) is defined along a horizontal spectrum in which ideal SRB is on the far right and sabotage is on the far left. In sabotage, the firm's intention is to harm persons outside the firm to gain at their expense. Ideal SRB is defined in a later section. The purpose of the model is to explain where on the SRB spectrum a firm will locate. The degree of a firm's SRB indicates much that is important about the firm's external relationships.

There are two classes of independent variables. The first relates to behavioural characteristics of the firm; the second relates to the external situation confronting the firm. The firm's SRB is its response to the external situation, a response reflecting its internal character. Decision making about the firm's SRB is assumed to be made by a coalition of people involved with the firm, most notably top management, but the nature of this coalition is not important for this analysis. What is important are three of the firm's internal characteristics: (1) ethical orientation, (2) patience, and (3) organizational capability. The first two are emphasized in the following analysis.

Internal characteristics

First, ethical orientation is defined along a spectrum that has three prominent points along it. On the far left is a point representing opportunism; the middle point represents non-opportunistic self-interest; and the far right point represents high ethical principle. Opportunism, following Oliver Williamson's usage, is present when in the effort to realize individual gains in transactions individuals are willing to be sly, crafty and dishonest. Non-opportunistic self-interest is present when individuals' ethical principles do not allow them to be dishonest or otherwise opportunistic, but there is no concern for others beyond what self-interest dictates. High ethical principle is present when individuals have a sense of high purpose involving the desire to find win–win solutions in their relations with others and experiencing others not simply as means but as ends.

Second, patience is also defined along a spectrum. On the far left is the short-term orientation, and on the far right is the long-term orientation involving a high degree of patience. Patience, thus, refers to the ability and willingness of an individual to make short-term sacrifices for the possibility of long-term gain. It corresponds roughly to the rate of discount, a variable often used by economists to denote the rate of return used in finding the present value of future returns. On the far left of the spectrum the rate of discount is very high and, thus, individuals greatly discount the possibility of future returns. The far right is opposite to this.

The third internal characteristic, organizational capability, refers to the firm's capability for (1) making rational decisions, (2) innovating and (3) learning. It is assumed in what follows that the firm's decision makers are at least average in these respects.

The three internal characteristics of the firm's decision makers are assumed to be subject to influence. For example, they can be influenced by organizational features such as the ethical climate, and they can to a degree be improved through the organization's training and development programmes.

External situation

The firm is assumed to have a social as well as an economic nature, and therefore it must respond not only to signals or demands emanating from the market but from other segments of society. It follows that the external situation variables must include factors reflecting both market incentives and broad societal influences. Also included here are variables reflecting special factors related to the specific sphere of activity involved (water pollution in this case).

First, market incentives derive from the product and resource markets in which the firm participates. In the sphere of water pollution, the cost, if any, to the firm of using up collectively owned water resources through its pollution is of special importance.

Second are the broad societal and community influences reflecting societal goals and values. These non-market societal influences may be experienced in specific spheres of activity such as when a community exerts pressure for a particular kind of socially acceptable behaviour.

Third are the special factors. For example, the following factors apply with respect to water pollution. It is assumed that (1) the amount of harm resulting from the pollution is known and non-negligible; (2) the damage results from this firm's pollution alone, not from combining with other pollution; (3) this type of pollution is not illegal, but it would not be considered acceptable by the people in the surrounding community (they also would not consider it the worst thing in the world); (4) immediate community activity to pressure the firm on account of the pollution is unlikely; and (5) there is no known equal or lower-cost alternative way to dispose of this polluting liquid.

Nature of the model

This model is designed to apply to situations in which there is no current government involvement. In this water pollution example, the government is

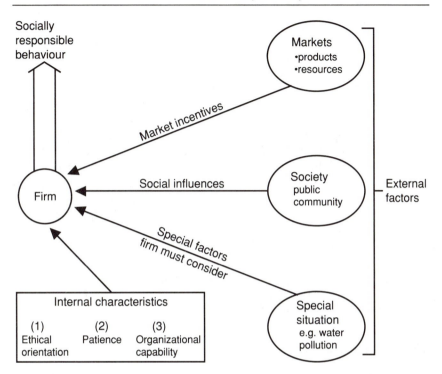

Figure 6.1 A socio-economic model of the firm's socially responsible
behaviour

not involved because the possible water pollutant is a previously unknown
substance. Thus, there are no laws, regulations or enforcement activities
relating to it. Otherwise, government-related variables would have to be
added to the model. The reason for excluding government-related variables
is that governmental activity is likely to be a consequence of the firm's earlier
socially responsible (or irresponsible) behaviour and, therefore, is not a fully
independent variable.

The essence of the model is depicted in Figure 6.1. In functional form, the
model is

$$SRB = f(EO, P, CAP, MK, SOC, SPEC)$$

where the first three independent variables are the firm's internal
characteristics, its ethical orientation (EO), patience (P) and organizational
capability (CAP). The second three independent variables represent the
firm's external situation, its market incentives (MK), societal influences
(SOC) and special factors (SPEC). The theory is a positive or descriptive one
in that it is designed to explain the degree of a firm's socially responsible
behaviour (SRB) in a specific sphere of activity. A particularly important and

novel feature of the theory is that the firm's behaviour is not simply a self-interested response to the external situation. As later analysis will reveal, the firm's ethical orientation and patience are particularly powerful determinants of its behaviour. These key variables have, with rare exceptions, been excluded from economic analysis. Although the theory is not a normative one, it has important normative implications (for example, for improving the firm's SRB) that will be developed later.

This theory represents at least a start in developing a theory of the firm's external relationships in the sense that it is a theory about how harmonious the relationship of the firm is with particular individuals and groups external to the firm. Among these external entities are victims, would-be victims, community organizations and leaders, and government. The key to the firm's relationship with those external to it is the degree to which its behaviour is socially responsible.

To understand the theory and the important role of the ethical orientation and patience variables, let us apply it to the water pollution case utilizing in sequence a number of different assumptions about the EO and P variables. Three scenarios are considered below. The first scenario is a special case that strongly resembles orthodox theory.

The classic negative externality scenario

In the first scenario, the firm's decision makers are assumed to be opportunistic and impatient (short-term orientation), values on the far left of the EO and P spectrums, respectively. Because there are no equal or lower-cost alternatives to the pollution, and because of their short-term orientation, implying unwillingness to look for advantageous long-term solutions, the firm will dispose of the liquid in the river. Because the decision makers know that the pollution is unacceptable to the community, and because of their opportunism, they will not be straightforward or honest with the community or the pollution victims. The firm will make every effort to deny the existence of the pollution, will not provide information about it, will not offer assistance or compensation to the victims, nor will it cooperate with concerned community leaders. In other words, it will attempt to avoid incurring costs by avoiding responsibility for the damage and attempt to maintain legitimacy through secrecy or deception.

This analysis of the classic negative externality scenario is at least superficially similar to the orthodox economic exposition, in which the firm is simply maximizing profit in a situation where there is a resource, the unpolluted river water, that is provided free to the firm rather than at a price reflecting its social opportunity cost. In both the orthodox analysis and this scenario, pollution is the expected result. But it should be emphasized that in the present analysis, the pollution outcome is not simply due to profit maximization, it is due as well to opportunism and impatience. The firm here is not behaving in a socially responsible manner, unless, of course, one holds the view that its social responsibility is only to its stockholders. A key to the irresponsible nature of the firm's action is that the firm is out of harmony with the society in which it is a part. In the orthodox economic analysis, this aspect is completely ignored. Consider another scenario.

Long-term oriented, non-opportunistic self-interest (the second scenario)

The decision

Assume that the firm's decision makers are (1) self-interested (but not opportunistic) and (2) patient. With a long-term orientation (low discount rate), these decision makers are now willing to consider sacrificing some profit in order to achieve the enhanced legitimacy that would follow from reduction of its pollution. The expectation is that the increased social acceptability of the firm's activity will, over the long term, lower certain costs associated with a lack of legitimacy. The latter are called *legitimacy costs*; the nature of these costs is considered below. Because these decision makers are, in addition to not being opportunistic, not burdened with high ethical principle, the decision to pollute is for them not a question of responsibility or ethical obligation, it is purely a matter of self-interest and efficiency. Similar to an investment decision, these decision makers will presumably choose to accept the higher current expense associated with lower pollution only if this cost is expected to be less than the present value of the future stream of lowered legitimacy costs. In this view, there is a simple trade-off between efficiency and legitimacy considerations. (For an alternative approach using the Prisoner's Dilemma analysis, see Appendix B.)

Legitimacy costs

A company's legitimacy costs are related to the public issues life cycle (see, for example, Buchholz, 1988, pp. 6–8). This cycle begins when a gap arises between a corporation's social performance and what the public expects of it. At this stage, businesses have many options concerning how to respond to the issue. If, however, the issue grows and businesses do not respond satisfactorily, the issue is likely to become a politicized media event, putting businesses on the defensive. In the next phase, legislation is passed, and regulations are promulgated. The final phase involves government action to implement the rules, enforce these, and, if necessary, litigation to force compliance. 'As an issue moves through this sequence, the options for business are narrowed to where they become almost non-existent' (Buchholz, 1982, p. 415).

The firm that takes a 'public-be-damned' attitude toward non-share-holders is a likely target for harsh and perhaps even punitive legislation. The firm that ignores the interests of society in a pell-mell pursuit of profit neglects the long-run consequences that could prove to be costly or even suicidal.

(Walters, 1977, p. 42)

Thus, a firm's legitimacy costs are the price it pays for not choosing socially acceptable behaviour; these costs are incurred in the long term not only in the form of financial penalties but as reduced autonomy with increased public control.

The public issues life cycle is suggestive of the nature of many of these legitimacy costs, but a few less obvious ones should be mentioned explicitly. One cost is the discomfort or harassment, as well as reduced prestige and prominence, that executives may experience as a result of pressure from activist community groups or others external to the firm (Manne and Wallich, 1972, p. 27). Along with this, corporations may experience reduced cooperation from a variety of external organizations, a deterioration of the business climate generally, and a more adversarial relationship with government (see Tomer, 1987, pp. 115–119). The firm may also experience lower cooperation from and motivation of its employees who find the social performance of their corporation uninspiring.

It should also be noted that firms pursuing socially irresponsible behaviour will experience increased uncertainty. This is true even if no one is presently objecting to this behaviour. Should societal values change, as they often do, bringing the issue to the fore, there is a high probability of starting down the public issue life cycle with its rising legitimacy costs. Thus, there is reason to believe that a firm will inevitably pay for its social irresponsibility, but the magnitude and timing of its cost will be highly uncertain.

The legitimacy costs considered above are the private costs, costs incurred by the firm as a consequence of their socially unacceptable behaviour; there are also the social costs incurred by others. An obvious example is the cost incurred by the victims of the offending behaviour. In addition, there may be costs of cleaning up the problem, judicial costs, enforcement costs and other costs associated with attempting to control the problem. Because these costs are not incurred and presumably not considered by the self-interested, long-term oriented firm, the firm's response to the negative externality situation, although better than the opportunistic, short-term oriented firm, is still likely to be sub-optimal from society's standpoint.

Strategic socially responsible behaviour

Firms that find it in their interest to be socially responsible (the second scenario) can be expected to develop a variety of strategies for attaining legitimacy. Firms' strategies will differ according to such factors as the degree of their ethical orientation and patience. Let us consider three strategies: (1) statesmanship, (2) accommodation and (3) public relations.

In the *statesmanship strategy*, the firm's leaders not only choose to incorporate social responsibility in their actions in a way that makes sense given their expected legitimacy costs but attempt to lead and educate the public and other businesses on the virtues of their chosen strategy. This strategy is likely to require a higher degree of organizational capability than the following two. In the *accommodation strategy*, the company's leaders are simply adapting in a self-interested way to signals from the society regarding what is acceptable and are not trying to play a leadership role. In the *public relations* strategy, the enterprise's leaders are in part accommodating and in part resisting society's demands, but they recognize that the firm requires legitimacy. To enhance the firm's legitimacy, the leaders take actions calculated to improve the public image of the firm while doing little to improve the social responsibility of the firm's behaviour.

SB	O		PR	A	ST	I

Figure 6.2 Spectrum of socially responsible behaviour

Recall the *spectrum of socially responsible behaviour* in which sabotage (SB) is located on the far left and ideal (I) socially responsible behaviour is on the far right (see Figure 6.2). The first scenario representing opportunistic behaviour (O) is on the left. The second scenario is represented by the three positions between O and I. Starting at the middle of the spectrum and moving right, one first encounters the public relations (PR), the accommodation (A) and finally the statesmanship (ST) strategy.

Principled behaviour (the third scenario)

The ideal

Ideal socially responsible behaviour is not based on a self-interested calculation, not even a long-term oriented one. Ideal strategies are based on a commitment to principle transcending narrow self-interest. The difference between a strategy based on principle and one rooted in self-interest and the problem with the latter are explained by John M. Clark (1957, p. 207):

> Self-interest is not really enlightened unless it is also enlarged until it identifies itself, to some extent at least, with the interests of others. And once this enlargement has taken place, it can never treat others as mere means. . . . And if 'enlightenment' goes this far, it has become ethical. It

has gone beyond the idea that 'what's good for me is good for the community' and has accepted at least some part of the idea that 'what's good for the community is good for me'; or that my economic relationships cannot be healthy unless they are part of a healthy community. If a businessman has gone this far, but still wants to insist that this regard for common interests is merely 'good business,' I have no quarrel with him. He has broadened his conception of 'good business' until it has become a moral one; that is sufficient. But if he has not gone this far, and if his enlightened self-interest is mere farsighted shrewdness, one can be sure that at some point or other the shrewdness will not be farsighted enough and trouble will result.

The ideal principled strategy is one that commits the firm to a harmonious relationship with its external social environment. Such a strategy may be a reflection of its leaders' higher self including their highest values, conscience and aesthetic sense of the business (see Lutz and Lux, 1988, ch. 6, on the higher self). Finally, such a strategy may reflect the leaders' vision for the firm and their sense of sacred duty.

The solution to negative externalities

This ideal socially responsible behaviour does not mean behaviour that has only positive impacts on others. It means self-regulated behaviour that has no socially unacceptable negative impacts. For example, the ideally behaving firm would not engage in any water pollution that the relevant affected parties find unacceptable. The firm would have to learn from society (community, government, media, etc.) what behaviour (pollution) is acceptable. The firm, of course, has a legitimate right to participate in the process of determining what is acceptable, and ideally it would seek standards (for example, pollution standards) that recognize both its own interests and the interests of those affected by its activities. That is, the ideally behaving firm would seek win–win solutions. In the process, the negative externality problem would be eliminated, because no appreciable damage would be inflicted on person(s) who were not fully consenting parties in reaching the decision regarding the firm's actions (recall Meade's externality definition).

Given competition in its product markets and significant costs of complying with societal standards, this ideal socially responsible firm could very well become uncompetitive if it were the only firm in its industry to behave in this way. Should this happen, it would be incumbent on the firm to take actions either (1) to gain voluntary adherence to these standards by its competitors or (2) to pressure government to impose regulations applying to all firms in the industry. Ideal socially responsible firm behaviour implies self-control, but it does not necessarily mean no governmental regulation. In situations where governmental regulation is necessary, this regulation may be expected to work much better in the presence of voluntary business cooperation than if businesses were to become adversaries to government and were to resist compliance with governmental standards.

The trade-off revisited

Do highly ethical decision makers trade-off legitimacy for efficiency in the same way as self-interested decision makers? Strictly speaking, the answer is no. If the firm's principled decision makers are acting out of a sense of high obligation to the common good, it does not make sense for them to be willing to trade a little less socially responsible behaviour for a little more profit. From an ethical standpoint, it is acceptable to pursue profits but only after fulfilling one's fundamental obligations to society. Of course, things may get a little murky if we inquire into the nature of these fundamental obligations. Are some obligations beyond trade-off, while others can be traded? Consider water pollution. Some types of pollution are totally unacceptable and other types are partially acceptable. The notion of a trade-off might apply to some extent to the latter but not the former. Nevertheless, it is generally true that ethical obligations and efficiency considerations are incommensurable and, thus, ethical decision makers have no basis for a quantitative trade-off of one for the other. Of course, business decision makers may have to grapple from time to time with tough ethical dilemmas involving choices between incommensurables.

The model: a recapitulation

The three scenarios above do not exhaust the model's possibilities but are suggestive of the model's ability to explain variations in businesses' socially responsible behaviour as well as indicating the range of its applicability. The essence is that for a given external situation, the firm's internal behavioural characteristics, especially its ethical orientation and patience, are the key to understanding its social responsibility. In the absence of these two variables, a firm behaving with a high level of corporate social responsibility simply does not make sense – at least not from the standpoint of economic theory. There are many facets of a firm's external relationships that involve some element of social responsibility. If we assume that the firm is solely motivated by self-interest, we cannot conceive of these relationships.

ISSUES RELATED TO THE FIRM'S SOCIALLY RESPONSIBLE BEHAVIOUR

A payoff to principle?

Although it would seem on the face of it that consciously principled behaviour is anything but profitable, there is, nevertheless, some evidence and a considerable amount of belief among businessmen that ethical behaviour pays off. According to an opinion survey of key business leaders, 'almost two-thirds (63 per cent) of executives are convinced that high ethical standards strengthen a firm's competitive position' (Cavanagh, 1990, p. 172). In a study of forty-two large corporations, Clarkson (1990, p. 10) found that

> Corporations . . . which balanced their proactive economic orientation with a proactive social orientation were profitable at average or above-average levels in their industries. . . . [Whereas] unbalanced concentration on the maximization of profits was counter-productive and resulted in lower ratios of profitability than their competitors. . . .

If what these findings imply is true, they represent a paradox. Perhaps companies that make efforts to acquire the discipline necessary to fulfil their ethical or social obligations have acquired an intangible asset that also serves them well in the traditional aspects of their business.

An investment in organizational capital

When business leaders commit their firm to socially responsible behaviour, for members of the organization, it means acquiring a kind of discipline which involves new ways of thinking and relating to others within and without the firm. Because acquiring this discipline uses up resources in the process of changing formal and informal social relationships, it may be considered an investment in organizational capital (Tomer, 1987, p. 24). Similarly, Hattwick (1986, p. 91) observes that 'the adoption of a code of business ethics can be viewed as an investment'. And Arrow (1973, p. 315) has pointed out that codes of ethics require discussion, incorporation in standard operating procedures and, in the process of transmitting them from one generation of executives to the next, education and indoctrination. In Bowen's (1978, p. 124) view, a reason why firms adopt socially responsible behaviour is to improve their intangible human relations which partake of the nature of assets. These intangible assets are believed to be the key to business success, and many 'policies and actions of the firm are directed toward bettering its position with respect to these intangibles' (p. 125).

Complicating factors

In the case of water pollution alone, not to mention other types of negative externalities, there are many complicating factors. A few of these should be mentioned. First, there are many instances when the pollution of a body of water occurs because of the combined effect of multiple sources of pollution. This tends to obscure the role that any one firm plays in the pollution. Firms lacking high principle will see the possible advantage to be gained if they can avoid being held accountable and, thereby, avoid incurring any legitimacy cost. This obviously discourages social responsibility.

The second complicating factor is that the pollution harm may not be known or knowable. Victimization could take a long time to become apparent; perhaps the victims will be members of the next (unborn) generation. Moreover, the water pollution harm may depend on the uncertain dilutive capacity of the river in which it is disposed. Such factors give unprincipled businesses further opportunity to avoid being socially responsible.

Socially responsible investing and buying

Interest in corporate social responsibility has spawned two kinds of relatively new activity: explicitly buying from and investing in companies perceived to be socially responsible. This buying and investing is believed to reinforce the socially responsible behaviour of these companies and to provide an incentive for other companies to become socially responsible. 'Conservatively estimated, $100 billion in U.S. investments were managed under social criteria by late 1985' (Lydenberg et al., 1986, p. 7). To guide consumers in their buying decisions, Lydenberg et al.'s *Rating America's Corporate Conscience* provides social responsibility ratings of many large American corporations. Among the criteria they use are: representation of women and minority in management positions, environmental record, charitable contributions, involvement in South Africa and weapons-related contracting (cf. Lewis and Webley, this volume).

Social responsibility and positive externalities

In the case of positive externalities, firms confer benefits on non-consenting others for which these firms do not receive compensation. For example, if companies train employees who are likely to leave the firm in a relatively short period of time, the next company that employs these workers will reap much of the benefit without paying for it. Thus, the firm's incentive to train these employees is insufficient considering the returns to society from investment in this training. If, due to this disincentive, companies do too little training of low-income workers, productivity will suffer, and this will exacerbate the social problems of poverty and inequality. Because of this negative outcome, it may be argued that the socially responsible company ought to do more of this training. This might make sense even for the self-interested firm because doing this would enhance the firm's reputation and, thus, its legitimacy. This is very similar to saying that a firm ought to do more pollution control (reduction of a negative externality) in order to reduce its legitimacy costs (become more legitimate). Whereas negative externalities relate to the negative impacts (pollution) of firm behaviour, positive externalities relate to the absence of positive impacts (training benefits) from the firm's behaviour. Thus, socially responsible firms may contribute more to the solution of social problems through positive accomplishments than might be expected considering the usual economic incentives.

A NORMATIVE VIEW: FOSTERING SOCIAL RESPONSIBILITY

If through socially responsible business behaviour significant progress towards solving social problems involving externalities is possible, then it is necessary to consider what needs to be done to foster this. Therefore, the following briefly summarizes the normative implications of the preceding analysis. It is beyond the scope of this paper to indicate precisely the nature of the governmental programmes that would help achieve these ends.

The character of the decision makers

The most obvious implication of the analysis is one that many economists are likely to be uncomfortable with; it is to improve the ethical orientation and patience of the firm's decision makers. Instead of the typical call for governmental incentives which appeal to self-interest and, if anything, strengthen self-interest motivation, the implication here is that we would be better off if decision makers were less self-interested and more motivated by obligations to others, or, as Paul Davidson puts it, more motivated by internal incentives. According to Davidson (1989, p. 44), in a monetary system, self-interest motivation is likely to be stronger and more durable than 'civic values'.

> The latter is, like a delicate, fragile flower, easily trampled and lost in any money-utilizing system of production organization – unless the society makes special efforts to nurture the belief in civic values. . . . A civilized society will try to sustain a productive harmony between external and internal incentives through the development of . . . human institutions.

To improve the humanity of the firm and its social responsibility requires ethical discipline on the part of organization members. First, this calls for an organizational environment that will foster ethical behaviour. A key to this environment is a humanized strategy that communicates the values, hopes and vision of the company's leaders. Ethical behaviour will thrive when members feel proud of the organization, are willing to be patient and persistent in applying the corporation's values and principles, and when members are encouraged to pause and reflect on where they are going and how they are going to get there (Blanchard and Peale, 1988, pp. 125–126). A second key to ethical discipline is the character and quality of the organization's members, especially the top management (Andrews, 1989, pp. 100–103). Character relates to a person's values and capacity for moral judgment. It is important that the corporation make an explicit effort to select people of high character. Other qualities such as the competence to recognize ethical issues and think through their consequences and the confidence to seek out different points of view are qualities that the organization can develop (p. 100). Developing ethical discipline in the organization may be viewed as an investment in organizational capital.

Fostering positive social influences

The case of very highly toxic pollution is instructive when considering how to improve the external social influences on the firm. If society's goals for elimination of less toxic types of pollution were just as high and clear as those for the highly toxic types, firms would more readily set high pollution elimination goals aligned with society's. Similarly, if the legitimacy costs associated with less toxic pollution were just as high as in the highly toxic case, this high socio-political cost would provide more disincentive to this pollution. In general, socially responsible behaviour is encouraged by high, clear goals and high legitimacy costs associated with the firm's negative external effects.

On 4 May 1989, Edward Woolard, chairman of the board of Du Pont, announced at the American Chamber of Commerce in London that Du Pont's goal is to reduce their air and water pollution to zero by the year 2000. The setting of high goals such as this requires several societal responses. Du Pont needs support, encouragement and praise for their high social aspirations. This development, along with specifics on Du Pont's plans and strategies, needs to be communicated to other firms in order to encourage them to set similarly high goals. In a variety of ways, institutional support needs to be given for corporate actions leading to the elimination of their negative external impacts.

Changes in social structure and process that would permit greater cooperation and coordination among economic institutions are also needed. It should be emphasized that this and other resource-using efforts to foster the social influences that encourage corporate social responsibility may be considered investments in organizational capital.

Governmental incentives

The issue of what to do about negative externalities like water pollution has often been posed as a choice between a tax on pollution (governmental incentives) or direct governmental controls involving pollution standards to be met by all firms. When posed in this way, the overwhelming majority of economists opt for incentives, either in the form of effluent fees or marketable pollution permits (see Blinder, 1987, ch. 5). This makes sense given the orthodox theory of the firm that assumes self-interested, short-term profit maximizing behaviour and an absence of ethical principle. If decision makers are rational in this way, the only possible way to reduce pollution is to raise the cost of pollution to the firm. Incentives are better, i.e. more efficient, than controls at doing this because firms with low pollution reduction costs will take on more of the pollution reduction task than those with high costs.

Assume now that the firms' decision makers are highly ethical or potentially so. What these decision makers need to know are society's standards, i.e. what is acceptable and what is not. Leaders of these firms also need encouragement and support for their socially responsible behaviour and discouragement for their unprincipled behaviour. If these are provided, many firms may be expected to voluntarily comply with the pollution standards. But if instead the main government anti-pollution initiative is to place a tax on pollution, the government is implicitly communicating that pollution is acceptable behaviour, albeit a more costly behaviour than before. While such incentives may help by increasing the efficiency of pollution reduction, they may actually discourage corporate social responsibility. Because pollution taxes are based on the assumption of short-term, opportunistic firm behaviour, they effectively sanction or legitimize this behaviour. This hurts because the war on pollution cannot be won without the willing cooperation of corporations. This is not to say that governmental incentives, especially pollution penalties, should not be used. If, however, incentives are to be used, they must be made compatible with socially responsible business behaviour.

It should be noted that pollution taxes involve substantial government monitoring and enforcement costs and cannot deal with previously unknown sources of pollution. With these taxes, the government is always trying to catch up and extend its incentives to new areas, some of which are not amenable to incentives. In contrast, the socially responsible firm would voluntarily decide either (1) to eliminate new sources of pollution before they ever came into existence or (2) to cooperate from day one with government on efforts to find pollution solutions.

CONCLUSION

Economic theory has for too long been dominated by an overly narrow conception of self-interest and has not appreciated that individuals and organizations are of society and, accordingly, must align their interests with the common interest. Because of this, economics' theory of the firm's external relationships has not been satisfactory. This article has attempted to remedy this deficiency by integrating the concept of social responsibility with economic theory. In the revised model of firm behaviour, an important ingredient is the ethical orientation of the firm's decision makers. This enables better understanding of the business–society relationship and enables considerable perspective on what needs to be done to deal with pressing social problems such as environmental pollution. A key to this is investing in intangible relationships and patterns of activity most likely to bring about socially responsible firm behaviour.

APPENDIX A
SOCIAL RESPONSIBILITY AND US COMPETITIVENESS

The lack of social responsibility of US corporations and the lack of governmental policies to encourage socially responsible behaviour appear to be damaging US international competitiveness. According to Robert Reich (1990, pp. 57–58), American companies do not feel a 'special obligation to serve national goals'; for them, short-term profitability comes ahead of national interests. 'Nor does our system alert American managers to the existence of such goals, impose on American managers unique requirements to meet them, offer special incentives to achieve them, or create measures to keep American managers accountable for accomplishing them' (p. 58). Therefore, too many US multinational companies in the interest of their own competitiveness have moved the base of their operations to foreign countries and have done too little to invest in the skills of the American workforce, actions damaging to US competitiveness.

APPENDIX B
THE PRISONER'S DILEMMA ANALYSIS

An alternative way to view the second scenario (long-term oriented, non-opportunistic self-interest) is using the Prisoner's Dilemma analysis. The firm in this analysis has two choices: (1) cooperate with the community (do not pollute) or (2) non-cooperation (pollute). Similarly, the community has two choices with respect to its behaviour towards the firm: (1) cooperate through actions towards the firm that are non-controlling and non-penalizing or (2) non-cooperation involving behaviour that is controlling and penalizing. If the firm's decision makers are opportunistic and short-term oriented, the predicted short-term outcome is that the firm pollutes and the community cooperates. The firm is acting as a free rider and taking advantage of the community. With the passage of time, however, the community will surely shift to non-cooperation, the ultimate result being the Prisoner's Dilemma solution, a jointly disadvantageous situation.

If the firm's decision makers are long-term oriented and self-interested (though not opportunistic), the decision makers may anticipate that the community's initially cooperative stance may degenerate if they choose to pollute. As a result, the firm may find it in its interest to cooperate by not polluting. At least, this is likely to be true in circumstances where the firm's payoff with community non-cooperation is very low compared to the mutual cooperation scenario. Thus, the Prisoner's Dilemma analysis comes to essentially the same conclusions as our earlier analysis which focused on legitimacy costs.

REFERENCES

Andrews, K. R. (1989) 'Ethics in practice', *Harvard Business Review*, September–October, 99–104.

Arrow, K. J. (1973) 'Social responsibility and economic efficiency', *Public Policy*, Fall, 303–317.

Baumol, W. J. (1974) 'Business responsibility and economic behavior', in Melvin Anshen (ed.), *Managing the Socially Responsible Corporation*, New York: Macmillan, pp. 59–73.

Blanchard, K. H. and Peale, N. V. (1988) *The Power of Ethical Management*, New York: Ballantine.

Blinder, A. S. (1987) *Hard Heads, Soft Hearts: Tough-minded Economics for a Just Society*, Reading, MA: Addison-Wesley.

Bowen, H. R. (1953) *Social Responsibilities of the Businessman*, New York: Harper & Bros.

Bowen, H. R. (1978) 'Social responsibility of the businessman – twenty years later', in Edwin M. Epstein and Dow Votaw (eds), *Rationality, Legitimacy and Responsibility: The Search for New Directions in Business and Society*, Santa Monica: Goodyear, pp. 116–130.

Bradshaw, T. and Vogel, D. (eds) (1981) *Corporations and their Critics: Issues and Answers to the Problems of Corporate Social Responsibility*, New York: McGraw-Hill.

Buchholz, R. A. (1982) *Business Environment and Public Policy: Implications for Management*, Englewood Cliffs, NJ: Prentice-Hall.

Buchholz, R. A. (1988) *Public Policy Issues for Management*, Englewood Cliffs, NJ: Prentice-Hall.

Byron, W. J. (1982) 'In defense of social responsibility', *Journal of Economics and Business*, 34, 189–192.

Cavanagh, G. F. (1990) *American Business Values*, 3rd edn, Englewood Cliffs, NJ: Prentice-Hall.

Clark, J. M. (1957) *Economic Institutions and Human Welfare*, New York: Knopf.

Clarkson, M. B. E. (1990) 'The moral dimension of corporate social responsibility', Paper presented at the Second Socio-economic Conference, George Washington University, Washington, DC, March.

Davidson, P. (1989) 'Achieving a civilized society', *Challenge*, 32, September/October, 40–46.

Friedman, M. (1962) *Capitalism and Freedom*, Chicago: University of Chicago Press.

Friedman, M. (1970) 'The social responsibility of business is to increase its profits', *New York Times Magazine*, 13 September.

Hattwick, R. E. (1986) 'The behavioral economics of business ethics', *Journal of Behavioral Economics*, 15, Spring/Summer, 87–101.

Jones, T. M. (1980) 'Corporate social responsibility revisited, redefined', *California Management Review*, 22, Spring, 59–67.

Kelman, S. (1981) 'Economists and the environmental muddle', *Public Interest*, Summer, 106–123.

Lutz, M. A. and Lux, K. (1988) *Humanistic Economics: The New Challenge*, New York: Bootstrap Press.

Lydenberg, S. D., Tepper, M. A., O'Brien, S. S. and the Council on Economic

Priorities (1986) *Rating America's Corporate Conscience*, Reading, MA: Addison-Wesley.

Manne, H. G. and Wallich, H. C. (1972) *The Modern Corporation and Social Responsibility*, Washington, DC: American Enterprise Institute.

Meade, J. E. (1973) *The Theory of Externalities: The Control of Environmental Pollution and Similar Social Costs*, Geneva: Sijthoff.

Reich, R. B. (1990) 'Who is us', *Harvard Business Review*, 68, January–February, 53–64.

Sen, A. (1987) *On Ethics and Economics*, New York: Blackwell.

Sethi, S. P. (1975) 'Dimensions of corporate social performance: an analytical framework', *California Management Review*, 17, Spring, 58–64.

Shapiro, I. S. (1984) *America's Third Revolution: Public Interest and the Private Role*, New York: Harper & Row.

Silk, L. and Vogel, D. (1976) *Ethics and Profits: The Crisis of Confidence in American Business*, New York: Simon & Schuster.

Smith, A. (1776/1937) *An Inquiry into the Nature and Causes of the Wealth of Nations*, New York: The Modern Library.

Sutton, F. X., Harris, S. E., Kaysen, C. and Tobin, J. (1956) *The American Business Creed*, New York: Schocken.

Tomer, J. F. (1980) 'Community control and the theory of the firm', *Review of Social Economy*, 38, October, 191–214.

Tomer, J. F. (1987) *Organizational Capital: The Path to Higher Productivity and Well-being*, New York: Praeger.

Walters, K. D. (1977) 'Corporate social responsibility and political ideology', *California Management Review*, 19, Spring, 40–51.

Part II

Case, questionnaire and experimental studies

Chapter 7

Fairness in consumer pricing

*Patrick J. Kaufmann, Gwen Ortmeyer and
N. Craig Smith*

Abstract   Two case studies illustrate problems of fairness in consumer pricing. The May D&F case involves charges of deceptive advertising as a result of the retailer's 'high-low pricing'; customers were allegedly deceived by artificially inflated 'regular' prices and discounts promoted from these prices. The GDC case involves charges that 10,000 consumers were deceived into purchasing homes at prices higher than 'fair market value'. Consumer policy and managerial issues are identified and analysis and recommendations provided. These cases are about fairness and trust within market exchange, and the responsibilities of sellers and consumers to provide and use information. Economic assumptions of non-fairness and *caveat emptor* are shown to be inadequate. The position that a fair price is the market price is questioned and an alternative suggested. Remedies which might be adopted by companies and pursued by policy-makers are proposed. By creating more realistic consumer expectations, they would reduce problems of fairness in pricing.

What is a fair price? This paper examines fairness in consumer pricing, using two intriguing legal cases brought before courts in the United States in 1989–90. The May Company case involved charges of deceptive advertising practices as a result of the company's 'high-low pricing' policy. Under this policy, the store was said to have deceived customers by artificially inflating its so-called 'original' or 'regular' (reference) prices and then promoting discounts from these prices as bargains. This practice has become so rife in the US retail environment that many consumers will only buy 'on sale', and then are sceptical about whether they have really bought at a fair price. In contrast, the General Development Corporation (GDC) case involved charges that the developer deceived nearly 10,000 home buyers into purchasing homes at inflated prices. The company was said to have used deceptive marketing practices to sell its Florida homes, primarily to out-of-state buyers unfamiliar with market conditions. The prices, allegedly based on improper appraisals, were around 20 per cent higher than 'fair market value'; a differential which was a substantial sum for the customer. While the May Company allegedly was reducing its prices deceptively and GDC allegedly inflating its prices deceptively, the issues common to both are deception and fairness in pricing.

Our analysis highlights implications beyond the retailing and real estate industries in the United States. Fundamentally, these cases are about fairness and trust within market exchange, the responsibilities of the seller in providing information to the consumer, and the responsibilities of the consumer to obtain and use that information. We may be said to employ a socio-economic perspective in identifying managerial, public policy and consumer interest issues and in providing some initial frameworks and recommendations.

THE MAY D&F CASE: WHEN IS A SALE REALLY A SALE?

In June 1989, May D&F, a unit of the May Department Stores Company operating twelve department stores in the state of Colorado, was charged with engaging in deceptive advertising practices in its Home Store department by the state Attorney General's office.[1] The Home Store department at May D&F includes housewares, cookware, mattresses, linens, textiles, small appliances and electronics. The state alleged that since 1986, May had used fictitious or exaggerated reference prices as a basis for comparison against its sale prices. These reference prices included designations such as 'original' and 'regular' price. The Colorado Attorney General gave several examples of suspect pricing, including: bedding sheets that had remained on sale for eight months; a cutlery set advertised and displayed 'on sale' for two years; a new style of luggage offered at its special 'introductory price' indefinitely (Nielson, 1989).

The court found that May D&F's promotional pricing was dictated by the company's 'Comparative Price Advertising' policy, developed in 1986 and in effect through August 1989.[2] This 1986 policy required that merchandise in the Home Store be offered at the so-called 'original price' for ten days at the beginning of each six-month selling season. Thereafter, the merchandise was discounted and advertising signs in stores, and item price tickets, indicated that it had been reduced from its original price. In addition, over the course of the six-month selling season, the merchandise could be discounted further for various sales of limited duration, including 'Fifteen-hour Sales' and 'Three Days Only' sales events. After any such sale, prices were returned to the first discount level and not to the original price. At the end of the six-month selling season, the original prices were restored for a further ten-day period.[3]

In August 1989, May D&F introduced a new comparative price advertising policy. Reference prices were lowered and were presented as 'regular prices' on signs in stores and advertisements, rather than as 'original prices'. In addition, these 'regular prices' were to be in effect twenty-eight out of each ninety selling days, with the ten days at the beginning of the selling season counting towards the twenty-eight days. This twenty-eight out of ninety days standard was derived from the standards given in Connecticut and Wisconsin state legislation governing deceptive price advertising. Customers who bought merchandise at the regular price were also able to return merchandise for a full refund under the store's new 'Satisfaction Guaranteed' programme, even though prices had been subsequently reduced. Finally, May D&F hired a manager of consumer affairs in April 1989 to monitor and ensure the credibility of May D&F's advertisements.

The Colorado Attorney General claimed that May D&F's comparative pricing policies, including both the 1986 and 1989 policies, constituted deceptive advertising. At trial, the state argued that the original prices were 'false, fictitious prices set not for the purpose of selling the items but for setting subsequent discounts' (Sadler, 1990), and elicited evidence that over 97 per cent of a sample of 5,340 household items were sold at sale prices (Fulcher, 1990). The state also charged that 'Consumers don't know what the original price of the item was nor the actual savings, if any, of the marked-down sales item' (Sadler, 1990).

Attorneys for May D&F denied that the retailer had engaged in any deceptive advertising or trade practices and offered, among a number of defences, that May D&F's advertisements were not misleading and caused no injury. They also argued that May D&F would be placed at a competitive disadvantage if forced to comply with a standard regarding either the proportion of time the merchandise must be at the reference price or the proportion of sales that must be made at the reference price. In particular, they would be at a competitive disadvantage relative to retailers who continued to promote without such restrictions.[4]

In June 1990, the Colorado Court, using the Federal Trade Commission (FTC) Guidelines[5] for purposes of interpretation, ruled that May D&F's 1986 and 1989 pricing policies violated the Colorado Consumer Protection Act (CRS Section 6-1-101 to 115) prohibiting false or misleading statements of fact concerning the price of goods, saying:

> May D&F's 'original' price for practically all of its merchandise in the Home Store was a fictitious high price established as a reference price for the purpose of subsequently advertising bargain reductions from that price. The clear expectation of May D&F was to sell all or practically all merchandise at its 'sale' price. May D&F's 'regular' price, pursuant to the 1989 policy, was certainly a step in the right direction, but May D&F's failure to disclose to the public its subjective and unique method of setting its 'regular' price for reference purposes, and its unique schedule or calendar for establishing when those 'regular' prices are in effect, have been shown at trial to affect consumers' choices and conduct concerning merchandise to their detriment.[6]

The judge permanently enjoined May D&F from its practice of advertising a 'regular' price as a reference price to be compared to the discounted price, unless May D&F fully and completely disclosed to consumers its method of determining the 'regular price' in the sale advertisement. The judge also permanently enjoined May D&F from using reference price terms with meanings unique to May D&F or reference price terms whose commonly understood meaning by consumers differed from that used by May D&F, unless May D&F defined the terms in the sale advertisement. Finally, May D&F was permanently enjoined from advertising sales of limited duration, like 'four-day-only sale', in such a manner as to communicate to consumers a false sense of urgency to purchase. May D&F was ordered to pay an $8,000 fine to the state, $2,000 for each of four consumers who had testified at the trial that they had been victims of May D&F's deceptive advertising, and to pay the costs incurred in prosecuting the case.[7]

The Colorado Attorney General subsequently filed a Notice of Appeal to the Colorado State Court of Appeals. He questioned the judge's decision to permit May D&F to continue pricing according to its 1989 policy under the condition that the company include in its advertisements a disclosure describing its method of determining prices. May D&F's October 1990 sale catalogue, for example, contained the following disclosure (on page 26):

Pricing Policy
Advertised merchandise in the Home Store may be available at these or similar sale prices in upcoming sales this season. Reference prices are based upon competitors' prices for similar merchandise, manufacturers' suggested retails, and other factors, including subjective ones. Regular prices are established by offering merchandise initially for ten consecutive days at the regular price, and afterward by offering the merchandise at the regular price for at least 28 out of every 90 days. The 10-day offering period is included in the 28 days. Original price is used with merchandise whose prices we have permanently reduced.

This disclosure was referenced at the bottom of many of the thirty-six pages of the catalogue, including every page that advertised Home Store merchandise. The Colorado Attorney General argued that since the judge ruled that May D&F's pricing policies were deceptive, he should have enjoined their use unconditionally. In addition, he questioned the judge's restriction of civil penalties only to those consumers who testified at the trial that they had been deceived, arguing that many more consumers had been harmed by May D&F's deceptive pricing policies.

Consumer research

Consumer research presented in expert testimony was critical to the arguments made by both sides in the case. It is indicative of opposing views of how consumers, in the current US retail environment, use sale and other price information in their purchase decisions. Dr Leo Shapiro, of Leo J. Shapiro and Associates, conducted a survey of 500 Denver metropolitan area households for May D&F (Shapiro, 1990). He concluded: 'Taken collectively, the results of this survey indicate that May D&F advertising is not misleading for households in the Denver metropolitan area. In fact, few households believe that May D&F advertised prices are better than those which they can find at other area retailers, even when advertising claims (e.g. 50 per cent off) are for substantial reductions.' He also concluded that 'By and large, consumers know what they are doing when it comes to using advertising effectively to help them source goods and services. They are aware of different retailers' approaches to advertising and promotion and are able to factor this knowledge into their own decision-making'. His conclusions were derived from responses to a series of questions, including (Shapiro, 1990):

- And, on balance, do you feel that May D&F's advertised prices are generally higher or lower than the other stores in your area who sell the same things?

May D&F's advertised prices are higher	72 per cent responding
May D&F's advertised prices are lower	6 per cent responding
May D&F's advertised prices are the same	20 per cent responding

- Specifically, when you see an advertisement from May D&F, that says 50 per cent off, do you believe that the item advertised from May D&F is going to be priced lower than any of the other stores in your area that sell the same thing?

  | No | 70 per cent responding |
  | Yes | 25 per cent responding |

- By the way, sometimes a store like May D&F will have a particular item or items that you can almost always find on sale in their store and in their ads. Do you believe that such an item from May D&F is going to be priced lower than any of the other stores in your area that sell the same things?

  | No | 70 per cent responding |
  | Yes | 21 per cent responding |

Shapiro's conclusions disputed the notion that consumers inferred exceptional value from May D&F's sale advertising, suggesting instead that consumers were aware of the regularity of its sale events and thus were sceptical when they saw a 'sale' price. Even though consumers viewed May D&F's sale prices with some scepticism, Shapiro argued that they none the less used them to determine when May D&F's prices were competitive with other retailers. This view suggests complete understanding by the consumer that the sale prices of the retailer practising high-low pricing are the true 'regular' prices and with that, the adoption of a decision criterion of buying primarily when the item is 'on sale'.

Professor Joel Urbany of the University of South Carolina, the expert witness for the state of Colorado, offered a different view, suggesting that including a reference price on sale advertisements significantly increased both the consumer's perception of the savings indicated by the sale price and the consumer's intention to purchase the item offered at the sale price (Urbany, 1990). His conclusions were based on an experiment in which half of the respondents received a sale advertisement that included both a sale price and a

Table 7.1 Results of pricing experiment (Urbany, 1990)

Per cent who agreed	Vacuum cleaner		Frying pan	
	Sale price only in ad	Sale and regular price in ad	Sale price only in ad	Sale and regular price in ad
'I'll save a lot if I buy from the advertising store'	11%	35%	29%	44%
'The product is a bargain at the advertised sale price'	14%	27%	29%	44%
'The retailer reduced the price a lot for this sale'	11%	35%	13%	41%
Choice: per cent who would consider buying today rather than comparison shopping	3%	13%	43%	46%
Chance: perceived chance of buying from the advertised retailer	22%	36%	43%	46%

reference 'regular' price, and the other half received a sale advertisement that included the sale price only. The respondents were a random sample of Colorado consumers. Two genuine May D&F advertisements were tested, advertising a vacuum cleaner and a frying pan, with the information identifying May D&F removed. When the regular price was included, the sale price represented a 30 per cent saving for the vacuum cleaner and a 35 per cent saving for the frying pan. Respondents were asked to assume that they were shopping for one of the two products. The results are shown in Table 7.1.

Respondents were asked other questions including their estimate of the number of days out of the last ninety that the retailer had offered the product for sale at the regular or original price. Fifty-two per cent of the respondents answered fifty days or more, and 30 per cent answered thirty or fewer. Respondents were also asked to estimate the percentage of sales typically made at regular prices: 58 per cent responded that at least 25 per cent of the sales were made at the regular price. Urbany's analysis found no major differences between those respondents recognizing the May D&F advertisement and those that did not. He concluded from these results that the presence of a reference price in a sale advertisement significantly increased respondent's perception of the savings represented by the sale price and the intention to purchase the advertised product. Urbany's results were used as support for the Colorado Attorney General's argument that May

D&F's high-low pricing deceived consumers by making them believe that the sale price was an exceptional and unusual value relative to the retailer's assumed day-to-day prices, when in fact it often was not. While there may be some methodological concerns about both studies, they do illustrate how retailer promotional pricing practices at least create confusion amongst consumers, if not deception, and raise issues of fairness.

Are consumers sceptical or are they being deceived?

It may be inferred from the Shapiro study that consumers are sceptical of retailer pricing policies, allowing for substantial puffery within advertising claims of price reductions. While this may be a defence of industry practices, it has troublesome implications for retailers. For example, mistrust of retailer advertising is likely to reduce store loyalty, presumably to the benefit of retailers not using high-low pricing.

An alternative perspective is that consumers are being deceived, believing that a sale still represents temporary exceptional value. Historically, sales conformed to this view, as those consumers willing to wait and take the risk of unavailability could obtain exceptional value when retailers attempted to clear stocks at the end of selling seasons. However, there have been significant changes in the US retail environment over the last twenty years, which have led to increased promotional activities such that sales have become weekly events in many stores. In particular, price competition has increased, with the abolition of retail price maintenance, the arrival of category specialists (such as audio equipment stores) and overcapacity. The increased mobility of consumers has also permitted greater comparison shopping. It is estimated that 60 per cent of sales in department stores took place at 'sale' prices in 1988 (McIlhenney, 1989). Urbany's study would suggest that his respondents, at least, are not aware of this.

Consumers can save by being vigilant and by comparison shopping, as an example cited in the *San Francisco Chronicle* indicates:

> A random survey of 'sale' and 'original' prices in Bay Area furniture stores found a difference of $1,680 between the highest and lowest 'original price' for a single Henredon sofa: Model No. 8670, with identical 'E-grade' upholstery, was advertised at Noriega Furniture, a small furniture retailer, at an 'original price' of $2,320, on sale for $2,170. A major department store offers the same sofa for $2,500 – '35 per cent off' the 'original price' of $4,000. A major furniture chain advertised the same model, originally priced at $3,009 'on sale at 20 per cent off' for $2,749. Another small furniture retailer in Marin County offers the same sofa at $2,476, twenty per cent off its original price of $3,095.[8]

However, comparison shopping not only requires some effort on the part of the consumer (discussed later), but has also become more difficult because of the frequency of sale events and the problems in making comparisons across stores. The sofa example is in some respects exceptional, more often it is difficult to directly compare furniture products in different stores, with retailers stocking 'exclusive' styles and fabrics. Likewise, in electronics, model numbers are often unique to the retailer. Not surprisingly, problems with promotional pricing practices more frequently arise with product categories where comparability is difficult: fine jewellery, furniture, electronics, ready-to-wear clothing.

In keeping with the conventional view of the sale as representing temporary exceptional value, the FTC has tended to view high-low pricing as deceptive. However, the agency has chosen to leave enforcement to the states, where most actions have been settled out of court with retailers agreeing to substantiate any reference prices used in advertising. Yet, as we argue below, providing more information on how prices were determined, as in the May Company case, may not be the optimal solution for consumers or, indeed, for retailers.

GENERAL DEVELOPMENT CORPORATION: OVERPRICING IS WRONG?

In March 1990, following a two-year federal grand jury investigation, General Development Corporation was charged with conspiring to defraud about 10,000 buyers of its 'overpriced' homes. Senior officers of the company also faced criminal charges (Brannigan, 1990). Eight months later, Judge Lenore Nesbitt, in a US District Court in Miami, accepted the company's third proposed plea bargain agreement, under which the company pleaded guilty to one count of conspiracy to violate federal mail fraud law in its house sales. The remaining fifteen counts against GDC were to be dismissed, though charges involving company officials were still standing. The company had filed for protection under Chapter 11 of the US Bankruptcy Code in April 1990. Under the terms of the plea bargain, GDC would provide restitution of as much as $160 million in claims by people who bought GDC homes based on inflated company appraisals of their value, between 1983 and 1989. The US Bankruptcy Court would determine the proportion of each claim to be paid. GDC was required to post a one million dollar cash sum for the administration of the restitution programme ('General Development gets court approval') (*Wall Street Journal*, 1990a).

The indictment called into question GDC's entire marketing operation. As a result, the company closed its worldwide homesite sales activities in April 1990, dismissing 1,100 employees, one-quarter of its workforce ('General Development is halting homesite sales') (*Wall Street Journal*, 1990b). Deprived of its principal means of revenue generation, the prospect of GDC surviving bankruptcy proceedings seemed unlikely.

Founded in 1955, GDC was one of the oldest and largest developers of planned communities in Florida. As well as 'homesites' (a plot of ground on which a house would be built) and housing, GDC was also involved in vacation timeshares, commercial property (in its communities), utility services, mortgage financing, resort and community operations and real estate services. In 1988, GDC had 5,300 employees, assets of just under $1 billion, revenues of $511 million and a net income of $22.5 million (GDC, 1988a). When last traded on the New York Stock Exchange, 5 November 1990, GDC stock was traded at around 0.5, though it had been as high as 12.25 in the preceding fifty-two weeks. As of 1988, the company had developed nine Florida communities, a process involving purchase of the land, planning of the overall community, obtaining necessary permits and approvals, building roads and canals, installing water and sewer lines, construction of recreational and shopping facilities, and building housing. The costs of the land improvements had been historically underestimated by GDC due to costs of compliance with more stringent environmental regulations as well as increases in engineering, maintenance and labour costs (GDC, 1988b).

GDC's communities were, for the most part, well established, with a total population of about 200,000 and containing some 95,000 homes, 40 per cent of which were built by GDC. Other Florida real estate developers, mostly now defunct, had been less successful. A key to success in community development is to attract people; if people do not move to a community it will not grow. Accordingly, central to GDC's activities was a housing programme (GDC, 1988b).

The target market of the housing programme was people who have the dream of Florida but were unlikely to explore 'the dream' at their own initiative. They were of moderate income, mainly out-of-state residents, living in the colder north-eastern regions of the United States, in cities such as Boston and New York; known as 'snowbirds', these people were attracted by the Florida climate (US v. Brown *et al.*, 1991).[9] Census data show that between 1980 and 1990, nine of the twelve fastest-growing US metropolitan areas were in Florida; the state's population increased 15.1 per cent between 1984 and 1989 (Shribman, 1991).

The division of GDC responsible for the housing programme had an extensive marketing organization in 1988: 2,500 employee representatives and 500 independent brokers, operating in sixty-five offices in northern markets in the US and in Canada, Europe and the Far East (GDC, 1988b). The product, as described in GDC brochures, was 'affordable Florida'. The route to this dream was via a homesite purchase through an instalment contract. In the early days this was '$10 down and $10 a month for ten years'. At the end of the contract period, GDC would have completed land improvements (providing roads, sewers, etc.) and with the final payment, the buyer would have possession of the land and could then build on it (GDC, 1988b).

Buying process

For many of its customers, GDC succeeded in making Florida a possible dream. Given GDC's objective of developing communities, and as 90 per cent of GDC homes sales were to homesite customers (GDC, 1988b), it is appropriate to view the homesite and home purchases as part of the same process in examining the alleged overpricing of GDC homes. The longer-term purpose of the homesite sale and a lengthy selling cycle are not inappropriate to a major life decision of the customer. However, while GDC had deeded 285,300 homesites by 1988, it had only sold 38,000 homes (GDC, 1988b); a low conversion rate, perhaps. The buying process may be conceived as comprising up to six stages, from the customer's initial contacts with GDC through to moving to Florida and living in the GDC home.

Initial contact with a GDC representative most likely arose through a referral by a friend or colleague, resulting in a visit to the customer's home. The next stage was the homesite purchase, with the lot selected from a community map provided by the GDC representative, and, in most cases, sold unseen in the customer's home. The average homesite price was $18,500 in 1988 (GDC, 1988b). Documentation provided prior to purchase explained the buyer's rights – to a full refund if GDC did not meet its obligations – and that homesite contracts did not impose personal liability for the development on the buyer, but would be subject to cancellation without refund if payments became overdue. As of 1988, the cumulative cancellation rate for homesite sales was 59 per cent (GDC, 1988b). A 'Bill of Rights' stressed the purpose of the homesite was 'for future use and not as a business investment . . . future value cannot be predicted . . . [GDC cannot] guarantee the profitability of any resale'. The contract required the buyer to acknowledge that no reliance had been placed on oral representations by GDC sales representatives in making the purchase decision. It also, in bold upper-case type, drew attention to the right of rescission up to seven days after signing the contract.

Under most homesite contracts, the buyer could exercise an option to visit the community within twelve months on a subsidized trip known as the 'Magic of Florida'. However, it was more likely that a visit would be made under the company's 'Southward-Ho!' programme, the third stage in the buying process. Generally three or more years after signing the homesite contract, the customer would be approached by a local GDC representative, and encouraged to visit a community on a 'So-Ho', to make a house purchase. Alternatively, the customer may have responded to an advertisement in the GDC *Vistas* magazine. The So-Ho provided a three-day visit to the community for two, for a nominal payment ($299 in 1989) plus a 'good-faith' deposit ($1,201), refunded if no purchase was made. GDC provided air travel, transportation to and from each airport, hotel accommodation, meal coupons and a tour of the community.

Some 55–60 per cent of So-Ho visitors would commit to purchase, the next stage in the buying process. However, with some not qualifying for financing and others exercising the seven-day right of rescission, around 45–50 per cent closed on the housing contract after mortgage approval and the house had been built, typically 120 days after the So-Ho. The average price of a GDC home (including land) was $72,000 (1985–90). The home did not have to be built on the customer's homesite; a lot equity transfer privilege provided the homesite owner with the option of exchanging the lot for any available lot in any GDC community, with the payment adjusted to reflect the current GDC prices of the lots. GDC provided a 'one-stop-shop' concept, allowing customers to determine in a single So-Ho trip: the site of the home, the style of building and its interior decor (from a range of standard designs), any extra amenities (double car garage, refrigerator), rental options (through GDC's rental division) and financing (through GDC's financing subsidiary, GDV). Around 90 per cent of GDC homesite owners buying GDC homes exercised the lot equity transfer privilege; over 80 per cent used GDV. The housing contract contained disclaimers regarding the value of the property and resale, refinancing and rental possibilities. These disclaimers were strengthened over the period 1985 to 1988. From 1987, for example, contracts stated, in bold print:

> Housing prices are based upon the cost of doing business, including but not limited to the fact that the Seller offers to prospective purchaser the ability to explore a house purchase while outside the State of Florida, and other benefits; therefore, they do not reflect the level of market prices of similar property sold by others on different terms.

Many purchasers would arrange for their homes to be rented, the next stage of the buying process. During the So-Ho, customers would be told historical rental figures and vacancy rates. The final stage in the buying process would be the move to Florida, some years later.

Customer complaints and the grand jury investigation

From 1985 onwards, there were increasing customer complaints and adverse publicity about GDC, particularly as the housing market turned soft and house prices no longer increased so dramatically, and as some buyers sought refinancing to benefit from lower interest rates. In the *Port St Lucie News*, 5 July 1987, for example:

> Linda and Dale Polish bought a GDC home in 1983 for $92,000, using a negatively amortized mortgage – one with increasingly higher payments – to afford the 17 per cent $69,000 mortgage. But as monthly payments increased, they found themselves unable to afford the payments and unable to resell the house, which they say is worth only $57,000 on the

open market. After making about $38,000 in payments, they have deeded the home back to GDC and are renting it from the company until October.

(Kleiner, 1987)

Following some 2,000 complaints and a series of local, unsuccessful, civil suits, GDC was subject to a grand jury investigation of suspected fraud and racketeering activities. The prosecutor and the court apparently concluded that GDC's marketing practices, described above, constituted a conspiracy to systematically defraud consumers. Of particular concern were:

- company appraisals based on other 'overpriced' GDC homes – not properties in the community at large – thus exceeding fair-market value (this appraisal method reportedly prevented GDC from selling its mortgages to the quasi-governmental agencies Fannie Mae and Freddie Mac);
- buyers susceptible to exploitation – out-of-state and unfamiliar with market conditions; many were also recent immigrants;
- community trips which were carefully controlled to prevent prospective buyers seeing comparable homes selling for lower prices;
- misrepresentation by sales representatives;
- the creation of a false impression as to increases in the value of GDC properties, through advertisements and the lot equity trade-in programme;
- the non-disclosure of local market prices;
- the settlement of actual or threatened litigation to avoid negative publicity.

The company and its senior officers were charged with seven counts of mail fraud, seven counts of interstate transportation of persons to commit fraud and two counts of conspiracy. United States attorney Dexter Lehtinen said the fraud 'permeated the entire corporation and was part of its institutional policy' (Brannigan, 1990). The essence of the prosecution's case was that GDC homes were overpriced and the company concealed this from buyers. GDC's reply was essentially that: its prices reflected costs; most of the practices of concern were created for legitimate business reasons, long before consumer complaints and not for reasons of concealment; and that the price disparity emerged as a result of the softening of the real estate market and increased competition from local builders. GDC's Securities and Exchange Commission filing states:

> The Company competes with many small homebuilders in each of its communities who typically offer housing units of generally similar quality and style to those offered by the Company, but at prices which are often substantially lower than those charged by the Company. The Company attempts to overcome such price disadvantages through the 'one-stop-shopping' afforded by the Company's various activities, which permits a prospective homebuyer to start the purchase of a Florida home in his own

state, take an inspection trip to Florida at nominal cost, select a community housing unit from a variety of types, styles and prices, and arrange mortgage financing and property management.

(GDC, 1988b)

Price disparities did exist; GDC conceded that its houses were priced on average 20 per cent higher than comparable products available from competitors. However, there did not seem to be evidence of profiteering by GDC and a cost comparison with local builders would find GDC's prices based upon some costs unique to GDC. Local builders were able to 'free-ride' on GDC's marketing activities. GDC's overpricing might not have occurred if these unique costs had been incorporated into the homesite price, though this would have made it more difficult to attract people to the communities. Likewise, an exclusivity arrangement with GDC as the only builder would also have avoided overpricing charges, but would again have slowed community development.

Overpricing is generally not illegal, though it may be unfair. If GDC customers were deceived, then there may be more certainty about an absence of fairness in the company's pricing policies. The company appraisals of property values were conducted on behalf of the lender, not on behalf of the customer, who would often not be aware of these appraisals, at least prior to purchase. This is not unusual; however, customers may assume that mortgage approval confirms a value close to the price paid. Historical increases in GDC properties, such as homesites, may add to this misperception, though factually accurate. Indeed, taken in its entirety, it is more understandable why the government claimed GDC's marketing created false impressions amongst consumers. It is possible that they were not aware of the 'bundle' they were buying, that the price reflected various marketing costs, including the benefits of one-stop-shopping and the security of the GDC brand name. It does seem unreasonable to suggest that consumers might expect a price differential of 20 per cent for this product category.

INITIAL ANALYSIS

We believe these cases exhibit some interesting common phenomena, despite the different industries involved. The commonalities give rise to some tentative conclusions for researchers and practitioners which we present at the end of the paper.

Both cases raise fairness issues; fairness in pricing requires just, honest and impartial treatment of both parties to an exchange in the determination of the price governing that exchange. More typically, the concern in consumer markets is with whether the consumer pays a fair price, one that is just and both honestly and impartially determined and conveyed. Fairness is more readily understood in its absence; accordingly, it is easier to give examples of unfairness in pricing to illustrate this definition. The term 'price gouging' vividly conveys the sense of unfairness experienced by consumers subject to price increases during temporary shortages of products such as petrol or food. The term 'price discrimination' also, to some degree, connotes the unfairness experienced where businesses have different prices for different customers, as tourists in foreign lands often find to their dismay. Finally, the practice of advertising low car rental prices in the United States, accompanied by hidden costs to the consumer within inordinately expensive or unnecessary collision damage waiver insurance, has rightly been described as a 'rip-off' by industry observers. However, there may be circumstances where a price paid is unfair to the seller rather than the buyer, as many retailers have argued in the current recessionary period; or as sellers in the housing market comment with respect to buyers who are 'bottom-fishing', pushing desperate sellers down to a price which leaves them substantially out-of-pocket; or where waiters receive no tips for their services, in countries where tipping is customary.

Conventional economics assumes both parties freely enter into an exchange and, acting out of self-interest, maximize their individual utilities.[10] Thus, within the classical, self-regulating model of the market, every exchange and each party involved, through an 'invisible hand', is part of and contributes to a far-reaching effect of 'an end which was no part of his intention' (Smith, 1971, p. 400). This model, however, relies on self-interest rather than fairness to realize common good.

Kahneman et al. (1986a) were not the first to observe the assumption of non-fairness among economists: 'It is often viewed as an embarrassment to the basic theory that people vote, do not always free ride, and commonly allocate resources equitably to others and to themselves when they are free to do otherwise' (p. 286). In empirical studies of fairness in economic transactions, Kahneman et al. show that even profit-maximizing firms have an incentive to act in a manner that is perceived as fair if the individuals with whom they deal are willing to resist unfair transactions and punish unfair firms at some cost to themselves. Accordingly, the economic model may be enriched by considering the preferences people have for being treated fairly and for treating others fairly.

It is beyond the scope of this paper to review the many simple but illuminating studies of Kahneman and his colleagues. However, some of their key conclusions with respect to the May and GDC cases should be noted. Aside from the more general conclusion that values play a key role in economic transactions, supporting Etzioni's argument of a 'moral dimension' (Etzioni, 1988), Kahneman et al. question the assumption of non-fairness which, in turn, has a bearing on the legitimacy of *caveat emptor* as a basis for accepting the practices described in the May and GDC cases. More specifically, they offer counter-intuitive conclusions on fairness in customer markets; for example:

- 'Survey responses suggest that charging the market-clearing price for the most popular goods would be judged unfair'; referring to within-season price variation in resort and ski hotels, they observe, 'If you gouge them at Christmas, they won't be back in March' (Kahneman *et al.*, 1986b, p. 738).
- 'Cost plus is not the rule of fair pricing'; in an experiment where respondents considered a scenario involving a supplier facing decreased costs, 'Half the respondents stated that fairness does not require the firm to pass on any part of its savings' (Kahneman *et al.*, 1986a, pp. 292–3).

Cost plus was a defence offered for GDC's pricing. Interestingly, in the May Company case, there was apparently no attempt to demonstrate that the retailer's high-low pricing did not result in profiteering. While perhaps difficult to obtain or unwise to reveal, Home Store financial performance data might indicate whether, in the aggregate, the company's pricing was fair, by not leading to inordinate gross profit margins over a period of, say, one year.[11] Yet, as Kahneman *et al.* indicate, cost plus may be an inadequate criterion for determining fairness in pricing. Individual consumers may have bought at May's regular price and paid too much. GDC's customers may have been paying for the company's inefficiencies or may not have wished to pay for the bundle of services provided under the one-stop-shop concept.

Price gouging, perceived as unfair, may lead to retaliation by the customer, as Kahneman *et al.* indicate. However, in the GDC case, the opportunity for retaliation is limited because the likelihood of repeat purchase is low for this product category. This factor has perhaps encouraged disgruntled customers, and lawmakers on their behalf, to retaliate in another fashion, through legal action. The consumer research conducted by Shapiro for May Company suggests this form of retaliation would be unnecessary as consumers were aware of the retailer's pricing policies: they could vote with their feet.

Perhaps the most basic point of comparison in analysing the cases can be found by questioning the assumption of non-fairness. If fairness is not to be expected within economic transactions (despite evidence that it may be found) then the consumer has every incentive to conform to *caveat emptor*: buyer beware. Companies may be expected to maximize their interests within the law; and neither the practices in the May Company case nor the GDC case were apparently clear-cut illegal. Accordingly, if *caveat emptor* were to be assumed it might be readily argued that there was no wrongdoing by May or GDC. Consumers could have made price comparisons before shopping at the May Company and had an incentive to do so given the store's somewhat unsavoury reputation, as evidenced in the Shapiro study. Likewise, GDC customers could have telephoned estate agents within GDC communities; studied advertisements in Florida newspapers of new, previously-owned or rental properties; or organized their own appraisals of GDC homes, before or within seven days of purchase. There are a number of possible explanations of why price comparisons do not take place and, accordingly, why *caveat emptor* is an inadequate model:

1 Consumer behaviour: Many studies of consumer decision-making processes have highlighted 'consumer satisficing' and a requirement for 'simplification' or convenience (Simon, 1957; Shugan, 1980). Less charitably, a lack of search activities by consumers may constitute laziness on the part of the consumer.
2 Information provision: Inadequate, incomplete or misleading information (regardless of disclaimers) make price comparisons difficult. This perhaps encourages simplification procedures such as over-reliance on the discount implied by the retailer's reference/sale price comparison.
3 Trust: Consumers may trust vendors, particularly when *caveat venditor* (seller beware) is tending to replace *caveat emptor*. However, trust is again a value not readily incorporated within conventional economics.

It seems reasonable to conclude that with greater search activities and less trust of the vendor by the consumer, and more information provision by the vendor, issues of fairness in pricing would not have arisen in the GDC and May cases. At least this may be argued in the abstract. There would need to be assumptions made about: the motivation of the customer to conduct adequate search activities; the quality of the information provided; whether this information is read and understood by the consumer; and the capability of the consumer to process this information. Yet, ultimately, the consumer would be the judge of his or her best interests and could be expected to act accordingly.

We would hope that, if the consumer were to make a mistake, this would remain his or her responsibility. Despite the shift away from *caveat emptor* evidenced in the courts' decisions on the GDC and May Company cases, we see a serious threat to the market mechanism if *caveat venditor* comes to predominate to the extent that a vendor, such as GDC, would be responsible for knowing the best interests of its customers or be penalized for events beyond its control, such as a softening of the real estate market. As Herbert Spencer (1891) so eloquently put it, 'the ultimate result of shielding men from the effects of folly is to fill the world with fools.'

Accordingly, we would not wish to see efforts to make overpricing illegal. Aside from problems of definition, it would be economically dysfunctional. Consumers are the best judges of their preferences and of utility. Consider the purchase of a one-carat diamond ring. A survey by *Fortune* magazine (Teitelbaum, 1991) reported the following prices for D VS 2 diamonds in 18-carat gold settings, during the week of 18 March 1991:

Tiffany, New York City	$20,000
Cartier, New York City	$18,700
Schmitter Burg, Milwaukee	$18,000

J. C. Penney, Dallas	$15,000
Zales, Dallas	$14,850
47th St District, New York City	$12,500

Is Tiffany guilty of overpricing when its price is 60 per cent higher than the price of a discounter in the same city? This difference is not explained by the cut of the gem or the amount of gold or style of the setting. As the article noted, 'A superior cut and setting usually account for only a fraction of the added cost. The rest is advertising, service, and Fifth Avenue overhead'. In other words, there is added value provided beyond the product itself. The 'augmented product' from Tiffany, to use marketing terminology, includes the less tangible benefits of the retailer's reputation, prestige and service.

The difference between the Tiffany example and GDC and May Company cases lies in consumer expectations and societal norms. GDC might argue that its brand name should allow it to command a premium price. However, the extent of this premium, though less in percentage terms than that commanded by Tiffany, was inappropriate for this product category and target market. It was also not signalled by a Fifth Avenue address and opulent facilities. With May Company, the consumer expectation was of exceptional value; the court apparently rejected the alternative argument presented by the defence that consumers expected misleading price information from May.

CONCLUSIONS

Under the conventional economic model and as many marketing academics would argue, a fair price is the market price, the price which consumers choose to pay. Yet this view would appear to be inadequate or incomplete, as the May and GDC cases indicate and as the courts' judgments strikingly confirm. We believe these cases present a worthy challenge to socio-economists: What constitutes fairness in pricing, if this is an appropriate requirement of economic transactions?

While these issues clearly need further development, our tentative conclusions are presented below in the form of remedies which might be adopted by companies and pursued by policymakers:

1. *Provide full information on how prices are determined.* GDC was more forthright about the basis for its prices in its later home sale contracts, though still less so than in its SEC submission (quoted above). Yet with increased disclosure, the company ran the risk of driving customers away or of customers free-riding, taking advantage of GDC-funded trips to the community and then buying from the less expensive local builders. Greater provision of information on retailer sale pricing practices might update consumer perceptions of the frequency and extent of price promotions and encourage comparisons of net prices. Consumers might, therefore, no longer

be deceived by high-low pricing. However, it is hard to believe that a consumer would pay close attention to and completely understand disclaimers of the form currently used by May D&F in its sale catalogue. This is confirmed by various consumer behaviour studies. It is also likely that some consumers would be less easily updated, particularly older or less educated consumers. With both cases, and more generally, this remedy does not address consumer laziness.

2. *Provide full information on market prices.* It was at least implied in the case against GDC that the company was to some extent responsible for providing information on competitor prices. Some retailers do provide this information. However, we see some serious disadvantages to this remedy. Operationally, it is likely to be difficult to obtain this information and to ensure its reliability, which in turn raises legal liability issues. Moreover, only price-competitive vendors have an incentive to provide this information. Finally, even assuming product comparability, it would be economically dysfunctional to force vendors to provide information on competitor prices as this would reduce consumer search activities and the incentive to augment products, as dicussed above.

3. *Adopt fair pricing.* While possibly incorporating to some extent remedies one and two, this remedy would focus more on consumer expectations. A fair price, as earlier defined, would be just and both honestly and impartially determined and conveyed. If GDC's prices were to be determined on the basis of costs, its customers could have been more fully informed of this and of what those costs comprised. In practice, given the extent of the price differential between GDC and local builders, this would have required either an exclusivity arrangement, where GDC was the only builder in its communities; more allocation of costs to the homesite purchase; or a significant reduction in the marketing expense, which at existing levels was apparently difficult to justify to customers. For retailers, fair pricing is likely to mean stable pricing. Given the problems in consumer motivation and ability to compare prices, and the retailer's need for customer trust and loyalty, an everyday low pricing policy has most to recommend it in the longer term. As some stores in the US (such as Sears) are finding, this switch is difficult and may take time. However, Dillards, for one, has found that it pays off, reducing the cost and inconvenience of organizing frequent sales events and in promoting customer loyalty. Recent reports from industry analysts Goldman Sachs have highlighted the store's decreased reliance on sales events as a significant factor in its impressive performance of late.

NOTES

1 The State of Colorado v. the May Department Stores Company, dba May D&F (District Court, Denver, Colorado: no. 89 CV 9274). A more detailed exposition of the May D&F case can be found in Gwen Ortmeyer, 'Retail promotional

pricing: when is a sale really a sale? (A) and (B)', Harvard Business School cases no. 9–591–111 and no. 9–591–112. Available from: The Publishing Division, Harvard Business School, Boston, MA 02163.

2 District Court Order dated 27 June 1990.

3 May D&F pricing was the responsibility of its buyers, who were also responsible for the advertising within their departments. Buyers set two prices when ordering merchandise, an 'initial mark-up price' and a 'promotional mark-up price'. The initial mark-up price reflected May D&F's usual or planned margin and was calculated using a formula that considered the costs of goods, the costs of doing business, and the company's profit goals. Merchandise was discounted to this price after being at the 'original price' for ten days. The promotional mark-up price was significantly greater than the initial mark-up price and was used as the 'original price', in effect for ten days at the beginning of the season. Buyers set this price by taking into account competitors' prices, manufacturers' suggested retail prices, the quality, popularity and brand name of the merchandise, and other subjective factors.

4 May D&F's Trial Brief, dated 7 May 1990.

5 Code of Federal Regulation of Commercial Practices, 1990, Volume 16, Part 233 – Guides Against Deceptive Pricing, Washington, DC: Federal Trade Commission.

6 District Court Order, 27 June 1990.

7 District Court Order, 27 June 1990.

8 'Why buyers should beware of "sale" prices', *San Francisco Chronicle*, 18 July 1990.

9 The primary source for the following material is US v. Brown *et al.* (1991). Other sources are noted where appropriate.

10 Under conditions of monopoly competition or in the house-selling or price-gouging examples above, it might be argued that freedom of action is less evident.

11 May Company's attorneys did note, in identifying extenuating circumstances, that the company's Home Store departments had realized poor gross and net margins during the period in question, in keeping with industry counterparts, but did not provide details.

REFERENCES

Brannigan, M. (1990) 'General Development to plead guilty in home-sales fraud, plans restitutions', *Wall Street Journal*, 19 March.

Etzioni, A. (1988) *The Moral Dimension: Toward a New Economics*, New York: Free Press.

Fulcher, M. P. (1990) 'May D&F sales compared', *Denver Post*, 18 May.

GDC (1988a) *1988 Annual Report*, Miami: General Development Corporation.

GDC (1988b) *From 10K. Annual report pursuant to section 13 or 15(d) of the Securities Exchange Act of 1934; for the fiscal year ended December 31, 1988*, Securities and Exchange Commission File Number 1–8967.

'General Development gets court approval for a plea bargain' (1990a) *Wall Street Journal*, 30 November.

'General Development is halting homesite sales' (1990b) *Wall Street Journal*, 4 April.

Kahneman, D Knetsch, J. L. and Thaler, R. H. (1986a) 'Fairness and the assumptions of economics', *Journal of Business*, 59, 285–300.

Kahneman, D., Knetsch, J. L. and Thaler, R. H. (1986b) 'Fairness as a constraint on profit seeking: entitlements in the market', *American Economic Review*, 76, 728–741.

Kleiner, K. (1987) 'GDC at center of growing storm', *Port St Lucie News*, 5 July.

McIlhenney, D. R. (1989) 'Introducing the NRMA retail market monitor, *Retail Control*, November.

Nielson, K. (1989) 'May D&F sued over advertising', *Rocky Mountain News*, 22 June, p. 63.

Sadler, L. W. (1990) 'Judge urged to fine May D&F', *Rocky Mountain News*, 25 May, p. 61.

Shapiro, L. (1990) *Expert witness report in the matter of the state of Colorado v. the May Department Stores Company*, No. 89 CV 9274.

Shribman, D. (1991) 'Mobility of US society turns small cities into giants', *Wall Street Journal*, 8 February.

Shugan, S. M. (1980) 'The cost of thinking', *Journal of Consumer Research*, 7, 99–111.

Simon, H. A. (1957) *Models of Man*, New York: Wiley.

Smith, A. (1971) *The Wealth of Nations*, London: Everyman. First published 1776.

Spencer, H. (1891) *Essays*, vol. III, London: Macmillan.

Teitelbaum, R. S. (1991) 'Hard times for diamonds', *Fortune*, 22 April, pp. 167–178.

Urbany, J. L. (1990) *Expert witness report in the matter of the state of Colorado v. The May Department Store Company*, No. 89 CV 9274.

US v. Brown *et al.* (1991) Defendants' memorandum in support of their motion to dismiss. In the case of United States of America v. David F. Brown, Robert F. Ehrling, Tore T. DeBella, and Richard A. Reizen; United States District Court, Southern District of Florida; Case No. 90–176–Cr.-Nesbitt; Memorandum filed 19 February 1991.

Chapter 8

Social and ethical investing
Beliefs, preferences and the willingness to sacrifice financial return

Alan Lewis and Paul Webley

THE ETHICAL INVESTMENT QUESTION

Unlike the majority of the papers in the current volume this one reports on some specific empirical findings generated to assess the influence of ethical considerations on economic behaviour and in particular the relationship between values, beliefs and investment decisions. Are people with liberal attitudes less likely to invest in companies operating in countries controlled by authoritarian regimes? Are environmentally conscious investors less likely to favour companies with poor pollution records, or, proactively, more likely to favour 'green' investments, e.g. companies that recycle paper and glass and seek alternatives to fossil fuels? In short: do people put their money where their morals are?

There has been a growth in so-called 'ethical' unit trusts in the UK and 'socially responsible' mutual funds in the USA in the last few years (Bruyn, 1987; Dominic and Kinder, 1984; Lowry, 1991; Lewis and Cullis, 1990; EIRIS). 'Socially responsible' funds, variously defined, probably account for as much as 20 per cent of personal and institutional investment in the USA. The findings reported here are from the UK where ethical investments have a smaller influence on the economy but where there are opportunities to monitor their development and to make Anglo-American comparisons.

The rationale for this research programme is that the attitudes, beliefs and perceptions of economic actors have economic consequences (Furnham and Lewis, 1986; Lea *et al.*, 1987) and in particular that economics has a moral dimension (Etzioni, 1988). The topic of 'ethical investment' seems an ideal test-bed for some of these new ideas; investment is a serious economic business and moral values look as if they must play a part in ethical investment. However, from the limited number of studies carried out to date (e.g. Lewis and Cullis, 1990; Luther and Matatko, 1991; Prestridge, 1989) it is not clear whether ethical investment is in fact ethical, whether there is a distinctly ethical component to the performance of ethical trusts and, most significantly from our point of view, whether investors are prepared to incur some costs in order to invest ethically.

Most of the contributors to the current volume share the view that ethics must play a part in economic affairs and so it goes that a growth in 'ethical' investments must be a function of a growth in ethical consumer demand. How might this have come about? This poses challenging questions for social historians, sociologists and the like. Have a large number of us seen the light, recognized that we have to do something to save the planet and not just leave it to governments? Or perhaps the 1960s really were a special time and this liberal-minded cohort have found themselves not only with the ideals but now also with the money. Craig Smith (1990) has traced the role of political pressure groups in influencing the withdrawal of investments in South Africa by Barclays Bank. Zealots can lead public opinion: would automobile emissions have been regulated as soon as they were in the USA without Ralph Nader? Similarly, the investments decisions of institutions, trade unions and pension funds can all be influenced by those energetic enough to represent individual investors in shareholders meetings and even when not initially successful have the tenacity to repeatedly push for votes on ethical issues.

These explanations are far from exclusive but they all have in common the idea that ethical investing is driven by ethical investor demand. A more cynical (or economic) explanation can almost do without ethics altogether. A rational investor wants to maximize profit and minimize risk. If there is little else to choose between investments on these two criteria another 'characteristic' might increase the visibility of a particular product; an ethical tag may simply be seen as an invention of marketeers eager to differentiate their product from the rest. Is the packaging of ethicals just a marketing trick? Certainly several of the leading ethical trusts in the UK are sensitive to such a charge and counter it by engaging respected scientists and broadcasters to vet the authenticity of investments, a vetting which is itself harped upon and used in marketing campaigns. Those outsiders concerned about authenticity become suspicious when looking at the performance of both social investments in the USA and ethical investments in the UK; it appears they perform as well as any other. But how can this be if portfolios are restricted on non-economic criteria? One is tempted to conclude that investment managers employ a kind of moral pragmatism which gives investors the chance to have their cake and eat it, to be good at little or no cost, although in defence of investment managers there is a case for arguing that ethical investments may be profitable ones, as companies who are careful to control toxic waste may also be those whose economic stability is enhanced by long-term planning and good industrial relations (a similar point is made in the current volume by Bowie).

THE EMPIRICAL WORK

All of these issues make the field of social and ethical investing intellectually fruitful and germane, but what is needed is the accumulation of some basic data on investors' (and potential investors') awareness, attitudes and preferences. This is pursued here in two ways: a small social survey of 100 comparatively wealthy UK residents; and through computer simulations of investment decisions. In the survey, respondents were asked what they thought ethical investments were, what they should be, how they believed they performed and whether they would invest in them given varying rates of return. The simulations gave participants the opportunity to invest in a number of different funds, an ethical green fund was hidden among them; participants' 'green' attitudes and values were also assessed with the hope of linking attitudes to investment preferences. In making such a link one has to be careful as a simple correspondence between the two is naive; e.g. as a recent survey showed (Mintel, 1991) young people have the most developed and positive attitudes towards green and ethical issues but favour ethical investing least; in order to put your money where your morals are you have to have the opportunity *and* the money.

STUDY 1: ETHICAL INVESTMENT: PERCEPTIONS AND PREFERENCES

Method

Subjects:

One hundred residents of areas of a medium-sized UK city with above-average house values (greater than £100,000 in 1990). (The UK currency of pounds sterling is used throughout. At the time of writing this value of housing would be the equivalent of approximately $US190,000.) Initially a request for help was mailed to a random sample of such households drawn from the electoral register. This was followed up by the interviewer calling on those who had agreed to take part and those who had not refused to take part. If an interview did not materialize, the interviewer called on next-door neighbours in similar housing until the target of 100 interviews was met.

Most of the respondents were in professional occupations including accountants, architects, solicitors, barristers, dentists, company directors, marketing personnel and one stockbroker. There were thirty-seven females and sixty-two males (demographic information for one respondent is missing). Approximately 50 per cent of respondents were between the ages of 20 and 39, 40 per cent between 40 and 59 and the rest over 60. Eighty-four people said that they had investments.

Interview schedule

The interview covered a range of issues using both open and closed questions. Respondents were asked what an ethical investment is, what it should be and whether they would invest ethically. They were presented with a hypothetical investment decision involving £1,000 windfall and different rates of return.

Results

What is an ethical investment? [open question]

Twenty-seven people had little to say in answer to this question except that they 'didn't know' or 'had no idea'. Four people suggested that an ethical investment might be one that is established or safe. Along the same lines was the reply that ethical investments are always unethical as 'they are always risky' (an alternative interpretation is that all investing is seen as a form of gambling).

Twenty-four people gave relatively undifferentiated answers to the effect that ethical investments have something 'to do with morals', 'doing good', 'avoiding immoral things' or 'something you care about . . . not tuna fish' (this probably refers to the accidental killing of dolphins by nets used to catch tuna). Eight people mentioned church, charity and religion: one individual that giving can make you feel good. A cynical reply from another respondent identified ethical giving with the church but added the rider that 'the Vatican invests in condoms you know'. Less disingenuous replies saw ethical investments as creating 'greater good for all', as being 'not for greed' but for 'promoting good-will in the economy'.

Fourteen people mentioned ecology, the environment and the 'greens'. Ethical investments are 'ecologically sound', 'won't damage humans or the environment' and are concerned with 'people as well as profits'. Replies in this category were more differentiated and linked re-afforestation, the World Wildlife Fund, 'water pumps for the third world', social and political issues and share ownership.

The largest category of replies (thirty-five people) mentioned specific exclusions. The majority cited South Africa, often in combination with the embargo on armaments, tobacco, alcohol and drugs. In this category there were also frequent references to environmental issues, which means that in total twenty-five people referred to the environment in some way. People in this group were more forthcoming and were happy to explain themselves. For instance, one retired bank manager talked about his own ethical investments, some of which gave reasonable returns whilst others 'were tantamount to a donation'.

What is an ethical investment? [closed question]

Here respondents had to indicate whether particular characteristics applied to all ethical investment, most, some or none of them. The exclusion of nuclear weapons rated highest among perceived characteristics, 73 per cent believing that this applied to most or all ethical investments. Exclusion of companies involved in 'South Africa', 'Pollution' and 'Tobacco' were some way behind with 57, 56 and 52 per cent, respectively. The nuclear power industry was clearly less salient, with 44 per cent saying that this was excluded by all, most or some of the ethical investments.

What should an ethical investment be?

Here respondents were invited to indicate what characteristics ethical investments should have. Responses were recorded on five-point scales anchored by 'strongly agree' (score 1) to 'strongly disagree' (score 5). The preferred characteristics were, in order, Pollution [1.60], Nuclear weapons [1.90], Tobacco [1.94], South Africa [2.45] and Nuclear Power [2.73]. Perceptions and preferences are very similar; the only real difference is that South Africa is much lower in the list of preferences.

Would you invest ethically?

Only six of the eighty-four respondents who had investments said that these investments were known to be ethical ones. Nevertheless, fifty-six people indicated that they would definitely invest ethically if the scheme had the characteristics they favoured and performed financially as well as any other. Enthusiam for investing ethically tailed off quickly as returns fall: 32 per cent were prepared to invest all or most of a windfall £1,000 ethically with a return of 9 per cent (compared to one of 10 per cent which they could obtain elsewhere); 22 per cent were prepared to do the same for an 8 per cent return; only 4 per cent for a 5 per cent return (see Figure 8.1).

STUDY 2: ETHICAL INVESTMENT IN A SIMULATION

Method

Subjects

Eighty-four undergraduate students studying a wide variety of subjects (biology, chemistry, music, English, economics, computer science, etc.) participated. Forty-one were female, forty-three were male. The mean age was 21.3 with a range from 18 to 42, with eleven participants being 25 or older.

Design

Two variables were investigated: the performance of the ethical trust (above average, average, below average) and 'green' attitudes (above the median,

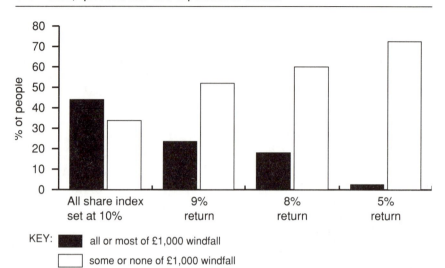

Figure 8.1 Preferences for ethical investments with varying returns

below the median). The dependent measures were the percentage of overall investment invested in the ethical trust in the last 'quarter' and the percentage of money invested ethically over all periods.

Procedure

Participants sat down at a computer and, after some screen displays giving guidance on using the keyboard, entered the practice phase. In this, subjects were presented with information about the past performance of five shares, simply labelled A to E. They were asked to invest as much or as little as they liked in each share from a capital sum of £40,000. The practice phase lasted for four 'quarters' and was designed simply to acquaint participants with the procedures they needed to follow to buy and sell shares and the way in which share-price information was graphically presented. They then started the experiment proper and received the following instructions:

> You have just inherited £40,000 from your uncle. You decide to invest in Scottish Equitable Unit Trusts, as this enables you to manage your investments whilst spreading the risks across a number of companies.
>
> Scottish Equitable have five trusts: 1, Global; 2, European; 3, UK Blue Chip; 4, Far East; 5, Ethical. A brief description of the investment policies of each is given in a leaflet. You may invest as much or as little of the £40,000 in as many of the different funds as you like. You will be able to change your investments quarterly.
>
> Uninvested money stays in the bank where it earns an interest rate of, on average, 5 per cent.

In order to help you with your investment decisions, each quarter you will be given some political or economic news (on teletext) and a graph displaying movements of unit trust prices and the *Financial Times* (FT) all-share index.

The teletext displays were near-perfect imitations of those used on Independent Television's Oracle service in the UK. They differed from the real thing only in being one column narrower. They covered a variety of political and economic topics, some being actual economic stories taken from the business pages of the daily papers ('A rise in unemployment and a report signalling that the US is likely to go into recession in the second half of the year yesterday prompted the US Federal Reserve Bank to cut its most influential interest rate'), others being fabricated ('Although not all the results are in, it is already clear that Labour have won yesterday's general election and will have a majority of around thirty seats over all other parties').

The leaflet on the investment policies of the five funds gave a brief (4–5 lines) description for each fund. For example:

1. Global

The Global fund searches for good investment opportunities wherever they are to be found. It includes companies from all five continents but a feature of recent investment has been a shift to the Pacific and, in particular, Australia.

5. Ethical

The Ethical Unit trust covers companies with significant business activity in health care and companies proactive on green issues (forestry, ozone layer, recyling of waste, sensitive use of land, acid rain, energy conservation, pollution, animal and plant welfare, healthy eating, community).

In order to make the task involving, participants were given a graphical display giving the recent history of the fluctuations in the prices of the unit trusts which brought them up to the day they were taking part in the experiment. Thus the world they entered in the experiment was an artificial one based on our expectations of the next one-and-a-half years (hence the need to have a teletext page about the results of the next British general election). To ensure good quality data, participants were asked at the outset to 'treat the task seriously: it is important that as far as possible you act as you would in real life'.

Participants were randomly allocated to one of three groups, ethical high, ethical average and ethical low. For those in the ethical high group the ethical trust performed above average, though not as high as the 'Global' share. For those in the ethical average group the ethical trust had an average performance in line with the FT all-share index. In the last group the ethical trust performed badly, its value decreasing steadily over the six quarters. The performance of the other unit trusts was the same for all groups; the 'Global' trust was a 'star' performer, the UK Blue Chip showed a slow but steady increase and the Far East and European trusts performed roughly in line with the FT all-share index.

After completing the simulation participants filled in a questionnaire. This included some manipulation checks, demographic data, some social identity measurements (items of the form 'being British is important to me' rated on a seven-point scale from 'not at all' to 'extremely important') and a twenty-item 'green' attitude scale ($\alpha = 0.80$). This comprised items covering a range of environmental issues such as pollution (e.g. 'all cars should have a catalytic converter', 'with modern techniques it is easy to deal with oil pollution'), animal experimentation (e.g. 'we should stop using animals to test cosmetic products'), nuclear power (e.g. 'nuclear power is a good alternative to limited fossil fuels'), South Africa (e.g. 'I would rather not buy South African products') and general issues (e.g. 'I am worried about the ozone layer', 'to go a short distance I would rather use a bike than a car'). A seven-point response format from strongly agree to strongly disagree was used.

Results

The results were analysed using two analyses of variance with ethical trust performance (high, average, low) and green attitudes (median split in each group, high, low) as independent factors and percentage of overall investment invested in the ethical trust in the last 'quarter' and the percentage of money invested ethically over all periods as dependent measures. For the overall percentage invested ethically there was a significant difference between those with more and those with less positive green attitudes ($F = 5.65$, $df = 1,78$, $p < 0.05$) and a significant difference between the performance conditions ($F = 4.08$, $df = 2,78$, $p < 0.05$). The interaction between the two factors was not significant. As Table 8.1 shows, those high on the green scale invested more in ethical trusts and better performance was associated with more investment.

The pattern of results for the percentage invested ethically in the last quarter was similar, but only green attitudes had a significant effect ($F = 7.65$, $df = 1,78$, $p < 0.01$) (see Table 8.2). The post-experimental questionnaire provided a check on how participants perceived the performance of the ethical trust and if they were taking the task seriously. Table 8.3 shows that although the majority of people in the ethical high and ethical low conditions perceived performance as intended, most of those in the ethical average condition saw the ethical trust as performing lower than the FT index. A re-categorization of people according to perceived performance of the ethical trust tells a slightly different story (see Table 8.4).

Though the pattern of results for those with less positive green attitudes is

Table 8.1 Overall percentage of money invested ethically as a function of trust performance and green attitudes

| Performance | Green attitudes | | |
	Lower than median	Higher than median	
Low	8.4	10.7	9.6
Average	10.5	19.1	14.8
High	14.8	21.0	17.9
	11.25	17.0	14.1

Table 8.2 Percentage of money invested ethically in the last quarter as a function of trust performance and green attitudes

| Performance | Green attitudes | | |
	Lower than median	Higher than median	
Low	12.9	16.2	14.6
Average	12.7	28.4	20.6
High	16.8	26.6	21.7
	14.2	23.7	19.0

Table 8.3 The relationship between actual and perceived ethical trust performance

| Actual performance | Perceived performance | | | |
	Low	Average	High	
Low	14	6	5	25
Average	14	7	7	28
High	7	6	15	28
	35	19	27	81*

* Note: Three participants omitted this question on the questionnaire

Table 8.4 Overall percentage of money invested ethically as a function of perceived trust performance and green attitudes

| Perceived performance | Green attitudes | | |
	Lower than median	Higher than median	
Low	7.2	12.7	10.0
Average	12.6	12.0	12.3
High	15.1	25.0	20.1
	11.0	17.0	14.0

comparable with the earlier analysis (the percentage invested ethically increases steadily with perceived performance), the pattern for those with more positive green attitudes is rather different. For those individuals, there is no difference between the percentage invested ethically when perceived performance is low and when it is average; when it is high the percentage invested ethically doubles.

Only eleven of the eighty-four participants reported not using the teletext pages for their investment decisions and most of them accurately reported the movement of the FT index, which suggests that the vast majority of participants took the task seriously.

DISCUSSION

Taking the computer simulations first we can conclude that people exhibiting 'green' attitudes reveal a greater enthusiasm for green ethical investments. By the last quarter of the exercise over 26 per cent of investments from among those with higher than median (more favourable) green attitudes were placed in the green ethical fund when it performed averagely or better (Table 8.2). For the last quarter the 'greens' invested more than other people in green investments in all three financial performance conditions. However, one should not over-emphasize the power of these findings; there were after all only five trusts to choose from, a completely even distribution of investments would therefore result in 20 per cent being placed in each. Nevertheless the 'green' supporters were happy to invest 27 per cent in green ethicals when they were performing well and still invested a similar amount when they were performing averagely.

An unexpected result was the apparent antipathy of those with lower than median attitudes, less than 17 per cent was invested ethically even when these funds performed well, a figure that fell to below 13 per cent in the average performance condition. The results for the last quarter were similar to those overall for this group (see Table 8.4 for 'perceived' performance rather than actual performance). It seems that regardless of attitudes green ethical investments were perceived to under-perform even when this was not the experimenters' intention. This perception was not found in the social survey. One way of accounting for this difference is that the survey concerned itself mostly with funds with restrictions, e.g. no investments in the tobacco industry, nuclear arms etc., which indeed does characterize the majority of ethical funds in the UK, whereas the green ethical fund used in the simulation was a proactive one investing in approved companies rather than excluding bad ones; it is simply an easier task to make a profit in the first case than the second.

Taking the simulations and survey together it seems that 'ordinary' investors cannot be relied upon to help make a better world, moral commitment in this context is highly price-elastic. If ethical funds perform reasonably well then sympathetic investors may choose them over others, while maintaining a mixed portfolio; as a foil to this there are other investors who would actively avoid them even if they perform well. The survey showed that the visibility of ethical investments in the UK is not great; around 50 per cent of the sample held undifferentiated views while those who knew better almost exclusively mentioned the restrictive nature of these investments rather than their possible proactive nature.

Of course some caveats need to be borne in mind. It is likely that real investors differ significantly from non-investors (and particularly from undergraduates) in their response to hypothetical investment decisions. This suggests that it is essential to carry out future experimental studies on investors or potential investors, who will have the necessary knowledge and background. It is also clear from the comments of participants that study 2 was enjoyable and involving, though there are evidently problems with the idea of the 'future world'. Certain events (e.g. a Labour victory in the next general election) were greeted with incredulity by some participants – an incredulity that turned out to be well founded. None the less, in combination with other methods, it appears that this is a worthwhile vehicle for future research.

In conclusion the observations suggest that there is pragmatism on both sides of the investment equation: some investors want to be good but they also want to make money; unit trust managers are happy to develop ethical funds but the criterion 'goodness' must not override financial performance. There are exceptions (e.g. the services offered by the Mercury Provident), but the impact of such investments on the economy as a whole is extremely small. An investor in the Mercury Provident buys shares in the company, although not quoted on the stock exchange as the directors (influenced by the philosopher and educationalist Rudolf Steiner) consider it to be a contaminating influence. Investors choose projects that they would like to support (e.g. Rudolf Steiner schools, organic farms and paper recycling businesses) and lend their money at a fixed rate of interest below that available elsewhere; investors can choose how much they want to 'give' in this way: by 1990 £2.5 million had been raised from 500 depositors. But even here perhaps a little pragmatism is at work: in May 1991 in response, say the directors, to demand from borrowers, Mercury Provident introduced a variable-rate deposit account paying interest only a little less than base rate (in the social survey it was revealed that people may be prepared to take a small loss compared with the base rate). Not all Mercury depositors were happy with this move, one of whom responded by asking if the fixed rate deposit was not raising enough money to have her interest reduced to 0 per cent. Nevertheless within four months the new variable-rate deposit account raised £250,000 and a second identical offer was launched.

Does one need morals to explain ethical investing? The answer is yes, but not in the naive way one might at first propose. It is not a question of simple self-interest, it is better to think of a multiple self (Elster, 1986; Mansbridge,

1990); a person undeified but with the usual mixture of good and evil, who when given the choice, and at little cost, chooses good. But is this enough to change the world, to solve for instance the problems of pollution? On this evidence the market cannot be relied upon and ethical values need bolstering via government intervention and tax incentives.

REFERENCES

Bruyn, S. (1987) *The Field of Social Investment*, Cambridge: Cambride University Press.

Cullis, J., Lewis, A. and Winnett, A. (1992) 'Paying to be good? UK ethical investments', *Kyklos*, 45, 1, 3–24.

Dominic, A. and Kinder, K. (1984) *Ethical Investing*, Reading, MA: Addison-Wesley.

EIRIS (The Ethical Investment Research Service). London.

Elster, J. (ed.) (1986) *The Multiple Self*, Cambridge and New York: Cambridge University Press.

Etzioni, A. (1988) *The Moral Dimension*, New York: Free Press.

Furnham, A. and Lewis, A. (1986) *The Economic Mind*, Brighton: Wheatsheaf.

Harte, G., Lewis, L. and Owen, D. (1990) 'Ethical investment and the corporate reporting function', paper presented to the British Accounting Association (Scottish group), Annual conference, September.

Lea, S. E. G., Tarpy, R. M. and Webley, P. (1987) *The Individual in the Economy*, Cambridge: Cambridge University Press.

Lewis, A. and Cullis, J. (1990) 'Ethical investments: preferences and morality', *Journal of Behavioral Economics*, 19, 395–411.

Lowry, R. (1991) *Good Money: A Guide to Profitable Social Investing in the '90s*, New York: Norton.

Luther, R. and Matatko, J. (1991) 'The investment performance of "ethical" unit trusts', paper presented to the British Accounting Association, April.

Mansbridge, J. (ed.) (1990) *Beyond Self Interest*, Chicago: University of Chicago Press.

Mintel International Group Ltd (1991) *Special Report: The Green Consumer*, 18–19 Long Lane, London, E0A 9HE.

Prestridge, J. (1989) 'Greens and ethics sprout forth', *Money Management*, November, 63–71.

Smith, N. C. (1990) *Morality and the Market*, London and New York: Routledge.

Chapter 9

Ethical issues in the world of finance
Two empirical studies

*Karl-Erik Wärneryd, Lars Bergkvist and
Kristin Westlund*

PROBLEMS IN BUSINESS ETHICS

Recent events in the world of finance

In many countries, spectacular events in the financial world have raised questions about the state of business ethics. Businessmen who were highly regarded have been publicly accused in the mass media, indicted in courts and sometimes sentenced for actions that have involved unethical and illegal transactions. 'The spectacle of rich, important financial titans being led in handcuffs from their offices somewhat tarnished the glow of investment banking' (de George, 1989, p. 197).

When the perpetrators of the financial swindles have been graduates from leading schools of business, questions have been asked about the ethical contents of the business training and the moral education given. Many schools of business, with the Harvard School of Business in the front line, have set up special programmes for establishing business ethics in the business curriculum. London Business School has a new, endowed chair in 'Business Ethics and Social Responsibility'.

The purpose of the studies

Two empirical studies in the Swedish world of finance are reported here. There were two main purposes behind the studies: (1) to investigate ethical attitudes and judgments of ethical conduct in the world of finance so as to reflect the social norms related to financial operations; (2) to compare a group of business school students with samples of executives, analysts, brokers and journalists active in the world of finance.

The main idea was to carry out an empirical study using brief scenarios based on actual events in the Swedish world of finance and to secure judgments of how unethical the described behaviours were according to representative opinion in the financial world. There was a special focus on whether the behaviour was assumed to be legal or not, and on how frequent it was believed to be.

The studies were based on the assumption that there are social norms influencing what is considered unethical in various professional groups. Asking for judgments of the unethicalness of the described behaviours should then reveal the social norms. An additional assumption that could not be tested in the studies is that social norms affect behaviour, at least in the long run, since they foreshadow the reactions from peers that a perpetrator will face if she/he is caught with unethical conduct. While there is an abundance of good normative discussions of ethical issues, there is as yet little empirical research elucidating how representative opinion in business judges actual cases.

THEORETICAL BACKGROUND

Ethics in theory and practice

Since ancient times there have been discussions about ethical problems. Cicero, for example, treated ethical problems and gave his opinion on ethical behaviour in business matters (see the introductory chapter). He used descriptions that are similar to the vignettes or brief case descriptions that were used in our studies. The type of ethical questions that Cicero raised are still of pertinence and great interest. He did not stop at presenting the problem, he also provided solutions. 'But I must record my opinion about these cases, for I did not write them down merely to raise problems, but to solve them. I believe, then, that the corn merchant ought not to have concealed the facts from the Rhodians.' Cicero apparently, by discussion of actual problems, attempted to establish norms that could guide behaviour.

The discussion of ethics still tends to be highly normative either on the basis of abstract ethical principles or as practical advice. There are comparatively few empirical studies of unethical behaviour and hardly any studies of the representative opinion controlling what is considered unethical in a profession. The empirical studies are usually not related to the abundant philosophical and legal discussions of ethics (Fritsche and Becker, 1984). Apart from the fact that it is extremely difficult to translate some of the concepts discussed into practical measurements, it may appear somewhat doubtful to ask people questions about unethical behaviour and expect candid answers.

From publicized anecdotal material and from our discussions with business executives there emerges a picture of the slippery road to unethical conduct, with some typical ingredients. There has often been success in the past, exhibited as high position and personal wealth. The reason for the unethical conduct is then characteristically a serious threat to the wealth or to keeping the position or an unusual opportunity where the gain is so large as to far outweigh the risk in the mind of the actor. It is said that when a person is sliding down a slope with several minor failures and the expectation of more to come, he or she is inclined to take a chance and do something unethical that neither he/she nor close colleagues would have dreamt of previously.

The two studies reported here focus on how actual behaviours are judged by colleagues and potential future colleagues. If there are clear norms for ethical behaviour and those are known, there should be less inclination to commit unethical behaviour, to run the risk of being caught and exposed to the critical judgments of others. It is not known to what extent or whether exposure but no legal sanction is deterring in advance of an event. Judging from what has happened in some Swedish cases, the way peers feel about a certain unethical conduct may be ruining to a person's career, meaning dismissal from the job. It also seems to mean serious damage to her/his self-image and self-esteem.

Principal problems

When unethical behaviour is illegal it may upon disclosure lead to indictment and sentence. The perpetrator is punished for breaking the law. One important function of the law is to deter potential lawbreakers from actually breaking the law. This is focused on in the economic, so-called deterrence, model of law compliance. In this it is assumed that the probability of being discovered and the severity of the punishment determine whether the unethical act will be committed. In criminology, ever since Jeremy Bentham (Russell, 1946, p. 803), it is generally held that the certainty of discovery is more important than the severity of the punishment (see e.g. Lewis, 1982, for a discussion of compliance problems in tax evasion).

From a psychological point of view, a few variables could be added to this discussion, in the first place what unethical acts mean to the self-image. So far, there is little empirical research on this aspect which is no surprise since it is hard to make amenable to research. Another important influence according to psychological thinking is the influence from what peers in the same social system think and do in ethical matters. Finally, as noted above on the basis of anecdotal evidence, there are situational factors or pressures that may trigger unethical behaviour that actually goes against a person's grain.

Similar reasoning in terms of deterrence can be applied when the unethical conduct does not break the law. Instead of punishments like fines and incarceration, such unethical behaviour on the part of an executive may be exposed to the public via the mass media and lead to losses of public and private esteem, even dismissal from attractive positions and perhaps rejection by colleagues. Dismissal and rejection sometimes follow the disclosure to the public even in cases where the presumed perpetrator in a court trial is found not guilty. The fact that individual executives in such cases have been summarily dismissed from their jobs is a sign that there is a high sensitivity to questionable ethics in Western society. Calls for explicit and clear ethical rules have ensued so as to make it possible for decision makers to know what is right or wrong.

Kant's categorical imperative tells us to ask of any projected action: What would happen if everyone acted like this? It is also explained as acting as if '. . . your action were to become through your will a general natural law' (Russell, 1946, p. 737). This may sound like a good rule, but people in the financial world are apt to question an example given by Kant: borrowing money is by Kant classified as behaviour akin to murder and theft. If everybody borrowed money, there would be no money to borrow! (ibid., p. 737). It is likely that, in the case of borrowing money, business executives think in terms that are not those of the categorical imperative. (In the light of the present financial crisis, some may think that it would have been better had they *not* borrowed money.)

It is interesting to note that in many cases the issue of unethical conduct has been raised when business executives have been indicted for breaking the law. Evidently, respect for the law is one important aspect of ethics. There are, however, discussions of unethical behaviour in cases in which the perpetrators have not broken any law, but have broken instead some kind of norms. From a public relations point of view, executive unethical conduct reflects on the company image. The perpetrator does not get much, if any, support from the company and is likely to be removed from the organization. This is especially the case when the unethical conduct involves an attempt to secure a personal profit, with no gain for the company. The situation may appear in a different light when the conduct is aimed at saving the company. When executives discuss ethical behaviour, there is often a PR or corporate image aspect to it. Unethical behaviour is shunned because it can be disclosed and damage the reputation or image of the company. Behaviour that may seem profitable to the company in the short run, is assumed to give unfavourable consequences in the longer run because of public distrust, unfavourable reactions from financiers, customers, consumers and the mass media.

Such considerations of reputation and image imply that business executives are driven by expectations of consequences (teleology, utilitarianism or consequentialism) rather than by absolute norms like the categorical imperative (deontology). According to deontological thinking, an act can be judged as correct or incorrect independent of its consequences. 'Let justice be done though the heavens fall' (Bullock *et al.*, 1988, p. 216). In teleological and utilitarian thinking the focus lies on the goodness of the consequences. Those acts are good that promote the general happiness. Fritsche and Becker (1984, p. 167) distinguish between two kinds of utilitarian theories of ethics: act utilitarian and rule utilitarian. In the former case only the consequences of the separate act are considered. Act utilitarians hold an act to be morally acceptable if it produces the most good for the greatest number. In the second case the consequences of not following the rule are considered and the consequences of the unethical act in itself are subordinate. Rule utilitarians pointing to the rules defend outcomes that give the greatest good for the largest number of people. In both cases the consequences thus refer to the social consequences, not the consequences to the person or business firm. This gives rise to the question whether behaviour can be ethical or unethical independent of motives. Can ethical behaviour which in the first place depends on efforts to avoid a stain on the company image be considered truly ethical? The pragmatic answer is, of course, affirmative.

At a highly abstract level, consequentialism and deontology may seem to be two irreconcilable alternatives. Ethical theory tends to be normative rather than descriptive and in normative utilitarian theory the focus is on social consequences. At a more practical level, there may be rules that are adhered to in an absolute way, independent of consequences and rules that are followed because of the fear of ill-consequences. In either case, ethical conduct may be fostered.

If there is definite provision in the law that a given behaviour is illegal and the executives know about the law, the knowledge factor should normally be decisive for whether the behaviour is displayed or not and for how the behaviour is judged by colleagues. The behaviour is judged as unethical if it is clearly against the law. It is intuitively clear that a behaviour can be legal and yet unethical, even though laws reflect social norms. There is also the possibility that, in some cases, business executives disagree with the spirit of the law and find a certain type of behaviour ethical despite the provisions of the law. This discrepancy should only rarely be seen as justifying an illegal behaviour. In presumably rare cases, an executive may, for example due to situational pressures, deliberately act against the law, with a more or less realistic hope of not being discovered.

In general, if ethical principles are not seen as absolute, there can be cases in which otherwise immoral acts become ethical because they have good social consequences. For example, a minor legal offence like stealing something to save a person in extreme danger would be considered ethical by most people. Unethical behaviour in order to save employment in a company would probably be judged differently from the same behaviour used to save private investment in a company.

If a certain behaviour belongs to a grey zone where, for lack of precise formulations, there is uncertainty about whether the law is really applicable and where precedents are missing, the judgments of legality or rather illegality will probably be influenced by the observer's general attitudes to ethical conduct. Some businessmen cling to the phrase 'If it's legal, it's moral'. Bowie (1988) calls the position that the only moral obligation of management is to obey the law the 'minimalist' position regarding business ethics. He argues that this position is untenable and points out that '. . . the law frequently requires corporate conduct to adhere to broad open-ended standards of morality' (p. 89). This means that a manager may appear before a court '. . . when neither she nor her company had done anything previously illegal nor contrary to stockholder interest, to be found morally and hence legally blameworthy' (Bowie, 1988, p. 90).

EMPIRICAL STUDIES

Compared with the huge amount of discussions of what constitutes ethical conduct in business, there are relatively few empirical studies of actual behaviour, except in the form of case reports. The empirical studies are commonly confined to questions of opinions about unethical tendencies or attitudes towards unethical conduct. Empirical studies have focused on ethical attitudes, often assessed with the aid of vignettes that briefly describe situations with ethical implications. In some cases, executives/managers and business school students have been compared. The attitude statements or vignettes used have with a few exceptions not included financial decisions or unethical behaviour in the world of finance.

In some studies there have been attempts to assess the importance of factors influencing ethical behaviour by ratings of factors according to their judged importance. An example is the study by Arlow and Ulrich (1988): business graduates (in their rather small sample) rated family training as the most important influence and, second, the conduct of superiors. In other studies the focus has lain on comparing unethical attitudes and judgments of groups with varying demographic and other characteristics. Gender seems to be of importance for judgments of what is unethical. Women are more inclined to find behaviours unethical.

Fraedrich and Ferrell (1992) investigated the tendency to revise decisions when a personal risk was introduced as a possible consequence. They found that the groups which they (on the basis of a moral content test) characterized as act-deontologists and act-utilitarians were more likely than rule-deontologists and rule-utilitarians to change their ethical decisions. Their sample consisted of managers in a retail organization.

In a recent study, using business students as subjects, Terpstra *et al.* (1991) tested experimentally a model that involved interaction between situational variables (size of profits and behaviour of peers) and personality variables (locus of control, competitiveness). They found support for the idea that unethical behaviour, which in their study concerned insider trading, was dependent on interactions between situational and personality variables.

There are many studies of ethical attitudes among executives and among business school students, but few of them relate to ethical issues in the world of finance. Special attention has, however, been given to the problem of insider trading (see, e.g., Parkman *et al.*, 1988; Moore, 1990).

A general tendency is that business school students are less prone than business professionals to find certain behaviours unethical (see, e.g., Stevens,

1984; Wood *et al.*, 1988; Jones and Gautschi, 1988). Among the vignettes used by Stevens (1984), earlier used by Clark (1966), one referred to insider trading: the executives were significantly more ethical in their responses to this item. Some authors seem to think that the attitudes of the students are a foreboding of deteriorating ethical attitudes in business in the future. At the same time some studies have noted an increasing concern with ethical issues among students which, however, conflicts with the fact that there is an increased tendency among students to cheat (Peterson *et al.*, 1991).

The original expectation (see, e.g., Stevens, 1985) was that business students would have stricter ethical attitudes than executives because of the influence of the theory-oriented environment. The differences found may, of course, be a sign of actual differences in attitudes or just differences in the conception of how ethical questions should be answered (different views of social desirability). A number of possible explanations have been brought forward and more can be added. Here are some attempts at explanation: (1) business executives often belong to firms and professional associations with formalized codes; (2) executives may need to balance the interests of various stakeholder groups (Kraft and Singhapakdi, 1991); (3) students may lack some of the emotions that practical experience can arouse due to personal contact with ethical conflicts; their judgments may be more cognitive.

FACTORS AFFECTING JUDGMENTS OF UNETHICAL CONDUCT

Judgments of unethicality can be assumed to depend on many factors; for example, whether the act is believed to be legal or illegal, whether it is believed to be frequent, the respondent's general attitude towards ethical issues, and on educational background and personal experience. These factors can be investigated through empirical studies, using surveys.

If a certain conduct is believed to be illegal, it should ordinarily be judged as highly unethical or more unethical than a behaviour that is seen as legal (departures from this canon can be interesting). If a certain conduct is believed to be frequent, it is likely to be seen as less unethical since 'many sinners' share the sin. An executive is likely to know more about persons involved in such affairs and may feel more empathy with the offenders. If there is a general belief in the efficacy of the law and of social norms, belief in a low frequency should be associated with less lenient judgments.

Behind these beliefs there should be an attitude towards ethical issues in the field of specialization and in business in general. The beliefs and evaluations that compose the attitude derive from more deep-seated values, business experience and education, among other factors. An interesting question is whether longer experience in a field of specialization leads to more lenient attitudes or on the contrary to stricter judgments.

On the basis of earlier studies, other boxes can be added to the model in

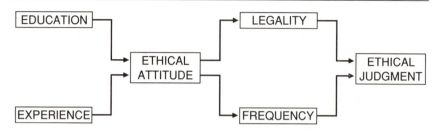

Figure 9.1 Factors influencing ethical judgments

Figure 9.1. Ethical attitude is influenced by long-term values, including the self-image (self-esteem) that the individual wants to maintain. In the first study reported here, it was not judged possible to ask the respondents any questions relating to personality variables: in the second study, a few questions of this kind were included in the questionnaire.

A social desirability effect is often suspected by critics of the survey studies which especially may apply where there are questions about unethical acts (see, e.g., Randall and Gibson, 1990, for a discussion). In the studies reported here, the aim is to find out about social norms from representative groups. A social desirability effect may be expected to reflect the norms and thus enhance what the studies attempt to elucidate. There may still be some social desirability effect; respondents may exaggerate the ethical contents of the extant norms, but such an effect would be less detrimental than in other types of studies.

Some prerequisites are important for the meaningfulness of survey studies on ethics. There must be involvement in the issue on the part of the respondent whether for defending a certain behaviour or because the respondent wants to further more ethical conduct. There should be anonymity of the respondent, of the business firm, sometimes also anonymity of profession (as is sometimes necessary in studies of tax evasion). In a study of social norms, it is interesting to look at the dispersions of the judgments of unethical conduct. If there are clear ethical norms, people will answer in such a way that there will be small differences between the answers from different persons (small standard deviations around the mean). A large dispersion around the mean judgment indicates that the norms are unclear or that there is inadequate knowledge about the norms. In fact, interpretable differences between groups of respondents are often found. People do differ in their judgments of what is ethical or unethical economic conduct. This reflects the fact that there are no established norms with respect to the ethics of a particular action. There are also clear cases where there is little difference of opinion, meaning almost unanimous rejection of certain actions as unethical.

STUDY 1

The questionnaire

A questionnaire was developed to produce judgments of ethical issues in two major ways. One way consisted of six cases that were anonymized brief descriptions of recent events in the Swedish financial world (written by Mr Sten Wikander, who for many years had been active in the world of finance before joining the staff of the Stockholm School of Economics). The cases are reproduced in the Appendix, translated into English. Commonly, when cases or vignettes are used, the respondent is instructed to imagine him- or herself in the role and make a decision to act. In the present study it seemed more natural to ask for opinions about events that had occurred and which could by most executive respondents easily be completed with an actor's name. Four scales were used. The respondents were asked to judge for each case:

1 whether the behaviour was ethical or unethical, on a ten-point scale (10 = to a very high degree an example of deficient ethics; 1 = in no way an example of deficient ethics);
2 whether the behaviour was frequent in Swedish business, on a ten-point scale (10 = frequent; 1 = does not occur at all);
3 whether the behaviour was frequent in Western industrial countries, on a ten-point scale (same as under 2);
4 whether the behaviour was legal, on a five-point scale (1 = the action is legal; 5 = the action is illegal).

The second part of the questionnaire comprised sixteen attitude statements, most of which were culled from attitude scales used in other studies. The respondents agreed–disagreed on a five-point Likert scale. Finally, there were questions about ethical policies in business firms. On a ten-point scale respondents could mark how commonly, in their opinion, ethical questions were discussed in Swedish business firms. On another ten-point scale they marked how frequent they thought that ethical policies were in Swedish business firms. A few background questions completed the questionnaire. The students reported on their studies and the executives on their education and business careers.

The samples

Two samples were used. The Stockholm School of Economics has a three-and-a-half year programme of study (leading to a Master's degree in Economics and Business) with specialization during the third year. All students who had chosen to specialize in financial economics, accounting or

Economic Analysis and Control during the academic year 1988–9 were included in the sample.

The sample of business executives consisted of the financial managers and those who were responsible for the finances of the eighty largest companies listed at the Stockholm stock exchange. All envelopes containing the questionnaire were addressed to a person. Of the 131 questionnaires mailed to students, sixty-five were returned, which gives a response rate of 49.6 per cent. For the business executives the response rate was eighty-two out of 144 or 56.9 per cent. The non-response is thus quite high as is common in this type of study and the results will have to be read with some caution.

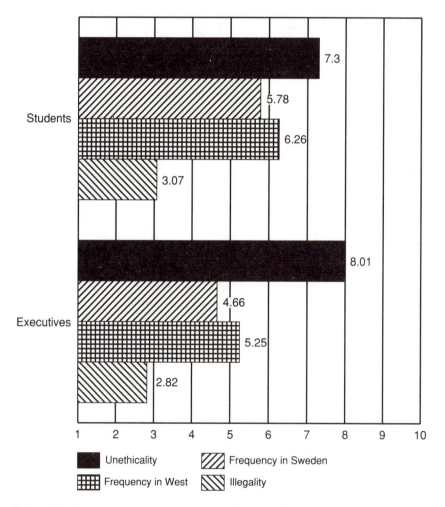

Figure 9.2 Average total scores on case judgment scales

The results of Study 1

Overall differences between students and executives

A more detailed report of Study 1 is given in Wärneryd and Westlund (1993). The first question to be answered is whether there are differences between the business students and the executives. First, some overall differences are presented. For each of the four judgment scales an overall index score was computed involving all six cases. In order to take care of a few missing response values, averages were used, based on the actual number of cases judged on each scale, thus allowing a score for each respondent.

Figure 9.2 shows that the students were more lenient in their judgments of the unethicality of the behaviours. At the same time they were more often than the executives convinced that such behaviours were frequent both in Sweden and in comparative Western countries. The students believed that the behaviours were on average more illegal. The differences between the groups are significant for all four scales.

While the students were more lenient in their judgments of unethicality, they believed that the behaviours were more often illegal than the executives did. Does this mean that they care less about illegal behaviour? It is often assumed, at least from the time of Socrates, that the young are more inclined to irregular behaviour than the previous generations. An alternative assumption that is often brought forth is that young people are more callous in their judgments and behaviour; for example, they tend to admit more tax evasion behaviour. The assumption is then that such tendencies disappear with increasing age.

Both groups thought that overall the unethical behaviours described in the questionnaire were more frequent in other countries than in Sweden.

The unethicalness of the six cases

For five of the six cases, the students judged the behaviour more leniently than the executives (Figure 9.3). The differences were significant for the first case 'Insider Trading 1' and the third case 'Private Interests'.

The former case describes a situation in which a chief executive officer (CEO) tries to salvage the remnants of his own wealth by getting rid of his own stock in the company six months before the bankruptcy. The implication is that he acted on inside information. The third case also has to do with self-interest in so far as a CEO looks to the interests of his family rather than to those of his company. It may be more acceptable to students that a person serves her/his self-interest rather than the interest of the company and other stakeholders.

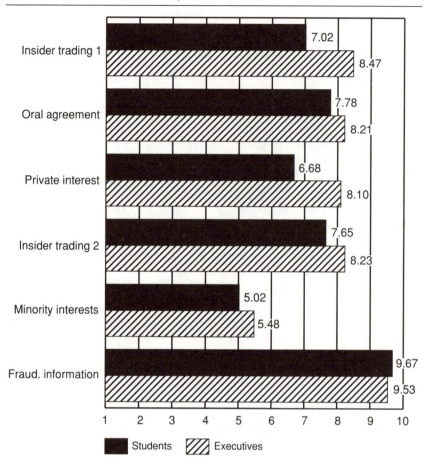

Figure 9.3 The unethicalness of the six cases

The role of illegality

The relationships between the perceived degree of illegality and the other judgment scales are one of the main questions of the study. It is clear that many respondents think of the behaviours as probably legal, but still unethical. To study the relationships further, Figure 9.4 was constructed to show the judgments of illegality and unethicality for each case. Those who classified the behaviour as illegal (response category 5) or probably illegal (4) are included in the illegal group. The fact that students gave higher estimates of illegality than executives and at the same time more lenient judgments of unethical behaviours does not preclude the possibility that within the groups there may be higher judgments of unethicality when the behaviour is considered illegal.

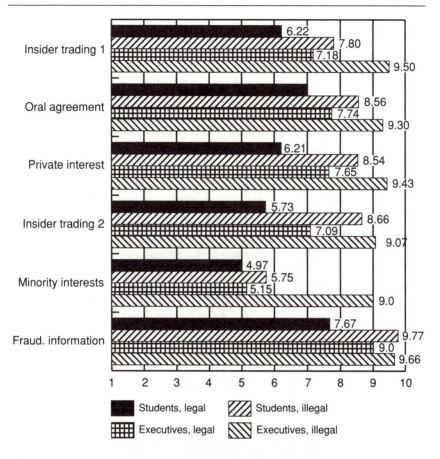

Figure 9.4 Illegality and unethicalness for the six cases

It is clear from the figure that, in both groups, those who thought that a behaviour might be illegal judged the behaviour more unethical. The differences are, except in two cases, highly significant. In one case, that of minority interests being hurt, very few students think that the behaviour is illegal. In the other case, only few executives think that the behaviour is legal, and all of them think that it is highly unethical. Except in the case of fraudulent information the students who think the behaviour is illegal give more lenient judgments than the executives. For this case the difference is trivial. While perceived illegality appears to be an important factor for the judgment of unethicality, there are still judgments of high unethicality made by those who thought that a certain behaviour was legal. The largest difference is found for Case 5 in the executive group. Those who thought the act was legal gave an average rating near 5 and those who believed it to be illegal rated it as very unethical.

The role of perceived frequency

Figure 9.2 showed that, in comparison with the executives, the students believed that the frequency of the misconducts was significantly higher. Looking at the separate cases according to Figure 9.5, one finds that the students stated higher frequencies for all of them (not significant for Cases 5 and 6).

If people believe in the efficacy of the law, they would be expected to presume lower frequency for illegal behaviours than for unethical, but legal behaviour. Figure 9.5 shows the estimates of frequencies in Sweden for those who thought the behaviour illegal in the two groups. While executives who think a certain behaviour is illegal tend to judge the frequency lower, there is an almost opposite tendency among the students.

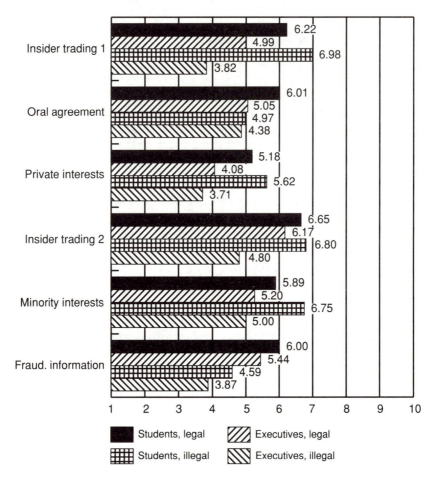

Figure 9.5 Illegality and frequency in Sweden

The frequency of the behaviours in Sweden is by both groups held to be lower than in other Western industrialized countries. For the student group the correlation between perceived frequency in Sweden and in other Western industrialized countries was 0.85 and for the executive group 0.76. Even the two insider trading cases were judged by both groups to be more frequent abroad. According to general opinion the Swedish legislation, even after new legislation in recent years, is more lenient about insider trading than is common in Anglo-Saxon countries, which could perhaps be expected to lead to more occurrences in Sweden.

Other factors influencing the judgments of unethicality

On the basis of earlier studies and some theory it was assumed that the judgments of unethicality for the executives would be affected by such factors as educational background, years of experience and the existence of ethical policies in the companies to which the executives belonged. Tests of these factors failed to reveal any significant differences among the executives and there was little indication of any interesting tendencies in the expected direction. There were too few women in the executive sample to make a gender comparison meaningful. The students were a rather homogeneous group with similar educational background, albeit with some differences in practical experience. Among the students there were no differences in judgments related to differences in practical experience.

The sixteen attitude statements in the questionnaire were used to construct an attitude index, 'Concern about Ethical Issues', based on eleven items (Cronbach's alpha = 0.66). A multiple regression analysis was run for each case and for the overall (summated) judgment of all six cases, using illegality, frequency in Sweden and the attitude index as independent variables. The groups were represented by a dummy (Students = 0 and Executives = 1). The results are shown in Table 9.1.

Table 9.1 demonstrates that perceived illegality contributes significantly to the variance in judged unethicality. The only exception is the sixth case which

Table 9.1 Study 1. Regression analyses of ethical judgments with the attitude index among the independent variables. Standardized coefficients

Case	Illegality	Sw. freq.	Group	Concern	Adj. R^2
Insider trading 1	0.407***	−0.149	0.213**	0.152*	0.285
Oral agreement	0.362***	−0.319***	0.189	0.245***	0.276
Private interests	0.293***	−0.070*	0.235**	0.142	0.158
Insider trading 2	0.380***	−0.223**	0.099	0.192**	0.257
Minority interests	0.357***	−0.108	0.107	0.023	0.129
Fraudulent information	0.143	−0.250**	−0.024	0.199	0.095
Overall index	0.303***	−0.152	0.278***	0.244**	0.209

*** $p < 0.001$ ** $p < 0.01$ * $p < 0.05$

was judged to be illegal by almost all respondents. As noted earlier (Figure 9.4), for the students there was one exception, namely Case 5 'Minority Interests', which very few students believed to be illegal. For the executives the exception, which is borne out by the regression analysis, is Case 6 'Fraudulent Information' which the large majority judged illegal and all condemned as highly unethical.

The model assumes that perceived frequency influences judged unethicality. If a certain behaviour is frequent, it should be judged less unethical to commit such an act because one is 'in good company' or, based on a highly different assumption, because really immoral acts are expected to be rare in a functioning society. The perceived frequency in Sweden is on the whole negatively related to judgments of unethicality. If the behaviour is judged unethical, it is generally assumed to be more rare. Few of the standardized coefficients of the frequency variable are significant, but there is an overall tendency.

The 'Group' variable again shows the differences between students and executives for Cases 1 and 3, and adds Case 3 'Oral Agreement' as another example of differences in opinions. The attitude variable 'Concern' adds something to the explanatory value for four of the cases and for the Overall index of judgments of unethicality. The total explained variance varies from 0.095 to 0.285. This may be taken to indicate that some of the cases do not perform too well. For the other cases the values are not unusually low, but indicate that the search for new explanatory variables should go on.

The judgments of the minimalists

Minimalists are, according to Bowie (1988), those who think that ethics is just a question of legality. The minimalists would be expected to mark as unethical only those cases which are judged by them to be illegal. Business students who have recently studied law may have more of a tendency in this direction than business executives who have seen more of reality.

Two of the attitude statements may be said to reflect minimalism: (1) 'If legislation is clear and precise, there will be no ethical problems'; (2) 'If one just stays within the limits of the law, one does not make any immoral business decisions'.

Ten of the sixty-five students and six of the eighty-two executives endorsed the first statement while only one student and three executives endorsed the second one. A group of minimalists was formed using those eighteen respondents who endorsed at least one of the statements. This group was compared to the rest of the samples. The eighteen minimalists judged the unethical behaviour significantly more leniently for Case 1 and Case 3. Five of the cases were more leniently judged and the sixth was, for all practical purposes, judged equally unethical by minimalists and others. Since ten of the eighteen minimalists are students, a check was made for each group separately. It showed that the tendencies were the same in both groups: the minimalists generally judged the cases more leniently. An interesting question concerns whether the minimalists believe more or less in the legality of the behaviours in the cases. The minimalists among the students judged all the cases except Case 6 as less illegal than the non-minimalists. In the executive group, four of the cases were judged as less illegal, Case 1 and Case 5 were judged as more illegal than in the comparison group. The groups of minimalists were very small, but the results suggest that the concept of minimalism may be worth further investigation.

STUDY 2

The samples

The second study used four samples: (1) financial analysts, (2) financial journalists, (3) money-market brokers and (4) students specializing in accounting, financial economics or economic control at the Stockholm School of Economics. The response rate for the analysts ($n = 156$) and the journalists ($n = 40$) amounted to 66 per cent and for the brokers ($n = 50$) to 47 per cent. The response rate for the students ($n = 89$) was 73 per cent.

The questionnaire

The main part of the questionnaire was the same as in Study 1. One of the cases was dropped and two new ones were added. One of the latter presented a case 'Breach of Trust' that was recent and still under debate. The second stated a problem of evaluating assets that is plaguing non-profitable Swedish banks at present. The attitude statements were increased to thirty-one, giving room for a few statements relating to personality dimensions (locus of control).

The results of Study 2

A full report of the results is published elsewhere (Bergkvist, 1992). Here the focus lies on a comparison with the 1988 study. This means that a comparison is made between the sample groups overall and for each case, and that the linkages between perceived illegality and frequency, on one hand, and judgments of unethicalness, on the other, are investigated. Finally, the role of some other factors is examined.

Overall differences between students and professionals

The overall differences between the business students and the three professional groups are presented in Figure 9.6. The overall index scores for all seven cases were calculated in the same manner as for the first study.

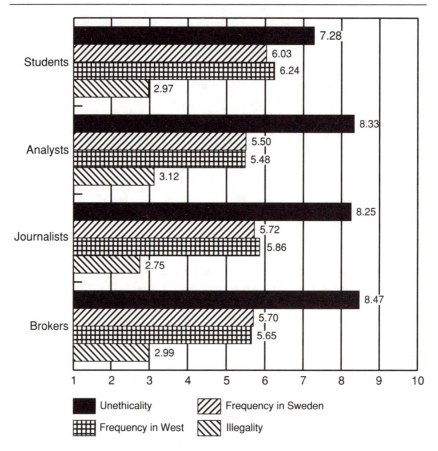

Figure 9.6 Average total scores on case judgment scales

Figure 9.6 shows results consistent with the first study. The difference between business students and professionals with practical experience seems to hold. The students made significantly more lenient judgments of the unethicality of the behaviours and believed that the described behaviours were more frequent both in Sweden and in comparative Western countries than did the professionals. As in the previous study the students believed that the behaviours were more illegal than did the professionals. All differences were significant on the 0.05 level.

The result from the first study that the described behaviours were assumed to be more frequent in comparative Western countries did not hold for the professionals. The differences between the two scales are negligible for all professional samples, whereas there was a highly significant difference for the student sample. The students still believe that unethical behaviours of the described types, although quite frequent, are less common in Sweden than in comparable countries.

THE UNETHICALNESS OF THE SEVEN CASES

Also with regard to the judged unethicalness of the different cases the results are similar to those of the first study. The students judged six of the seven cases more leniently. The differences were highly significant for four cases: 'Insider Trading 1', 'Private Interests', 'Insider Trading 2' and 'Breach of Trust' (Figure 9.7).

The Case 'Insider Trading 2' describes a situation in which the chief executive officer (CEO) of a listed investment company offers insider tips and the financial means to take opportunity of those to some key employees.

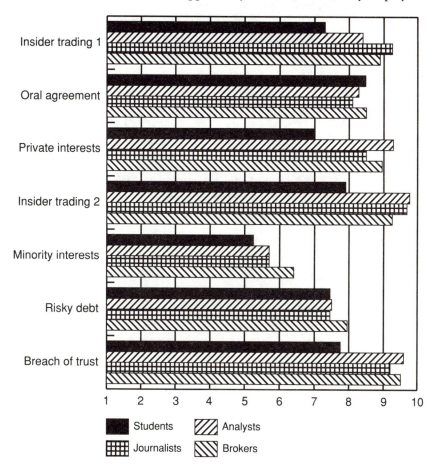

Figure 9.7 The unethicalness of the seven cases

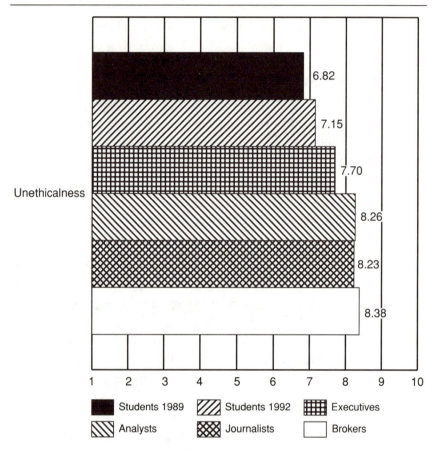

Figure 9.8 Average total scores of unethicalness

The new case 'Breach of Trust' describes a situation in which the CEO of a listed company sells a large number of his private shares to his company which loses a substantial amount on the deal. This case was under much debate during the data collection as the CEO and the chairman of the company were on trial for their behaviour. They were later acquitted.

A COMPARISON OF THE RESULTS OF THE TWO STUDIES

In order to make a comparison of the total scores of the two studies possible, new total scores based on the five cases used in both studies were calculated. As with the earlier total scores, averages adjusted for missing response values were used.

Figure 9.8 shows that there was a clear tendency to make harsher

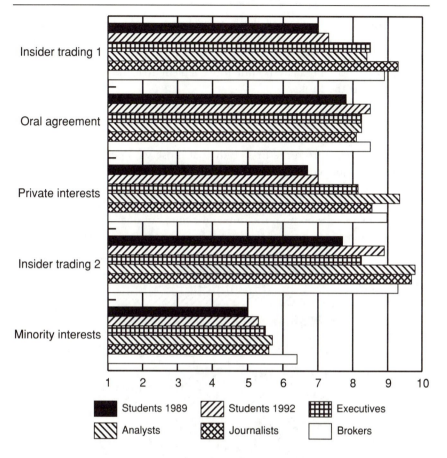

Figure 9.9 The unethicalness of the cases used in both studies

judgments. The difference between the two student samples can probably be interpreted as changing attitudes over time, since their background and experience are identical. More attention has been given to ethical problems both in the curriculum of the Stockholm School of Economics and in public debate. It is more ambiguous whether the difference between the executives of the first study and the three other professional samples in the second study reflects different social norms in the groups or whether the difference is to a large extent explained by the development over time involving an intensified public and professional debate.

The difference between the two student samples remains when a comparison is made for the judgments of each of the five cases used in both studies. The differences between the executives and the other professional groups are less clear.

As can be seen in Figure 9.9 the executives judged three cases (Cases 3, 4 and 5) more leniently than all three other groups. Case 2 'Oral Agreement' was judged about equally harshly by the executives as by the analysts and the journalists, while the executives' judgment of Case 1 'Insider Trading 1' was similar to that of the analysts, but more lenient than the judgment of the journalists and the brokers.

The role of illegality and perceived frequency

The clear tendency from the first study that those who perceived a situation as more illegal judged it as more unethical remained in the second. Among the analysts and the students all seven cases were judged significantly more harshly by those who classified the different cases as illegal. In the other groups all the results point in the same direction, but due to the small sample sizes the differences were not significant for the separate groups. Figure 9.10

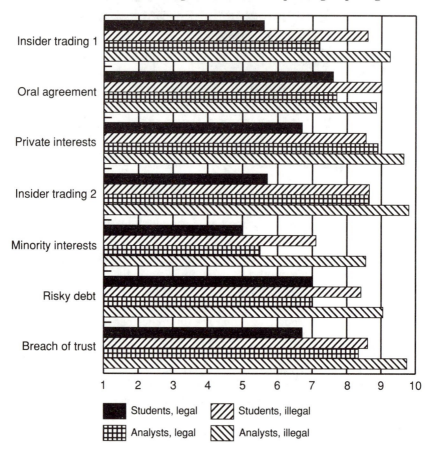

Figure 9.10 Illegality and unethicalness for the seven cases

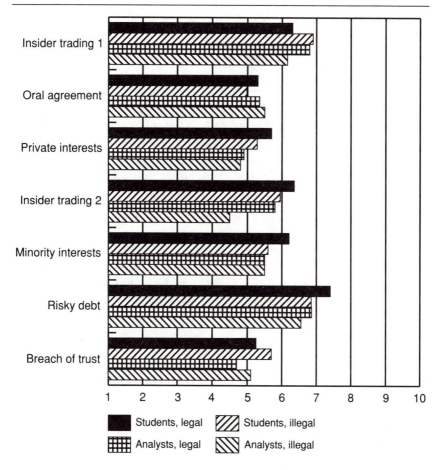

Figure 9.11 Illegality and frequency in Sweden

is based only on the largest group, the analysts. As can be seen from the figure, the differences are large and going in the expected direction for most of the cases.

In the first study the executives were found to believe that an illegal behaviour was less frequent than a legal, while the students showed an almost opposite tendency. Figure 9.11 shows that, except in two cases in both groups, both students and analysts who classified a case as illegal perceived it as less frequent than those who classified it as legal.

There was a tendency in the first study to regard the described behaviours as more frequent abroad than in Sweden, but the correlations between the estimated frequencies were very high. The perception of frequency in other Western industrial countries was highly correlated with perception of frequency in Sweden in the second study as well. This time only the students,

Table 9.2 Study 2. Regression analyses of ethical judgments with the attitude index among the independent variables. Standardized coefficients

Case	Illegaility	Sw. freq.	Group	Concern	Adj. R^2
Insider trading 1	0.428***	0.003	0.240***	0.100*	0.251
Oral agreement	0.240***	−0.064	0.006	0.064	0.055
Private interests	0.292***	0.096*	0.376***	0.079	0.252
Insider trading 2	0.394***	−0.013	0.394***	0.012	0.363
Minority interests	0.399***	0.009	0.109*	−0.001	0.153
Risky debt	0.357***	0.063	0.063	0.072	0.129
Breach of trust	0.378***	0.124***	0.325***	0.105*	0.337
Overall index	0.285***	0.102*	0.405***	0.116*	0.271

*** $p < 0.001$ ** $p < 0.01$ * $p < 0.05$

however, showed a tendency to perceive the described situations as more frequent in other Western countries. The students held six of the seven cases to be more frequent abroad than in Sweden, but the differences were very small. All groups believed that Case 6 'Risky Debt' was more common in Sweden. As mentioned above, the case deals with the problem of evaluating assets, a phenomenon much mentioned in the mass media during the data collection. In the three professional groups the difference in frequency perceptions for Sweden and other Western countries was very small and none of the groups in Study 2 showed any tendency to regard the described situations as more common now in Sweden or abroad. This may be a sign of a decreasing belief in the high ethical standards of Swedish finance as a possible consequence of the spectacular disclosures that have occurred over the last few years.

Other factors influencing judgments of unethicality

As in the first study several questions relating to background variables were asked. The samples were, however, as in the first study quite homogeneous and few background variables had any significant effect on the ethical judgments. To allow a comparison with the first study a regression analysis with the same variables as in the analysis presented above was made. The results are shown in Table 9.2.

The attitude index 'Concern' was based on the same eleven items as in the analysis of the first study (Cronbach's alpha = 0.42, which is not very satisfactory). The three professional samples were treated as one group and represented by the dummy variable group (Students = 0 and Professionals = 1).

The tendencies from the first study remain in this analysis with one exception: the role of perceived frequency. The perception of illegality contributes significantly in all cases to explaining the variance in judged unethicality. The more lenient judgments of the students are reflected in the standardized coefficients of the dummy variable. There is a tendency for the attitude index 'Concern' to have a positive influence on ethical judgment. A major difference from the first study is the influence of the frequency variable. It is not significant in five of the seven cases, and it has a positive influence on ethical judgment in the two cases where it is significant, and also on the overall index.

The adjusted R^2 ranged from 0.05 to 0.36. The largest difference in adjusted R^2 was for Case 2 'Oral Agreement', which dropped from 0.28 to 0.06. One of the new cases, 'Breach of Trust', is quite well explained by the variables used ($R^2 = 0.337$), whereas the other case 'Risky Debt' is less well explained ($R^2 = 0.129$). For the latter case, only 'illegality' gave a significant contribution to the explained variance.

In the first study, a group of 'minimalists', who saw a strong relation between legality and ethics, was found to judge the misconducts more leniently than the rest of the respondents. A similar comparison in the second study revealed no consistent differences between the minimalists and the non-minimalists.

DISCUSSION

The main purpose of the study was to explore how executives, analysts, brokers and journalists who regularly work with financial problems felt about some recent examples of unethical conduct in the world of finance and to compare them with business students with a specialization aimed at similar careers in business. It is not an attempt to study individual tendencies towards unethical behaviour. The rationale behind the study is the idea that the occurrence of unethical conduct is influenced by what one's peers think. The two studies are an attempt to find out what the present and future colleagues think about a chief executive officer's questionable conduct. In this way the study is different from most studies of ethical issues in business. As a rule the questions posed in studies ask the respondents to impersonate a decision maker and make a decision in a hypothetical situation with ethical implications.

In our studies we asked for judgments of the degree of unethicalness of behaviours that had actually occurred. If there is a tendency to judge more behaviours more unethical, this can be taken as a sign that the respondents think of the situation as unsatisfactory from an ethical point of view; does it also indicate that the respondents and their colleagues in their behaviour will be more directed by ethical considerations? This question cannot be answered on the basis of our material and it is in general a very difficult question to answer. It is likely that those who find more of the behaviours highly unethical are more inclined to discuss and influence social norms, at any rate if they are dissatisfied with the situation.

A respondent cannot be expected fully to reveal her or his own tendency towards unethical behaviour in financial affairs even if complete anonymity is assured, but he/she may reveal more or less involvement with ethical issues and concern over the state of affairs. The degree of involvement in ethical issues was measured directly by the attitude statements which were used to form an index 'Concern'. This variable gave some, though not very impressive, contribution towards explaining the variance in the judgments of unethicalness. Another indicator of involvement in ethical issues is the number of spontaneous comments in the questionnaire. In the first study, thirteen executives (15.8 per cent) and nineteen students (29.2 per cent) commented on ethics. In the second study, there were even more spontaneous comments: fifty-nine analysts/journalists (30.1 per cent), thirteen brokers (26.0 per cent) and twenty-two students (24.7 per cent) gave such comments. Since this is, in our experience, an unusually high number of comments, we tend to interpret it as a sign of high involvement in the issues.

The analyses show that the perceived illegality of the behaviour is the most important factor in explaining the judgments of unethicality. The 'Breach of Trust' case in our second study was tried in court after our data collection and the CEO was acquitted. The case will be tried later in a higher court. Will the judgments of unethicality which were very stern be influenced by the fact that the conduct has been found not to be illegal? Later studies can give an answer. The cases of misconduct that are taken to court are informative since the evidence used against the suspected perpetrators is usually available and reported on in the news media.

The behaviour in most of our cases was judged as very unethical even by those who believed it to be legal. There is thus a clear distinction between what is illegal and what is unethical: the norms are higher for what constitutes ethically acceptable behaviour. While in general illegal conduct should receive harsh judgments from peers and from the public, it cannot be excluded that the judgments may be lenient in some cases. Certain types of tax evasion seem more acceptable than many other forms of unethical behaviour, judging from the results of empirical tax evasion research (Lewis, 1982).

The role of the perceived frequency of the misconducts is somewhat puzzling. The expected negative correlation between judgments of unethicality and perceived frequency does not always appear. The estimates of frequency are relatively low which may be part of an explanation. Another part may be simply that many respondents may think that there are too many of certain misconducts.

Social norms are by definition not coded in an index that can easily be handed over to the newcomers in a profession. Some professional groups have written codes of behaviour, quite a large number of companies have written ethical policies. When the norms are explicit, they are probably known and respected by more members of a professional group than when there are no such agreed-on moral codes. When there are no written rules or when the rules do not cover a certain conduct, the question of the role of social norms becomes urgent. To what extent are there concordances in opinions among the professionals so that it is permissible to speak about existing social norms? A look at the dispersions (standard deviations) of the judgments reveals that the students have larger dispersions around the mean judgment than the others, with a few exceptions where the dispersions are similar. There is thus less agreement among them about the norms to apply. A second observation is that there are differences in the dispersions for the cases. Case 6 'Fraudulent Information', which was used only in the first study, shows less dispersion than the other cases. The fact that the conduct in a case is judged as extremely unethical is a sign that there is consensus and that there are definite social norms. When the mean judgment falls in an extreme category, it follows that the dispersion is lower.

A subsequent question is to what extent actors respect the norms. A mediating factor may be the awareness that if someone is caught with the unethical conduct, the verdicts of the colleagues will be grave or lenient. Social norms are not created by force or deliberation, they emerge. If the social norms guiding judgments of unethical behaviour are too inarticulate or inadequate, ways to change them are to start work on developing a written ethical code, stimulating discussion to bring forward opinions about actual and hypothetical cases (cf. Cicero), and making attempts to increase the awareness of ethical problems and of the fact that there are social norms.

The differences in judgments and in attitudes towards ethical issues between students and executives cannot be fully explained. Judging from the results of our analyses, students seem to rely more on law than executives. Still, the students' assessments of illegality are higher than those of the executives. This can perhaps be interpreted as a sign that the students perceive the law to be less imperative, that they have less respect for the law and believe that this is also characteristic of business. The students perceive the business world as more wicked; they believe the frequency of unethical conduct is higher than do the professionals, but at the same time they think less of the seriousness of the misconducts. They did, however, on average judge the conducts as highly unethical. Misbehaviours are judged even more severely by peers. This may have consequences if the judgments are made known in appropriate ways. A relevant observation in this context is that the attitude statement 'As boss you should serve as a good example in ethical matters' was the most endorsed attitude statement in all groups in both studies.

Practical experience in the line of business should give a better basis for estimating the frequency of a certain unethical behaviour. For certain types of unethical behaviour, perhaps most types, practical experience should also give a better feeling for the consequences of a certain unethical behaviour. In some cases, such a feeling may lead to lenient judgments, in other cases to stricter judgments. In all regression analyses the experience measures tried failed to yield any significant contributions towards explaining variance. The measures used referred to the number of years in the line of business; in the present work position, and as executive, better measures may be possible.

CONCLUSIONS

As repeatedly stated, the purpose of a study like this one is not to disclose unethical behaviour or inclinations towards such behaviour, the purpose is simply to find out about norms of business ethics by using actual cases. Like other norms they may vary over time and in space. They can certainly be influenced by events, debates and possibly also training in which ethical problems are discussed and really brought to the students' attention.

Interesting, interpretable data can be gathered through anonymous surveys. Several indicators suggest that there was a high degree of involvement in the studies. Many respondents spontaneously gave long comments which is rather unusual in surveys. The questions were phrased in a guarded way so that no one would have to reveal unethical practices in their own careers or in their firms. It may be possible to be a little blunter in some contexts, but there is a risk of an even bigger non-response.

A general conclusion is that perceived legality which presumably has some correlation with legal reality is of great import for ethical judgments. If a behaviour is believed to be illegal it is also, as a rule, judged to be highly unethical. The question is then when a conduct which is believed to be legal is judged as unethical. Using insider information is illegal in Sweden but litigation is comparatively rare, yet it is commonly judged as unethical by our respondents (comparative information on insider legislation in the UK and the USA can be found in *The Economist*, 7–13 November 1992, p. 89). On the basis of psychological thinking, it seems likely that acts undertaken to secure personal profit are more apt to be considered unethical than acts that purport to serve a purpose with less direct self-interest.

APPENDIX

Cases used in Study 1

Case 1 Insider trading 1

The chief executive officer (CEO) of a company listed on the stock exchange realizes that his company has such serious problems that, within six to nine months, it is likely to have to go into liquidation. The problems have largely arisen as a consequence of the strategy that the CEO himself has chosen to pursue. The CEO owns considerable stock in the company. The current value of this stock ownership is some millions SEK ($US1 is approximately SEK 18.00). This value is half of the corresponding value a year ago. The CEO chooses to sell his shares in the company. Six months later the company goes into liquidation.

Case 2 The sanctity of oral agreement

A small group of companies together hold the practical voting majority in a company listed on the stock exchange and make an oral agreement to carry out together a cleansing and restructuring process in the company. The restructuring is expected to require a few years. Company A which takes a leading role in the group of companies makes an official declaration that its involvement in the company is of a long-term nature. Slightly more than a year later, A faces certain problems when making its annual statement and sells the stock owned to a competitor of the jointly owned company without informing its partners. The chairman of the board of A declares that 'it was only an oral agreement'.

Case 3 The influence of private interests

The chief executive officer (CEO) of an industrial conglomerate with a parent company listed on the stock exchange is becoming interested in a new processing procedure in the energy field. For a company owned by his children, the CEO acquires the licence for the process valid among other things in Sweden. Shortly thereafter, on the initiative of the CEO, the conglomerate founds a subsidiary company for exploiting the new process. The new company acquires the right to use the licence at a very high cost. The decision is made by the board of the subsidiary company and there is no formal ground for a conflict of interest. The new process turns out to be a very costly fiasco.

Case 4 Insider trading 2

The CEO of an investment company listed on the stock exchange is anxious to motivate and to attach more closely to himself some leading staff members. He introduces the principle of offering them, before a planned purchase of a company, the chance to buy stock in the latter with a favourable loan. The purchase usually results in considerable rises in stock value.

Case 5 Minority interests

The parent company in a group of industrial companies acquires by means of shares with higher voting power slightly less than 10 per cent of the capital stock and slightly more than 49 per cent of the votes in another company listed on the stock exchange. Enough shares are distributed among 'good friends' to secure that the parent company has more than 50 per cent of the votes. The group of companies is already active in the same industry as the dominated company and there are plans to coordinate the businesses. When some leading representatives of 'the minority' (who thus hold slightly more than 90 per cent of the capital stock) complain, the CEO of the parent company threatens them that he will reproach them in a press release for having foiled the merger (which was correct from an industry point of view).

Case 6 Fraudulent information

The chief executive officer (CEO) of a rather small unlisted company tries to interest some institutional buyers to buy stock in his company. As a basis for a discussion with those he composes data on among other things the volume of orders and outstanding tenders which are not truthful. He is convinced that with larger financial resources he will be able to achieve satisfactory results. This is, however, not accomplished despite large infusions of capital and the company goes bankrupt after one-and-a-half years.

Note: The headings were not in the questionnaire.

Cases used in Study 2

Cases 1–5 from the first study and the following two new cases.

Case 6 Risky debt

The board of a commercial bank discusses the size of reservations for possible credit losses that have to be made in the current year's annual statement. The chief executive officer (CEO) argues that the conservative principles normally employed would lead to very large reservations. This would provide a more accurate picture of the bank's financial status, according to the CEO, but the reservations might affect the confidence in the financial system to such an extent that serious harm is done to the national economy. The board decides that the reservations should be done according to less conservative principles than the bank has employed in earlier years.

Case 7 Breach of trust

The chief executive officer (CEO) of company A, which is listed on the stock exchange, privately owns a large share of stock in company B. He is also a member of B's board. Shortly before B's annual statement is made public, A's CEO sells his shares in B via a stockbroker. The buyer is company A, whose chairman took the decision to buy. When A's CEO was informed about the identity of the buyer, he did not take any measures. The annual statement of B is made public shortly and the price of the stock falls drastically, since the company's finances are very weak. Six months later, the loss incurred to A by the deal is SEK 13 million.

REFERENCES

Arlow, P. and Ulrich, T. A. (1988) 'A longitudinal survey of business school graduates' assessment of business ethics', *Journal of Business Ethics*, 7, 295–302.

Bergkvist, L. (1992) 'Empirical business ethics–ethical judgments in the financial community', paper presented at IAREP/GEW Joint Conference, 27–30 August, Goethe University, Frankfurt/Main.

Bowie, N. E. (1988) 'Fair markets', *Journal of Business Ethics*, 7, 89–98.

Bullock, A., Stallybrass, O. and Trombley S. (eds) (1988) *The Fontana Dictionary of Modern Thought*, 2nd edn, London: Fontana.

Clark, J. W. S. J. (1966) *Religion and Moral Standards of American Businessmen*, Cincinnati, OH: South-Western.

De George, R. T. (1989) 'Ethics and the financial community: an overview', in O. E. Williams, F. K. Reilly and J. W. Houck (eds), *Ethics and the Investment Industry*, Savage, MD: Rowman & Littlefield, pp. 197–216.

Fraedrich, J. P. and Ferrell, O. C. (1992) 'The impact of perceived risk and moral philosophy type on ethical decision making in business organizations', *Journal of Business Research*, 24, 283–295.

Fritsche, D. J. and Becker, H. (1984) 'Linking management behavior to ethical philosophy: an empirical investigation', *Academy of Management Journal*, 27, 166–175.

Jones, T. M. and Gautschi, F. H. (1988) 'Will the ethics of business change? A survey of future executives', *Journal of Business Ethics*, 7, 231–248.

Jones, W. A. (1990) 'Student views of "ethical" issues: a situational analysis', *Journal of Business Ethics*, 9, 201–205.

Kraft, K. L. and Singhapakdi, A. (1991) 'The role of ethics and social responsibility in achieving organizational effectiveness: students versus managers', *Journal of Business Ethics*, 10, 679–686.

Lewis, A. (1982) *The Psychology of Taxation*, Oxford: Blackwell.

Moore, J. (1990) 'What is really unethical about insider trading?', *Journal of Business Ethics*, 9, 171–182.

Parkman, A. M., George, B. C. and Boss, M. (1988) 'Owners or traders: who are the real victims of insider trading?', *Journal of Business Ethics*, 7, 965–971.

Peterson, R. A., Beltramin, R. F. and Kozmetsky, G. (1991) 'Concerns of college students regarding business ethics: a replication', *Journal of Business Ethics*, 10, 733–738.

Randall, D. M. and Gibson, A. M. (1990) 'Methodology in business ethics research: a review and critical assessment', *Journal of Business Ethics*, 9, 457–471.

Russell, B. (1946) *History of Western Philosophy*. London: Allen & Unwin.

Stevens, G. E. (1984) 'Business ethics and social responsibility: the responses of present and future managers', *Akron Business and Economic Review*, Fall, 1–11.

Stevens, G. E. (1985) 'Ethical inclinations of tomorrow's managers', *Journal of Business Ethics*, 4, 291–296.

Terpstra, D. E., Reyes, M. G. C. and Bokor, D. W. (1991) 'Predictors of ethical decisions regarding insider trading', *Journal of Business Ethics*, 10, 699–710.

Wärneryd, K.-E. and Westlund, K. (1992) 'Ethics and economic affairs in the world of finance', *Journal of Economic Psychology*, 14, 523–539.

Williams, O. E., Reilly, F. K. and Houck, J. W. (eds) (1989) *Ethics and the Investment Industry*, Savage, MD: Rowman & Littlefield.

Wood, J. A., Longenecker, J. G., McKinney, J. A. and Moore, C. W. (1988) 'Ethical attitudes of students and business professionals: a study of moral reasoning', *Journal of Business Ethics*, 7, 249–257.

Chapter 10

Ethical regulation of economic transactions

Solidarity frame versus gain-maximization frame[1]

Paul E. M. Ligthart and Siegwart Lindenberg

In 1963 Macaulay was struck by the fact that business parties hesitated to regulate their transactions formally. He noticed an almost common practice to rely on 'a man's word'. His work sparked much interest in the relational aspects of contracting.

Since then, this topic has been addressed particularly by Williamson (1975, 1985). His transaction cost theory criticizes the neoclassical reliance on legally enforceable contracts. Except in some spot exchanges, people are not fully informed, and opportunistic others will exploit this strategically. This will be especially hazardous when transaction-specific investments have to be made because they retain their value only in the particular relationship. Consequently, the anonymous relation on the market needs to be replaced by an identifiable relationship between the partners. Williamson called this process of transition 'the fundamental transformation' which implies extra investments to mitigate the dependency, for instance by the exchange of hostages or through the establishment of an hierarchical relationship.

The relational perspective on contracting also drew attention to ethical regulation of dependencies. For example, Ouchi (1980) pointed to solidarity norms in clans. According to him, regulation based on solidarity also occurs in situations where individual performance takes place in a team context but is difficult to measure. In such a situation, goals other than material advantage become more important, such as maintaining a good relationship with the other members of the clan. The solidarity norms provide (some) protection against exploitation.

THE INTEGRATION OF SOLIDARITY NORMS AND GAIN-MAXIMIZING BEHAVIOUR

Introducing the relational or solidarity dimension as a separate mechanism of regulation besides market and hierarchy is useful, but also poses a problem, previously addressed by Weber (1961). Weber analysed the transition from an extreme split between the ingroup and outgroup morality to a more general normative regulation of economic transactions. He concluded that a strong form of solidarity is accompanied by opportunism *between* groups and a norm of equality *within* groups. A comparable conclusion can be drawn from more recent group categorization research based on the social identity theory (e.g. Tajfel and Turner, 1986; Brewer and Kramer, 1986). The sharp distinction between groups leaves relations between them unregulated. On the other hand the accompanying norms of solidarity within the group can be a serious obstacle to individual initiative (and thus contracting). Long-term economic relationships cannot prosper in either case. Rather, such relationships need a general form of normative regulation among all potential contracting partners.

When one introduces the normative dimension into economic transactions, one should thus not only explain when solidarity norms are advantageous (like Ouchi, 1980), but also when solidarity norms are disadvantageous for economic transactions. Such a combined approach has been suggested by Lindenberg (1988). He uses a decision-making model[2] in his solidarity theory in which gain maximization and solidarity norms appear as different frames that structure the action situation. A situation is structured by a dominant goal that determines selection and ordering of alternatives. How does this work? Given a choice situation, there are various cost and benefit aspects, each related to a potential general situational goal. In this 'competition' of potential goals one will emerge as the strongest: the one that discriminates most between alternative courses of action. This general dominant goal constitutes the frame of the decision maker and alternatives are selected and ordered in accordance with this frame. However, other aspects in the choice situation do not disappear. They affect the salience of the dominant goal and thereby the probability with which each alternative will be chosen.[3] For example, when the dominant goal is 'gain', the situation will be screened for opportunities for gain and the alternative courses of action are ordered from highest to lowest expected gain. Yet, when I do business with somebody I know quite well, the wish not to risk losing this relationship may influence the gain-frame by lowering its salience. Thereby the choice probability for alternatives that are not optimal from the point of view of maximizing gain will be increased. When the salience of a frame is low, it does not structure the situation well and it is likely to be replaced by another frame that structures the situation better. In this way, it can happen that **frame switches** occur, i.e. that conflicting goals will weaken each other as frames, a fact that will prove to be quite important for contracting, if the framing theory is right.

On the basis of these arguments, Lindenberg distinguished three relationships based on two frames. Figure 10.1 shows an outline of both frames related to the different forms of solidarity relationship and the underlying principles of the individuals' behaviour. The pure case of a totally non-exploitative relationship is one of **strong solidarity** with norms to help

FRAME	Forms of solidarity	Principle in the individual's behaviour	
		Gain-maximization	Solidarity norms
SOLIDARITY-FRAME	Strong-solidarity	Indirect	Dominant
GAIN-FRAME	Weak solidarity	Dominant	Indirect via 'signalling behaviour'
	Opportunism (no solidarity)	Unlimited	Absent

Figure 10.1 The different forms of solidarity orientation in terms of the principles of gain-maximizing behaviour and normative behaviour

the other in need, not to hurt the other, and to minimize the social distance to the other. In such a relationship, the frame is the goal to conform to the solidarity norms. The model of the totally exploitative relationship (pure opportunism) is unbridled gain maximization with no concern for the relationship and therefore no help, no restraints against hurting the other or increasing the social distance whenever that is instrumental for maximizing gain. Such a situation is thus framed by 'gain' with a very high salience.

There is an important third relationship: **weak solidarity**. It consists of the interplay of two frames: the gain-frame (the salience of which is lowered by the wish to maintain a non-opportunistic relationship) and a relational frame in which the appropriate relational signals are chosen (and the salience of which is lowered by the wish to maximize gain). The gain frame is the prevalent one but whenever claimed gain levels threaten the maintenance of a non-opportunistic relationship, the salience of gain is lowered so much by the relational goal that a frame switch occurs and the situation is structured according to the most appropriate relational signals. For example, you may make profit off an acquaintance but there are profit levels that would clearly hurt the other and thus signal an utter disregard for the relationship. Thus, in weak solidarity, a gain frame is influenced by the goal to maintain a non-opportunistic relationship and, periodically, this goal will even become the frame in which the choice of relational signals dominates the situation. What is the most important relational signal?

The relational frame is not identical to strong solidarity because the goal is only to avoid opportunistic behaviour in the other. Only one of the three solidarity norms will influence the signals: the norm not to hurt the other. This leads to equity as distributional standard. The argument is as follows. In negotiations, claims are made about the distribution of gain that is produced by the transaction (and thus by both partners together). There are mainly two aspects that influence the share a partner will claim (see Lindenberg, 1988): power-related aspects (such as alternative deals, information asymmetries, etc.) and input-related aspects (such as costs, investments, contribution to the production of the joint good, etc.). Use of power-related aspects in negotiations capitalizes on the ability to hurt the other and will thus give the wrong signals when there is weak solidarity. For this reason, weak solidarity will stress the importance of input-related aspects, i.e. equity considerations, as a legitimate base for claims.

Whereas **strong solidarity** is an effective curb on opportunism, it is bad for contracting because of its relational emphasis on helping and equality. **Weak solidarity**, by contrast, is good for contracting because it leaves gain legitimate (as long as it remains within the bounds of equity) and it discourages opportunistic behaviour. These arguments are summarized in Figure 10.1.

The solidarity theory provides a general framework for explaining the direction (positive and negative) of the effects of norms on economic behaviour. Furthermore the generality of the model consisting of two general principles (or motives) incorporates many otherwise fragmented phenomena concerning norms. This model thus avoids 'the threat of a slippery slope of a lengthy list of non-economic motives' (Kahneman et al., 1987, p. 103).

HYPOTHESES

The core prediction of the solidarity theory is that the relationship between transaction parties tempers gain maximization and it does so *differently* for a weak and a strong-solidarity frame: legitimate (equitable) profit making versus no profit making. The present study will focus on an empirical test of the framing element of the solidarity theory.[4]

In this study, the effects of the two forms of solidarity on the partition of a joint agreement space will be examined. A joint agreement space exists when the buyer offers more than the minimum selling price. Given a fixed maximum offer, the seller determines how this extra value is divided between the seller and the buyer. The solidarity theory can predict how the solidarity frame affects the partitioning of this agreement space. The seller with a strong-solidarity frame will order the alternatives according to the solidarity norms. The partition of the agreement space has the zero-sum aspect that a profit for the seller is a loss (i.e. harm) for the buyer. Thus, the preferred alternative will be the one without profit, where the selling price equals the purchase price. The individual with a weak-solidarity orientation will order the alternatives along the line of profit, but due to the impact of relational signalling, the equitable profit alternative will be highly probable. When the seller is compensated for his costs (mainly the purchase price) an equal split of the extra value is legitimate when both parties have equal input levels. The opportunistically-oriented individual also orders alternatives by profit, but now the maximum profit alternative will be on top (i.e. the buyer's maximum offer).

In the study the subjects were presented with a scenario of buying and selling a book in which the joint agreement space is 40 guilders (approximately 20 dollars). This amount results from the difference between the maximum selling price of 50 guilders and the purchase price of 10 guilders. The following hypotheses are deduced from the solidarity theory regarding the partition of this joint agreement space.

Solidarity hypothesis

(a) In the case of an *opportunistic orientation*, the subject will sell the book for a price where his profit is at its maximum: the maximum selling price of 50 guilders.
(b) In the case of a *weak-solidarity orientation*, the subject will sell the book for a price where partition of the joint negotiation space is equitable. In this scenario, the selling price would be about 30 guilders (the purchase price of $10 + (50 - 10)/2 = 30$).
(c) A subject with a *strong-solidarity orientation* will not try to make any profit. In other words, he would sell the book at cost (10 guilders).

In order to test the impact of salience, the salience of gain is varied. It is hypothesized that (**salience hypothesis**):

Subjects with a higher salience for gain will ask a higher price from the buyer than subjects with a lower salience.

THE EXPERIMENT, METHOD

Subjects. A total of 155 subjects, female and male students from the universities of Groningen and Maastricht, participated in this study. The subjects were invited in groups of six subjects. Each subject was assigned at random to one of the experimental conditions. The subjects received a compensation for their participation.

Design. The design contained one within-subject factor and two between-subjects factors. The within-subject factor 'solidarity orientation' had three levels: opportunism, a weak-solidarity orientation and a strong-solidarity orientation. The solidarity orientations were operationalized as forms of personal relations which had to be imagined by the subject. It was expected that when a subject was dealing with a stranger or with an acquaintance, he would have primarily a gain-frame. In the case of the acquaintance, the relational dimension will temper the salience of gain-maximization (weak-solidarity), making for a lower and equitable price. For the subject dealing with a good friend, solidarity norms were expected to dominate (strong-solidarity). Additional to this within-subject factor, a between-subjects factor **'salience of gain'** was introduced in the scenario. The salience of the dimension 'gain-maximization' was varied by assigning roles to the subjects. One role was the professional bookseller, who has to live off his profits (high salience), the other role was the student, who does not depend on making a profit by selling anything (low salience). The factorial design was thus as follows (the operationalizations are mentioned in parentheses):

Design:

Solidarity orientation (within subject)

(between subjects)	Opportunism (stranger)	Weak (acquaintance)	Strong (good friend)
Salience Low (student) High (bookseller)			

Besides these factors, a sequence factor was introduced to counterbalance the possible sequence effects. The three levels of the within-subject factor solidarity orientation were presented to each subject in one of the six possible sequences.

Procedure. The experiment was presented to the subjects as a study concerning books. Each subject received a booklet in which a scenario was presented. The scenario described a situation in which the subject was in a position to sell a particular book to someone who was prepared to pay, at most, 50 guilders for it.

One of the scenarios (the weak-solidarity orientation, low salience) was as follows (the italicizing of the key words is added):

The situation:

Imagine you are a *student* in this city. You advertised in the local university paper in order to sell some secondhand textbooks. *An acquaintance* phoned and told you he was looking for a particular textbook. You did not own that book, but you were willing to look for the book. The *acquaintance* was willing to pay at the most 50 guilders for the book.

Last Saturday you visited a flea-market. You noticed some stands selling textbooks. You remembered the telephone conversation and you started looking for that book. After a short time – about 5 minutes – you found the book. The book cost 10 guilders. You bought the book.

Imagine an *acquaintance* with whom you are experiencing this.

What is the first name of the *acquaintance*: . . .

The last sentence in the scenario (concerning the first name) was not asked in the opportunism condition, because the stranger was supposed to be nameless.

The scenario was followed by a questionnaire which contained questions such as the level of the selling price, the amount the subject wanted to receive for the effort of searching for the desired book, the amount of profit the subject wished to make, the subject's monetarized value of the book, the involvement with the other party. Furthermore, some questions were asked concerning the check on the experimental manipulation, such as the perceived value of profit and of the relationship itself and separately, the relative importance of each of these aspects in considering the selling price.

Following the first scenario, the subject was asked to fill in these questions again for each of the other solidarity orientations. Instead of repeating the whole scenario the subject was instructed to imagine the same situation in which another person had phoned. The three solidarity orientations were presented to the subject in one of the six possible sequences.

At the end of the questionnaire following only the first scenario, seven selling prices were presented one at a time. These selling prices were (for all subjects and in order of appearance): 20, 50, 30, 0, 40, 25 and 10 guilders. The subject was then asked for each proposed selling price about its acceptability, the amount wanted for the effort of searching for the book, and the profit wanted given the person depicted in the scenario.

At the end of the booklet the subjects were asked questions concerning how seriously they had answered the questions and how well they could imagine the different situations.

The questions varied in their response mode. Some questions required an amount of money to be filled in, other questions required an answer on a seven-point scaled bar (unipolar) with labels at the extremes (i.e. totally unimportant to extremely important), or on a nine-point scaled bar (bipolar) with labels at the extremes and in the middle. It is important to note that this last type of scale had a meaningful midpoint. For example, the scale measuring the relative importance of profit versus relationship was labelled as follows: (0) the relationship is much more important than my profit; (4.5) both are equally important; (9) my profit is much more important than the relationship. The midpoint divides the scale into two different frames and is therefore meaningful.

RESULTS

The results were analysed mainly by using the Multivariate Analysis Of Variance-module (MANOVA) in Spsspc 4.0. The significant univariate results

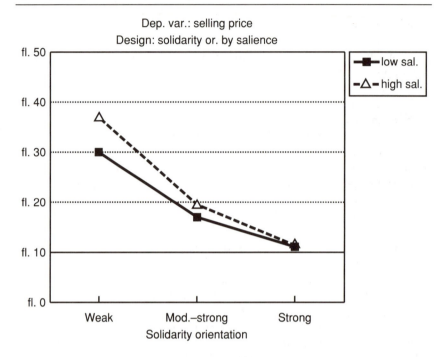

Figure 10.2 The effect of solidarity orientation by the salience of gain on the selling prices asked; the purchase price is fl. 10.–

were only taken into account if there was also a significant multivariate effect. The significance level is 0.05.

Did the experimental manipulation work the way we thought it should? In the Appendix, there is a complete description of the checks on the manipulation. Here it is enough to say that the manipulation worked with one

Table 10.1 The results of the MANOVA; dependent variable is the selling price asked by the subjects, the factors are solidarity orientation (weak, moderately strong, strong) and salience of gain (low, high)

Mult. effect	Mult. F	Sig.	Univ. effect	T-value	Sig.
Constant	1116.2 (1,150)	0.001	Solidarity	33.4	0.001
Salience	7.0 (1,150)	0.009	Solidarity	−2.6	0.009
Solidarity orientation	250.2 (2,149)	0.001	Wk–mod. str.	16.3	0.001
			Mod. str–str.	11.0	0.001
Solidarity orientation by salience	6.1 (2,149)	0.003	Wk–mod. str.	2.9	0.005
			Mod. str.–str.	1.4	0.161 n.s.

important exception: it was not possible to achieve a purely opportunistic relation. Subjects related to a stranger had a weak-solidarity orientation, whereas subjects dealing with an acquaintance and those dealing with a friend had a strong-solidarity orientation, although the former had a much lower salience than the latter. As a consequence, the opportunistic orientation was left out of the analysis and the analysis had to be carried out with the actual frame the average subject had in each condition rather than the frames he or she was designed to have. The consequences for the hypotheses will be dealt with when the results are examined. The results of two dependent variables will be examined, that is the selling price the seller (i.e. the subject) charged the buyer and the acceptability of some proposed selling prices for the seller within his or her relationship with the buyer.

The selling price. The means are depicted graphically in Figure 10.2, the results of the MANOVA are summarized in Table 10.1. The results of the MANOVA-analysis show that the solidarity orientations had a main effect on the level of the selling price. Subjects charged a higher price to a stranger (the weak-solidarity orientation) than to an acquaintance (the moderately strong-solidarity orientation). The lowest price was asked from the good friend (the strong-solidarity orientation). All univariate differences were significant (wk–mod. str.: $t(df = 151)$: 16.3, $p < 0.001$ and mod. str.–str.: $t(df = 151)$: 11.0, $p < 0.001$). These results are in line with what is predicted by the solidarity theory. The predictions of the absolute selling price are also borne out quite closely: fl. 11.52 in the strong-solidarity condition (predicted fl. 10.00) and fl. 33.47 in the weak-solidarity condition (predicted fl. 30.00).

The MANOVA results also show, as expected, a main effect of salience of gain on the selling price (mult. $F(df = 1,150)$: 7.0, $p < 0.009$). The high salience subject sold his books for a higher price than the low salience subject did. The former subject's (bookseller) mean selling price was fl. 22.95, whereas the latter subjects (students) asked fl. 19.45 on average. Although this difference is small, it is in line with the prediction from the salience hypothesis.

The interaction effect of solidarity orientation by salience of gain shows that the effect of salience (the difference between the high and low salience subjects) is much smaller when subjects had a strong-solidarity frame than when they had a weak-solidarity frame. As can be seen in Figure 10.2, the selling price of the high salience subjects drops much more between the weak-solidarity and the moderately strong orientation than the selling price of the low salience subjects ($t(df = 150)$: 2.9, $p < 0.005$). The subjects with a high and low salience of gain did not differ significantly in their decrease of the selling price between the two orientations within the domain of the solidarity frame, i.e. between the moderately strong and the strong-solidarity orientation ($t(df = 150)$: -1.4, $p < 0.161$ n.s.). This interaction effect between salience of gain and the solidarity frame was not included in the predictions, although it can be explained by the solidarity theory. According to the

Table 10.2 The means of the involvement variable by solidarity orientation (within subject) and salience of gain (between subjects)

	Solidarity orientation		
Salience of gain	Weak	Mod. str.	Strong
Low	1.87[a]	4.61[b]	6.23[c]
High	2.07[a]	4.60[b]	6.10[c]

[a,b,c] The means that have different indices differ significantly ($p < 0.05$)

framing theory, direct effects within the frame exert a greater influence than indirect effects (from outside the frame). The strengthening of the wish to make as much profit as possible is most likely in a situation where making a profit is the primary goal (frame). Thus, the difference in the importance of profit will show up more in a weak-solidarity orientation where gain is the primary goal than in a strong-solidarity orientation where solidarity is the primary goal.

This interpretation is strengthened by the fact that the differences are not due to different levels of involvement. The results for the involvement variable show no main effect (mult. $F(df = 1,150)$: 0.01, $p < 0.906$) and no interaction effect for salience of gain and solidarity orientation on the level of involvement with the other person (mult. $F(df = 2,149)$: 0.61, $p < 0.545$). As expected, the more important the normative, relational dimension is in the three solidarity orientations, the greater is the involvement with the other (see Table 10.2). The factor solidarity orientation has a main effect on the level of involvement. The conditions differ significantly from each other (the contrast between weak and moderately strong-solidarity orientation: $t(df = 151)$: -16.4, $p < 0.001$; the contrast between moderately strong and strong-solidarity orientation: $t(df = 151)$: -13.1, $p < 0.001$). Thus, the involvement differs by solidarity orientation (as expected), but not by role of the subject, which is in accordance with the theory.

To summarize, when the actual frames of the average subject are taken into account, the results concerning the level of the selling price support the solidarity and salience hypotheses. The predictions described in the solidarity hypothesis concerning the weak and strong-solidarity condition are quite close to the subjects' observed prices. Furthermore, regarding the salience hypothesis, the results support the implication from the framing theory that direct effects are stronger than indirect effects.

The acceptability of proposed selling prices. In the above section, the results were discussed in terms of the level of selling price asked by the subjects. These results showed there is indeed a (non-linear) framing effect. However, there is another method to check on the central framing hypothesis concerning the difference between the gain and solidarity frames

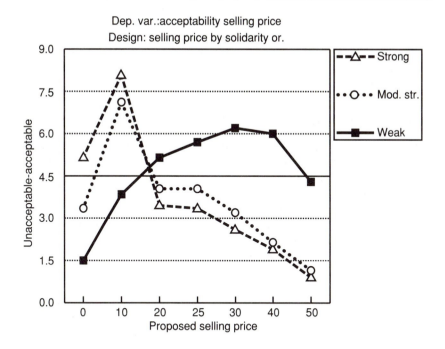

Figure 10.3 The effect of the solidarity orientation by the level of the proposed selling price on the acceptability of asking such a selling price

(see Figure 10.1): to examine the acceptability of the several proposed selling prices. A question about the acceptability of proposed selling prices was asked in the context of the first scenario. This is a between-subjects factor. Framing means that a situation is seen as qualitatively different in one frame from another frame. Thus, if there is a framing effect then the three conditions should not form a continuum. Rather, the acceptability curves for the solidarity frame (moderately strong and strong-solidarity orientation) should resemble each other and be qualitatively different from the acceptability curve for the gain-frame (i.e. the weak-solidarity orientation, in which profit was supposedly the primary goal). The means of acceptability of the proposed selling price are graphically presented in Figure 10.3. Note again the meaningfulness of the midpoint (4.5) of the scale for this variable.

Figure 10.3 indeed shows a similar pattern for the moderately strong and strong-solidarity conditions in contrast to the curve for the weak-solidarity condition. Except for the proposed selling price of 20 guilders, the means of both strong-solidarity orientations are significantly different from the means of the weak-solidarity orientation. These results corroborate the findings for the within-subject factor, that were depicted in Figure 10.2.

Furthermore, it is clear from Figure 10.3 that the selling prices the subjects find most acceptable are in accordance with the prediction for strong and weak solidarity: with a strong-solidarity orientation subjects find a proposed selling price of 10 guilders most suitable, with a weak-solidarity orientation, subjects find 30 guilders most acceptable.

SUMMARY AND DISCUSSION

This study focused on two central tenets of the solidarity theory: that the relationship between transaction parties tempers gain maximization and that a weak-solidarity relationship does so differently from a strong-solidarity relationship.

The results showed a substantial effect for the type of solidarity orientation on the level of the subjects' selling price, as well as on the acceptability of the proposed selling prices. In the weak-solidarity orientation condition, it was predicted that subjects would ask an equitable selling price (about 30 guilders). It was reasoned that these subjects structured the situation primarily according to the gain maximization but with relational signalling. Making a profit is most important to them, although the choices made are tempered by the importance placed on the relationship. The results confirmed this prediction, the subjects asked 33.47 guilders and found 30 guilders to be the most acceptable price. In the second condition, when the subjects had a strong-solidarity orientation, a selling price equal to cost price, i.e. 10 guilders, was predicted. The subjects would be primarily focused on conforming to solidarity norms and thus would avoid making profit off a friend. This too was confirmed. The mean selling price the subjects asked was 11.52 guilders and the most acceptable price was indeed 10 guilders. The prediction that in a purely opportunistic relationship subjects would ask the maximum price could not be tested. Individuals always felt some involvement with another person, even if the latter was a stranger. Thus, at least in this experiment, the purely opportunistic orientation could not be reproduced. Perhaps this does support the contention that an established market economy is permeated with weak-solidarity (see Lindenberg, 1988) and it casts some doubt on the standard assumption of a purely opportunistic orientation in micro-economics.

It should also be mentioned that the effects could have been produced by some implicit time-perspective in the relationship. People might have expected to interact more frequently in the future with a friend than with an acquaintance and a stranger. If that is so then arguments relating to the super-game literature might be important. However, in a sequel experiment (to be reported elsewhere) we did control for time-perspective and did not find pricing differences.

One aspect of the framing theory is the impact of salience of the frame on choice. This was tested by the salience hypothesis. As predicted, the subjects in the high salience condition in general valued profit more than subjects in the low salience condition. Furthermore, as could be expected, the importance of profit influenced choice much less when the frame was solidarity rather than gain. A solidarity frame really pushes profit opportunities into the background.

All in all, the experiment confirmed that relationship is an important factor which must be taken into account in economic transactions. Furthermore, the results showed that a relationship can be described in terms of two global dimensions, gain and the normative or relational dimension, and that those dimensions 'frame' situations differently. The framing theory of choice offers a coherent framework for explaining the impact of norms without denying self-interest and rational choice.

APPENDIX

Checks. The subjects could imagine the situations very well (mean 6.5; s.d. 1.5) and took answering the questions very seriously (mean 6.1; s.d. 0.7). Both variables were measured on a seven-point scaled bar. No subject had to be removed from the analysis on the basis of low scores on these variables. The means did not vary significantly between the conditions.

The six different sequences of the within-subject factor **solidarity** affected some of the dependent variables. Subjects were influenced especially in the sequences where the stranger-condition preceded the other two conditions or the good friend-condition followed one of the other conditions. In general, it appeared that the subjects reacted less extremely to the stranger if this was the first condition than the subjects who confronted a stranger in the second or third condition. However, the three scenarios were analysed independently of the order in which they were presented. All possible sequences had been used, so overall, the sequence effect was cancelled out.

The experimental manipulation was checked by looking at the variables: the **relative importance** of profit versus relationship (a nine-point scaled bar), which was measured separately and the value of the relationship, the value of profit (both seven-point scaled bars).

A direct test of the subjects' type of frame is to look at the form of solidarity orientation (operationalized as the type of relationship) and the relative importance of profit versus the relationship. The variable 'relative importance' was measured directly and describes the importance of profit over relationship (or the relationship over profit) in determining the selling price. The means are shown in Figure 10.4. Along the Y-axis the type of the solidarity frame is indicated: above 4.5, profit is more important than the relationship (weak-solidarity frame), below 4.5, the relationship is more important than the profit (strong-solidarity frame).

The results of the MANOVA analysis show a significant multivariate effect on the relative importance of the type of relationship (solidarity mult.

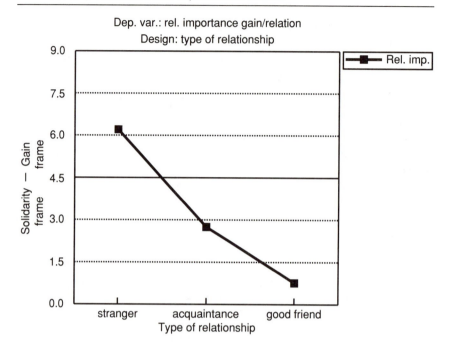

Figure 10.4 The effect of three types of relationship on the relative importance of profit over the relationship (midpoint = 4.5)

$F(df = 2,148)$: 466.3, $p < 0.001$). All three contrasts among the three types
of relationships were significant (stranger–acquaintance contrast: $t(df = 148)$: 17.9, $p < 0.001$, and acquaintance–friend contrast: $t(df = 148)$: 13.5, $p < 0.001$).

The results depicted in Figure 10.4 show that in terms of the impact, the
subject dealing with a stranger had in fact a weak-solidarity orientation rather
than an opportunistic one. The mean value (6.19) lies in the domain in which

Table 10.3 The means of the value of the relationship and the profit for the
different solidarity orientation conditions (between subjects)

Solidarity orientation	Mean value relationship	Mean value profit	n
Stranger	3.1[a]	5.0[a]	55
Acquaintance	5.3[b]	2.7[b]	50
Good friend	6.1[c]	2.3[b]	49
Overall	4.8	3.4	154

[a,b,c] The differences between the means with different indices within each column are
significant

profit is the dominant principle, but this dominance is not as extreme as can be expected in an opportunistic orientation. Furthermore, the subject related to an acquaintance actually had a moderate form of a strong-solidarity orientation (the mean value is 2.71) instead of the expected weak-solidarity orientation. The subject related to a good friend showed, as expected, a strong form of a strong-solidarity orientation (the mean value is 0.75). In short, the actual frame of the average subject in the stranger and acquaintance conditions differs from the frame he or she was designed to have according to the experimental operationalizations.

The results of the separate measurements of the value of the relationship and the value of the profit show the same pattern. The means of these variables are summarized in Table 10.3.

Both value variables have a significant multivariate effect for the type of relationship (type of relationship, mult. $F(df = 4,294)$: 38.9, $p < 0.001$). The simple effects among the three conditions show that the value of the relationship differs between all three levels of the solidarity orientation (tested between subjects; stranger–acquaintance contrast: $t(df = 103)$: -7.3, $p < 0.001$, and acquaintance–friend contrast: $t(df = 97)$: -3.9, $p < 0.001$). In other words, subjects who were in contact with a stranger valued the relationship less than subjects related to an acquaintance, and these subjects valued the relationship less than the subjects in the good friend condition.

The value of profit differs between the levels of the relationship (simple effects tested between subjects; stranger–acquaintance contrast: $t(df = 103)$: 7.9, $p < 0.001$), but there is no difference between the good friend and acquaintance conditions (acquaintance–friend contrast: $t(df = 97)$: 1.2, $p < 0.236$). As expected, the value of profit did differ between the subjects who had a low salience and those with a high salience of the frame. The high salience subjects (acting as a bookseller) placed a higher value on profit than the low salience subjects (student) (salience of gain, mult. $F(df = 2,147)$: 9.0, $p < 0.001$; univariate contrast between low and high salience ($t(df = 147)=$ -3.1; $p < 0.002$)). The means were 3.9 and 2.95, respectively.

The results of the two variables support the general tendencies which were anticipated in the use of the relational operationalizations. Along the line of stranger, acquaintance and good friend the value of the relationship increased and the value of the profit decreased. However, like the results of the variable **relative importance** mentioned above, the absolute mean values of **relationship** and **profit** suggest that even the 'stranger' relation was still constrained by some relational considerations (see Table 10.3). Subjects related to a stranger still valued the relationship at a level of 3.1 on a seven-point scale. In addition, these subjects only valued the profit at a level of 5.0 on a seven-point scale.

NOTES

1 We gratefully acknowledge Professor Dr H. A. M. Wilke for comments on the early versions of the paper.
2 This model – the discrimination model – is also tested in a more general context (see Braspenning, 1992).
3 The precise mathematical form is not central to this paper and will therefore not be presented (see Lindenberg, 1988).
4 Other hypotheses on contracting, based on the solidarity theory, have been worked out (see Lindenberg, 1988; Lindenberg and Ligthart, 1989). These hypotheses will be tested in subsequent studies.

REFERENCES

Braspenning, J. C. C. (1992) 'Framing: de prospecttheorie en het discriminatiemodel. Een empirische vergelijking en validering', dissertation, University of Groningen.
Brewer, M. B. and Kramer, R. M. (1986) 'Choice behavior in social dilemmas: effects of social identity, group size, and decision framing', *Journal of Personality and Social Psychology*, 50, 3, 543–549.
Kahneman, D., Knetsch, J. L. and Thaler, R. (1987) 'Fairness and the assumptions of economics', in R. M. Hogarth and M. W. Reder (eds), *Rational Choice: The Contrast between Economics and Psychology*, Chicago: University of Chicago Press, pp. 101–116.
Lindenberg, S. (1985) 'An assessment of the new political economy: its potential for the social sciences and for sociology in particular', *Sociological Theory*, 3, 99–114.
Lindenberg, S. (1988) 'Contractual relations and weak-solidarity; the behavioral basis of restraints on gain-maximization', *Journal of Institutional Economics (JITE)*, 144, no. 1, 39–58.
Lindenberg, S. M. and Ligthart, P. E. M. (1989) 'The effect of different forms of solidarity on economic transactions: an experimental study'. Grant proposal for the Netherlands Organization for Scientific Research (NWO).
Macaulay, S. (1963) 'Non-contractual relations in business: a preliminary study', *American Sociological Review*, 28, 55–67.
Ouchi, W. G. (1980) 'Markets, bureaucracies, and clans', *Administrative Science Quarterly*, 25, 129–141.
Tajfel, H. and Turner, J. (1986) 'The social identity theory of intergroup behavior', in S. Worchel and W. Austin (eds), *Psychology of Intergroup Relations*, Chicago: Nelson-Hall, pp. 7–24.
Weber, M. (1961) *General Economic History*, New York: Collier.
Williamson, O. E. (1975) *Markets and Hierarchies: Analysis and Antitrust Implications*, New York: Free Press.
Williamson, O. E. (1985) *The Economic Institutions of Capitalism: Firms, Markets, Relational Contracting*, New York: Free Press.

Part III

A new economics?

Chapter 11

Ethics, ideological commitment and social change

Institutionalism as an alternative to neoclassical theory[1]

Peter Söderbaum

THE CONSEQUENTIAL ROLE OF ECONOMIC THEORY

The current political debate is very much based on ideas that have been around for a long time and that often can be connected with political philosophers and economists of previous centuries. According to John Maynard Keynes, 'practical men, who believe themselves to be exempt from any intellectual influences, are usually the slaves of some defunct economist' (cf. Fusfeld, 1986, p. ix). An example of this is Adam Smith's ideas about division of labour, specialization, the market mechanism and the 'invisible hand', which is part of the thinking patterns of many politicians and business leaders. The behaviour of self-interested individuals is expected to be coordinated through the market mechanism in a way that benefits all concerned.

Keynes's argument points to the possible importance of paradigm issues in economics. But the argument is a bit simplistic. After all, 'practical men' have some choice in terms of 'defunct economists' and even a specific economist like Adam Smith may be interpreted in more ways than one. Also the one-way slavery relationship does not tell the whole story. 'Practical men', such as politicians and business leaders, are not completely powerless in relation to economists. And economists may respond to business interests or other political power groups in an opportunistic way by rationalizing and legitimizing thinking habits and behavioural patterns of various actors. Scholars may also respond to societal pressures by avoiding issues that are regarded as controversial by some groups. For instance, the simplistic economic man assumptions, utility theory, etc., of neoclassical economics can be regarded as a way of avoiding or downplaying ethical issues.

In this paper, I will therefore look upon the relationship between economists and practical men as one of mutual interdependence. It will be suggested that this interdependence can fruitfully be discussed in terms of the supply and demand of economic theory. I will even take a stand in favour of some diversity on both the supply and the demand side of the 'market' for economic theory. The quest for monopoly on the supply-side of economic theory is as easily understood as for other kinds of 'commodities'. I will, however, argue that workable competition among producers and groups of producers of economic theory is preferable from a societal and democratic point of view.

Whether a theory or paradigm is fruitful or not, or more or less useful than some other theory, is somehow related to the problems faced. Here I will choose environmental and natural resource problems as the point of departure, although I believe that the discussion of paradigms that follows is relevant for a broader range of socio-cultural issues.

Current environmental problems raise many questions concerning our ideas about wealth and progress in society. They also challenge conventional views of economics, resource management or resource allocation as well as ideas about social change and motives for human behaviour. It may be noted that considerable degradation of the environment has occurred in a period when neoclassical economics has dominated the thinking habits of many important actors on the public scene. In attempts to understand and perhaps explain the process of environmental deterioration, the dominant paradigm of economics can therefore not be ruled out for consideration. This paradigm issue has to be confronted rather than avoided. What are the alternatives to neoclassical economics? Would some unorthodox economics have done better?

ENVIRONMENT AND DEVELOPMENT AS AN EXAMPLE

Problems of environment and development have been the subject of two United Nations conferences, one in Stockholm (1972) and the other in Rio de Janeiro (1992). Some local and regional problems that were known in 1972 have been handled with some success. Other problems known at the time of the first conference, such as 'acid rain' are more serious today. Also new problem areas have been added in the period between the two conferences. The degradation of the ozone layer and possible climatic change are cases in point.

It is not possible here to go into detail about specific environmental problems. In broad and admittedly simplistic terms it can be argued, however, that the seriousness of the problems at a global level is related to the size of the human population times the average load on the environment of each individual. The latter factor is in turn connected with the life styles of individuals (with related production and consumption activities) in various parts of the world. Human activities of production, consumption, etc., are embedded in a global ecosystem or biosphere which essentially is a finite system. Physical resources are extracted from this ecosystem and pollution and waste are returned to the ecosystem. In relation to the human subsystem with physical man-made capital etc., the global ecosystem has a 'source' and a 'sink' function. These two functions are related, for instance, in the sense that a higher extraction of non-renewable resources such as oil and coal will mean more pollution and waste and thereby increased pressure on the assimilative capacity of ecosystems.

Comparing now the time of the two conferences, the global environmental situation is in many respects more serious today than it was twenty years ago. The human population on this planet has increased and is now at the level of 5.3 billion and the average 'load' on the environment from these individuals has probably not decreased. Although no one-dimensional indicator is available, the scale of human activities seems to be increasing. If there is an 'ecological space' on this planet which is limited and rather unchanging, the part of it occupied by humans is increasing in relation to other forms of biological life. That non-human life forms are losing ground is indicated, for instance, by losses in biodiversity. Some kinds of environmental degradation which are the result of human activities, like depletion of the ozone layer or climatic change, may directly affect all kinds of life and ecosystems.

The environmental and development problems faced can be described as complex. They are multifactorial and multidimensional and uncertainty is the normal case rather than an exception. Many impacts and changes involved are irreversible (for instance species lost) rather than reversible. Environmental and development issues also raise important questions about values, ethics and ideology. Individuals belonging to different cultures may differ in their ideas about and relations to nature. Other aspects of ethics concern ideas of progress and our relations to future generations. As an example, present life styles will affect the natural resource base available in the future.

How do mainstream, neoclassical economists deal with these issues that are 'new' at least in terms of the size of potential impacts? The answer is that they essentially rely on the well-established logical structure of the neoclassical paradigm and add a new field of study, 'neoclassical environmental economics' (Randall, 1987; Pearce and Turner, 1990; Tietenberg, 1992). 'Resource economics' is a label sometimes used when emphasis is on the stocks of renewable and non-renewable natural resources (cf. the 'source' aspect in the previous discussion).

It will not be argued here that this neoclassical analysis is without value in every respect. There are some environmental problems which can be illuminated through this approach, for instance those related to the use of the price mechanism as part of environmental policy. The fact that a small but increasing number of neoclassical economists now show an interest in environmental issues is also a step forward. My point is rather that there are serious limits to neoclassical analysis and that other perspectives and paradigms should be encouraged as well.

For instance, neoclassical environmental economists suggest cost–benefit analysis as the approach to value issues and project appraisal at the societal level. But if the problems faced are multidimensional, reducing this complexity to one-dimensional 'present values' by referring to money as 'the common yardstick' is questionable. Here an analysis in terms of impact profiles can be more compatible with the problems faced. Similarly, the idea that the economist knows the correct values or prices (or valuational rules) to be applied, becomes suspect if the problems faced are ethical and ideological in nature, a point that has been made by Ezra Mishan, himself an author of textbooks in cost–benefit analysis (Mishan, 1980, 1982; see also Self, 1975; Fischer, 1990).

Each such specific idea of correct prices or correct valuational rules, that permits a recommendation of the 'best' or optimal alternative from a societal point of view, obviously has a specific ideological and political content. The specific ideology of cost–benefit analysis has been identified by some as a modified version of GNP growth (or net-value added) ideology (Johansen, 1977; Elzinga, 1981). Reliance on economic growth as the main criterion of progress may not pose much of a problem for some citizens and politicians. But other groups, for instance environmentalists, are highly sceptical about such an emphasis on GNP growth. In a democracy, many ideas of progress in society rather than one should be allowed and even encouraged. Economists at the universities do not have the right to pick out one of the competing valuational views as the correct one for purposes of analysis at the societal level.

The idea of adding or aggregating impacts in monetary terms for all the individuals affected may at first appeal to our ideas of democracy but has its limits. In a case where an open landscape at a particular place is threatened, adding the willingness to pay (WTP) of each affected 'consumer' will give us a precise number in money terms but will not be of much help if the environmental problems faced are connected with the current preferences and life styles of the same consumers. Some argue that present environmental problems are symptoms of a crisis in the dominating Western world-view (Clark, 1989). If this is so, then the problems also have to be discussed at the levels of alternative ideologies, paradigms and world-views. In other words, the positivistic idea of standing outside and objectively measuring the preferences of individuals is not the only possibility for the scholar.

In a similar manner, 'economic man' assumptions applied to the consumer, the entrepreneur or (as part of public choice theory) to politicians, bureaucrats, etc., have a specific ideological content. Assuming that individuals in all possible roles are motivated by self-interest may serve the purpose of making analysis more tractable and simple but will not do much to raise issues of ethics and social responsibility in society. Rather these assumptions serve the purpose of legitimizing thinking and behavioural patterns that themselves are essential components of the problems faced.

INSTITUTIONAL ECONOMICS

The contemporary situation concerning schools of thought or paradigms in economics can be described in more ways than one. I will distinguish between Marxian economics to the left, institutional economics in the middle and neoclassical economics to the right. Also within the neoclassical school, there are some tensions between those who believe in a mixed economy and are less afraid of state regulation and Austrians who all share a strong belief in market solutions.

Criticism of the neoclassical paradigm often evokes expectations of some other perspective that is similar in its logical structure, for instance alternative ideas of what the consumer or business company is maximizing. Institutional economics – which can be traced back to American institutionalism in the nineteenth century, with Thorstein Veblen as one of the prominent figures – does not meet such expectations in all respects. Also, some heterogeneity seems to prevail, for instance in the sense that institutionalists organized in the USA-based Association for Evolutionary Economics are not always pointing in the same direction as institutionalists in the European Association for Evolutionary Political Economy.

Among European institutionalists of recent times, Gunnar Myrdal, winner of the Bank of Sweden's prize in memory of Alfred Nobel, is of particular importance in relation to this paper. Myrdal emphasized the political element in economic theory and I will here suggest that this awareness and explicitness about values and ideology in social research is a first characteristic of institutional economics.

A second characteristic of institutional research is holism and interdisciplinarity. The problems faced in our societies are not economic, sociological or psychological problems but just problems, and they are all complex and require an open attitude to other disciplines and a willingness to listen and learn. Analysis which is reductionist either with respect to scope and subject matter or with respect to approach (for instance one-dimensionality through aggregation) is questioned in favour of a broader analysis, where more factors are included and where disaggregation and the search for patterns are emphasized. The label 'institutional' may not be the best today in discriminating against other approaches. It originally referred to a willingness to include and critically examine the institutional arrangements of a specific society (organization, rules of the game and power relationships) rather than regard these conditions as exogenous and given.

A third feature of institutional analysis is its evolutionary, i.e. historical or dynamic, character. Institutionalists look for patterns in historical time (Wilber and Harrison, 1978). Patterns that are specific or unique are not necessarily of less interest than regularly occurring patterns. It is furthermore not regarded as particularly helpful to try to grasp all relevant factors in one mathematical formula, for instance one equation for the welfare of all members of a society. Rather, open-ended models are preferred where simple calculations in monetary or other terms may enter as parts of a study, i.e. represent partial analysis.

A similar open-minded attitude is seen as fruitful in relation to issues of methodology. Positivism is regarded as only one of several possibilities. Other approaches like hermeneutics and action research may serve a complementary purpose.

As the reader may understand, this open-ended view of institutionalism means that the approach has much in common with and indeed may be difficult to distinguish from some other perspectives that have been suggested as alternatives or complements to neoclassical economics. I will here refer to these other approaches as 'relatives' of institutionalism. I am thinking of socio-economics (cf. the Society for the Advancement of Socio-economics), social economics (cf. *Review of Social Economy*) and humanistic economics (cf. the *Human Economy Newsletter*). Economic psychology is another field which differs from the mainstream of economics, for instance in the sense that Herbert Simon's work on 'bounded rationality' etc. from his early contribution in *Administrative Behaviour* (1945) to *Reason in Human Affairs* (1983) has at best had a limited influence on mainstream texts. Parts of ecological economics and interdisciplinary economics can be included among the relatives to institutionalism (cf. *Ecological Economics, Journal of the International Society for Ecological Economics*, and *Journal of Interdisciplinary Economics*, respectively).

Some of the mentioned features of institutional economics will be elaborated below. I will also indicate what an institutional alternative to cost–benefit analysis may look like.

THE POLITICAL ELEMENT

As already indicated Gunnar Myrdal emphasizes the political element in economic theory and analysis:

> Valuations are always with us. Disinterested research there has never been and can never be. Prior to answers there must be questions. There can be no view except from a viewpoint. In the questions raised and viewpoint chosen, valuations are implied.
>
> (Myrdal, 1978, pp. 778–779)

Against this background, I will suggest six statements (or sets of statements) concerning the schools of thought mentioned:

1 None of the schools is purely scientific. Each contains various valuational and ideological elements. For this reason Marxists and many institutionalists already speak about their approaches as 'political economics'. But this label should rightly be used for all schools. Thus, for instance, socio-economics represents one category (admittedly a bit heterogeneous) of

political economy. (When the label political economics is sometimes used by mainstream economists, the focus is generally on subject matter that is seen as 'political', e.g. institutions, democracy, etc., and not on the ideological colouring of the analysis.)

2 The political element in all kinds of economics is one of the reasons why the idea of one and only one paradigm as being the 'correct' one should be abandoned. There have always been and will always be competing schools of thought in economics. One school may gain ground considerably in relation to another between two points in time and schools may lose all their adherents. But the Kuhnian idea of 'paradigm shift', i.e. one school completely superseding the other, seems to be less relevant for economics and other social sciences than for natural sciences. This point has been made by Alan Randall, himself a textbook writer in neoclassical environmental economics (1986).

3 Competition between paradigms and, more generally, tensions between different perspectives play an important and constructive role in research and education. It is fruitful to regard paradigms or perspectives as complementary in relation to some purposes and mutually exclusive in other cases. Therefore, a scholar's preference for one school, such as institutional economics, need not imply that this person regards all as wrong with some other school such as neoclassical economics.

4 Our decisions as scholars to rely mainly on one paradigm rather than another are partly political decisions which reflect our personal beliefs and ideologies. Empirical tests along positivistic lines can play a role in challenging, for instance, the economic man idea of neoclassical economics. However, ethical reasoning about the social fruitfulness and dangers of various ideas concerning human motives and human behaviour can be of equal importance (cf. Lutz, 1991).

5 Departments of economics are not only places for 'scientific' research and education but also political propaganda centres. To the extent that one paradigm dominates the scene at a department (or at several departments of economics in a given country) to the exclusion of other paradigms, the specific ideology or political propaganda built into the paradigm will be more influential. If as part of teaching economics it is repeatedly assumed, for instance, that companies maximize monetary profits, then the teacher is obviously not doing much to open the mind of the student for more holistic, multidimensional thinking or ethical reasoning. It can also be expected that those who are the students of economics at a certain time later will become the actors that are observed, for instance in studies of a positivistic and allegedly value-neutral kind. If these actors point to profits as the one and only goal of business activities, then the explanation may partly lie in the education previously received.

6 From the point of view of democracy, competiton between paradigms at specific departments or in a country means a sounder situation than

monopoly. Borrowing a bit from Bruce Caldwell's 'methodological pluralism' in his book *Beyond Positivism* (1982), 'paradigmatic pluralism' can be suggested as a key concept (Söderbaum, 1990). As already indicated, such paradigmatic pluralism also contains some degree of ideological pluralism, using the word 'ideology' in a broad sense.

Some of these ideas concerning economic theory in society can be brought together by applying the concepts of supply and demand at the level of economic ideas. It is possible to think of a market for economic theory or theories in a metaphorical sense (Söderbaum, 1991c). The reasons why some groups criticize neoclassical economics and call for a 'new' economics, socio-economics or ecological economics, etc., are not purely scientific reasons (whatever that may mean). It is true that there are conceptual and theoretical aspects involved but also valuational elements (to use the term preferred by Myrdal). In other words, there is a demand for alternatives to neoclassical theory. Similarly, there may be a considerable demand for parts of conventional economic theory. As already indicated, some groups of 'practical men' may be very happy with the now dominant school of neoclassical economics because it rationalizes or legitimizes their present modes of thinking and patterns of behaviour.

Neoclassical economists (just as institutional economists) at the universities have their vested interests in a specific world-view and may align themselves with 'practical men' who somehow have established a similar world-view. Coalitions or networks of a more or less conscious nature may be established. This means, among other things, that success for a new paradigm such as socio-economics (or ecological economics) will be as much a matter of public and political debate and acceptance as one of dialogue among economists and other scholars. For instance, advocates of socio-economics have to articulate a supply of economic theory and can then hope for some response not only from their colleagues in the social sciences but also from various groups in society who express a demand for the theory. Just as is the case with normal marketing activities in business, it is a good strategy to listen to the consumer. The supplier of economic theory can learn from the consumers and modify the product or assortment of products accordingly. It is quite possible that many of the best ideas to reconsider economic theory come from 'practical men' (or practical women, for that matter). In that sense, some essential inputs into economic theorizing, i.e. influence on the supply of social or economic theory is not exclusively a product of scholarly work at our departments.

TOWARDS HOLISTIC THINKING

According to the philosopher Georg Henrik von Wright, there is a tension in science generally between reductionist–mechanistic modes of thinking on the one hand and holistic–evolutionary approaches on the other (von Wright, 1986). Reductionist–mechanistic approaches have dominated physics, chemistry and biology since Isaac Newton and have succeeded in some respects. Considering especially the environmental problems now facing humankind, von Wright calls for an increased emphasis on holistic and evolutionary approaches.

A similar tension seems to prevail in the social sciences. Neoclassical economics belongs largely to the reductionist–mechanistic side of this dichotomy. The mechanistic aspect of neoclassical theory is best exemplified by equilibrium analysis in terms of supply and demand. This theory is reductionist in the sense that it is based on beliefs about far-reaching simplification and specialization as fruitful in attempts to improve efficiency of various activities or the accumulation of wealth at the micro level and in society at large. This 'propensity to simplify' also concerns the subject of economics itself. There is a tendency to believe that economics can be distinguished fairly well from other disciplines and that economic factors or impacts are distinguishable from those that are 'non-economic' (Myrdal, 1973). Economics, furthermore, can neatly be subdivided and research can be carried out in one area relatively independently of other specialities. For instance, the idea that environmental issues are best dealt with as a new speciality, neoclassical environmental economics, while leaving other subfields untouched, is highly questionable. It is a mistake to believe that economists dealing with international trade, taxes and financing or agricultural production, etc., can go on as they did before, relying on the environmental economists to deal with environmental problems.

Additional instances of simplification and reductionism relate to *ceteris paribus* reasoning, i.e. the idea of keeping all factors constant except one. Conventional economic man assumptions also reflect a tendency to simplify in the sense that the complexity of human motives is reduced to a utility function or to money income. For reasons of tractability, human beings are seen as consumers and income earners while other roles, such as being a citizen, are ruled out for consideration.

In the case of conventional cost–benefit analysis, impacts of a multidimensional nature are transformed or reduced to one-dimensional impacts. What are perceived as serious conflicts of interest by some, are transformed to harmony in calculations of optimal resource allocation. Money is regarded as a common denominator and advocates of this approach believe that they can carry out an objective and value-free or neutral analysis. It is generally believed, moreover, that analysis for public sector purposes can be limited to one sector at a time, the link with other sectors being reduced to a matter of relative monetary profitability. Marc Sagoff, a philosopher at Maryland University, argues that certain ways of conceptualizing an issue tend to conceal problems rather than address them:

The notion of allocatory efficiency and related concepts in the literature of resource economics, as I shall show, have become academic abstractions and serve today primarily to distract attention from the moral, cultural, aesthetic and political purposes on which social regulation is appropriately based.

(Sagoff, 1988, p. 6)

According to the institutionalists then, man should not be reduced to 'a lightning calculator of pleasures and pains, who oscillates like a homogeneous globule of desire and happiness under the impulse of stimuli that shift him about the area, but leave him intact' to use a phrase coined by Thorstein Veblen. The complexity of human motives should be allowed for, for instance by referring to a 'dual self' (Lutz and Lux, 1988) or a 'multiple self' (Elster, 1986). There is an 'I-aspect' for all healthy individuals but also a 'We-aspect', as suggested by Etzioni (1988). And ethical aspects of human choice and behaviour should be articulated and openly addressed rather than avoided in economic analysis. A move in this direction is also suggested by Amartya Sen (1987), former president of the International Economic Association.

Some simplification cannot be avoided in economic analysis. What should be avoided is oversimplification, and where to draw the line between the one and the other can of course be debated. Institutionalists and many other unorthodox economists point in the direction of more holistic approaches. They may agree that some specialization is useful and beneficial but they also suggest disadvantages with reductionism in its different forms and a responsibility for each individual to improve the understanding of his or her role in a broader context. Economics is a part of all social sciences which in turn are a part of all sciences. The meaning of economics is a concern for all scholars and all citizens rather than only for the economists themselves. Economists can learn from other social sciences just as scholars in other disciplines can learn from economists. The relationship between disciplines is better regarded as one of overlapping than of clear boundaries. Interdisciplinary or transdisciplinary thinking should be encouraged rather than avoided.

What then is the alternative to the monetary reductionism and ideologically closed nature of conventional cost–benefit analysis? I think that an alternative follows logically from the criticism offered. While the idea of optimality can be regarded as rather innocent at the level of one individual, i.e. when one individual is the only decision maker and the only person affected, it often becomes problematic when many decision makers are involved and many persons and interests are affected. At the level of collective decision making for a society, optimization using a specific approach such as cost–benefit analysis can only be used if the decision makers and affected parties agree about the reasonableness of that specific idea of societal evaluation. Since the typical decision situation where conservation and environmental issues are involved is one of conflicting interests and world-views, cost–benefit analysis is no longer an alternative.

In this situation the role of the analyst should be one of 'illuminating' the decision situation in a many-sided way, rather than 'solving' it. Many-sidedness in this case refers to: (1) possible valuational standpoints or ideologies, (2) alternative courses of action, (3) impacts (non-monetary as well as monetary), and (4) activities and interests affected. The approach is disaggregated rather than aggregated in the sense that impact profiles or impact patterns are presented rather than one-dimensional figures in monetary terms. Rationality is no longer a matter of maximizing or minimizing one variable subject to constraints but rather a matter of pattern recognition. As human beings we are able to recognize a friend in the street, we can recognize a large number of symbols and words (Simon, 1983, pp. 25–29), buildings, plants, ecosystems, etc. We often have clear visual ideas of buildings or landscapes that we like or dislike.

According to the philosophy here indicated, the conclusions of the analyst will be conditional rather than absolute. Valuational standpoint A may point to one alternative as the best whereas valuational standpoint B may be compatible with the impact profile of some other alternative. A more holistic idea of rationality emerges. The specific ideological profile of decision maker D1 is matched against the impact profiles of each alternative with the purpose of looking for the best possible fit. Decision maker D2 should similarly look for the best fit and a set of decision makers, for instance belonging to different political parties, may then vote according to the usual majority principle.

Positional analysis (Söderbaum, 1987) is one approach of the kind indicated which has been applied to decision situations concerning land use, transportation, energy systems, etc. But also some forms of systems analysis or policy analysis emphasize compatibility with democracy and try to avoid the traditional expert role of 'solving' the problem. In relation to environmental problems, environmental impact statements (EIS) is a case in point. This approach, however, may be limited in scope to a specific kind of impacts and is not 'many-sided' in the sense of illuminating all kinds of impacts.

The idea of illuminating a problem or decision situation for all parties affected and all decision makers means that the analysis is as much an input into a public dialogue as a basis for decision making. Illuminating conflicts between various activities, interests and interested parties may also be a basis for reconsideration of values and ideologies among decision makers. This is a situation which is very different from the usual neoclassical attitude of regarding values as exogenous and given.

METHODOLOGICAL AND IDEOLOGICAL PLURALISM

Positivism is still the dominant epistemological position among neoclassical economists. This philosophy has lost ground among philosophers and some groups of unorthodox economists. Bruce Caldwell's methodological pluralism seems to be a preferable position to methodological monopoly for one approach. Such a move from monism to pluralism will open up for differences in purpose. Institutionalists, for instance, do not regard explanation, i.e. identification of causality based on the testing of hypotheses, as the only road to useful knowledge. Neither is prediction accepted as the only criterion of success in scholarly work. Instead understanding and the revealing or uncovering of patterns is a better description of the purpose of institutional analysis.

Without abandoning old ideals of objectivity in some situations and for some purposes, institutionalists try to be conscious and open-minded about the subjective factors of the scholar (cf. Myrdal, 1969). Intersubjective confirmation of information or knowledge is certainly of importance but it should also be recognized that knowledge in the social sciences is always in some respects personal knowledge. As already indicated there is furthermore an ideological and political aspect of knowledge and research activities. In response to this problem, Myrdal recommends an open declaration of valuational standpoints in scholarly work. As already indicated, in some situations, the analyst can try to consider more than one valuational standpoint and refer to conditional (rather than absolute) conclusions in relation to such possibilities.

A related issue has to do with the subjectivity of the actors under study. Here interpretative approaches like hermeneutics, often used in the humanistic disciplines, can be considered as well as action research (where the scholar learns by participation). If the research purpose is to understand what goes on in society, interpretative approaches should by no means be excluded. An example from the environmental field will make this point clear.

In most countries, there are examples of environmental conflict. What is the proper role of economists in relation to such conflicts? A case in point is a planned motorway between Oslo in Norway and Hamburg in Germany, the so-called Scan-Link. Two years ago, students at the Technical University of Gothenburg wanted to debate this issue. They called in representatives of the Scan-Link consortium, i.e. those who were in favour of the project, as well as experts and laymen representing those who opposed the project. In addition a clergyman was present to discuss the ethical issues involved and the present writer was called in as an economist from a different part of the country. I understood afterwards that one of the organizers expected me to critically evaluate the issue in terms of cost–benefit analysis. Was the Scan-Link project profitable in a monetary sense or not? Were there more profitable alternatives?

I could say a few words also in the conventional terms indicated, but my main strategy was one of trying to understand the development concepts or ideas of progress of the two opposing parties. It was striking how the developers reasoned in conventional economic terms of GNP growth, investments in infrastructure, international competitiveness and the just-in-time principle. This was an application of the ideology of the European Round Table of Industrialists, where car manufacturing companies like Volvo have a role. The opponents of the project emphasized some version of ecological ethics pointing to the unhealthy state of forests and other ecosystems in the area and our responsibilities to future generations. They questioned unchecked internationalization, suggesting that some degree of self-reliance is a positive value. While not opposing improvements of roads altogether, they suggested that investment in railway transportation was a preferable alternative.

The two opposing parties, especially the developers, accepted my interpretation of the two views of progress in society. They also accepted my point that there is no value-neutral way to find out the optimal 'solution' from a societal point of view. Conventional cost–benefit analysis is – as already noted – part of a specific ideology which can be described as a modified version of a value-added or GNP-growth ideology. Applying cost–benefit techniques therefore is close to taking a stand for GNP growth as the main societal objective. (It can be added that the Scan-Link project under discussion was shown to be unprofitable when cost–benefit techniques were applied. The project was accepted by the Swedish government as part of negotiations with Volvo, ruling out even the normal evaluating procedures of the Swedish Road Planning Agency.)

It is striking how the view taken by the consortium is easily expressed in terms of mainstream neoclassical economics, while the opponents get little help from conventional economics in articulating their view. Ecological ethics and self-reliance are not taken seriously by the average neoclassical scholar. The discussion about sustainability, following the Brundtland Report (World Commission, 1987) is regarded as confused or interpreted to make it fit into the established world-view of neoclassical economics as 'sustainable GNP growth' or as not reducing the total stock of wealth of a society as measured in monetary terms (Mäler, 1990).

A different way of responding as an economist is to enter into a dialogue with environmentalists and help them in their attempts to articulate a different development view and, if possible, the rudiments of a different economics. There is a demand for ecological economics, i.e. a partly different language of economics, and the thinking behind this demand is not necessarily inferior to the well-established thinking habits of the average conventional economist.

Few scholars in economics and other social sciences are completely unemotional, objective and value-neutral in relation to the 'object' under study. A final epistemological issue then concerns such subjective commitments of the student. Pure positivists would probably deny or downplay emotional relationships of any kind to the subject matter under study. Statements about the existence of such commitments would be interpreted as signs of a low scientific quality. Without denying possible problems with subjective engagement in relation to particular issues, I will here contend that subjective engagement of the scholar is often an asset rather than something to be minimized. Those who, like environmentalists, are engaged in specific societal issues, may understand the problems better than those who claim to be uncommitted. And no healthy person is uncommitted in every respect. Those who bother less about environmental problems may bother more about specific theories and methods. Is obedience to neoclassical economics as a commitment necessarily less problematical than engagement for the survival of humankind on this planet? Is survival less respectable than economic growth in simplistic terms as a purpose for research in economics and other social sciences?

IDEOLOGICAL COMPETITION AND NETWORKING AS ELEMENTS IN SOCIAL CHANGE

As part of the so-called public choice literature, neoclassical economists have in recent times shown an increased interest in institutional arrangements. Instead of interest being limited to consumers and producers of goods and services, Economic Man-assumptions are extended to new categories of actors such as bureaucrats and politicians. Bureaucrats are assumed to assert their self-interest in terms of prestige, which may be connected with the budget that they control, whereas politicians are expected to maximize their votes.

The model of social change that emerges is one where various actor-categories, such as farmers or labour unions, engage in rent-seeking activities, i.e. try to increase their share of the total pie in terms of monetary income through negotiations, lobbying, etc. Success in these rent-seeking activities is expected to depend on success at organizing oneself. It is predicted that relatively small groups, in which each individual has a lot to gain or lose, e.g. farmers, will be more successful than large groups with more diffuse interests, such as citizens with a concern for the environment (Olson, 1965, 1982). Clearly this theory does not offer much hope for the environment. Economics, once more, stands out as the dismal science.

There are some useful features about the public choice approach. It points to the presence of self-interest and egoistic motives in all kinds of human behaviour. Ideas of politicians or bureaucrats as exclusively serving the people or as completely altruistic lose ground. In this sense, models built on rent-seeking behaviour certainly have some explanatory value.

But such simplistic models fail to recognize the complexities of human life and behaviour. Alternatively, it may be assumed, as already indicated, that man is a complex being with incessant tensions between various egoistic and other related motives. Human beings have many roles and take part in many activities, i.e. are related to many interests rather than to one. Farmers are not only farmers and bureaucrats are not only bureaucrats. A farmer may certainly be a member of a farmers' union, but he or she is also a citizen and a consumer. In addition, he or she may be a parent and perhaps an organized environmentalist. It can furthermore be assumed that our farmer practises organic farming. All these different ambitions are parts of a valuational or ideological orientation. Similarly, a bureaucrat may have his or her particular ideological orientation comprising many interests rather than just one.

It may well be that two individuals, who in conventional public choice terms are assigned to different actor-categories, such as farmer A and bureaucrat C, are closer to each other in terms of ideological orientation than farmers A and B (cf. Söderbaum, 1991a, 1991b). Individuals with a similar ideology, such as the ecological ethics orientation previously discussed, may join together in network-building for a sustainable society and to compete with groups of actors, characterized by a more conventional value orientation. In this manner, social change is no longer limited to a matter of narrow and shortsighted behaviour of the rent-seeking kind. It is argued that the actor-network model indicated improves our understanding of social change compared to a situation with only the conventional public choice theory. At the same time some hope is given to those of us who take the environment seriously.

CONCLUDING COMMENTS

Few would deny that markets can function as a very beneficial decentralizing mechanism in a society. At times one can even share the enthusiasm of all those who believe in Adam Smith's invisible hand. But the realities of environmental and socio-cultural problems makes me argue in favour of hands that are made visible as often as possible. Prices do not tell the whole story and price signalling is only part of the functioning of an economy.

In most cases, the prices at which goods and services are sold and purchased do not reflect the costs of third parties, for instance environmental costs. In OECD countries, governments have accepted the 'polluter pays' principle but the implementation of this principle is still in its infancy. One explanation of this reluctance to use environmental charges or taxes to modify the functioning of the market may lie in a strong belief in the invisible hand of Adam Smith. Many economists and practical men and women seem emotionally to prefer Smith's simplistic message.

In this essay, I have suggested that the issue of world-views and paradigms cannot be avoided if we want to approach environmental and other contemporary issues in a rational way. I have emphasized pluralism and competition between advocates of various perspectives rather than monopoly. There is a choice in terms of paradigms, and knowledge about the options is indispensable.

Another theme in this paper relates to the importance of ethical or ideological issues. It has been argued that the economist should participate, together with philosophers and colleagues in the social sciences, in attempts to articulate conventional and alternative ideas of development and progress. How can we assist in articulating the meaning of ecological ethics or ecological sustainability? The role of the economists in public debate is then different from the neoclassical view that values are exogenous and given and should be measured as they are, for instance as part of cost–benefit analysis.

Little will happen to prices or in terms of technology if values and attitudes remain the same. If we want to cope with environmental problems, all possible parts of the problem have to be scrutinized. Prices and market forces will play a role, but in addition to 'price-signalling' there is 'word-signalling' and public debate which may be even more fundamental. There is voice in addition to exit as suggested by Hirschman (1970) and ideological or valuational debate is probably at least one of the keys to a sustainable future.

NOTE

1 Paper presented at the conference 'Interdisciplinary studies of economic problems', Stockholm School of Economics, 16–19 June 1991.

REFERENCES

Caldwell, B. (1982) *Beyond Positivism. Economic Methodology in the Twentieth Century*, London: Allen & Unwin.

Clark, M. E. (1989) *Ariadne's Thread. The Search for New Modes of Thinking*, New York: St Martin's Press.

Elster, J. (ed.) (1986) *The Multiple Self*, Cambridge: Cambridge University Press.

Elzinga, A. (1981) 'Evaluating the evaluation game: on the methodology of project evaluation. With special reference to development cooperation', Stockholm: Swedish Agency for Research Cooperation with Developing Countries (SAREC), Report R1.

Etzioni, A. (1988) *The Moral Dimension. Toward a New Economics*, London: Collier-Macmillan and New York: Free Press.

Fischer, F. (1990) *Technology and the Politics of Expertise*, London: Sage.

Fusfeld, D. R. (1986) *The Age of the Economist*, Glenview, IL: Scott Foresman.

Hirschman, A. O. (1970) *Exit, Voice and Loyalty*, Cambridge, MA: Harvard University Press.

Johansen, L. (1977) *Samfunnsökonomisk lönnsomhet. En dröfting av begrepets bakgrunn og innhold*, Industriökonomisk Institutt, Rapport nr. 1. Oslo: Tanum-Norli.

Lutz, M. A. (1991) 'Emphasizing the social: social economics and socio-economics', *Review of Social Economy*, vol. 38, no. 3, 303–320.

Lutz, M. A. and Lux, K. (1988) *Humanistic Economics*, New York: Bootstrap Press.

Mishan, E. J. (1980) 'How valid are economic evaluations of allocative changes?', *Journal of Economic Issues*, vol. 14, no. 1, 143–161.

Mishan, E. J. (1982) 'The new controversy about the rationale of economic evaluation', *Journal of Economic Issues*, vol. 15, no. 1, 29–47.

Myrdal, G. (1969) *Objectivity in Social Research*, New York: Random House.

Myrdal, G. (1973) *Against the Stream. Critical Essays on Economics*, New York: Random House.

Myrdal, G. (1978) 'Institutional Economics', *Journal of Economic Issues*, 12, 771–783.

Mäler, K.-G. (1990) 'Sustainable development', in *Sustainable Development, Science and Policy*. Bergen, 8–10 May, Conference Report. Norwegian Research Council for Science and the Humanities, Oslo.

National Center for Food and Agricultural Policy (1986) Annual Policy Review, Washington DC: Resources for the Future.

Olson, M. (1965) *The Logic of Collective Action. Public Goods and the Theory of Groups*, Cambridge, MA: Harvard University Press.

Olson, M. (1982) *The Rise and Decline of Nations. Economic Growth, Stagflation, and Social Rigidities*, New Haven: Yale University Press.

Pearce, D. W. and Turner, R. K. (1990) *Economics of Natural Resources and the Environment*, Hemel Hempstead: Harvester Wheatsheaf.

Randall, A. (1986) 'Institutional and neoclassical approaches to environmental policy', in T. T. Phiggs, P. R. Crosson and K. A. Price (eds), *Agriculture and the Environment*, 7, pp. 205–224.

Randall, A. (1987) *Resource Economics. An Economic Approach to Natural Resource and Environmental Policy*, 2nd edn., New York: Wiley.

Sagoff, M. (1988) *The Economy of the Earth. Philosophy, Law, and the Environment*, Cambridge: Cambridge University Press.

Self, P. (1975) *Econocrats and the Policy Process. The Politics and Economics of Cost–Benefit Analysis*, London: Macmillan.

Sen, A. (1987) *On Ethics and Economics*, New York: Blackwell.

Simon, H. A. (1945) *Administrative Behavior*, New York: Free Press.

Simon, H. A. (1983) *Reason in Human Affairs*, London: Blackwell.

Söderbaum, P. (1987) 'Environmental management. A non-traditional approach', *Journal of Economic Issues*, 21 (March), 139–165.

Söderbaum, P. (1990) 'Neoclassical and institutional approaches to environmental economics', *Journal of Economic Issues*, vol. 24, no. 2 (June), 481–492.

Söderbaum, P. (1991a) 'Actors, roles, and networks: an institutional perspective to environmental problems', in C. Folke and T. Kåberger (eds), *Linking the Natural Environment and the Economy. Essays from the Eco-Eco Group*, Dordrecht: Kluwer, pp. 31–42.

Söderbaum, P. (1991b) 'Environmental and agricultural issues: what is the alternative to public choice theory?', in Partha Dasgupta (ed.), *Issues in Contemporary Economics*, vol. 3, Policy and Development. (International Economic Association conference, vol. 100), 2, pp. 24–42, London: Macmillan.

Söderbaum, P. (1991c) 'Supply and demand of economic theory', *Methodus. Bulletin of the International Network of Economic Method*, vol. 3, no. 1 (June), pp. 124–128.

Tietenberg, T. (1992) *Environmental and Natural Resource Economics*, 3rd edn, New York: Harper-Collins.

Von Wright, G. H. (1986) *Vetenskapen och förnuftet* (Science and Reason), Stockholm: Bonniers.

Wilber, C. K. with Harrison, R. S. (1978) 'The methodological basis of institutional economics: pattern model, story telling and holism', *Journal of Economic Issues*, 12 (March), 61–89.

World Commission on Environment and Development (1987) *Our Common Future*, Oxford: Oxford University Press.

Chapter 12

Interpersonal relations
A disregarded theme in the debate on ethics and economics

Benedetto Gui[1]

INTRODUCTION

In a recent speech the French philosopher Paul Ricoeur (1991) gave the following definition of 'personal ethos': 'aspiration to a thorough life; with and for others; within just institutions'. He then better specifies the three dimensions of this definition as: (1) 'self-esteem', as a necessary precondition for a responsible relationship with others; (2) solicitude for the other, to be intended as a 'you', following a 'recognition' of similarity ('friendship', 'amity'); (3) the relation with the other, intended as 'everyone' ('justice').

Scholarly work by economists on 'ethics and economics' has mainly investigated the third dimension of this 'ternary structure': the 'institutional dimension'. There exists, in particular, a large literature that deals with redistributive issues, and examines the relation between some notion of 'justice' and other key systemic attributes such as freedom and efficiency (see for example Schokkaert, 1992).

I will not try to develop the first dimension, which is inside the self, although I agree with Ricoeur that it is also important, even in the economic sphere. Indeed, apart from some exceptions,[2] the man of economics is still the 'economic man', that is a static and monolithic entity that lacks most of those features that make the study of human behaviour fascinating, such as: value conflicts, preferences that evolve in dialogue with others, the inner desire of personal realization, and so on.

In this paper I will focus instead on the second dimension of ethics, concerning face-to-face, interpersonal relations. The second section documents the disregard for this dimension on the part of economic theory, even when ethical issues are explicitly raised. Then, in the third section, I argue that the negative effects of selfish behaviour in interpersonal relations represent an additional reason for questioning – even on consequentialist and welfarist grounds, common in economic theory – the traditional tolerance towards selfishness on the part of this discipline. Finally, the fourth section sketches some implications of the inclusion of 'relational goods' among economic goods.

THE DISREGARD FOR INTERPERSONAL RELATIONS IN ECONOMIC DISCOURSE

As is well known, economics has seldom suffered from an excess of idealism in describing the moral attitude of individuals. Francis Edgeworth was particularly explicit in this regard when he stated: 'The first principle of economics is that every agent is actuated only by self-interest' (1881, p. 16).

Although in the majority of theoretical works the usual assumption is one of maximizing individual utility – with utility only depending on one's consumption – several attempts can be found at enlarging the motivation of agents on the social side, so as to better understand otherwise unintelligible phenomena, first of all donations. However, as I will try to show, the normal habit of economists remains treating relations among agents as relations 'at arm's length': a genuine human relation with the other 'yous' involved does not enter the picture.[3]

Altruism in the marketplace: irrelevant, or even detrimental?

An extreme example in this regard is provided by Philip Wicksteed (1910), who was trying to defend the economic discipline from the charge of describing people as irreducibly egoistical, but in doing so, paradoxically, formulated the crudest exclusion of 'solicitude' from the field of study:

> The specific characteristic of an economic relation is not its 'egoism' but its 'non-tuism'. . . . What makes an economic transaction is that I am not considering you except as a link in a chain, or considering your desires except as a means by which I may gratify those of somebody else – not necessarily myself. . . . The economic relation does not exclude from my mind everyone but me, it potentially includes everyone but you [pp. 180 and 174].

'Non-tuism' is not only seen as a positive characteristic of economic transactions that would distinguish them from other types of social interaction; it is also recommended on normative grounds. David Collard – the author of a book on 'nonselfish economics' – rephrases Wicksteed's position as the claim that 'unselfishness is not relevant to the process of exchange'. And adds: 'This is an enormous advantage from the informational standpoint and certainly saves one from continuous anxiety about the indirect effects of one's daily market behaviour' (1978, pp. 25–26).

Taking into consideration the goals or the preferences of our partners in economic transactions – this view implies – would impose additional costs of information collecting and processing, but would not improve at all the allocation of resources. In fact – Collard continues, citing Archibald and Donaldson (1976) – 'optimality is attainable in the everyday world in which we do not even know the names of all our fellow-citizens, much less their preferences'.

The fear of these authors is that unselfishness would introduce extraneous decision criteria into the market mechanism, whose alleged efficiency in allocating private goods rests on decentralized choices based only on prices and individual preferences: concern for others in the exchange process might interfere with the market logic and prevent prices from acting as reliable signals of the relative scarcity of the various goods with respect to citizens' needs. This is why a cold attitude in economic transactions – as in front of the shelves of an ideal unmanned department store – represents the ideal standard of economic behaviour. This attitude could well – or, some authors say, should – be combined with the altruistic willingness to transfer purchasing power to the poor; however, this should occur outside of the marketplace and, in a sense, subsequently. It is just this view that inspires the following neat sentence of Nobel prize winner James Meade, a scholar who cannot be charged with social unconsciousness:

> In my view the ideal society would be one in which each citizen developed a real split personality, acting selfishly in the market place and altruistically at the ballot box . . . it is, for example, only by such 'altruistic' political action that there can be any alleviation of 'poverty' in a society in which the poor are in a minority.

> (1973, p. 52)

Whether the transfer of wealth to the poor should take place through the state budget, authorized by people's votes, or through voluntary philanthropy – a possibility that Collard carefully examines – is at this point a secondary question.[4] In this view the only issue of ethical relevance is income distribution, or, if one prefers, distributive justice. As I said in the introduction, the third dimension of ethics, that of just institutions, seems to exhaust the economist's concern.

Altruism in the marketplace: beneficial?

The above view is not satisfactory for at least two reasons. First of all, it completely disregards the role played by interpersonal relations in social (and therefore also economic) life, a point that I will develop in the next section. Second, this view overestimates the ability of market interactions among selfish agents to assure an efficient production and allocation of material goods.

The circumstances under which 'markets fail' are several, but ethical discussion has only addressed some of them, first of all the case of public goods – those that, once produced, benefit several people at the same time. Here the link between payment and benefit that characterizes market allocation of private goods, is broken, so consumers have little incentive to contribute to their cost. When compulsory contribution is unfeasible (as often occurs), if these public goods are to be produced voluntary provision is the only possibility, and in some cases is an effective one. However, voluntary contributions are largely incompatible with a narrow self-interested motivation.[5] Here is a typical instance in which, on both positive and normative grounds, one has to take into consideration broader individual motivations. In fact, in an increasing number of writings that address the issue of voluntary contributions to public goods, reference is made to internal drives that counter untrammelled self-seeking. See among other proposals: Sugden's (1984) theory of reciprocity, that assumes a moral commitment not to give less than others do; Margolis's (1982) idea that people devote a share of their income to society's good; Kantian ethics (e.g. Bordignon, 1990); a desire for 'social approval' (Hollander, 1990); Higgs's (1987) hypothesis that individuals align their own perceived identity to the standards of the community. Notice that these lines of reasoning imply a significant amendment of the research programme, particularly common among economists, that explains differences in individual behaviour in terms of external conditionings (rewards, punishments, prices, prohibitions), while prudentially assuming universal individual selfishness.

Another instance of market failure that lends itself to introduction of ethical considerations is asymmetric information: the more informed party (the seller, the borrower) can take undue advantage of the less informed party (the buyer, the lender) by misrepresenting the truth. Here individual behaviour has first of all an immediate direct effect on a well-identified other and on the quality of the interpersonal relation between the two parties. However, this face-to-face aspect is not explicitly considered in economic discourse. The focus, in fact, is not on the actors directly affected, but on the (indirect) effects that each pattern of individual behaviour exerts on the society-wide equilibrium. The concern is about the inefficient loss of opportunities for trade caused by widespread (and therefore anticipated) dishonesty. The following sentences clearly reveal this attitude.

> One of the characteristics of a successful economic system is that the relations of trust and confidence between principal and agent are sufficiently strong so that the agent will not cheat even though it may be 'rational economic behavior' to do so.

(In the light of nearby sentences, 'successful' means 'efficient'.[6])

> Norms and rules thus act as constraints which are advantageously respected. No society without a moral order can function and survive in competition with other societies with more moral order.

(Brunner, 1987, p. 377)

A similar attitude can also be found in Schotter (1981), Johansen (1977) and Yaari (1991) among others. Paraphrasing an auto-ironic sentence of George Stigler, one could say that 'the economist is a person who, reading of the mugging of an old woman, laments the additional expenditure in crime prevention that this will cause in the future'.[7]

In some instances of asymmetric information, selfishness is not a path to an efficient outcome. Certain actions may benefit some individuals, at the same time improving overall efficiency, whereas they can only be recognized or taken by others with more information or better access to the appropriate transactions. If the transaction costs of setting up a satisfactory agency relationship between the uninformed (the principal) and the informed (the agent) are prohibitive, the agent's concern for the uninformed will lead to improved overall efficiency.

An inadequate concept of altruism

As I said above, more and more often the traditional assumption of self-seeking is questioned, and some form of concern for others is introduced into economic discourse. In various cases an explicit reference to 'altruism' is found. However, not even here fully-fledged interpersonal relations enter the scene: the notion of altruism that is adopted is inadequate with this regard. This explains why some paradoxical results are obtained when face-to-face benevolent interactions are the object of study.

A look at a recent article by Bernheim and Stark (1988) on altruism in the family, published in the influential *American Economic Review*, clarifies these statements. As is common in the economic literature,[8] altruism is modelled by having the utility of agent B depend on agent A's utility, in addition to agent B's own consumption, and vice versa. In this way altruism reduces to a mere passive interdependence in utilities (B would be disturbed by A's unhappiness, and vice versa), which are ultimately derived from consumption. Thus, if we keep income transfers out of the picture, the problem of a woman who is looking for a partner consists in choosing one with whom this passive utility link works best (from her point of view). This is why a woman with low 'felicity' (the satisfaction derived from own consumption) might prefer, *ceteris paribus*, to choose a less altruistic partner: in fact – the authors explain – so he will suffer less from her unhappiness, then will be less depressed, and therefore the negative feedback on her utility will be smaller.[9] The disregard for the genuinely relational aspect of the situation considered is astonishing. So we are taught that, when one is hurt by misfortune, the partner's sympathy is in itself irrelevant; the recipe for happiness – or for less unhappiness – is having at one's side an unconcerned, and therefore content, partner.

The inadequacy of this concept of altruism for understanding the kind of complex relations the two authors dare to tackle, also emerges from the analysis carried on in section 2B of the same article. Here, in a 'prisoner's dilemma' situation in which agents have to choose between 'cooperation' and 'non-cooperation', altruism does not affect at all the agent's attitude towards cooperation as such, but only the appreciation for the consumption of the other agent. Hence the paradoxical result that more altruistic agents may be less successful in sharing their endowments of consumption goods than less altruistic ones. Imagine that the two agents consume two goods, one of which is monopolized by A while the other is monopolized by B, and that they cannot rely on exchange contracts. Each agent prefers to consume more of each good, but also prefers a more balanced combination of the two goods. Here non-cooperation means that each (altruistic) player decides independently the share of the good he possesses to be donated to the other, according to his own preferences. Unless altruism is extremely strong, the resulting equilibrium entails an unbalanced (and therefore inefficient) division of the two goods. Cooperation, instead, entails pooling the two baskets and splitting them equally, a fully efficient allocation. The problem, as usual with such games, is how to sustain cooperation, given that each agent is subject to the temptation to defect while the other cooperates, which would give the defector a larger combination of goods. Repetition of the game can induce cooperation, but only under certain circumstances. It all depends on a comparison between the utility gain associated with defection now, and the utility loss associated with the consequent retaliation by the other player in future periods. How, then, does the degree of altruism affect the no-defection condition? On the one hand, higher altruism reduces the threat of stopping cooperation (the more altruistic the players, the less far from an equal division is the non-cooperative equilibrium); on the other hand, greater altruism also reduces the temptation (more altruistic players weigh less their own consumption relative to that of the other). The authors show that for certain values of parameters the former effect dominates the latter, which means that altruism may reduce the chances of obtaining cooperation.[10]

THE IMPORTANCE OF INTERPERSONAL RELATIONS EXTENDS TO ECONOMIC LIFE

Are we sure, this is my point, that we are not forgetting something important: the quality of interpersonal relations among agents? One could object that economics only deals with the sphere of material goods, which would justify its disregarding interpersonal relations. However, we must recognize the increasing share of services in household expenditure, many of which are largely immaterial and often relational (think of commercial entertainment, not to speak of a session with a psychologist). The borderline between such activities, usually included in the economic sphere, and other allegedly non-economic activities, such as a gathering with acquaintances or a conversation with a friend, is clearly blurred. The relation of substitutability that clearly holds between the former and the latter suggests that drawing conclusions regarding the desirability of an economic course of action, without taking into account interpersonal relations, is unwarranted. This applies very well to a recent article by Arnott and Stiglitz, where they point out some undesirable allocative effects of group solidarity. During their detailed formal analysis they ignore the fact that solidarity can have direct utility effects; it is only in the conclusion that they let the doubt come forth that mutual help could have a value in itself, i.e. that there could be 'non-monetary rewards from cooperation' (1991, p. 188).[11]

That something important is missing is much more than a doubt in the words of a highly respectable, albeit somewhat unorthodox, scholar:

> While we have considered which quantity of each good accrues to each, we have never taken into account the quality of economic relations between the persons involved, nor what they do to and with these persons, apart from modifying the basket of goods they have at their disposal. Indeed, this is so important that the omission invalidates all our prescriptions.
>
> (Kolm, 1984, p. 18; my translation)

Relational goods

Despite the neglect of the issue by economists, interpersonal relations do matter in economic life – which, by the way, represents a large share of human life. Here I might say that interpersonal relations shape the evolution of our personality, and are an important ingredient of human realization; or that we have a moral obligation to treat other persons not as means, but rather as ends, so a merely instrumental interpersonal behaviour is below the standard of human dignity. However, in order to avoid the charge of idealism – a charge so common within the pragmatic social sciences – I will put it in more prosaic consequentialist terms, and say that interpersonal relations are a valuable economic good: a consumer good that significantly contributes to individual welfare; and possibly also a production good, an asset that can improve productive performance or resource allocation.

The quality of interpersonal relations in trading situations, in leisure time and on the job, surely has a bearing on our evaluation of these situations either as consumers strictly speaking (of vendor services, of sport and vacation facilities), or as consumers broadly speaking (of the characteristics of the work environment).

However, as I have said, production and resource allocation are also affected by interpersonal relations. Decision-making processes, team coordination and the exchange of information within organizations are among the aspects more directly involved. The quality of interpersonal relations is also significant in the case of repeated or enduring exchanges among organizations, for which the term 'relational exchanges' (Goldberg, 1980) has been coined.[12]

Due to a lack of attention by economics, scientific evidence on the economic relevance of interpersonal relations is easier to find in other social sciences. For instance, Lea *et al.*, reviewing various works in occupational psychology, conclude that: 'the social environment is one of the most important properties of a workplace, from the point of view of both worker happiness and the plant's efficiency' (1987, p. 170).

If all this is true, even in economic discourse we should explicitly consider the existence of 'relational goods', that are inherent in the relationship among people and can be described as a climate of mutual attention, openness and care (see also Donati, 1991). My point is that these relational goods are under-produced (or under-maintained) when people behave selfishly. This inefficiency represents a further instance of what is usually called 'market failure' – i.e. the inability to reach efficiency through decentralized self-regarding incentives. However, in this case one had better speak of 'selfishness failure', since it is not a change in the mode of allocation – from the market to the government – that can correct this failure, but a change in what is normally assumed to be the standard individual attitude in market transactions: selfishness.[13]

Relational goods and motivation

Relational goods are by definition public goods, in that they are enjoyed by at least two people. In their 'production' the usual incentive problem arises: each person is tempted to let the other(s) bear the cost. For instance, in situations such as a working team, the willingness of each member of the team to devote time and goodwill to listen to and help solve the problems of colleagues is required in order to promote the establishment of a friendly and cooperative atmosphere, which then benefits directly all the members of the team, and indirectly also those interacting with them, in addition to possible positive effects on group productivity. As with public goods in general, private incentives to devote resources to relational goods do exist when one can expect reciprocation in the future. However, with self-regarding motivations, the outcome is usually insufficient and biased. The typical example is that of a trader who, by showing kindness and attention, hopes to attract or maintain the customer. The latter, however, can easily distinguish the underlying motivation, whether it be instrumental courtesy or a genuine regard: the boundaries of the region of mutually advantageous acts are sooner or later crossed.

That interpersonal relations not only concrete behaviour matters, but also motivation as perceived by the other, is stressed by Kelley and Thibaut (1978). According to these authors there exist two interrelated levels of interdependence between persons, the 'given' level, that of direct and factual outcomes, and the 'dispositional' level, that of 'symbolic' outcomes, which somehow disclose attitudes and traits (e.g. concern or fairness). With reference to all types of interpersonal relationship, although his language fits especially marital relationships, Kelley writes: 'the events in a personal relationship are evaluated on a dual basis. Their affective consequences derive partly from the specific rewards and costs they entail but also partly from what the events reveal about each person's underlying dispositions' (1986, p. 12).

An example of this general statement with reference to the economic sphere is provided by Hirsch, a scholar very aware of the importance of interpersonal relations: that in some industries, such as medical care, the quality of the output depends in an essential way on the attitude of the personnel (1976, p. 86). In other words, a genuine participation in one's own problems by doctors and nurses is a non-negligible component of the service patients expect of a hospital.

Relational goods are then an instance of cooperation, that also benefits those who invest in care and attention for their neighbours, if the others reciprocate. The old objection then applies: if moral behaviour is eventually beneficial also to the actor, is it not just a form of enlightened self-interest? The paradox cannot be fully solved easily. However, a possible way out is supplied by the 'dispositional level' of interpersonal relations, that is by the ability of humans to intuit the dispositions underlying the actions of their fellow creatures. As Stefano Zamagni, drawing from Robert Frank (1988), recently put it: 'in order for such predispositions to be advantageous, others must be able to discern that we have them . . . moral values do not lead to material advantage unless they are heartfelt' (1991, p. 30).

CONCLUSIONS

In this paper I have tried to document the neglect of interpersonal relations on the part of economic theory, and argued that this can contribute to an invalidation of some of its traditional views. In particular, I have tried to show that the relatively high status that selfish behaviour enjoys in economic theorizing, stands at least partly on this neglect.

I see a few implications of a greater awareness by economists of the importance of interpersonal relations. First, 'relational goods' can be made the object of formal economic analysis. Especially in the last two decades economic analysis has been able to overcome, at least to a certain extent, the oversimplistic description of human reality that had characterized its inception. Some of the contributions I have mentioned in this paper are good examples of this tendency. Second, even when explicit consideration of interpersonal aspects in economic modelling is unfeasible, awareness that this element is missing should suggest additional caution when evaluating the results obtained. Third, economics has long suffered from a materialistic bias, according to which the output of the economic system is a list of commodities (even though the implicit reference remains industrial production, services are included, although immaterial, provided they are sold in the market or their cost of production is measurable). However, the very idea of individual (and therefore subjective) utility, that plays such a great role in economic theorizing, implies that the aim of the economic system is to supply efficiently all those 'goods' that people value. Some of these – interpersonal relations among them – pertain rather to the socio-economic process than to what we see as its output. Explicit consideration of this fact should contribute to correct the bias.

The sphere of interpersonal relations, on which I have focused in this paper, may seem to belong to a less pressing level of concern with respect to the urgency and size of problems such as mass poverty or inequality. It is my conviction, however, that the second dimension of ethics – that of 'solicitude' in interpersonal relations, and therefore of the recognition of other 'economic agents' as 'yous' – is a necessary step for confronting the macroscopic challenges of world economy.

NOTES

1 The author thanks the participants in the conferences 'Persona e sviluppo', Centro Ricerche Personaliste, Teramo (Italy), January 1990, 'Etica ed economia', University of Verona (Italy), April 1990 and 'Ethics and economics', University of Siena (Italy), July 1991, for useful comments on previous drafts. Financial support by the Italian Ministry for University and Scientific and Technologic Research (MURST) is gratefully acknowledged.
2 See among others: Akerlof (1983), Akerlof and Dickens (1982), Boulding (1969), Hirschman (1985), Kolm (1984), Lutz and Lux (1979), Perroux (1958), Sen (1987, ch. 3) and Vanek (1977).
3 The need to distinguish relations with the other as a 'you' from relations with the other as a 'he' is also stressed by Buber (1923). That face-to-face morality has been somewhat disregarded is also noticed by Downie (1986).
4 Here the problem arises of coordinating the actions of several altruists concerned about the poor. See Collard (1978, pp. 26–28).
5 Even if the game is repeated an indefinite number of times – so that a cooperative reply by others in future periods can be the reward of an agent's cooperation today – only under special circumstances is cooperation an equilibrium strategy for selfish players (see Taylor, 1987).
6 The quotation is from Nobel laureate Kenneth Arrow (1971, pp. 221–222), an author remarkably sensitive to ethical issues (see also: 1974, ch. 1).
7 The original auto-ironic sentence is in Stigler (1981, p. 151).
8 See among others: Boulding (1962, appendix); Collard (1978, p. 7); Lindbeck and Weibull (1988); and Becker (1976), who also gives the following verbal definition of altruism: the 'willing[ness] to reduce [one's] own consumption in order to increase the consumption of others' (p. 818).
9 By the way, this effect is interpreted by the authors as showing that 'nice guys finish last'. Quite the opposite, I would say, since in this strange world nice guys would thus avoid being associated with an unhappy woman.

10 This line of reasoning seems more fruitful with reference to an asymmetric situation in which an agent who is willing to cooperate has the problem of inducing a selfish partner to do the same. It is in this case that, if the former is an altruist, the threat of punishing the latter by breaking cooperation may be too weak (altruism would lead the altruist to donate a certain amount anyhow). In fact this second situation resembles Buchanan's 'samaritan's dilemma'.

11 The main message of the paper is that informal solidarity discourages loss preventing activities, and therefore renders market damage insurance unprofitable. The authors admit two countervailing forces: peer monitoring may force people to take preventive steps; or – they add in a footnote – loss prevention may be induced by the potential victim's altruism.

12 The importance of these exchanges in economic life is increasingly recognized, together with their distinctive complexity with respect to isolated exchanges, that have long represented the stereotype of economic transactions. Indeed, some authors introduce with this regard the category of 'network', as a distinct mode of economic coordination that strongly relies on trust (see Powell, 1991).

13 Other situations that might be identified as 'selfishness failure' have been considered in the literature. An example is the possibility to escape the non-cooperation trap in a prisoner's dilemma game thanks to agents' altruism (see Collard, 1978, ch. 1).

REFERENCES

Akerlof, G. (1983) 'Loyalty filters', *American Economic Review,* 73 (1), 54–63.

Akerlof, G. and Dickens, W. T. (1982) 'The economic consequences of cognitive dissonance', *American Economic Review,* 72, 307–319.

Archibald, G. C. and Donaldson, D. (1976) 'Nonpaternalism and the basic theorems of welfare economics', *Canadian Journal of Economics,* 9 (August), 492–507.

Arnott, R. and Stiglitz, J. E. (1991) 'Moral hazard and nonmarket institutions: disfunctional crowding out or peer monitoring?', *American Economic Review,* 81 (1), 179–190.

Arrow, K. (1971) 'The economics of moral hazard: further comment', in K. Arrow, *Essays in the Theory of Risk Bearing,* Chicago: Markham, pp. 220–223.

Arrow, K. (1974) *The Limits of Organization,* New York: Norton.

Becker, G. S. (1976) 'Altruism, egoism and genetic fitness: economics and sociobiology', *Journal of Economic Literature,* 14 (3), 817–826.

Bernheim, D. and Stark, O. (1988) 'Altruism within the family reconsidered: do nice guys finish last?', *American Economic Review,* 78, 1034–1045.

Bordignon, M. (1990) 'Was Kant right? Voluntary provision of public goods under the principle of unconditional commitment', *Economic Notes,* 3, 342–372.

Boulding, K. E. (1962) 'Notes on a theory of philanthropy', in F. Dickinson (ed.), *Philanthropy and Public Policy,* New York: National Bureau of Economic Research.

Boulding, K. (1969) 'Economics as a Moral Science', *American Economic Review,* 59 (1), 1–12.

Brunner, K. (1987) 'The perception of man and the conception of society: two approaches to understanding society', *Economic Inquiry,* XXV (3), 367–388.

Buber, M. (1923) *Ich und Du,* Leipzig: Insel-Verlag.

Collard, D. (1978) *Altruism and Economy,* Oxford: Martin Robertson.

Donati, P. (1991) *Teoria relazionale della società,* Milan: Franco Angeli, pp. 156–158.

Downie, R. S. (1986) 'Moral philosophy', in J. Eatwell *et al.* (eds), *The New Palgrave,* London: Macmillan.

Edgeworth, F. Y. (1881) *Mathematical Psychics* (reprinted by the London School of Economics, 1932).

Frank, R. H. (1988) *Passions within Reason*, New York: Norton.

Goldberg, V. P. (1980) 'Relational exchange: economics and complex contracts', *American Behavioral Scientist*, 23 (3), 337–352.

Higgs, R. (1987) 'Identity and cooperation: a comment on Sen's alternative program', *Journal of Law, Economics and Organization*, 3 (1), 140–142.

Hirsch, F. (1976) *Social Limits to Growth*, Cambridge, MA: Harvard University Press.

Hirschman, A. (1985) 'Against parsimony: three easy ways of complicating some categories of economic discourse', *Economics and Philosophy*, 1 (1).

Hirschman, A. (1986) *Rival Views of Market Society and Other Recent Essays*, Harmondsworth: Penguin.

Hollander, H. (1990) 'A social exchange approach to voluntary cooperation', *American Economic Review*, 80 (4), 1157–1167.

Johansen, L. (1977) 'The theory of public goods: misplaced emphasis', *Journal of Public Economics*, 7, 147–152.

Kelley, H. H. (1986) 'Personal relationships: their nature and significance', in R. Gilmour and S. Duck (eds), *The Emerging Field of Personal Relationships*, Hillsdale, NJ: Lawrence Erlbaum, pp. 3–19.

Kelley, H. and Thibaut, J. W. (1978) *Interpersonal Relations: A Theory of Interdependence*, New York: Wiley.

Kolm, S.-C. (1984) *La bonne economie: La réciprocité generale*, Paris: Presses Universitaire de France.

Lea, S. E. G., Tarpy, R. M. and Webley, P. (1987) *The Individual in the Economy*, Cambridge: Cambridge University Press.

Lindbeck, A. and Weibull, J. W. (1988) 'Altruism and time consistency: the economics of *fait accompli*', *Journal of Political Economy*, 96, 1165–1182.

Lutz, M. A. and Lux, K. (1979) *The Challenge of Humanistic Economics*, Menlo Park, CA: Benjamin/Cummings.

Margolis, H. (1982) *Selfishness, Altruism and Rationality*, Cambridge: Cambridge University Press.

Meade, J. (1973) *Theory of Economic Externality: The Control of Environmental Pollution and Similar Social Cost*, Sijthoff-Leiden.

Mounier, E. (1962) 'Le personnalisme', in E. Mounier, *Oeuvres*, vol. III, Paris: Du Seuil, pp. 427–525 (original edition: Du Seuil, 1948).

Perroux, F. (1958) *Economie et Civilization*, Paris: Editions Ouvrières.

Powell, W. W. (1991) 'Neither markets nor hierarchy: network forms of organization', in G. Thompson *et al.* (eds), *Markets, Hierarchies and Networks. The Coordination of Social Life*, London: Sage Publications, pp. 265–276.

Ricoeur, P. (1991) 'Il tripode etico della persona', in A. Danese (ed.), *Persona e sviluppo*, Bologna: Edizioni Dehoniane, pp. 65–86.

Schokkaert, E. (1992) 'The economics of distributive justice, welfare and freedom', in K. Scherer (ed.), *Justice: Interdisciplinary Perspectives*, Cambridge: Cambridge University Press, pp. 65–113.

Schotter, A. (1981) *The Economic Theory of Social Institutions*, Cambridge: Cambridge University Press.

Sen, A. (1987) *On Ethics and Economics*, Oxford: Blackwell.

Stigler, G. (1981) 'Economics or ethics?', in S. M. McMurrin (ed.), *The Tanner Lectures on Human Values*, vol. II, Salt Lake City: University of Utah Press, pp. 144–191.

Sugden, R. (1984) 'Reciprocity: the supply of public goods through voluntary contributions', *Economic Journal*, 94, 772–787.

Taylor, M. (1987) *The Possibility of Cooperation*, Cambridge: Cambridge University Press.

Vanek, J. (1977) 'Through participation and dialogue to a world of justice', Ithaca, NY, Department of Economics, Cornell University, Mimeo.

Wicksteed, P. H. (1910) *The Commonsense of Political Economy*, London: Macmillan. (Citations refer to the 1933 edition by Routledge & Kegan Paul, London.)

Yaari, M. (1991) 'Rationality and morality: a Humean view', paper presented at the International School of Economic Research, Siena, July.

Zamagni, S. (1991) 'Extended rationality, altruism and the justification of moral rules', paper presented at the International School of Economic Research, Siena, July.

Chapter 13

Economy and ethics in functionally differentiated societies

History and present problems

Josef Wieland

ETHICS AS A SYMPTOM OF CRISIS: INTERNAL AND EXTERNAL EFFECTS OF THE ECONOMY

The emergence of ethical discussions is always an expression of the crisis in what has been taken for granted, of the fact that practices that have been viewed as unproblematical till now have themselves become problematic. Therefore it would be useful first of all to define the character of this crisis from the perspective of an economist.

On the economic level – and this will determine my approach in the following – there is a crisis of overproduction, viz. the overproduction of negative external effects.

Economic theory defines externalities as the utility or costs of the actions of firms or individuals that devolve upon other economic subjects without a corresponding payment of money or compensation for costs. I would like to reformulate this definition in a systems-theoretic way because I believe that this will open up useful perspectives on the problem. Negative external effects, then, are those that are generated in the economic system and create costs in other social or individual systems without the latter being compensated for this. In a more general sense this is a matter of the consequences of economic action in other contexts. The squandering of resources and the polluting of the environment, the undesired societal effects of new technologies and the problems of industrially organized provision for food and health; all these problem areas in modern societies are negative external effects of the economic system, according to our definition, in so far as they are connected with its operation.

Economists, however, approach ethics not only as the reflection of a crisis in this sense but also as the requirement of a minimum standard of morality in the economy (Matthews, 1981; Etzioni, 1988), something whose absence, it seems, would render a modern market economy with a division of labour ultimately impossible. In all cases where one furnishes services in a complex and imprecisely specifiable way (e.g. in a client–expert relationship or in an owner–manager relationship), in cases of long-term contractual and material commitments (e.g. employment contracts, supplier contracts) and in cases of asymmetries of information between contractual parties, there is the risk of opportunism by one of the partners (Williamson, 1979, 1985). Generally recognized examples of opportunism are, among others: pirated versions of books, photos, sound recordings and software. Here property rights are transferred without compensation, or they are simply not enforceable.

The ethical–economical problem lying behind all these examples is that the attempt to enforce adherence to contracts or the full enforcement of property rights would lead to prohibitive costs. Transaction costs would be so great that the economic order would not be able to function (North, 1981). These considerations show that, from a purely economic perspective, the question of morality can only be a temporary phenomenon, whose effectiveness is given credit as long as the costs of economic and legal mechanisms of regulation are prohibitively high. Were these only low enough, the question of a minimal standard of morality could be solved with economic means. But in the course of this paper it will be shown that from a systems-theoretic perspective, it follows that there are systematic reasons why this cannot be the case in complex and differentiated societies.

It is important now to understand the distinctions between both these types of relationships between ethics and the economy. In the case of the consequences of economic action in other contexts, we are actually concerned with *external effects* in the sense that this is a matter of the relation of the economic system to structurally and functionally different systems. In the case of a minimal morality and transaction costs we are concerned with relations within the economic system, i.e. with *internal effects*. Therefore in the following, in contrast to the standard economic terminology, I use the term 'internal effects' when these are generated in the economic system and are directly relevant there. What are the essential distinctions between internal and external effects?

First of all, although internal effects are directly relevant in the economic system, this is not necessarily true in the case of external effects. Ecological damage and new technologies can, of course, be connected with positive effects in the economic system, at least for some time, while the negative effects devolve upon other, existing or future, social or natural systems. Accordingly, it is the possible systemic uncoupling of negative and positive effects of economic externalities that is thematized in the term 'external effects'. For the examples of 'internal effects' discussed above, this is not the case. Viewed systemically, the positive and negative effects of internal effects comply with one another but they are not equally distributed. On the one hand there is a profit, on the other a loss. This is the source of the problem of a minimal morality.

A further important distinction is the complete quantifiability of internal effects that, in the case of external effects, encounters, in part, methodological problems, in part, fundamental provisos. How can the utility of the existence of a kingfisher be calculated against the loss of social welfare from the fact that a factory is not being built? To do this, one would have to assume the qualitative equivalence and, with it, the substitutability of natural and artificial things (Hampicke, 1987, p. 93). This results in the decisive aspect that compensation payments via market prices to the internalization of externalities are impractical in this case. This is clear in all cases of ecological and human catastrophes caused by economic operations that would have to be internalized by fantastic and incalculable compensations and which, because of their frequently irreversible character, could not be compensated at all. But it is precisely this kind of negative external effect that initiated the ethical discussion within economics. The conceptual distinction proposed above tries to address this situation.

This differentiation constitutes two distinct concepts of ethics. While in the case of *internal* effects ethics is a programme to reduce transaction costs (Posner, 1975, p. 185f; North, 1981), in the case of *external* effects ethics seeks responsible and rational action in modern and systemically differentiated societies.

Both ethical variants are relevant and legitimate concerns of *one* ethics of the economy admitting their basic differences. One consequence of this proposal is a distinction of levels of discussion within one ethics of the economy: an ethics of the economic system and an ethics between the economic and other social and natural systems.

The reason for proceeding in this way lies, first of all, in the fact that both ethical types can be reduced to a common problem motif. This says that there are non-economic conditions of the economy, non-functional conditions of functionality. Speaking concretely, this means that if we could not assume that a significant number of economic actors does feel itself bound to the imperative of fairness and honesty because these are obligatory societal standards (thus not only because they are useful), then the economy would not be possible (North, 1981). If I understand it correctly, this was already the way Thomas Hobbes broached the problem at the beginning of the modern period: an enduring community with unrestrictedly egoistical profit maximizers is impossible. Hobbes used this to infer the inevitability of social contracts and the Leviathan, the enormous state-machine that forces the observance of the rules of the games that limit and, at the same time, benefit all. But we will say more about this later.

To begin with, we must establish that the cases of internal as well as external effects require an ethics that has to be compatible with the economy but not absorbed by it. It must be compatible because both kinds of effects can lead very quickly to costs or profits within the economic system but, in the long run, can also affect the bases of its existence.

It cannot be absorbed by the economy because it is not possible for quantitative and qualitative reasons to internalize all – and this again in the standard language of economists – external effects through prices. In other words, for structural reasons one always has to reckon with imperfect competition and an imperfect market, thus with market failure. This is precisely why institutions, law and the binding force of norms are established to restrict individuals' preferences for specific choices of actions and thus enable social order. The decisive perspective of these restrictions is not that they question the economy as such but its immanent efficiency. Transaction costs and externalities are genuine arguments for efficiency and not ethical arguments against the market. However, the fact that they can be shown to be points of connection for ethical arguments shows that efficiency and ethics are indeed essentially different but not, in principle, incompatible (Buchanan, 1985; Lindenberg, 1983).

To the extent that ethics completely adopts the language of economics it provides economics, as one might expect, with no problems of internalization. More problematical, as we will see for good reasons, is the idea of the non-economic conditions of the constitution of the economy because the categories of modern economics no longer depict this dimension. But also in the first case methodological problems are very important because the alternative to non-economic conditions of the economy is the infinite reduction of ethical behaviour to an economic calculation of benefits – either as the value of following a norm that expresses preferences or as the calculation of the consequences of an action (Gäfgen, 1988, p. 89).

It is now necessary to undertake a general reconstruction of the emergence and the actual state of these difficulties. This will form the basis for the attempt to systematize these difficulties through combining a deterministic systems- and an individualistic action-theory. This should clarify the foundation on which a unified concept of an economic ethics can be built.

THE EMERGENCE OF THE ECONOMY AND ECONOMICS AS FUNCTIONALLY DIFFERENTIATED SYSTEMS

In considering a scientific and practical problem a knowledge of its history is always useful. In the case of the relation of economics and ethics, however, this is a requirement of any understanding of the present situation. From the perspective of modern economics this has, to the present day – and this means for about 2,500 years – been a relationship of domination in which economics played the role of the dominated party. And even today one can still see the presence of such ideas of domination, of course in much more subtle ways. But I would now like to demonstrate that there is no basis for this any more.

It was ancient Greek thought that ordered the relation between ethics and economics so that the latter played a subaltern and relative role. Economics, as a part of practical philosophy, was not only subordinate to ethics and politics but also – and in common with these two – to a metaphysics that was to be realized in this world, either as the platonic idea of the good or as the Aristotelian highest good.

In this regard truly successful economic action realized aesthetic, ethical and goal-directed rationality claims at the same time. Medieval philosophy transferred the realization of the greatest happiness from the earth to heaven; which surely negated neither the complex demands on economic action nor its subalternate status, but increased them instead.

Unfortunately, this is not the place to make a detailed investigation of these things (Wieland, 1989). Instead, I am concerned only with the viewpoint of the hierarchical differentiation of societies. In this case, *hierarchical differentiation* means the teleological arrangement of all spheres of societal action in terms of a fixed, highest goal.

With the collapse of religious claims of domination due to a pluralistic expansion of society that created new action possibilities and expectations, the interpretation of the world as an hierarchically differentiated whole fell away. Now ethics, politics and economics were understood as merely relatively autonomous subsystems of society that effect specific performances for these and that steer themselves according to their own internal criteria. At the same time this meant that, henceforth, systems that are *functionally differentiated out* neither can nor may raise claims to domination – i.e. claims to steering – any longer over one another but are essentially equal.

What the economic system was expected to perform, the production of wealth and welfare, was certainly not a new idea. Aristotle, for example, says that the goal of economics is wealth (Nicomachean Ethics, 1094a9). What was new was Adam Smith's argument that the means–end rational pursuit of individual interests within the context of a self-organized market system realizes the common interest at the same time, viz. the well-being of nations as well as justice (of exchange and distribution). Economic action need only follow means–end rational perspectives. Ethical and aesthetic rationality have their place now only in their own specific systems that are separate from economics. This meant a drastic reduction in what was expected from economic action; the bursting of the hierarchical combination of economic, ethical and aesthetic rationality claims. This is accompanied by an absolution of responsibility for actions because these can be projected, as it were, on an objectivating mechanism. Only then was it possible to interpret the economy as a functional nexus among things instead of as an action-nexus among human beings, as was the case in antiquity and the Middle Ages. This is when the ethical problem of the economy and economics arose because human action is accessible to ethical consideration while the functional nexus of things is not.

The objectivation and depersonalization of domains of life correspond to increasing individualization and personal independence. This, in turn, was interpreted as an increase of freedom (Simmel, 1901/1989). The separation of subject and object, their reciprocal autonomization, is a characteristic of the modern period and this is something to which economics referred from the very beginning, accounting for it either in a structuro-theoretical or in an individualistic way, in the very process of unfolding it.

The fact that this release of the individual and the rationalization of objectified societal function-domains to self-organizing systems (Angell, 1926; Viner, 1937; Mayr, 1971; Wieland, 1991a, 1991b), the mechanization of society as it were, increased the efficiency and effectiveness of these subsystems is what Adam Smith intended to address for the economy in his book *The Wealth of Nations*. His thesis that a just society and universal well-being are possible only through and not in opposition to a self-referential economic system not only goes against ancient and medieval modes of thought but was directed, above all, against the mercantilistic primacy of the political system. The famous statement that we do not expect our daily bread from the goodwill of the butcher, brewer and baker but from the fact that these perceive their own interests and seek their own advantage (Smith, 1776/1976, I.ii.2) emphasizes this viewpoint as well as Adam Smith's statement of the self-regulating market mechanism anchored in the self-interests of the individual. The latter is in his own words, 'a system . . . an imaginary machine to connect together in the fancy those different movements and effects which are already in reality preformed' (Smith, 1795/1980, IV.19).

On *the level of this system* human beings no longer exist. It is an intelligible form, a pure functional nexus, an ideal thing–thing world. Resources stream into it in reaction to prices.

The newness, in the eighteenth century, of the idea of the economy as a self-referential automatism lying behind the surface of the economic process, can be seen in the fact that Adam Smith himself repeatedly emphasizes the difference between the tangible economic fact and the abstract concept of it which corresponds to an abstract object and that he tries to explain it through, as he himself says, 'tedious' examples (Smith, 1776/1976, I.iv.18, I.v.5).

Of course, he already saw that, beside autonomous claims to steering, this system ultimately depended on ethically liable individuals and political and legal institutions and, in this way, also on the performances of other social subsystems. Only the ethical and the political system could supply sympathy, a sense of justice, voluntary acceptance of ethical rules and positive laws; things without which the economic machine might very well function but not endure. It is this aspect of durability that had already led in ancient thought to the co-evolving relation of ethics and the economy (Wieland, 1989) and in which Adam Smith saw a boundary of the economic mechanism (Smith, 1759/1976; Wieland, 1991a, 1991b). To be sure, the wages of labour, according to Smith, are regulated by the law of the supply and demand for labour. But he also distinguishes a sub-boundary that is defined as 'consistent with common humanity' (Smith, 1776/1976, I.vii.24). The system as the execution of functional connections does not recognize this boundary. If one assumes a sufficiently high supply of labour then the price of labour within the logic of the system can fall below the minimum for existence (Sen, 1987, p. 26f). The fact that this is not merely a theoretical consideration is historically relevant. Beyond this boundary is where the destruction of man begins or, in revolt, the destruction of the community and with it also the destruction of the economic mechanism. Formulated systems-theoretically, the problem of modern economics for Smith is that a self-referential mechanism in which all system events are connection-possibilities within an operationally closed loop can achieve enduring stability only if it realizes its environmental dependence and takes this into account.

The fact that the problem of the integration of modern societies lies in the functional autonomization and simultaneous interdependence of societal subsystems had already been noted by the English physician and writer Bernard Mandeville with his handy as well as razor-sharp formulation of the public virtues of private vices (Mandeville, 1795/1966). If luxury, profligacy, prostitution, criminality and war are indeed ethically disreputable but economically profitable and with it contribute to the increase of well-being, while asceticism, chastity, honour and peace are ethically preferable but have a negative economic effect, then ethics and the economy are no longer compatible. The good consequences of bad deeds and the bad consequences of good ones express not only the existence of societal subsystems obeying their own logics but also their difficulties in compatibility. It was Karl Marx then who clearly expressed the confusion resulting from this concerning the norms that guide action:

> When I ask the political economists: am I obeying economic laws if I make money from giving my body to someone else's lust [. . .], or do I not act economically if I sell my friend to the Moroccans [. . .], the political economist answers me: you are not acting against my laws but look around and see what morality and religion have to say; my economic morality and religion have nothing to object, but what should one believe in more, political economy or morality?
>
> (Marx, 1844/1981, p. 550f)

To this day, modern societies have been faced with this question. And it also ultimately underlies the present economic discussion. Marx emphasizes each action-sphere's distinct normativity and brings out the features of their disparateness and contradictoriness. In the defence of David Ricardo, who was the first person to isolate economics completely from ethics and politics and who consequently drew the reproach of theoretical amorality from a French economist, Marx formulates the problem in a way that has remained valid till today:

> The relation of political economy to morality, if it is not otherwise arbitrary, accidental and therefore unjustified and unscientific, if it is not

shown to be an illusion but is intended essentially, can only be that of economic laws to morality; if this is not the case or if the opposite occurs what can Ricardo do to change it? Moreover, the opposition of political economy and morality is itself only an illusion and, as it is an opposition, not an opposition. Political economy merely expresses moral laws in its own way.

(Marx, 1844/1981, p. 551)

Modern economy expresses in its semantics what the ethical system communicates to it. A discursive relation between both *systems* is therefore impossible. The economic system is operatively closed. To be sure, it is communicatively open but evaluates what is communicated exclusively according to its own criteria. This is precisely what reveals the system's self-referential character and its claim to a uniquely internal steering (Luhmann, 1984, 1988; Wieland, 1988).

ETHICS OR ECONOMICS?

Can one explain prostitution and slavery economically? Can one explain morality economically? Whom should one believe: morality or the economy? These questions, that have arisen with the emergence of the modern economy based on the functional differentiation (objectivation and individualization) of society, occupy the present economic discussion in the form of a General Theory of Rationality and an Economic Theory of Morality. Of course, it seems that – and this is important – the presuppositions of this discussion have changed. Here too, to begin with, I would like to use a rough sketch of the broader theoretical development to present the background against which the true form of the present discussion of an ethics of the economic system emerges.

It is no longer remarkable that the establishment of an autonomous economic system was accompanied by the effort to detach theoretical reflection on it from the traditional old-European complex of practical philosophy (politics, ethics, economics). This undertaking developed, of course, with much greater difficulty (even, to the present day (Biervert and Wieland, 1990)) than one would naturally think. And this had (and has) its basis in the peculiar character of the economic system: to be the intelligible form of empirical phenomena.

The decisive question was and is: is economics determined by its object or by its method?

From Aristotle to Adam Smith it was unquestioned that the task of economics was to investigate the production, distribution and consumption of wealth. Then in 1836 John Stuart Mill formulated the decisive objection against this way of looking at things. The economy cannot be determined by means of its object since it shares this with other human, societal and engineering sciences. Instead, Mill proposed to determine political economy formally from the point of view of its method since every science is inseparably connected to its method (Mill, 1844).

This discussion about object determination versus method determination has accompanied political economy ever since (Dietzel, 1882; Sombart, 1930). Its background was captured by an economist of the early twentieth century:

> This is a matter of securing a domain for the economy in which it is autonomous while it determines the facts according to its requirements and while the process is determined according to its laws.
>
> (Strigl, 1923, p. 19)

When one compares this statement with one of William Stanley Jevons from the year 1871, in which he justifies the necessity of an economic theory by saying that no other science is concerned with investigation of the 'laws of human enjoyment' (Jevons, 1871/1970, p. 102), then one can easily see that the focal point of the justification had moved: from the necessity of investigating what is economic to the maintenance of competing claims to autonomy *vis-à-vis* politics and ethics.

Then in 1932 Lionel Robbins published the formal definition of economics that has been accepted within the profession ever since: 'Economics is the science which studies human behaviour as a relationship between ends and means which have alternative uses' (Robbins, 1932, p. 16).

Efforts at eliminating all explicitly ethico-normative and aesthetic elements from economics seemed even more difficult. Essentially there were three lines of discussions that ran in this direction (Biervert and Wieland, 1987). Decisive first of all was the elimination of all ethical content from the category of utility, which was organized first by William Stanley Jevons through the rejection of a normative concept of utility and then continued and completed by Léon Walras and Vilfredo Pareto by the elimination of hedonism from the concept. Walras had already viewed the economic concept of utility (pure science) as ethically indifferent. But Pareto rejected it completely and replaced it with the concept of the idea of utility (ophelimity) that exclusively expresses subjective preferences as they are enunciated. Pareto demonstrated the radicality of this change when he used the example of morphine addicts who view morphine as useful to argue that: 'Thus there are things that are very detrimental and yet are said to be economically useful' (Pareto, 1900–1904, 1103). Where Mandeville had held up a mirror to society in the form of satire now one encountered: *de gustibus non est disputandum*.

The increasing rejection of cardinally measurable and interpersonally comparable utilities, that partially stemmed from methodological problems, and the ascendancy of an ordinal concept (Rosenberg, 1980) were a second factor in this direction because an interdependent connection of the estimation of utilities in favour of an individualistic formation of preferences was theoretically blocked. Subsequently, Kenneth Arrow, Amartya K. Sen and John C. Harsanyi made clear that an individual who orders preferences ordinally does not allow ethical statements beyond statements of the efficiency of a welfare economics.

The third line of discussion closely connected with this context was the effort to conceive economics scientistically and to direct its interest, above all, towards mathematically manipulable quantities. Thus there is a way to economics as a 'pure science' that leads from Jevons to Walras that is to be distinguished from 'art' (Walras, 1926/1977). This cleared the way for the concentration of analysis on the pure systems level of a self-referential system.

The scientific reflection on the economic system (Hobbes, 1561/1841, p. 232ff) extracted the economic as a causal structure lying behind the surface of daily economic activity. The analytical description and explanation of events, the intelligible form, thus became a part of the empirical course of events and acquired a normative power to guide actions.

At the preliminary end of this development, then, one found the economy as an Arrow–Debreu world; a price-inducing allocation mechanism for which, under specific conditions (above all, of perfect competition and no external effects), one can show a general equilibrium of interdependent markets (Arrow and Debreu, 1954). In this state of allocative efficiency, welfare could never be increased for anyone without decreasing it for someone else. In such a context, equity of exchange is not a personal relation but refers to a function system of interconnected and interdependent exchange acts that guarantees the freedom as well as the possibility of exchanging homogeneous goods (de Gijsel, 1984, p. 26). Theoretically, at least, the system's capacity for self-organized equilibrium was demonstrated in this way.

For the present discussion it is important that because of this the interpretation of the economic system as a functional mechanism among things has become paramount.[1] Walras had already eliminated the human–human and human–thing relation from economic analysis and restricted it to the thing–thing level (Walras, 1926/1977, p. 115ff). Pareto distinctly says that, 'Science proceeds by replacing the relationships between human concepts . . . by relationships between things' (Pareto, 1900, p. 150). Only this step makes it possible to reformulate ethics as efficiency statements about the use of resources, given initial property rights and an order of preference.

In this world a human being is always a maximizer of utility according to George Stigler. And here the truth holds that the ethical system rests on utility maximizing behaviour (Stigler, 1981). On the economic system level, then, all ethics dissolves into the difference of cost and benefit. The system does not speak or understand any other language. To be sure, George Stigler does not restrict the validity of his statement to the system level. Instead, he falsely infers from this to human behaviour pure and simple.[2]

A turning point in the discussion of the relationship between the economy and ethics was when, in reaction to the empirically empty abstractions of the general theory of equilibrium (such as completely specified property rights, transaction costs equal to zero, complete information and infinitely fast adaption), these abstractions themselves became an object of research when they were internalized in the theory by means of open utility functions (Alchian, 1965). This interest in the explanation of non-market phenomena that are also important for economic productivity led to the establishment of the Rational-choice theory that included quite heterogeneous approaches and points of reference: individual and collective action (e.g. marriage, addiction, organizations, political parties), political and social institutions (e.g. constitutions, elections, law, property rights, contracts) were now the subject of economic analysis. This extension of the economic explanation of the world led to the projection of a General Theory of Rationality that we would now like to consider.

Gary S. Becker is one of the leading theorists in this context. And he has applied this mode of economic explanation to many areas of human behaviour: marriage, divorce, sexuality, reproduction, criminality, drug use, suicide and others still. Within the context of this approach children assume the form of long-term consumer goods that, on one hand, evoke costs and, on the other, produce psychical income. The family becomes a community of independent persons with interdependent utility functions. And every death tends to be a 'suicide' because one would have been able to delay it if one had invested more resources in keeping oneself alive (Becker, 1976).

The works of Robert B. McKenzie and Gordon Tullock go in a similar direction. The authors are not concerned with normative statements nor do they explicitly maintain the realism of their approach (Biervert and Wieland, 1990). Instead, they understand economic theory as an approach, as an analytical perspective of professional economists. The core of this perspective is that everything that people do and allow can be considered under the assumption of the utility maximization, market equilibrium and stable preferences (Becker, 1976; McKenzie and Tullock, 1978, p. 51f). The interesting point here is that these authors do not dispute the fact that human behaviour can also be motivated in non-economic ways. But, for them, economic rationality is the framework, the 'point of reference' (Becker, 1976), for non-economic motivational factors. The economic calculus for maximizing utility 'overrides' all other motives (McKenzie and Tullock, 1978, p. 11). Such statements have earned these authors the reproach of 'economic imperialism'. This is no longer a case of autonomy claims for economics, economics demands primacy!

As far as the relationship of ethics and economics is concerned, this means the complete reversal of the situation as it was at the beginning of the modern period; a situation that, I believe, documents how the economic system had become the leading system of Western societies.

Of course, the economic approach to human behaviour is burdened with series of epistemological and methodological difficulties, e.g. a tendency to tautology or *ad hoc* arguments. One must also ask whether a theory that explains everything really explains anything. These objections, however, will not be developed here (Biervert and Wieland, 1990; Rosenberg, 1979). The systemic discussion presented here evokes a different view of the problem: 'economic imperialism' and the general theory of rationality are attempts to answer the over-differentiation of modern societies. We will say more on this presently.

James M. Buchanan's considerations of an Economic Theory of Morality are to be seen as a non-imperialistic approach within the context of a general theory of rationality (Buchanan, 1975, 1977; Homann, 1988, 1990). This theory is not concerned with the question of the content or legitimation of the moral system but with an economic justification or grounding of ethics (Homann, 1988, p. 220f). Justification follows from egoistical interests, their evaluation and a collective consideration of gain. Accordingly, morality is a public good and a capital good for which one has to pay.

As a public good, morality represents universally accepted constraints on action that, for their part, can be reduced to individual considerations of gain. In this way stable and calculable behavioural expectations emerge that enable one to plan one's life in society. The costs associated with these constraints, perhaps the deferment of immediate gain, constitute the capital-good aspect of ethics. Ethics is, as it were, an investment in foreseeable societal order through which a permanent perception of gain in the economic system is possible. Formulated neoclassically, behavioural constraints follow to the point where the marginal costs are equal to the marginal utility in units of freedom as action possibilities (Homann, 1988, p. 231). Here too I am only interested in the systemic consequences of this approach, although I believe that an economic theory of morality still is deficient in the justification of intergenerationally effective behavioural constraints. To be sure, within the context of this theory, one can explain why individuals within a generation might have no interest in an erosion of the moral stock of capital of their society precisely because of the losses and costs of reforming it anew that are connected with this. But for a utility maximizer this erosion is not a problem if the costs only fall on the next or the subsequent generation. In principle, this argument also holds for international relations in which one can externalize the costs of national or private actions outside the domain of constitutional contracts. Ecological ethics, many aspects of an ethics of technology and a just international economic order revolve around this problem.

What an economic theory of morality shows, however, is that the avoidance of external and internal effects is economically rational and justifiable in a whole series of cases in so far as it focuses on the stability and durability of behavioural expectations. Furthermore, it shows that an ethics that cannot connect onto what is economic is literally a utopia and really has no place. But at the same time this theoretical approach is not capable of qualifying this connectivity.

On the one hand, the economic calculus is in no way preferable to the ethical calculus. On the contrary, James Buchanan restricts the economic explanation of the constitutional conditions of post-constitutional economic action to the contractual process (Buchanan, 1975, p. 182f). He rejects a purely economic explanation of what is social as something confusing and misleading to economics (Buchanan, 1977, p. 236; Brennan and Buchanan, 1984, p. 385f). Not only does he see that an ethical explanation of what is social is possible but his argument is that a purely economic foundation of social actions can never exclude the contractual infringements by individuals as something detrimental to the community (the problem of free riders). As the voluntary constraining of action, ethics can be effective, according to Buchanan, wherever the economic calculus does not guarantee this (Buchanan and Tollison, 1984, pp. 109, 114f, 173f).

On the other hand, however, the relation between ethics and economics is only vaguely described so that economics is 'more or less codecisive in the justification' (Homann, 1990, p. 17) of moral norms. It contains an extremely 'important contribution' to the justification of morality that does not dispute the rights of pedagogical, psychological, technical, legal, philosophical and theological considerations in the justification of morality (Homann, 1988, p. 235). In formulations like 'more or less codecisive' or 'important contribution' the real problem of the determination of the relationship between distinct system types remains unsolved. What should be the rules of mediation and decision in case of a conflict between economical and ethical rationality? What institution controls the means to implement the decisions that have been made in cases of conflict?

These are difficult questions and no one has a ready answer for them at present. In the following I would like to restrict myself to illuminating the system structure that lies behind this question.

DIFFERENTIATION PROBLEMS: LOSS OF EFFICIENCY AND COSTS OF COORDINATION

Let us first recapitulate the discussion till now. The core of the problem lies in the existence of functionally differentiated systems whose specific performances are steered by system-internal codes that, in turn, lead to autonomy claims *vis-à-vis* other subsystems. The specific performance of the economic system is the production of material wealth. The specific code which it follows is the positive formation of the cost–benefit difference. The economic principle of achieving the maximum gain with given means, the postulate of scarcity or the hypothesis of the maximization of utility, are only different versions of this guiding difference. It is this semantic, and only this one, that steers all operations of the system and connects them into an operationally closed, but communicatively open, unity.

The interconnection of operational closure and communicative openness shows that the economic system indeed can hear the message of ethics but must reformulate it in its own language so that it can be effective on the operational level. All approaches of economic theories refer precisely to this connection for which the question is: ethics or economy? This means at the same time that neoclassical theory, or more exactly the general theory of equilibrium, adequately thematizes the *system level* of the economy.

An initial result of this theory of functionally differentiated societies is that a successful external steering of the economy by ethical parameters is not possible. Another is that there can be no communicative discourse between ethics and the economy on the systems level. Systems indeed reflect their respective environments on the system level, on the basis of their own operational conditions. In this situation the condition of the possibility of an ethics of the economic system cannot lie in the system of mainstream economics, because standard economics can reformulate ethics only as a problem of efficiency. A general theory of rationality, however, amounts to an ethics that is completely absorbed by the economic calculus. But this is precisely where one encounters an inestimable danger to the economic system which may very well enjoy a steering autonomy but at the same time depends to a great degree on the steeering autonomy of its environment. Wherever the economic code is incapable of adequately reducing problematic societal complexity, the expansion of economic rationality that falls to other system logics tends to lead to the destruction of the economic system's mirror of reflection. In the end it turns blindly in circles.

This is the ultimate basis of the weakness and impossibility of an actual general theory of rationality as well as the necessity of the talk of the non-economic conditions of the economy. The former emphasizes the autonomy (and in some cases the primacy too) of the economic system, the latter interprets autonomy as an element of interdependent dependences.

My thesis now is that this contemporary discussion of the ethics of the economic system points to a much deeper societal problem, viz. the problem of an overdifferentiation (Buss and Schöps, 1979; Halfmannand Japp, 1981).

First, the basic problematic is the one of the relation of functionally differentiated systems among themselves. We found that it was coterminous with the beginning of functional differentiation. And it is no accident that social theories of differentiation are strong in the analysis of autonomy claims but weak in the explanation of the integration of subsystems into a functional whole. Second, and this follows from the first point, evolved functionality is accompanied by the loss of efficiency and effectiveness due to coordination costs. Third, and this follows from the basic problematic too, in the course of societal differentiation there seems to be an increase of relevant, intended and unintended effects of system activity on other systems. In any event, I am inclined to view the motives of the present discussion about an ethics of the economic system elaborated above, viz. internal and external effects, as the expression of this problematic situation of societal overdifferentiation.

From this point of view, the theoretical efforts to establish a general theory of rationality are nothing less than the attempt, through the expansion of the economic form of rationality and the internalization of non-market phenomena, to give the societal steering problems that have emerged in the course of societal differentiation a theoretical form that will make them accessible to steering from the leading system: the economy. This simply means increasing complexity for the purpose of reducing complexity.

It is therefore incorrect to begin in an *a priori* and unilinear way from a positive correlation between functional differentiation and an increase of efficiency. Instead, costs accrue that can overshadow gains in differentiation. In this situation dedifferentiation is not a step backwards into a seemingly less complex situation but a thematization of the necessity to supplement differentiation with the specific logic of distinct subsystems (Buss and Schöps, 1979, p. 317). In this way emphasis is put on functional interconnection and non-functional extension with a view to reducing system incompatibilities and their resulting losses of efficiency and coordination costs. This is a matter of solving the problem of integration of differentiated societies by means of structural assimilation and the inclusion of the logics of other systems in any system. In this way, a theory of dedifferentiation reacts to the same phenomena as a general theory of rationality, but it reacts in the opposite direction. Both ways of solving the problem are possible: the extension of the economic system's steering code to everything of societal and personal importance, and the interweaving of different logics. In practice, the latter means that functions, interests and discussable themes are not to be referred to in an *a priori* manner to the exclusive domain of competency of one subsystem but are intermediary in such a way that their meaning, scope and effectiveness are attributable to different societal subdomains (Buss and Schöps, 1979, p. 324).

A SYSTEMATIC OF THE INTERCONNECTION OF THE ECONOMY AND ETHICS

Our considerations of dedifferentiation are in need of further justification since, at first glance, they seem somehow to contradict our earlier assumptions concerning the autonomy claims of societal systems based on the classical formulation of the theory of functional differentiation (Spencer, Durkheim, Simmel, Weber, Parsons and Luhmann). As far as the justification of economics is concerned, I would like to conclude with a discussion of several aspects.

First of all, it seems important to me to have a clear concept of the system itself. Who has already seen the economic system, the circulation of money or the market as an efficient allocative mechanism? Obviously, these are cases of theoretically educed, abstract world-structures that are ascribed the power to guide actions. They are the result of a societal and scientific discourse that in our case begins in the modern period with the socio-philosophical justification and the instrumental formation of the economic system. The peculiarity and also the problem of the social sciences (crystallized in endless epistemological and methodological discussions) lies in the fact that they deal with forms of being that they themselves have helped to create. This constructive idea avoids the functional mistake of ascribing the causal advantages of efficiency and effectiveness to functional system-differentiation. To treat differentiation as an historically emergent form of thinking that was a successful answer to a problematic historical situation allows one to modify this form of thinking when the problematic situation changes.

A further point is the fact that an exclusively functional consideration can only deal very poorly with the complexity of acting individuals. This complexity has its roots in the self-reflexivity of social actors that is expressed in the action-guiding role of expectations, thus in the projection of the future as a part of the present motives of action. In other words, individuals are by no means forced to carry out system imperatives. They are more than mere character masks. They enjoy a degree of freedom that derives from the fact that, in contrast to the system, the economic, ethical and aesthetic code of rationality is accessible to them. This does not mean that they could act in permanent disregard of system logics. But it perhaps means that, as a rule, there is no system logic that admits of only one action-alternative. Instead, equi-final solutions are possible. Precisely because what one normally calls economic reality or the force of things are also always sought after, it is possible to conceive ethics and economics as reciprocally connectable. If, in fact, at any time we were faced with the sole alternative of carrying out the fixed laws of the economy or of failing through inefficiency, then one could no longer see where the often touted individualism of the economic actor could be effective. Formulated economically, this means that wherever there is uncertainty of action because of incomplete information and complex circumstances it makes no sense to assume the maximization of utility as a motive of action. The definition of the economic code as the positive formation of the cost–benefit difference reflects this circumstance because it replaces the maximization hypothesis with an adequate selection criterion for economic decisions (Alchian, 1950).[3]

Thus because of cognitive competence individuals have to be ascribed an essential capacity for strategy (Elster, 1984, 1989). The capacity for 'rational choice' then does not refer only to the maximization of given and permanently assumed ideas of utility but to 'constraints' themselves, thus to the forming of constraints on action. Jon Elster has analysed such situations using game theory and exemplified them through the example of Ulysses. Ulysses was bound to the mast in order to resist the enticements of the sirens. His self-binding was an act of the 'rational self-conditioning of rationality' (Wiesenthal, 1987, p. 18) so that he could remain capable of action in the short as well as in the long run.

In this version of the problem of rationality, ethical preferences are no longer assumed as given and stable but the utility of the concept of utility is itself an object of reflection. Its difference from the classical theory resides then in a concept of utility that does not confuse functional efficiency with rationality. The result of this for economic theory is, I believe, the task of extending and restructuring its concept of personal preferences because the standard assumption that the order of an individual's preferences is independent of all other individual preference orders no longer holds up from the perspective of an ethics of the economic system. John C. Harsanyi's differentiation of ethical and subjective preferences (Harsanyi, 1955, p. 315) and Amartya K. Sen's requirement of a theoretical structure that allows an individual many preference orders and the formation of a meta-preference order (Sen, 1977) go in this direction. An ethics of the economy can be understood as an act of individual and collective self-binding, as a possibility of the rational choice of action constraints.[4]

In this way a theory of functional differentiation is connected with an action theory, action-orienting systems with action-capable individuals and system-properties with individual interpretations.

Therefore an ethics of the economy as it is presented here by its very definition cannot be any particular, subtle institution for the maximization of profits. Instead, it enables the economic system and its actors to see themselves from the perspectives of other rationality claims that are, none the less, indispensable for their existence. This is where one has to take account of the objection that such behaviour ultimately derives from the economic calculus. This is the case to the extent that it is a matter of the self-reflexive reference to economic rationality to the conditions of the economic system's continued existence. The difference is that self-interested utility maximization is not confused in this case with the discovery of rational decisions pure and simple. The infinite regress of what I have called the non-economic bases of the economy to the self-interests of individuals is possible as long as the concept of self-interests is conceived as genuinely and exclusively belonging to the economic sphere. But this is not the case.

Self-interest is the modern formulation of a much more fundamental human capacity, viz. the ability to strive for something. Aesthetic as well as economic and ethical rationality follows from rationally guided striving. Only together do these constitute rationally reflected self-interest.

This leads to the thesis that an ethics of the economy is not sufficiently defined by the economic system's capacity to reflect the logics of other systems. Instead, ethical action in the economy means the capacity to integrate different and possibly conflicting system perspectives. The acceptance of conflicting forms of logic involved in economic actions leads to the differentiation of economic decision-making processes into their moral (and naturally also technical, legal, psychological, social, political) and economic aspects. These aspects are not mutually reducible and to produce an economic decision means to balance out all these autonomous claims.

Seen from the perspective of the architecture of theory this cannot be realized on the macro level of action-oriented systems, nor on the micro level of individuals that are in principle capable of action, but only by mesosystems capable of action: organizations. The concept of mesosystems does not indicate a specific form of organization but the form of organization pure and simple. Correct as it is that an ethics of the economic system is impossible without an individual that is capable of action in the strategic sense, it is just as true that this kind of capacity for action usually has narrow boundaries. These boundaries are dramatically extended by organizations that are ascribed the capacity to act.

Firms, labour unions, associations and other collective actors in the domains of the economy, politics and ethics are of decisive importance for any concept of an ethics of the economy because they are the point of intersection between the system and the individual. There is a drift within the tectonics of modern societies in which organizations such as companies are gaining in governing capacity with regard to complex social and societal decisions. Organizations are the systematic locus of the ethics of the economy. For, on one hand, they are the existence-form of the respective system imperatives (macro level of society), and, on the other, the individuals (micro level of society) constituting them are capable of polycontextual thinking. Mesosystems (or organizations) can therefore realize the macro system's internal and external effects as such and reconstruct them discursively (by individuals) and in a way relevant for action in different system logics without their information value being lost. This is precisely what is impossible, for different reasons, on the macro and micro levels. Competing autonomy claims that refer back to the system's macro level are accessible to relativization only on the meso level because individuals are capable of a multi-rational and polycontextual clarification and conditioning of distinct and possibly conflicting rationality claims.

The different levels of relating the economy, economics and ethics thus open up, as it were, like a Russian *matrioshka* doll. This too contains distinct entities that only together constitute its essence. This may help to clarify what I have attempted to present here: the different levels and structural possibilities of a discussion of an ethics of the economic system that focuses on a unified concept of an ethics of the economy.

NOTES

1 Even though this has become the dominant interpretation of economics since the end of the Second World War it is still not the only one. These interpretations, whether this is the Austrian Aprioristic School or Socio-economics, argue for the inclusion of the human–human and the human–thing relation within economics; whether this is as irretrievable subjectivity or as psychological, socio-psychological, sociological, legal or political parameters of action. See A. Etzioni, op. cit. In this context Keynesian theory is also important because the thesis of a long-term underemployment equilibrium calls the capacity of the self-regulation of the system into question. See Keynes (1934/1974).

2 It should be noted that this reification of the intelligible form is not often encountered in the economic discussion and is a permanent source of confusion and false fronts in methodological questions. It is no accident that *homo oeconomicus* is not a concrete, living being but a stimulus-reaction machine adapted to its environment.

3 The fact remains that maximizing behaviour under the conditions of competition and uncertainty is itself a method of reducing uncertainty *ex ante*. The fact that this method is counterproductive in complex circumstances, thus misses its goal, was the starting point for our discussions. Nevertheless, the positive formation of the cost–benefit difference is an *ex-post* criterion to which effectiveness can be ascribed if it succeeds in supplying the conditions under which it is possible to determine which difference is adequate with regard to future developments. Ultimately this is a matter of the choice of rational constraints on action.

4 Of course, this formulation contains a new difficulty, viz. that of defining the concept of reason more exactly. It will be decisive in this connection to clarify the problem of action within a future that is in principle open. In practice this means: how is the choice of action-constraints at time t_0 connected with the expectation of possible innovations at time t_1. Innovations can make action-constraints superfluous. But the converse is also true. The development, stagnation and collapse of societies are very similar in this point and therefore no ethics of the economic system can escape answering this question. An entire abyss of questions opens up here that I would not like to address. Nor do I have a convincing answer for them. However, I believe that the continued pursuit of the idea of the rational choice of action-constraints is absolutely indispensable because it leads to the core of any ethics of the economics system.

REFERENCES

Alchian, A. A. (1950) 'Uncertainty, evolution, and economic theory', *Journal of Political Economy*, 58 (2), 211–221.

Alchian, A. A. (1965) 'The basis of some recent advances in the theory of management of the firm', *Journal of Industrial Economics*, 14, 30–48.

Angell, J. W. (1926) *The Theory of International Prices: History, Criticism, and Restatement*, Cambridge, MA: Harvard University Press.

Arrow, K. J. and Debreu, G. (1954) 'Existence of an equilibrium for a competitive economy', *Econometrica*, 22, 265–290.

Becker, G. S. (1976) *The Economic Approach to Human Behavior*, Chicago: University of Chicago Press.

Biervert, B. and Wieland, J. (1987) 'Der ethische Gehalt ökonomischer Kategorien – Beispiel: Der Nutzen', in B. Biervert and M. Held (eds), *Ökonomische Theorie und Ethik*, Frankfurt a.M. and New York: Campus, pp. 23–50.

Biervert, B. and Wieland, J. (1990) 'Gegenstandsbereich und Rationalitätsform der Ökonomie und der Ökonomik', in B. Biervert, K. Held and J. Wieland (eds), *Sozialphilosophische Grundlagen der Ökonomie*, Frankfurt a.M.: Suhrkamp Verlag, pp. 7–32.

Brennan, G. and Buchanan, J. M. (1984) 'The normative purpose of economic "science": rediscovery of an eighteenth century method', in J. M. Buchanan and R. D. Tollison (eds), *The Theory of Public Choice II*, Ann Arbor: University of Michigan Press.

Buchanan, A. (1985) *Ethics, Efficiency, and the Market*, Oxford: Oxford University Press.

Buchanan, J. M. (1975) *The Limits of Liberty. Between Anarchy and Leviathan*, Chicago: University of Chicago Press.

Buchanan, J. M. (1977) *Freedom in Constitutional Contract*, College Station and London: Texas A & M University Press.

Buchanan, J. M. and Tollison, R. D. (eds) (1984) *The Theory of Public Choice II*, Ann Arbor: University of Michigan Press.

Buss, E. and Schöps, M. (1979) 'Die gesellschaftliche Entdifferenzierung', *Zeitschrift für Soziologie*, 8, 315–329.

de Gijsel, P. (1984) 'Individuum und Gerechtigkeit in ökonomischen Verteilungstheorien', in *Jahrbuch Ökonomie und Gesellschaft*, Frankfurt a.M. and New York: Campus, pp. 14–66.

Dietzel, H. (1882) 'Der Ausgangspunkt der Sozialwirtschaftslehre und ihre Grundbegriffe', *Zeitschrift für die gesamte Staatswissenschaft*, 39, 336–362.

Elster, J. (1984) *Ulysses and the Sirens. Studies in Rationality and Irrationality*. rev. edn, Cambridge: Cambridge University Press.

Elster, J. (1989) *The Cement of Society. Studies in Rationality and Social Change*, Cambridge: Cambridge University Press.

Etzioni, A. (1988) *The Moral Dimension. Toward a New Economics*, New York: Free Press.

Gäfgen, G. (1988) 'Der Wandel moralischer Normen in der Entwicklung der Wirtschaftsordnung: Erklärung und ethische Folgerungen', in H. Hesse (ed.), *Wirtschaftswissenschaft und Ethik*, Berlin: Duncker & Humblot.

Halfmann, J. and Japp, K. P. (1981) 'Grenzen sozialer Differenzierung – Grenzen des Wachstums öffentlicher Sozialdienste', *Zeitschrift für Soziologie*, 10, 244–255.

Hampicke, U. (1987) 'Ethik, Natur und Neoklassische Ökonomie', in B. Biervert and M. Held (eds), *Ökonomische Theorie und Ethik*, Frankfurt: Campus Verlag, pp. 78–100.

Harsanyi, J. C. (1955) 'Cardinal welfare. Individualistic ethics, and interpersonal comparison of utility', *Journal of Political Economy*, 63, 309–321.

Hobbes, T. (1561/1841) *Leviathan: Or, the Matter, Form, and Power of a Commonwealth, Ecclesiastical and Civil*, in *The English Works*, London: John Bohn, vol. III.

Homann, K. (1988) 'Die Rolle ökonomischer Überlegungen in der Grundlegung der Ethik', in H. Hesse (ed.), *Wirtschaftswissenschaft und Ethik*, Berlin: Duncker & Humblot.

Homann, K. (ed.) (1990) *Wirtschaftswissenschaft und Ethik*, Tübingen: Mohr.

Jevons, W. St. (1871/1970) *The Theory of Political Economy*, Harmondsworth: Penguin.

Keynes, J. M. (1934/1974) 'Poverty in plenty: is the economic system self-adjusting?', in *Collected Writings of J. M. Keynes*, London: Macmillan, vol. 13.

Lindenberg, S. (1983) 'Utility and morality', *Kyklos*, 36 (3), 450–468.

Luhmann, N. (1984) *Soziale Systeme. Grundriß einer allgemeinen Theorie*, Frankfurt: Suhrkamp Verlag.

Luhmann, N. (1988) *Die Wirtschaft der Gesellschaft*, Frankfurt: Suhrkamp Verlag.

McKenzie, R. B. and Tullock, G. (1978) *The World of Economics*, Homewood: R. D. Irwin.

Mandeville, B. (1795/1966) *The Fable of the Bees or Private Vices, Public Benefits*, Oxford: Oxford University Press.

Marx, K. (1844/1981) 'Ökonomisch–philosophische Manuskripte aus dem Jahre 1844', in *MEW Ergänzungsband: Schriften bis 1844; Erster Teil*, Berlin: Dietz.

Matthews, R. C. O. (1981) 'Morality, competition and efficiency', *The Manchester School of Economic and Social Studies*, II, 289–309.

Mayr, O. (1971) 'Adam Smith and the concept of the feedback system', *Technology and Culture*, 12 (1), 1–22.

Mill, J. S. (1844) *Essays on Some Unsettled Questions of Political Economy*, London: Parker.

North, D. C. (1981) *Structure and Change in Economic History*, New York: Norton.

Pareto, V. (1900) 'Sul fenomeno economico. Lettre a Benedetto Croce', *Giornale degli Economisti*, 21.

Pareto, V. (1900–1904) 'Anwendungen der Mathematik auf Nationalökonomië', in *Enzyklopädie der mathematischen Wissenschaften mit Einschlüß ihrer Anwendungen*, Leipzig: Teubner-Verlag, vol. 1, part 2.

Posner, R. (1975) *Economic Analysis of Law*, Boston and Toronto: Little Brown.

Robbins, L. (1932) *An Essay on the Nature and Significance of Economic Science*, London and Basingstoke: Macmillan.

Rosenberg, A. (1979) 'Can economic theory explain everything?', *Philosophy of the Social Sciences*, 9, 63–84.

Rosenberg, A. (1980) 'A skeptical history of micro-economic theory', *Theory and Decision*, 12, 79–93.

Sen, A. K. (1977) 'Rational fools: a critique of the behavioral foundations of economic theory', *Philosophy and Public Affairs*, 6 (4), 317–344.

Sen, A. K. (1987) *On Ethics and Economics*, New York: Blackwell.

Simmel, G. (1901/1989) *Philosophie des Geldes*, Frankfurt a.M.: Suhrkamp.

Smith, A. (1759/1976) *The Theory of Moral Sentiments*, Oxford: Clarendon Press.

Smith, A. (1776/1976) *An Inquiry into the Nature and Causes of the Wealth of Nations*, Oxford: Clarendon Press.

Smith, A. (1795/1980) *Essays on Philosophical Subjects*, Oxford: Clarendon Press.

Sombart, W. (1930) *Die drei Nationalökonomien*, Berlin: Duncker & Humblot.

Stigler, G. J. (1981) 'Economics or Ethics?', in *The Tanner Lectures on Human Values*, Salt Lake City: University of Utah Press.

Strigl, R. (1923) *Die ökonomischen Kategorien und die Organisation der Wirtschaft*, Jena: Fischer Verlag.

Viner, J. (1937) *Studies in the Theory of International Trade*, London: Allen & Unwin.

Walras, L. (1926/1977) *Elements of Pure Economics and the Theory of Social Wealth*, Homewood: Fairfield.

Wieland, J. (1988) 'Die Wirtschaft als autopoietisches System. Einige eher kritische Überlegungen', *Delfin*, X, 18–29.

Wieland, J. (1989) *Die Entdeckung der Ökonomie. Kategorien, Gegenstandsbereiche und Rationalitätstypen der Ökonomie an ihrem Ursprung*, Bern/Stuttgart: Haupt.

Wieland, J. (1991a) 'Die immanente Ethik des natürlichen Preises bei Adam Smith – über die Beziehungen des Marktsystems zu seinem Rand', in A. Meyer-Faje and P. Ulrich (eds), *Der andere Adam Smith. Beiträge zur Neubestimmung von Ökonomie als Politischer Ökonomie*, Bern/Stuttgart: Haupt, pp. 223–248.

Wieland, J. (1991b) 'Adam Smiths System der Politischen Ökonomie. Die Emergenz des ökonomischen Systems der Moderne', in W. Krohn and G. Küppers (eds), *Emergenz und Selbstorganisation*, Frankfurt a.M.: Suhrkamp, pp. 363–387.

Wiesenthal, H. (1987) *Introduction to J. Elster, Subversion der Rationalität*, Frankfurt a.M./ New York: Campus.

Williamson, O. E. (1979) 'Transaction cost economics: the governance of contractual relations', *Journal of Law and Economics*, 22, 231–261.

Williamson, O. E. (1985) *The Economic Institutions of Capitalism*, New York: Free Press.

Chapter 14

Social ownership

A comparison of the property rights, social choice and economic justice approaches

Robert Stallaerts

SUMMARY

In this article, we confront three main approaches to the problem of social ownership. We first analyse the most common objections to the concept of social ownership, as formulated by the property rights school (e.g. Furubotn and Pejovich). Though some of the arguments are contested by other authors, their approach seems now to have been accepted as the standard view on the problem of common ownership. The main arguments for privatization strategies are based upon this approach. Next we recall some of the principles and requirements a desirable social economic order should satisfy. We take here into consideration the implications of some criteria formulated by the social choice approach of J. Roemer. We then extend the discussion to the moral foundations of some theories of justice (Rawls, Barry) and explore whether one can find a good justification for the concept of social ownership on these grounds.

INTRODUCTION

The question of social ownership has been debated long and hard. Many contemporary authors argue that the inefficiency of social ownership has been proven and that privatization strategies should take precedence. We will once more review the issue, trying not to focus just on one approach, but enlarging the discussion in some unusual but hopely fruitful directions. Finally, we shall fall back upon some well-known intuitions, but we hope the new formulation shall contribute to the debate. The category of social ownership has been first extensively studied by the property rights economics, a forerunner of institutional economics. Of course, it had its place earlier in socialist political economy,[1] that however lacked analytical rigour and that will not be considered here. In the early 1970s, Furubotn and Pejovich (1974) developed their arguments about the intrinsic deficiencies and difficulties of the self-managed economy. Their conclusions did not go totally unchallenged (Stephen and Smith, 1975), but mainstream economics did take over their argument, as exemplified by Jensen and Meckling (1979). This critical current seems now also dominant in Yugoslavia (Posljednji Dani Društvenog Vlasništva, 1990).

We then leave this traditional pattern of thinking on social ownership for some normative economics of welfare and social choice theory. We analyse what are the consequences when we want to introduce axiomatically some ethical principles. We follow Roemer (1988) showing us some of the implications of social ownership.

Finally we look into theories of justice developed by Harsanyi and Rawls for a justification of social ownership as a moral and socially just institution. Can social ownership be derived as a necessary, desirable and just institution by decision makers? If so, has this some practical implications in the real world?

At least we try to show that it can be fruitful to enrich the traditional discussion with these two viewpoints.

PROPERTY RIGHTS ECONOMICS

We summarize in a non-formal way the main points of the property rights advocates. We define social property in a way it fitted the Yugoslav situation. Social property is a special form of collective property of the means of production and of other resources such that they belong to the community and not to one collective, group or individual. So, in theory, everybody and nobody owns these means.[2]

Furubotn (1974) was one of the first to criticize such an arrangement analytically. His main argument holds that workers will not be interested in future investment in their own firm out of profits or savings, because they have no claim on the principal. They prefer to consume or invest in self-owned assets. In any case, they will first exhaust bank loans. They will only invest own means when the rate of interest equals the bank rate plus a remuneration for their forgone principal. Moreover workers want to recuperate their investment in a rather short time period, at most the time of their future working career in the firm.

Jensen and Meckling (1979) label this the horizon problem. The authors further argue that workers will not even be much interested in maintaining the real worth of the means of production. Accounting tricks will diminish real depreciation. A part of the real value of the capital stock will be transformed into current income and distributed to the workers.

The property rights structure of the Yugoslav self-managed firm generates some more problems. The authors distinguish the horizon problem from the common property problem, a slight variation on our first investment problem. Workers are self-interested welfare optimizers. Their interests will necessarily clash. Newcomers are at once granted the same claims on current income. Senior members will react with policies of under-investment or restriction of membership. In either case, Pareto-optimality will not be reached.

The non-transferability of the claims causes related problems. As the worth of firms cannot be valuated on a stock market, the pattern of allocation of the means of production will necessarily display inefficiencies. Moreover, employees suffer from serious portfolio problems as the ability to diversify assets has been curtailed. In sum, the property rights structure of social property does not provide a viable solution to the problems of risk and uncertainty.

Finally, there exists a control problem in the self-managed firm. In the view of the author it has to be ascribed more to the institutional set-up than to the property rights structure of the economy.

There has been some discussion about technical points in the literature. Stephen (1980) has attacked Furubotn's assertion that self-managing collectives will first use external resources before financing investments out of retained profits. He shows that welfare maximization should reverse this priority rule. However, Milanovic (1983), while granting Stephen this point, argues that in fact the cooperative will then fail to use the resource with the lower social opportunity cost. The relevance of this discussion fades out a little, as borrowing of external funds has been conditioned on partial self-financing.[3]

Most of the above arguments are picked up by today's privatizers. (Poslednji Dani Društvenog Vlasništva, 1990). The introduction to this book tells us that social property hampers the installation of political democracy and an efficient market economy. Most authors elaborate on this theme, focusing on the economic implications of social property. Only privatization can bring a solution to the economic crisis. For example, Mencinger (1990) argues that full responsibility will not be taken up until ownership titles are clearly distributed. The functions of risk taking and efficient undertaking require well-defined rules fixing rights and responsibilities. Kalogjera (1990) argues for the transformation of the social capital into shares and the introduction of a capital market. The federal law on the circulation of social capital has incorporated a great deal of the privatization philosophy.[4] It is not clear, however, how much of the social economy should be privatized and whether the issuing of internal shares should be supplemented by the issuing of external shares. A Slovenian law proposal transcends the hitherto extending practice in Yugoslavia of issuing internal shares and starts creating regulations for transferable shares.[5]

We now return to the discussion of principles and like to comment as follows. Just one institutional characteristic has been picked out: the social property. But it is clear that the whole legal and institutional surroundings will determine how the economy really works. Economic policy will greatly influence the performance of the institution of social property. Further, a certain type of economic agent has been selected: a short-time self-interested welfare maximizer. How realistic is this individualistic creature? It looks at least an extreme representation.

Finally, and in the light of the previous remarks, most problematical aspects of the social property institution could be remedied. In my view, the most serious challenge lies in the risk and uncertainty argument. Is a good working capital market an inevitable condition for an efficient developed economy? Are there other institutional arrangements possible that respect social ownership and at the same time resolve problems of efficiency and evaluation of worth? On the other side, can this argument alone decide the question? We argue it should not. A trade-off has to be considered between the desirability and moral value of social property and some loss of efficiency.

The limits of the property rights approach have to be carefully stated. As Furubotn and Pejovich (1972) characterize the approach, the organization *per se* is not the central focus: rather, individuals who are assumed to seek their own interests and to maximize utility subject to the limits established by the existing organizational structure.[6] So the strength of the approach turns into its weakness: social welfare functions are either ignored or ruled out on grounds that such constructs have use only when choices are to be made by some agency or group external to the individuals directly affected.[7] The property rights approach is based on assumptions that show an extreme individualist basis of choice. In the next section we try to transcend this bias.

THE SOCIAL WELFARE APPROACH OF J. ROEMER

On the crossroads of welfare economics and social choice theory, Roemer does research on the implications of the concept of social ownership. What does it really mean in axiomatic terms to impose the requirement of social ownership? This can be seen as an exercise in normative economics, or just as a description of the implications of a normative approach. It is in this last perspective that Roemer undertakes his project, but we propose to take a stronger stand.

Roemer (1988) gives no exact positive definition of social ownership. Instead, he follows an axiomatic approach. Social ownership is defined as the axiomatically defined restrictions a constitution or allocation mechanism needs to respect in certain environments. Roemer then analyses the implications of this formulation.

Take for example the following situation. Two agents display an unequal ability to work. They own jointly the land on which corn has to be cultivated by investing each (unequal) labour. Here the normative principles are thus given by the private ownership of their skills and the public or joint ownership of the land. In fact, they also share a common utility function and their labour can be translated into units of standard labour, so that a production function can transform the labour and land into corn. An economic environment consists of land, a production function and a utility function and the skill levels of the individuals. An economic constitution or allocation mechanism is a rule that assigns some feasible allocation of labour and corn to both individuals. Of course there are a lot of these rules. One needs to specify conditions that restrict the economic constitutions to a class that displays the desired features. These restrictions on the behaviour of the rules will be translated into axioms.

Roemer needs five axioms to fix the self-ownership of capabilities and the right on public ownership of the external world, supplemented by some other technological requirements.

Axiom 1: Pareto optimality

The first axiom defines efficiency by Pareto optimality. This means that it should be impossible to find another feasible allocation that gives both of the agents greater utility.

Axiom 2: Land monotonicity

When the amount of land has increased, then both agents should be at least as well off in terms of welfare as before. The axiom is intended as a necessary condition of public ownership of the land.

Axiom 3: Technological monotonicity

When the technology (the production function) has improved, at least as much corn should be produced as before. Each agent should be at least as well off in terms of welfare as before. Technological monotonicity represents the public property right that agents have in technology, which is taken to be part of the external world.

Axiom 4: Limited self-ownership

When one agent is at least as skilled as the other, then he should be rendered at least as well off as the other. This right on self-ownership is limited in the sense that one could argue that an agent with more skills should be strictly better off. The axiom implies that equally skilled agents should be rendered equally well off.

Axiom 5: Protection of infirm

A less skilled person should not suffer for the greater ability of the more skilled. This can be formalized by stating that the less skilled person should not be worse off than in a world where both agents would be equally (the other also less) skilled. This axiom does not imply that the better skilled should share the fruits of his skill differentially to the less skilled. It only prescribes that there are no negative externalities from being less skilled.

When these five restrictions are imposed on economic constitutions, then Roemer can prove that there is only one that satisfies these conditions. It is the unique constitution that assigns in any environment the Pareto optimal allocation of corn and labour that equalizes the utility levels of the agents.

This is a very strong requirement. So the conclusion can go either way. Or one sticks to these conditions and then a strong institutional design has to be set up to satisfy the conditions. Or one thinks these conditions are too strong and gives up some of the axioms, e.g. those that imply common ownership.

Of course, the weight of each axiom to the final result has to be verified. For example, Christie (1989) has criticized Roemer's monotonicity requirements as too strong and as unworkable in the real world. Roemer (1988) himself gives much weight to the common ownership features. They are most responsible for the equalization of welfare. Common ownership fades out self-ownership of capabilities. Common ownership also clashes with strict self-ownership. People's capitalism – that takes equal distribution of the means of production as a starting point before a free market does its work – also clashes with the five axioms.

Roemer defines an economic environment as a vector of economic elements. The moral character of a constitution is defined by the restrictions imposed on them. Should it not be possible to define an ethical environment, so adding some moral elements to the economic vector? In fact, moral elements could then be seen as additional restrictions on the economic constitution. This focuses the discussion on the ethical question.

Roemer has analysed the strong implications of the concept of social ownership. It leaves unanswered the question why we should impose social ownership. We propose an answer to this question in the framework of a third approach.

THEORIES OF JUSTICE

Rawls (1972) is of course the most well-known contemporary advocate of a theory of justice. In reality, Harsanyi (1955) formulated an earlier version of the hypothetical situation in a search for generally acceptable ethical preferences.[8] The ethical component is given by the fact that persons have to make choices while not knowing which place they will occupy in society. They have knowledge about the society, the possible roles, technology and so on, but their personal interests cannot play in the choice. This forces them to an impartial choice, imagining they could occupy any place in the society. Harsanyi thus uses a thin veil of ignorance, in contrast to Rawls. The choice situation of the Rawlsian actors is much more uncertain, covered by a thick veil, granting only a minimum of information in the hypothetical situation.

For our purposes the Rawlsian situation fits better, as we suppose some institutions still have to be chosen by the actors in the hypothetical situation. The point we want to derive so far is that an institutional set-up can be morally justified by the hypothetical situation with a thick veil.

There has been some discussion in the literature (Barry, 1989) as to whether a decision on principles taken in the hypothetical situation should be carried over in real life. The point is in my view heavily related to the acceptance of pure procedural justice. Principles and institutional choices are justified because they are the result of a fair procedure. If one does accept that the hypothetical situation is a fair situation, then one has to accept the outcomes of decision making in that situation. Is the hypothetical situation a relevant frame for our decision making? We think we do not dispose of decisive arguments, but we find it a valuable moral point of view. The original situation is a prototype of a situation that guarantees an impartial decision. One could argue that there is not enough information in this situation to decide anything, or one could hold that decisions can be taken only when led by one's interests. Both objections are not wholly valid. The original situation seems to have enough structure to derive principles and desired characteristics of institutional set-ups. The second objection rejects a model of man that is not only driven by personal interest. Some common goals in society cannot be defined as the aggregation of the preferences of all the individuals. Real life shows that these ideals exist and in my view they are also morally justified. Of course, we accept there can be a lot of discussion about the exact derivation of results in the hypothetical situation, not in the least about the relevant decision procedures. We conclude that some reservation should be made to our future assertations and derivations, but we hold that none the less there is some moral justification for our thought experiment.

What we now want to argue, and this is the central thesis of this section, is that the institution of social ownership can be derived logically and with enough force within the hypothetical situation. So we find a general moral justification for social property, that should not be rejected by rational decision makers in society. This proposal is of course not self-evident. Rawls (1972) himself argues that his theory of justice does not pre-judge the choice of regime.

We first follow Pazner and Schmeidler (1976) who in the contractarian framework of Rawls, seek to determine *ex ante* a determinate distribution of economic resources. Rational individuals in the original position can be expected to agree unanimously on the egalitarian distribution of resources. When they do not know which position they will take in society, decision rules will lead them to this egalitarian position.[9]

Now we recall Roemer's result on the implication of social property. He showed that common property necessarily leads to an equal distribution. So, we now suggest that common property could do the job Pazner and

Schmeidler require as the logical outcome of the contractarian approach in the hypothetical situation. Rational individuals in the hypothetical situation should choose a basic structure of society where common property of the means of production is a fundamental feature. This choice could be seen as an insurance policy granting equal opportunities to all members of society once the veil of ignorance is lifted.

CONCLUSION

In the first part we have presented arguments of the property rights theorists against the common property as an inefficient institution. We pointed out the underlying anthropological assumptions and value options of the approach. Social choice theory in Roemer's interpretation has laid bare some logical implications of common property. In the theory of justice, using Pazner's egalitarian interpretation of Rawls's contractarian approach, we have finally found a convincing justification for the institution of common property.

NOTES

1 The point of departure could perhaps be found in the work of Kidric (1952).
2 Mali Leksikon Samoupravljača (1972, p. 6) and Strahinjić (1980, p. 45).
3 In 1972 a Yugoslav law was enacted specifying that a bank could not make a loan to a business firm for investment in fixed assets unless the firm secured at least 20 per cent of the total cost from its own funds (Furubotn, 1974, p. 269).
4 For a discussion of this law, see B. Kovać, 'Nacionalizacija i privatizacija', *Ekonomska Politika* (1989), pp. 23–26.
5 'Slovenija. Strogo kontrolisana privatizacija', in *Ekonomska Politika* (1991), pp. 17–18.
6 Furubotn and Pejovich (1972), p. 1137.
7 Furubotn and Pejovich (1972), p. 1157.
8 Of course, one could go back to Hume, Smith and other philosophers who put the impartial spectator on stage.
9 This is equally true for the minimax, the minimax regret and insufficient reason decision rules (Pazner and Schmeidler, 1976).

REFERENCES

Barry, B. (1989) *Theories of Justice*, Berkeley, University of California Press, vol. I.
Christie, D. (1989) 'John Roemer's economic philosophy and the perils of formalism', in R. Ware and K. Nielsen (eds), Analyzing Marxism, Supplement, *Canadian Journal of Philosophy*, 267–280.
Furubotn, E. (1974) 'Bank credit and the labor-managed firm: the Yugoslav case', reprinted in: E. Furubotn and S. Pejovich, *The Economics of Property Rights*, Cambridge, MA: Ballinger, pp. 257–276.
Furubotn, E. and Pejovich, S. (1972) 'Property rights and economic theory: a survey of recent literature', *Journal of Economic Literature*, 4, 1137–1162.
Furubotn, E. G. and Pejovich, S. (1974) *The Economics of Property Rights*, Cambridge, MA: Ballinger.

Harsanyi, J. C. (1955) 'Cardinal welfare, individualistic ethics and interpersonal comparisons of utility', *Journal of Political Economy*, 309–321.

Jensen, M. C. and Meckling, W. H. (1979) 'Rights and production functions: an application to labor-managed firms and codetermination', *Journal of Business*, 4, 469–506.

Kalogjera, D. (1990) 'Puteve preobrazbe vlasništva', *Poslednji Dani Društvenog Vlasništva*, 7–21.

Kidrić, B. (1952) 'O nekim teorijskim pitanjima novog privrednog sistema'. *Komunist*, 1–2. Reprinted in V. Merhar, (ed.) (1979) *Boris Kidrić. Socijalizam i ekonomija*, Zagreb: Globus, pp. 166–197.

Mali Leksikon Samoupravljača (1972) Beograd, Savremena Administracija.

Mencinger, J. (1990) 'Dileme privatizacije društvene imovine u Sloveniji', *Poslednji Dani Društvenog Vlasništva*, pp. 23–29.

Milanović, B. (1983) 'The investment behaviour of the labour-managed firm: a property-rights approach', *Economic Analysis*, 4, 327–340.

Pazner, E. A. and Schmeidler, D. (1976) 'Social contract theory and ordinal distributive equity', *Journal of Public Economics*, 3–4, 261–268. Reprinted in L. Hurwicz, D. Schmeidler and H. Sonnenschein (eds) (1985) *Social Goals and Social Organization. Essays in Memory of Elisha Pazner*, Cambridge: Cambridge University Press, pp. 311–319.

Posljednji Dani Društvenog Vlasništva (1990) Opatija 6–8, Rujna. Zagreb Poslovna Skola.

Rawls, J. (1972) *A Theory of Justice*, Oxford: Oxford University Press.

Roemer, J. E. (1988) 'Public ownership of the means of production', in J. E. Roemer, *Free to Lose*, Cambridge, MA: Harvard University Press, pp. 148–171.

Roemer, J. E. (1989) 'A public ownership resolution on the tragedy of the commons', *Social Philosophy and Policy*, 2, 74–93.

Stephen, F. H. (1980) 'Bank credit and the labor-managed firm: comment', *American Economic Review*, 4, 796–799.

Stephen, F. H. and Smith, B. (1975) 'Capital investment in the Yugoslav firm', *Canadian Journal of Economics*, 4, 609–617.

Strahinjić, C. (1980) Zastita samoupravnih prava radnika i drustvene svojine i uloga i zadaci sindikata. Beograd: Institut za Političke Studije.

Ustav, S. F. R. J. (1974) Beograd, Savremena Administracija.

Part IV

Interdisciplinary perspectives

Chapter 15

Niklas Luhmann's sociology of the economic system
Some moral implications

William Ossipow

INTRODUCTION

The development of Western civilization has been characterized since the sixteenth century by a continuous process of dissociation. Modern world separates what traditional societies held strongly together. At the end of the Middle Ages, there was the dissociation of politics from moral as expressed by Machiavel; then, the dissociation of science from religion and theology with Galileo; the eighteenth century dissociated sexuality from love as can be read in Sade's novels. In the economic field, which is our concern here, the same thing happened at the beginning of the eighteenth century. Mandeville's *Fable of the Bees* and, half a century later, Smith's *Wealth of Nations* are the major landmarks of a similar shift. Both these books theorized the dissociation of economic activity and its motivations from the traditional moral teaching.

Modernity, our present condition, is the result of this historical process, based on the power of analytical mind which gave rise to sophisticated specialized activities, for instance industry or technology, and to the development of various sciences. This development has probably gone so far and produced such bewildering fruits that periodical attempts are made to bind anew what our historical evolution had separated. It is the basic interpretation I give to the *socio-economic* movement of thought. In this respect, A. Etzioni's book *The Moral Dimension* (1988) outstandingly illustrates the struggle for a renewed alliance between economics and ethics.

Niklas Luhmann's work offers an impressive sociological account of our dislocated world (he would say of our 'differentiated' world). Moreover, it is a brilliant advocacy of modernity understood as the era of functional differentiation. And the task is hard for those who would try to take into account the achievements of his thought without giving up the moral claim in social life, including economy and economics.

My aim in this paper is to think about the link which could be made between the scientific view of an autonomous economic system and the ethical requirements. My basic question concerns the place of moral discourse with respect to the claimed amorality of modernity.

I shall successively deal with the following points: first, the general concepts of Luhmann's sociology; second, his theory of the economic system; and third, his point of view on moral. As a conclusion, I will present some ideas of mine about how it can be possible to keep some place for the moral concern in the socio-economic system.

LUHMANN'S GENERAL THEORY ON SOCIETY

Luhmann belongs to the great tradition of theoretical sociology: he continues the Durkheiman interest of differentiation and social evolution; he stands next to Weber with his concern for the specificity of modern times; he borrows from Parsons the concept of functional subsystems. Nowadays, Luhmann's work is the most brilliant herald of an abstract theory of the social world relying upon systemic concepts.

The classical theory of systems – Ashby, von Bertalanffy, Deutsch, Easton[1] – made a distinction between open and closed systems. The first have exchanges between themselves and their environment by means of inputs and outputs. These exchanges are considered by classical theory as essential to the functioning of systems. The closed systems, on the other hand, were mainly treated as a theoretical case without any counterpart in real world. Following the so-called Chilean school of the systemic approach (Maturana, Varela),[2] Luhmann operates a major turn in social theory by considering systems as being closed and this very closure as being the primary condition for their opening.

In this perspective, a system is a unity quite distinct from its environment. It is separated from it, from what is not itself, by boundaries. The environment of a system is defined as all what is not the system. Owing to the sharp distinction between system and environment, one can say that closed systems constitute **identities**. What is specific to this approach is the stress on the very basic fact that closed systems produce their own boundaries and, doing so, create their own identities. This peculiar capacity allows us to qualify them as **autopoietic** systems:

> Such systems are called, following Maturana, 'autopoietic'. Autopoietic systems are closed systems in the sense that they cannot receive their elements from their environment but produce them by a selective arrangement. I could also say . . . that everything used as a unit by the systems, whether its elements, its processes, or the system itself, has to be constituted by the system.

(1990a, p. 115)

The most obvious examples of closed systems can be found in living systems. They actually constitute, maintain and reproduce themselves out of their own internal dynamism. If inputs from the environment (for instance oxygen or food) are a necessary condition for their existence, they are by no means a sufficient condition for it. Death precisely shows how a living organism suddenly lacks the internal energy to use external resources, even if these resources are available in the environment. Death is then the loss of the autopoietic property of living systems. A living being has an identity of its own (obviously, my cat is not my neighbour's cat) whereas a corpse disintegrates and becomes very soon merged with the environment, dust amidst dust. This confusion is specifically the loss of boundaries, the loss of an identity.

Luhmann divides systems into three kinds: the living systems (biology), the conscious systems (psychology) and the social systems which are the object of sociology (1990a, p. 3).

Conscious and social systems, not less than living systems, are closed and reveal autopoietic features. They too must be distinguished from what is not themselves and acquire an identity of their own. It is commonly considered as a psychic pathology when somebody considers himself as being someone else, for instance, I believe I am Napoleon. Here again, there is a lack of identity. The same happens in a world where nation-states are the basic units, when territories are not clearly integrated with one or the other state system, as it is the case with, for example, Kashmir or Bosnia.

Luhmann defines social systems essentially as communication systems. 'The system of society consists of communications. There are no other elements, there is no further substance but communications. The society is not built out of human bodies and minds. It is simply a network of communication' (1990a, p. 100). And elsewhere, he underlines: 'Social systems use communication as their particular mode of autopoietic reproduction' (1990a, p. 3).

Communication has no environment and social systems do not communicate with their environment. Indeed, if a system could communicate with the environment, it would imply that the environment could communicate, that it would itself belong to the communication system, which is obviously contradictory. This logical impossibility clearly indicates that communication systems are closed systems.

Communication is basically a selection process, a choice among a set of possibilities. The main vehicle for communication, natural language, displays this essential feature: the expression of thought is adequately realized through the right selection among available words. Artists, writers, scientists are those people who master particularly well their own communication choices.

Society is the totality of all communications. Some sociologists would define society as the totality of human interactions. But Luhmann argues that interactions require the physical presence of individuals, whereas society implies much more than these brief encounters. It is the whole world of meaning which is made possible by communication.

Society, thus defined, is always a differentiated system. This property is closely linked with the properties of language itself, the function of which is to produce meaningful differences, for instance between masters and slaves, rich and poor, red and pink, and so on. Traditional societies were divided into social strata, as for instance the Indian caste system. Modern societies are differentiated along functional lines. This means that the formation of a communication system derives from a functional requirement. Communications tend to become specialized, devoted to particular tasks. Again, the appearance of specialized social systems cannot be separated from the appearance of specialized languages, or semantic systems. This link between system and language can be illustrated by the invention in recent years of computer science which is altogether a new scientific field of its own (a system) and a new language.

When semantic systems develop, inventing new concepts and new words to speak about reality, they increase the range of possible choices. In Luhmann's words, it increases the complexity not only of the communication process but also of the world itself about which the communication process takes place. Thus, it is the very dynamics of communication and language which leads to a more complex and differentiated world.

Within society, a process of formation of partial autopoietic units – the subsystems – takes place. This process of differentiation into functionally specialized systems increases the global complexity of the system, where 'by complexity we mean the number of possibilities from which, through experience and action, we can choose – either through structural reduction or through conscious decision-making' (1982, p. 218). But, at the same time, when global complexity increases, means are developed to reduce it, in order to master it. There is a process Hegel and Marx would have called dialectical in the concomitant movement of increasing and reducing the complexity of reality.

The reduction of complexity is performed by the specialized subsystems which have to be considered, in their turn, as closed and autopoietic systems.

The concept of functional **autonomy** is essential to the understanding of social systems. Autonomy is the result of the choice of a **specific point of view** on reality. And, as society (and language) become more complex, the different points of view on reality tend to multiply. The differentiation of the social systems primarily means that there is a way of considering society from a legal, scientific, moral, economical, etc., point of view:

> Starting from special conditions in medieval Europe, where there existed a relatively high degree of differentiation of religion, politics, and economy, European society has evolved into a functionally differentiated system. This means that function, not rank, is the dominant principle of system building. Modern society is differentiated into the political subsystem and its environment, the economic subsystem and its environment, the scientific subsystem and its environment, the educational subsystem and its environment, and so on. Each of these subsystems accentuates, for its

own communicative processes, the primacy of its own function. All of the other subsystems belong to its environment and vice versa.

(1990a, pp. 177–178)

A functionally specialized subsystem is a means of reducing complexity, because it considers reality only from one point of view out of many others. The scientific system, for instance, is not concerned by the beauty of flowers. It takes flowers as objects of knowledge with the goals and means of science, which are not concerned by beauty.

The multiplication of various specific points of view has one important consequence: in modern society, there is no longer one unique perspective, one dominant system which would be the reference for the whole society. If, in the past, religion or politics played this role, modern society is a system 'broken down internally into partial systems' (1987, p. 105). Modernity has built a dislocated world where no system can legitimate another one and where social systems can only rely on 'self-legitimation' (1987, p. 108). Indeed, we intuitively accept that scientific research and scientific achievements are not justified because of their moral, political or economic aspects, but merely by the increase in true knowledge science allows. If, for instance, the moral or political point of view should regulate scientific activities, the danger of new Galileo trials or of Lyssenko's proletarian biology would be great.

As autopoietic and autonomous entities, social systems constitute themselves their identity, their boundaries with their environment through a sort of sovereign decree. Only scientists can say what is science and set limits between what is science and what is not, for instance between astronomy and astrology. Only law can trace the border between what belongs to law and what does not (the beauty of flowers). Thus an autonomous social system is a system of its own 'with its own natural law, its own regulations, its own logic of decision-making' (1982, p. 200).

Luhmann repeatedly stresses that communication is an improbable process, I would say a sort of miracle allowing society to exist. This important thesis, developed in Chapter 4 of *Essays on Self-reference* (1990), assumes that communication is a selection process and that, at the very beginning, two persons have very little chance to make identical selections. For instance, at the semantic level, it is not at all certain that they would give the same meaning to words, and that they would understand each other. Exchanged signs are not *a priori* and unconditionally acceptable to each partner.

The miracle of society is related to the transformation of improbable communication into probable communication. This transformation is made possible if what is exchanged in the communication process is generally accepted. Following T. Parsons, Luhmann calls a medium the means of the symbolic exchanges which take place in society and, if accepted, allow it to exist.

Natural language is the most general and diffused medium of communication. It is based on shared meanings which allow mutual understanding, once these common meanings are widely accepted in a linguistic area. As society becomes more complex and more functionally differentiated, new types of media appear, each suited to a particular subsystem.

> With reference to social systems, Parsons mentions, as examples of this type of medium, money, power, influence, and value commitments. To this list, I would add truth in the realm of science, and love in the realm of intimate relationships. The various media cover the major branches of the social system that have a civilizing influence and the main subsystems of modern society.
>
> (1990a, p. 90)

The various media are semantic agencies which increase the probability of acceptance of a communication. They direct the selections in a sense which motivates people. This very help to motivation constitutes the secret which makes improbable communication turn into a probable and successful one. To give a trivial but well-known example, the pleasure in sexual intercourse motivates people to have such a relationship. Without it, there would be no motivation for reproduction.

A medium is a semantic device realizing the coordination of actions. Natural language is not only a generalized, i.e. universally accepted, medium, but also an unspecific one since language is used in extremely various circumstances. Functionally differentiated subsystems, such as law, science, politics or economy, have developed generalized and specific media such as law, truth, power or money. All these media allow, in their specific field, exchanges to take place.

As a semantic device and vehicle of meaning, the media rely on binary codes, i.e. codes which have two values. For the natural language, the fundamental binary code which structures the whole semantic construction, is the opposition of **yes** and **no**, affirmation and negation. The binary codes which regulate the functionally differentiated subsystems are, according to Luhmann, the following:

Systems	*Media*	*Codes*
Law	Law	Legal–illegal
Science	Truth	True–false
Politics	Power	Government–opposition
Economy	Money	Profitable–not-profitable

Any event occurring in the world may gain a meaning by applying the binary code. First of all, an event may be relevant or irrelevant to a specific system.

We already gave the example of the beauty of flowers which is irrelevant for law or science. It may be relevant, for instance in economy, if there is a social acceptance that beautiful flowers have a value of exchange and are objects of trade.

The binary codes express the specific semantics of the various systems. They have a positive value (true, legal, profitable). The positive value is attached to a psychological preference which gives people the motivation and energy to act and which is an incentive for coordination. For the actors, it is better to tell the truth, or to have power, or to have plenty of money than the contrary. But, in spite of the fact that binary codes incorporate a positive value, attractive to people, Luhmann strongly underlines that both values of the code, the negative as well as the positive one, are semantically necessary. Indeed, it is mere logic to say that if anything has a positive value then nothing has value. If any behaviour is legal, the very distinction between a legal or illegal behaviour vanishes and, consequently, the reign of law is ruined. The same applies of course to the other semantic distinctions. If 'anything goes' in science, as Feyerabend puts it in *Against Method* (1975), there is no science any longer.

It is of equal importance to point out another feature of the binary code: although it incorporates a psychological preference, it does not give any criterion to evaluate informations or events. There is no natural or eternal (or *a priori*) rule to decide whether an information or event comes under the positive or negative value of the code. Science is, of course, devoted to truth, but a particular theorem may prove to be false. It is the task of each social system to elaborate its own rules of evaluation through, for instance in science, the whole corpus of methodology of research.

The day-to-day application of the codes obeys no everlasting rules. The history of science shows how conceptions of science and methodology have evolved over centuries; in law, legal provisions may change and jurisprudence may be reversed. In the stock exchange, an investment which today seems profitable, may prove to be a loss. Application of the codes thus depends on the circumstances and on a hermeneutic reasoning. The code is just a schema of differences. How events and informations distribute themselves between the two values of the code depends on a decision.

This thesis implies a further distinction Luhmann makes between the level of the code and the level of the programme, i.e. the application of the code. At the level of the programme, any evaluation happens to be contingent: any event is considered so, but it may be considered differently as well. A behaviour is today judged illegal but another justice may consider it as legal. Here the self-referential circle (which Luhmann treats as a paradox) fully appears: the code may be applied to itself. Once again, a behaviour may be judged legal but, in appeal, the very judgment may be considered as legal or illegal. According to Luhmann, there is no objective way of getting out of the circle, or of the paradox. Only an arbitrary decision coming out of the system itself is able to stop the paradoxical self-application of the code. In this respect – the stress on paradox and contingency – Luhmann's sociology is not far from Sartre's early philosophy.

Every time a social activity is successfully performed with the help of a specific medium it gives a further incentive to use it again. It is a typical reinforcement process which increases the probability of acceptance of the medium. If the use of money makes people more wealthy and more comfortable, the trust in money will tend to be generalized. 'Order is created by virtue of the fact that communication, though improbable, is nonetheless made possible and becomes the normal situation in social systems' (1990a, p. 91).

Despite the fact that social communication is improbable, society and its functional subsystems do exist. Communication works through law, power, money or truth. Modern world may stem from a miracle; it is actually routinized. Luhmann's general sociology is the theory of our brave normal world.

THE SOCIOLOGY OF THE ECONOMIC SYSTEM

Luhmann's sociological conception of economy is to be found in an important article 'The economy as a social system', which constitutes Chapter 9 of *The Differentiation of Society* (1982).

The concepts of his general theory are to be applied 'analogously' in 'the realm of economy' (1982, p. 191). As can be expected, economy will be understood 'as a functionally necessary subsystem of society' (ibid.).

Luhmann does not accept the common idea that economy has to do with human needs and that its function is to remove scarcity. What is specific to economy, he argues, is

> the possibility of deferring a decision about the satisfaction of needs while providing a guarantee that they will be satisfied and so utilizing the time thus acquired. From this point of view, the fundamental problem of the economy lies in the dimension of time.
>
> (1982, p. 194)

The specific function of economy is to guarantee that needs will be satisfied in the future.

Money is the specific means to establish equivalences between needs. Since 'money is chronically scarce', even in wealthy nations, 'scarcity does not decrease; it increases with the heightening of economic efficiency' (1982, p. 195).

In archaic societies, economy was far from being differentiated from other social tasks. Luhmann reminds us of the importance of social solidarity in small-scale societies and of the central role played by the exchange of gifts. In the context of this traditional framework, economic activities are largely mixed with interpersonal, political or religious tasks and duties. The differentiation of the economic sphere appears with the rise of markets where surplus is exchanged. Luhmann considers the institution of the market as a decisive step towards dissociation between the thing and its owner. And only this dissociation could lead to generalized exchange, not only of things or objects, but also of land, capital and invisible services. For a market to be effective, it is a necessary condition that things be separated from their owners and that they can change hands.

Economic exchange is a form of social communication. Here again, Luhmann underlines that the economic exchange, as it happens on markets, is *a priori* highly improbable as is any other form of communication. When two persons are engaged in an economic deal, they have to accept mutually what the other offers, and they must come to an agreement on a rate of equivalence between the things which are to be exchanged. But the deal will become easier, i.e. more probable, more accepted and normal once it is abstracted from moral, personal, religious or political considerations. The great merit of markets is to rely on abstractions (for instance money) and to establish impersonal relations. Economic exchange does not depend any longer on considerations such as social honourability of the buyer or the seller.

> As often has been said but not clearly understood, the market makes 'impersonal' relations possible: it neutralizes the relevance of the other roles of the participants, and it removes the mutually binding moral controls that evaluate persons and thus moral *engagement* as well.
>
> (1982, p. 199)

In modern times, the rise of large firms made possible the dissociation between markets and households. The huge widening of market activities was decisive for the differentiation and autonomization of economic activity which became 'a system of its own, with its own natural law, its own regulations, its own logic of decision making' (1982, p. 200).

With money as an institutionalized medium, 'economy builds its own values, its own goals, norms, criteria of rationality, and directions of abstraction, by means of which the behavioral choices in its domain are oriented' (1982, p. 200). In the words of the Chilean school Luhmann will use in later works, economy appears as an autopoietic and self-referential system: a system which constitutes its own boundaries and which functions on its own rules. As the economic system functions with the help of a specific medium, money, and elaborates specific rules which are not valid outside economy, it allows 'risky and improbable heightenings of abstraction and specification to arise . . .' (1982, p. 200). The self-referential feature of economy allows that 'in an economic context labor can be treated as a commodity, because it has properties similar to those of other particular quantities – and because in the religious, political, family, educational, or medical systems it cannot be so treated' (ibid.).

On one hand, the differentiation of functional systems makes economy more autonomous from moral, religion or politics. Historically, liberalism has been the awareness of the necessary autonomy of economy in a modern society. On the other hand, the economic point of view should not interfere in other social subsystems: in modern times marriage is for love, not for money[3] and one should be entitled to a fair trial, whether rich or poor (1982, p. 201).

The self-referential nature of the economic system and its autonomy make acceptable such behavioural maxims as 'in financial matters friendship ceases' (ibid.). Obviously, to make money is the strongest motivation of economic actors. Luhmann is fully aware that 'unnaturally one-sided' experience and behaviour are encouraged in the autonomous and efficient modern economy: 'The market economy demonstrates that morally reprehensible, egoistical, profit-oriented behavior may nevertheless have virtuous consequences' (1990a, p. 133).

In archaic societies, economy was based on a normative attitude, i.e. an attitude which proved to be, according to Luhmann, incapable of adaptation. An example of such an attitude is the prohibition of interest rates. Modern economy, on the other hand, is based on a cognitive attitude which proves to be able to learn and to adapt itself to change. There is an obvious shift which has disconnected economy from traditional moral: 'It seems that the constancy of morality over time, which is supported by all of society, can be replaced by the constancy over time of purely economic opportunities' (1982, pp. 202–203).

The success of money as the specific medium of economy occurs when it becomes a generalized symbol in the sense defined earlier. Money is the specific means which allows to reduce the complexity of the economic world. In modern economies, choices – hence complexity – are almost infinite. But money makes possible precise selections among this infinity.

In the course of economic development, the same operation, which gave birth to money, was applied to money itself: money which was originally a means of exchanging things thus becomes itself an object of the exchange process. 'The exchanging of possibilities of exchange' comes out of the self-referential and reflexive features of the system. This evolution led to the tremendous internal differentiation of economy with the rise of the commercial, industrial and financial subsystems.

LUHMANN'S THEORY OF MORAL AND ETHICS

Moral is a particular form of communication which has to do with esteem or contempt of persons as such, i.e. which is not considered on the basis of a partial and functional point of view such as worker, consumer, citizen, sexual partner and so on, but as a whole person (*die ganze Person*) (1990b, pp. 17–18).

Moral communication relies on a binary code which includes two values, a positive one (good) and a negative one (evil). Moral cannot be identified only with the positive value, since a behaviour may be qualified either as good or as bad. For instance, to consider that being faithful to one's spouse is an eternally valuable moral rule would dogmatically reduce the complexity of the (sentimental) world as well as the capacity of selection, i.e. would reduce human freedom.

The binary code is a scheme of semantic distinctions which does not give by itself any directives on how it should be applied. In the moral field too, Luhmann states the difference between the level of the code and the level of the application of the code (level of the programme). Even if the moral code is largely used by people, it does not mean that, when evaluating concrete problems, there is a social consensus at the level of the programme.

Because moral has to do with the human person as a whole, it cannot have a partial view. But, as mentioned earlier, society evolved in a dialectical movement towards more complexity and towards a functional differentiation which is designed to help mastering this complexity. The functional differentiated social subsystems are those social devices which reduce and master complexity by constituting their own (partial) point of view, their own specific medium and binary code, their own working rules, their own values. It has the very important consequence that functional media and codes have replaced, in the most important social fields like law, science, economy or politics, the antique moral code. Moral concern still exists when individuals are in a situation to consider the person as a whole, but it exists outside the functionally differentiated social systems. A scientist must not be valued because he is a nice man or a good father, but solely on the basis of his scientific records and merits. In the economic field, an investment should not be decided because it is good for mankind but because it is profitable to the individual or to the firm. As quoted before from Luhmann, labour can be considered, in economy, as a commodity because in other social domains, people are not considered as a commodity but as citizens, lovers or persons. Thus, Luhmann repeatedly states that there is no congruence between the two values of the functional binary codes and the values of the moral code (1991b, pp. 23–24). The functional subsystems have to perform their tasks at a level of higher amorality (1991b, p. 24), if they are expected to perform them at all.

The disconnection of the systems from moral makes Luhmann suspicious towards good intents either in politics, where virtue may turn into terror (as during the French Revolution) (1990a, p. 133), or in economy, where socialist planning has proved disastrous because it took into account social ethics (1991, p. 498).

Luhmann concedes a residual role to moral: the protection of the specific codes of the functional systems. He gives the following example (1991, p. 499): in sport, doping is forbidden because doping removes the distinction which is essential to the specific sport system, i.e. the distinction of those who win and those who lose the game on purely sporting criteria. In the same way, the modern liberal state should protect the autonomy of the economic system.

If my interpretation is correct, this function of protection of specific codes devoted to moral is nothing else than a redundant statement: specific and functional codes do exist, and it is good, i.e. worthy of protection that they exist.

Ethics, according to Luhmann, are the reflexive theory of moral. Whereas traditional moral thought was inquiring for what is substantially good or bad, ethics are an inquiry into the grounds or the very possibility of moral judgment (with Kant, for instance). Ethics have evolved by questioning the relevance of the traditional moral distinctions such as the distinction between virtue and vice. Thus Mandeville's *Fable of the Bees*, a sort of manifesto of the modern economic ethos, demonstrates that vices may have beneficial consequences (1990a, p. 133; 1990b, p. 28). Weber's famous distinction between ethics of conviction and ethics of responsibility (1990b, p. 28) also belongs to ethics; according to Weber, it appears that strongly held moral convictions may have harmful consequences.

In our modern society, i.e. in a functionally differentiated social world, it is the present task of ethics to take into account the actual structure of society and to limit the field of application of moral (1990b, p. 40). According to Luhmann, it is the most urgent task of ethics to warn against moral (1990b, p. 41).

AND THEN, WHAT PLACE FOR MORAL?

Luhmann's impressive and provocative view on the relationship between social systems – and, among them, economy – and moral must be carefully evaluated. On one hand, if we reject his view, we are in danger to be blind to the hard reality of modernity and to the theoretical account of it by sociology. On the other hand, if we merely accept it, we support the cynicism of considering the fact of social differentiation as the norm of social relations.

The discussion of Luhmann's theory must then be carried on with nuance. I suggest three different levels of discussion. Each of them would deserve much more study than can be done here:

- The first question relates to the empirical level: Is Luhmann's theoretical account of modern society a true description of it? Do things really happen as he says?
- The second question is at the interpretation level: How exactly should his

concept of amorality be understood? Is Luhmann himself disconnected of any tradition of moral thought?

- The third question is at the level of moral theory: After such a questioning of moral in social life, what place is left for it? How is it possible to justify moral concern in social activities, particularly in economy?

(a) Concerning the first point, I am convinced that Luhmann's theory has underlined central features of modernity. The stress on the differentiation of social systems and on their autonomy is in deep accordance with the experience of modern man. We, in the academic world, are proud of the scientific autonomy of our universities and laboratories. As citizens, we hope that democratic power is disconnected from money. In arts, we do not think any longer that music or painting should serve God, or the people, or the party.

Many behavioural consequences have resulted from the evolution of social systems towards more differentiation and autonomy. In economy, the fact that actors are profit-oriented is firmly established. Profit is a structural condition of a firm long-term survival and constitutes a necessary constraint on behaviour. Economics have actually reflected this constraint in theorizing, which is altogether a scientific achievement and the ideological justification available for managers' and shareholders' quest for profit.

The historical success of the neoclassical paradigm in economics and of utilitarianism as a moral theory may be considered as a proof that both express the very ethos of the economic system.

At the same time as liberal economy developed, a deep movement of protest arose against it. Socialism and Marxism can be interpreted as the moral and political rejection of its growing autonomy and amorality. But this rejection is a testimony of the very reality of what is rejected.

(b) The fact that Luhmann advocates the amorality of the social subsystems should not be misunderstood. The semantic distinction between what is amoral and what is immoral has to be taken into account. Immorality is what goes bluntly against any moral principle. Amorality is what has no relation with moral, what is independent of moral. The immoral man reverses moral values, considering good what is commonly considered as being evil. Immorality is a moral, even if a reversed one. Amoral behaviour, on the other hand, depends on quite different rules than moral ones, for instance system-specific rules. In this sense, calculate, write or invest money are amoral activities. In Wittgenstein's words, specific systems and moral systems are different and incommensurable language-games.

However, there is at least one weak link between Luhmann's theory and traditional moral. Nowhere does Luhmann suggest that people should behave against the law. Now, to behave in accordance with an existing law has relevance for moral philosophy. Aristotle stated that one of the basic meanings of justice is to behave according to law (see his Nicomachean Ethics, V, 2 and 3). The same point is true for utilitarian ethics.

Nowadays, economic activity is governed by a whole corpus of legal rules which have incorporated some basic moral principles such as the obligation to respect contracts. In relation to economy, law has the function of protecting economic operations from disturbing behaviours: violence, lies and so on. But, in so far as law has had an increasing importance for the regulation of economic activities, moral has had a diminishing one because there is no longer a consensus on substantial moral issues, either in the economic realm or in other fields of social life (Luhmann, 1991, p. 498). For instance, there is no single and widely accepted conception of what is economic justice. Some have a utilitarian view of justice, others an egalitarian one, others rely on Paretian optimum and so on.

In such a context, it is quite normal that moral has been largely replaced by law in the function of integration and regulation of society.

(c) Luhmann's rupture with traditional moral thought is obvious. His sociology does not deal with great ethical concepts such as virtue or vice, justice, common good, duty or sanctity, except for questioning or 'deconstructing' them by demonstrating their historical relativity and their essential contingency.

For people interested in the relevance of moral in social and economic life, his theory is a hard blow, but also a challenge to think about the problem in a new way. To conclude, I would like to suggest some reflections on what should be a moral discourse.

First, it is necessary to remind Luhmann's theory of the improbability of communication. 'Order is created by virtue of the fact that communication, though improbable, is nonetheless made possible and becomes the normal situation in social systems' (Luhmann, 1990a, p. 91). Despite the brilliant analysis of the improbability of communication, it is quite clear that Luhmann makes a sociology of stabilized systems, a sociology of the 'normal situation' where the media perfectly perform their functions. He describes how things work in the day-to-day functioning of the systems. In this perspective, amorality is almost fully covered by normality: is it not normal for people to desire a high salary or a high return on their investments? Is it not normal that there are poor and rich people?

To qualify moral discourse, I suggest following Richard Rorty when he makes a distinction between normal and abnormal discourse (or hermeneutics) (1980, p. 320). Rorty borrows from T. Kuhn's concept of normal science, that is 'the sort of statement which can be agreed to be true by all participants whom the other participants count as rational' (ibid.). Normal discourse, or normal science, is what comes out of a consensus of experts or specialists. Abnormal discourse has subjective features, is considered by specialists as 'irrelevant', 'kooky' or 'revolutionary' (1980, pp. 338–339). It can also be understood as 'emotional' or 'fantastic' (1980, p. 339).

I would like to argue that Luhmann's theory is a typical normal discourse and that the paradoxical function of moral discourse is to be abnormal. We have seen earlier that the specific medium is what allows a highly improbable communication to take place and, when accepted, to become institutionalized and routinized. This could be called the passage from improbability to normality. And Luhmann's theory takes this systemic normality as its focal object. It describes how things are going on when market is the central economic organization, when property is recognized and protected. Thus Luhmann writes the sociological meta-theory of neoclassical economics, which is in itself a normal science, object of a wide consensus. I would say that Luhmann's theory is twice normal: first, as the sociological meta-theory of economics; second, as the theory of the normal and socially accepted motivations, actions and operations taking place in the economic system.

As an abnormal discourse, moral cannot aim at meeting the consensus of scientific community. It stands in the face of functional discourses as Antigona faced Creon. The paradoxical function of moral discourse is to point out the abnormality of normality. It has to underline that the habits and institutions to which we are accustomed may constitute, either in their very principle or in their daily functioning, an injury to humanity, to what makes human beings human. In this respect, the prophetic discourse of the biblical tradition is an outstanding example: against the prevailing mood, without any purpose of reaching a consensus, it points out the sins and harms of the people and calls for justice and sanctity.

Moral discourse may have its origin either in the practical field or at the theoretical level. Militants or trade unionists feel the duty to utter this peculiar abnormal discourse and to say what is unacceptable, although it is quite normal, in social life. At the theoretical level, things are more difficult. Karl Marx's work has long remained paradigmatic by arousing the hope of a possible scientific discourse about the evils of capitalism. The social strength of Marxism has been its ability to mix in a fascinating way a rationalist purpose and a moral protest. Nowadays, the strict differentiation between science and moral makes the Marxian point of view uneasy. We do not consider any longer 'militant science' as science. Thus moral discourse is sent back, if it has to keep its significance, to its prophetic radicality and to its ultimately incommensurable relationship with the various rules of the subsystems.

Moral discourse reminds us that people, in economy or elsewhere, are not mere 'commodities' or any other mutilated entities. Of course Luhmann knows all that perfectly well. But functionally differentiated subsystems may tend to forget this basic fact. The point of moral discourse is certainly not to convert scholars to a virtuous theory but, ever again, to introduce into social visibility the idea that human beings are, as Kant put it, not to be considered as means, but as ends.

NOTES

1 See Ashby, W. R. (1960) *Design for a Brain*, New York: Wiley; von Bertalanffy, L. (1968) *General System Theory*, New York: G. Braziller; Deutsch, K. W. (1963) *The Nerves of Government. Models of Political Communication and Control*, New York: Free Press; Easton, D. (1965) *A Systems Analysis of Political Life*, New York: Wiley.
2 Maturana, H. and Varela, F. (1980) *Autopoiesis and Cognition: The Realization of the Living*, Dordrecht, Boston and London: Reidel; Varela, F. (1980) *Principles of Biological Autonomy*, North-Holland and New York: Elsevier.
3 On this point, see N. Luhmann (1986) *Love as Passion*, Cambridge: Polity Press.

REFERENCES

Etzioni, A. (1988) *The Moral Dimension. Toward a New Economics*, New York: Free Press.
Feyerabend, P. (1975) *Against Method*, London: New Left Books.
Hayoz, N. (1991) *Société, politique et etat dans la perspective de la sociologie systémique de Niklas Luhmann*, Genève: Département de Science Politique, Université de Genève, Etudes et Recherches, no. 25.
Luhmann, N. (1982) *The Differentiation of Society*, New York: Columbia University Press.
Luhmann, N. (1987) 'The representation of society within society', *Current Sociology*, 35, 2, 101–108.
Luhmann, N. (1990a) *Essays on Self-reference*, New York: Columbia University Press.
Luhmann, N. (1990b) *Paradigm Lost: Ueber die ethische Reflexion der Moral*, Frankfurt: Suhrkamp.
Luhmann, N. (1991) 'Politik und Moral. Zum Beitrag von Otfried Höffe', *Politische Vierteljahresschrift*, 3, 497–500.
Rorty, R. (1980) *Philosophy and the Mirror of Nature*. Oxford: Blackwell.

Chapter 16

Ideology and morality in economics theory

Monroe Burk

PURPOSE AND INTENT OF THE PAPER

The purpose and intent of this paper are two-fold:

1 To demonstrate that neoclassical economics theory is not a science but an ideology; that the quality of this ideology is poor; and that this ideology inhibits sound social responses to social problems, and is prejudicial to a morally based world order.
2 Inasmuch as a public policy science cannot rely on neoclassical economics theory either as a positive or as a normative science, to suggest that scholars interested in advising society on interventions to improve the general welfare pursue three lines of effort: (a) erect a unified normative social science, capable of providing guidance to the social process of governance, (b) obtain guidance from the neurosciences and life sciences for insights on individual human behaviour, (c) adopt philosophic and ethical premises suitable for a science of governance.

The creation of a suitable unified normative social science requires the destruction of the neoclassical economics paradigm which has its philosophic and ethical roots in utilitarianism, a doctrine resting on the central importance of the individual. The extirpation of neoclassical economics from the popular culture is an essential prerequisite to laying a basis for the examination of alternative philosophic and ethical systems, such as communitarianism and deontology. Each of us is born ego-conscious, a perception reinforced in Western European cultures by prevailing religious doctrine. This perception is challenged only during conflagrations, such as war or natural disaster, when the notion of community comes to the fore. After such cataclysms, people in Western European cultures typically revert to individualism as the natural state. When, in the following sections, I attack neoclassical economics as an unworthy ideology, this charge typically resonates not in the cognitive centres but in the limbic centres of the brain; it is felt as an attack on ego-consciousness, on self. My arguments are likely to be unconvincing unless one is prepared to be self-critical and self-reflective, ready to question one's own centrality in human existence.

To the neoclassical economist fully cognizant of the technical discussion to follow, the arguments offered in these pages might be accepted as relevant to policy analysis but not to either positive or normative economics and therefore of no interest to him. Positive neoclassical economics, he will argue, is a useful partition of a phenomenology-society – into the area of its provisioning by rational people under conditions of scarce resources. In this area, resources are manifestly scarce; moreover, it is only a matter of common observation that each person attempts to better himself and his family, and tries to achieve those things he values with the least expenditure of time and effort and of resources. To other areas of inquiry, he leaves governance and community life, where behaviour is affective or even irrational. Hence, he concludes that neoclassical economics is valid science and an addition to the stock of knowledge. As a normative science, he argues, neoclassical economics reveals what is efficient, both to the individual in the attainment of private objectives, and to society, in the attainment of public goals, chosen in democratic society by the electorate. The neoclassical economist typically is not concerned with the usefulness of the theory to governance; it suffices for him that the theory is useful and applicable in problems involving maximization of returns from the use of scarce resources.

The fallacy of this position lies in its inadmissible partitioning of the phenomenology-society – into a set of characteristics which is amenable to treatment by the theory in which he has an interest. It assumes that human behaviour is separable into economic, social and political spheres, and that economic behaviour is not also social and political behaviour. It also assumes that people act rationally when confronted by economic problems, and may or may not act rationally when confronted by political and social problems. Moreover, it assumes that behaviour lies outside of morality and of justice. It is the burden of this paper to point out that these assumptions are false. Can the provisioning of the household be partitioned from nurturing a child and emotionally as well as economically supporting a spouse? Is it acceptable that one bring home a paycheque every week by selling cocaine on the streets? Can the pursuance of national objectives, even by a democratic society, be partitioned from the objective of preserving the species *Homo sapiens sapiens* and the global environment? Is it appropriate to wipe out mature forests for the sake of providing jobs for the lumbermen? As the paper will show, human behaviour cannot be partitioned: every social human act has a component in morality and justice, and is simultaneously an economic, political and social act. Neoclassical economics therefore lacks the ability to describe actual behaviour because no behaviour is simply economic.

THE NEOCLASSICAL ECONOMICS PARADIGM

The economics faculties of the leading universities teach neoclassical economics; textbooks for principles of economics courses and for more advanced theory courses in economics contain, for the most part, neoclassical economics. Neoclassical economics has a distinctive paradigm, which I shall describe presently. The central importance of neoclassical economics lies in the fact that, in its populist version, it is considered to be an explanation of the capitalist system, and that it is part of the *Weltanschauung/* Mind Set/Myth structure of democratic capitalist societies. Since, as I later demonstrate, neoclassical economics provides little guidance to governance and thus has negligible social use, it remains of central social importance as an icon.

Despite its cultural and scientific standing, many distinguished economics professors, both in their theory courses and in their descriptive courses, are critical of neoclassical economics and introduce their students to the several varieties of institutional economics and socio-economics, as well as to Marxian economics. Although schools of business administration usually teach neoclassical economics as a distinct subject, under other headings, such as management, international trade, labour relations, etc., the subject matter they teach can be called institutional economics. Moreover, sociologists, political scientists and scholars in international relations usually have much to say about economic matters from the perspective of the acquisition and use of power and the resolution of conflicts.

A particular language usage, involving the words 'economic' and 'economical' adds to the cultural confusion. The first word has to do with the provisioning of society, and the second with the most efficient way any task can be performed, given a scarcity of means. Neoclassical economics is based on the efficiency notion, as explained more fully in the next section. The notion of efficiency is an integral part of Western culture but is not universal, as other cultures place great importance on not offending the spirits whom they believe govern them, reaching a particular state in the after-life, or achieving aesthetic expression. Our language usage illustrates our culture which reinforces the integration of neoclassical economics into it.

NEOCLASSICAL ECONOMICS DESCRIBED

An axiomatic system

Neoclassical economics evolved from its classical roots (Smith, Ricardo, Malthus, Mill) into an axiomatized mathematical model. The utility axiom states that the consumption and enjoyment of goods and services by people can be described by a particular mathematical function; one which is continuously differentiable, strictly increasing and strictly concave. That is, starting from zero consumption, people will strive to consume goods and services without limit, but each increment of consumption will bring lesser satisfaction than the previous increment. In this respect, all goods and services are fungible, so that a lesser amount of food, for example, can substitute for a greater amount of clothes. The production axiom posits a production function which is continuously differentiable, strictly increasing, homogeneous of degree one, strictly quasi-concave and subject to feasibility constraints. Time and effort spent in production are disutilities. Confronted with those two mathematical functions, the individual chooses his optimum point by solving the equational system and making economic decisions accordingly.

The paradigm underlying neoclassical economics theory is a deductive axiomatic system of a type made familiar by Euclid and used extensively in mathematics and theoretical physical sciences.

The employment of an axiomatic system to describe or approximate the real world cannot escape ontological examination. An axiomatic system implies that the real world – or at least the particular phenomenology under review – can be completely captured by what is contained in the axioms; that is, nothing is left out. Since, in fact, the axiomatic system captures only the endogenous variables and not the exogenous ones known to exist, there must be a system for controlling for these (as in a laboratory) or there must exist a complete model for each exogenous variable. This implies that the entire universe is subject to causal laws which, potentially, can be known by man. It is of interest that the great thinkers of history, such as Newton, who tried to axiomatize the real world (as opposed to a conceptual world, such as that of logic and mathematics) failed to do so; they are inevitably forced to make *ad hoc* addenda in the same manner as I describe neoclassical economists doing.

Since, in fact, few people know enough calculus, or enough information about the situation at hand, to form mathematical equations and solve them, one would have thought that neoclassical economics would have rejected the axiomatic system long ago. The theory was, however, saved by defining the phenomenology under consideration to fit the theory: to pose the question what people would do if they were rational and know the facts. The theory thus has the status of being an 'as-if' or 'mental-experiment' theory, and not a theory of reality. The real world differs markedly from the world captured by neoclassical economics. To adherents to that theory, however, that is its strength, as it abstracts from reality. People who live in the real world, however, must ask themselves when is an orange tennis ball an orange, and when is a pin-up picture on a dorm wall a flesh-and-blood woman in a dorm room.

Sociological content

The paradigm presumes that each individual acquires a set of preferences for goods and services; neoclassical economists refrain from inquiring into the laws governing the formation of preferences. Moreover, it accords the same level of justification to each person's preferences; rock and opera, saturated fat, playing sports and being a couch potato are matters of no concern to those who accept the neoclassical economics paradigm. Each person is autonomous and sovereign over his preferences; that is, each person asserts his own criteria for the reasonableness of his consumption behaviour and need not defend these criteria before society. So, for that matter, are means–ends choices: a person intending to travel to London from America is as entitled to go east as west, provided that he does get to London. The only relationship accounted for between people, and between people and collectivities, are transactions freely entered into. If two people are actually bound together by love or affection, those affects are entered into the preference set; similarly, if a person is motivated to save the whales or the virgin forest, that is also entered into the preference set. Thus, if one person chooses to observe high moral principles, and the other not, the level of satisfaction and happiness of the immoral person is as much to be cherished as that of the moral person. The greatest social welfare, meaning the aggregate of individuals' levels of satisfaction, is a natural consequence of this system, inasmuch as people would not enter a transaction unless they hoped to benefit from it. Thus, if the only permitted relationships between people are transactions, a society conducted in this manner must be one which always maximizes social welfare.

Dubious scientific status

In presenting and defending the theses that the neoclassical paradigm cannot form the basis for a science and is merely an ideology, I do not intend to impugn the profession of the economist or to charge that economists are guilty of non-professional conduct. It should be said at once that most people with professional titles of economist have a great deal of institutional, legal and factual knowledge of some segment of the economy, together with knowledge of mathematics and statistical theory, as well as the history of thought and of the current state of economic theory. Academic economists engaged in drawing implications from neoclassical economics theory and testing these theories against reality, as represented by statistical series, are undoubtedly as scientific as academic theorists in other professions. *The behaviour which runs the risk of being unscientific is presenting policy advice to legislators and the public based solely on the neoclassical economics paradigm or testifying in support of public policy measured with disingenuous argumentation drawn from neoclassical economics theory.*

The neoclassical economics paradigm has a number of defects as a basis for science. The major defect is that no implication drawn from this paradigm can be falsified by confronting it with reality, either by way of a crucial experiment or by observation of an event not predictable by an alternative theory and yet to occur. While retro-prediction is a suitable method of confirming theories in some sciences (e.g. 'predicting' that an eclipse must have occurred in 7000 BC), it is not in economics, unless one can first demonstrate that economic history is determinate – that the past predicts or holds the basis of prediction for the future. This defect arises in neoclassical economics because its conceptional apparatus cannot be reduced to a phenomenon observable and measurable outside of the conceptual apparatus itself. No psychologist can confirm the report of a subject that he is happy or satisfied; no philosopher can dispute with a subject the criteria of reasonableness he uses in forming his preferences or choosing a means to an end. The notion that economic actors behave to advance their interests is self-reflective: whatever the behaviour of the actor, it is defined as being in the actor's best interest; whatever the end result achieved by the economic actor, it is defined as intended.

The second defect is that neoclassical economics contains a feedback loop; hence, the mathematics to describe it must be of a dynamic character (that is, describe a path and not merely a cycle). This feedback loop is created by stating that economic actors are rational; hence, they must be capable of absorbing all new information about the economy, including the information predicted by economic theory. Thus, the state of the real world at t_0 must be different from its state in t_1. A large number of mathematical techniques have been tried in an effort to dynamize neoclassical economics, one of the latest being recursive analysis and, another, determinate chaos. In these and similar systems, an equation, reduced to an algorithm and placed into the computer, will run for as many periods as one wishes, t_m always being determined by t_{m-1}. Such a mathematical system cannot be successful for determining the true course of history because shocks from outside the defined system (political events, earthquakes, changes in weather patterns, etc.) throw the mathematically predicted path off course. Hence, the mathematical system used must be one which permits current data to be entered for every period, such as is done in meteorology. Such new data cannot be observed in economics or in day-to-day events, according to the tenets of neoclassical economics theory, because the important events are in the minds of people: changes in preferences and new knowledge about the world, changing expectations. Its propositions cannot be shown to be false.

Thus, a system of thought or theory which predicates that human behaviour is rational (in a real world in which events change from moment to moment) cannot lead to predicted outcomes; unless, of course, the new state of affairs at every moment can be assessed anew and predicted in advance.

Another line of criticism is that neoclassical economics is inconsistent with other behavioural sciences, particularly neurosciences, psychology and psychiatry. While these sciences recognize that the cognitive capacity (the basis of rational behaviour) is considerably more developed in man than in his biologic cousins – chimps, gorillas, etc. – it is still very imperfect and limited. Most behaviour in man, as is true for lower animals, is explainable through mechanisms other than cognitive. The average man, after all, has an IQ of 100, and is driven by instinct and affect; moreover, his ability to perceive changes in his environment is limited by his imperfect senses. Rationality is probably the last and most improbable basis on which to erect a theory of human behaviour. Thus, neoclassical economics theory cannot meet the test of being consistent with the known facts about the real world.

Dismissing these criticisms as academic, economists and others in the social science area who use the rational-man paradigm point out its usefulness. It is said to provide an insightful perspective, in the same sense that physicists can apply a relationship which holds for a vacuum to the world of atmosphere, correcting the prediction for the vacuum by known factors. This procedure is possible for physics, because the arguments used in physics are cardinal numbers, e.g. Avogadro's number, speed of light, but is not possible for economics, where the quantities entering a problem under study can only be determined from the data in the problem and not from outside it. Moreover, it is said, the neoclassical economics paradigm provides a vocabulary with which to talk about economic phenomena. This, however, has no bearing on whether the universe of discourse is treatable as a science. Adepts in the Ptolomeic system, alchemy, phlogiston, astrology, phrenology, IQ measurement, and Marxism invented conceptual systems and specialized vocabularies comprehensible to themselves but incomprehensible to others.

Usefulness for governance

The last defence of the neoclassical economics paradigm to be considered is that it is useful for policy making, inasmuch as it is able to predict the consequences of proposed policy, given certain parameters and assumptions. Thus, the neoclassical economist would argue, it is possible to predict with confidence that if people were provided with welfare transfer payments, their incentive to work would be reduced. This observation is really of little help, however, if counterbalanced by some offsetting factor, such as moral obligation.

Neither the neoclassical economics paradigm, nor the theory elaborated from it, can be considered a policy theory for four weighty reasons:

(a) A policy theory contains a philosophically supportable and objective function. There are two discernible objective functions in neoclassical economics. The first is social welfare, that is, the fulfilment of wants and desires of individuals, as defined by their preferences. Since individuals are permitted, by the terms of the theory, to have immoral or unworthy objectives, the social welfare hardly classifies as an ethically defensible objective function. The second discernible objective function is efficiency in the use of scarce resources. Those resources which are of greatest consequences to mankind, however, are not scarce resources but free resources, such as air and water, or resources/values which arise in communion, fraternity and mutual support, e.g. love of spouse or children, love of humankind.

(b) A policy is addressed to a body or institution capable of carrying out this policy, that is, a collectivity or a polity. Neoclassical theory contains no theory of collectivity or of polity; it does, however, contain a theory of the firm, presumed to be bent on maximizing its present-value net worth. Since all collectivities are led by elites, with the support of the rank and file, this introduces a contradiction internal to the theory: each person bent on maximizing his own self-interest will surely be incapable of supporting general policy for the benefit of all. Without a theory of the polity integral to it, one cannot presume that a policy recommended to the polity would actually be carried out effectively.

(c) Neoclassical economic theory can suggest the existence of a tendency, but to find the strength of this tendency one must do econometrics or statistical studies. Such quantitative studies may and frequently do make use of any theory or hypothesis, some of which may contradict economic theory.

(d) Neoclassical economics theory does not have the conceptual apparatus to deal with existing social problems. This thesis was tested by making a list of current social problems, gleaned from scientific and popular literature. The problems were classified as individual life style, interpersonal relationships and collectivity problems (see Exhibit 16.A, p. 334). Neoclassical economics has little to say about the first two classes of social problems, except perhaps to dismiss them as non-social problems. For example, if discrimination on the basis of race or sex actually exists, then they must be efficient practices. As to the third group of problems, neoclassical economics has the basically same set of policy recommendations for all of them, indiscriminately: internalize costs, privatize and deregulate. In effect, neoclassical economics tries to wrest jurisdiction over problems like despoliation of the environment from scientists, ethicists and concerned citizens, and impose its own schema.

Summary

In short, neoclassical economics is neither a positive nor a normative science. What it appears to be is an ideology. It is used extensively as a rhetorical device in support of policies arrived at independently. In its populist version, it enters into the *Weltanschauung*/Mind Set/Myth structure of our culture, and thus becomes a lens through which individuals observe the world about them and guide their behaviour. To the extent it contributes to a materialistic, hedonistic, greedy and avaricious life style, it is greatly to be deplored. Its most destructive impact, however, is to debar other paradigms, and in particular the socio-economics paradigm, from a respectful hearing.

THE POSSIBILITIES OF IMPROVING NEOCLASSICAL ECONOMICS

As already indicated, in practical economic work – as differentiated from academic work – neoclassical economics is a pencil or charcoal sketch from life: the painting fills out as realistic details are added. Often, unfortunately, a finished painting does not work because the details have smothered the design. A closer analogy is mechanical engineering: one designs a machine according to well-known principles, builds a prototype, tests it and then adds devices which keeps the feedstock in place or prevents the machine from blowing up. When the modifications overwhelm the machine, however, it is necessary to redesign using a different principle, or to redefine the task. In practice, schemes or proposals emanating from the economics division of a bureaucracy are usually so modified as they move through other divisions, that they lose their original rationale.

Since, in real situations, the business or government decision maker must get the relevant facts, some of which exist only in the minds of participants or are subject to chance occurrences in the future, his first problem is to determine the optimum outlay for information collection and analysis. This decision is a difficult one to make because it is seldom known in advance what information will turn up and how it bears on the problem at hand. There is thus an incentive to guess what the facts might prove to be and to delay decision making until events clarify the situation. The study of how to make sensible rules about guessing and timing constitutes much of decision theory, and this area of study can be used to put some realism into suggestions originating in economics divisions.

When the principals must use agents to complete and monitor transactions, their relationship with agents must be those which minimize agent defection. A formidable literature, by Coase, Williamson, North and others, modifies neoclassical economics in these directions.

In today's economy, the prevailing market structure is not perfectly competitive, as envisaged in general equilibrium models (e.g. Arrow–Debreu), but oligopolistic. Some oligopolies can be modelled as stable structures, others not, and the subject is complicated. The game-theoretic approach introduced by von Neumann and Morgenstern promised an advance, but the game-theoretic approach cannot deal with the secret agendas of principals and agents, nor with their limited cognitive powers. Moreover, as many such transactions are subject to government scrutiny, they involve not only legal questions but the ability to influence government through lobbyists, political contributions and bribery. It is invariably unwise to limit oneself to the content of neoclassical economics in these settings.

In the area of trade and distribution, the chief practical concerns are often with devices used to alter consumer preferences, influence retailers to stock items and motivate sales people – subjects better treated in psychology than in neoclassical economics.

Most economists consider that macro-economics rests on the neoclassical foundation, and much literature is devoted to proving this. But a fundamental error in mathematical logic occurs when this connection is drawn. Standard neoclassical economics deals with decision making by an individual acting as principal, or by a management team, acting on behalf of a collectivity, such as a business corporation. Each decision maker has its own utility function or desiderata which it seeks to maximize. The presumed aim of a decision maker in a particular economic group, such as a consumer, worker, manufacturer, etc., to maximize his objective function is the only thing which unites the individuals in a class; otherwise, no two individuals in the same class are identical. To operate mathematically with the class as the variable implies that individual differences within the class exert no effect. Since this is untrue, neoclassical economics deals with the problem by stating that it deals with a 'representative' consumer, worker, entrepreneur, etc. This is somewhat analogous to stating that Associate Justice Clarence Thomas is representative of Afro-Americans when, in actuality, his only characteristic which might be called representative is that he is of African descent. In more formal language it can be said that no class of decision makers possesses the same properties relevant to the problem at hand; hence aggregation is impossible. Macro-economics should thus be considered as a separate theory or as an addition, in the direction of improving its reality, to neoclassical economics. Unfortunately, the kind of macro-economics used to forecast business conditions has a very low success rate and, in practice, is not very useful in problems of governance.

In short, at the practical level, neoclassical economics is less of a framework than a movable scaffold. While this section has hardly exhausted the list of efforts within economics itself to make neoclassical economics more useful, it represents some fifty years of trying by recognized geniuses, such as von Neumann, Arrow and Simon. My own conclusion is that neoclassical economics often constitutes an impediment rather than a help in the analysis of a real-world problem because it prevents piercing through the layer of assumptions about consumer sovereignty and consumer preference contained in it. This becomes particularly obvious in real-world problems dealing with former communist and third world countries and with problems arising from dysfunctional subcultures in our own society. The analysis ought to penetrate to culture and institutions, and beyond these, to philosophy and ethics.

While it is true that only individuals can make choices, choices are made from options, and the range of options is constrained by the prevailing *Weltanschauung*/Mind Set/Myth structure in a local community, by existing institutions, and by individual characteristics. Moreover, people make choices which do not fit the neoclassical economics notion of rational. Economic analysis must begin at more fundamental levels than consumer preference and consumer sovereignty.

One of the more fruitful approaches to a culturally oriented economics, to be discussed next, is socio-economics, which explicitly introduces morality into the discussion, and alters the philosophic base from utilitarianism to communitarianism.

THE SOCIO-ECONOMICS PARADIGM

The most serious effort in recent years to alter the cultural basis of economics, and thereby its philosophic basis, was that made by Amitai Etzioni. The socio-economics paradigm formulated by Etzioni holds that the neoclassical paradigm is only half right. While the socio-economics paradigm recognizes that human behaviour is indeed often explainable by self-interest, it insists that, at other times, human behaviour is explainable by the existence of an obligation or compulsion to act according to moral principles, and to the apparent prejudice of narrow self-interest. Although this formulation is accommodating to the neoclassical paradigm, it is actually antithetical and irreconcilable with it.

The socio-economics paradigm assertion that there exists a drive within human beings to obey external rules (irrespective or not of whether humans invariably obey them) states that they do so not through calculating rationally the adverse consequences of violating such rules, but that it is human nature to discover such rules and consider them seriously in decision making. What a human may experience when acting contrary to these rules is shame, or loss of humanity. The characteristic of affect is that its quantitative force feeds on itself and leads to personality dysfunction, and, if not resolved, to neurotic or psychotic states.

The view of neoclassical economics on morals is a polar opposite to the Old Testament view contained in Etzioni's socio-economics paradigm.

For 100 years, counting from the publication of the *Wealth of Nations* in 1776, economics has been informed by moral ideas. From Petty, Locke and the Enlightenment philosophers came the notion that human freedom required the state to protect the natural rights of man, among which is the right to private property. From Smith and his predecessors (e.g. Hobbes) in moral philosophy came the notion that an invisible hand resolved the clash of egocentric behaviour into the social good. From Jeremy Bentham came the idea that the moral worth of an act was not an absolute but was determined by whether it raised the happiness of a population. From the Reformation and the Renaissance came ideas which led to the viewpoint that the individual and not society as a whole or humankind was the primary constituent of the universe.

Economics, towards the end of the nineteenth century, became dissatisfied with the explicit moral tone of economic theory. Under the influence of positivism, writers attempted to make economic theory value-free and thus like natural science. Jevons, Menger and Pareto created an intellectual basis for abstracting and mathematizing economics. In the mid-twentieth century, the New Welfare Economics claimed to have expunged morality from economics theory, first, by burying moral values into personal preferences and thus beyond the concern of economists, and second by adopting the concept of social welfare as the *summum bonum*. In the light of the first portion of this paper, one may suspect that those who participated in eliminating morals from economics were also interested in creating an ideology supporting a particular version of democratic capitalism.

It is, of course, as impossible to take morality out of economics (which is a theory of human behaviour in an economic setting and not a theory of production and distribution) as it is to take the smile from the Cheshire cat. All human behaviour involving the exercise of free will has moral content; we do not say this of animal behaviour or of the behaviour of people in subhuman conditions – under torture, or in conditions of starvation or homelessness.

The claimed signal merit of the socio-economics paradigm is that it alters the philosophic basis of neoclassical economics from utilitarianism to communitarianism. The idea of morality is contained in neoclassical economics theory, but is contained as part of the preference set of each individual. Each individual is free to define morality for himself, for it is he who has a pact with God or with Nature. Each individual may rationally choose to ignore his own standards of morality by taking the consequences of his immoral acts. Those consequences that are remote, such as damnation and hell-fire, he may logically choose to ignore. It is by the same token, one should notice, that the individual can opt to violate civilian law by computing the presumed benefits to himself from lawless acts and mathematical expectations of his punishment (the probable punishment times the probability of being detected, charged and convicted). A communitarian-based morality, in contrast, states that society (or the God of that society) establishes the rules of right conduct and that a member of that society is compelled to follow moral rules if he wishes to remain in that society.

Without neglecting the contribution of socio-economics, it has a number of deficiencies:

1 The socio-economics paradigm cannot lay the basis for a comprehensive positivist economic theory, since it suffers from the same and additional inadequacies as does the neoclassical paradigm. The idea that man is egocentric and rational is a powerful tool in creating a deterministic

science; the notion that man oscillates in his choices between the egocentric-rational and the moral destroys that element of determinacy. Since, as already demonstrated, no comprehensive theory of economic behaviour can be deterministic, it is a further contribution to clarity of thought to show that socio-economics cannot provide a basis for a comprehensive positivist economics theory.

There is, however, no inherent logical barrier to positivist institutional economics – the study of the institutions and relationships prevailing in certain sectors of society, such as labour relations, labour markets, banking, investment banking, etc. In these fields one finds writers who attempt to bring to bear all relevant fields of knowledge to their area, including the prevailing moral code. Here, as elsewhere, it is sensible to remember that men are under moral rules.

2 There is nothing in philosophy to suggest that all of reality must be explainable by positivistic science. Indeed, it is probably a conceit of man that physics is an adequate positivist theory of matter. For many purposes, normative theories are very useful; e.g. the normative theory of democracy permits us to distinguish political systems with the trappings of elections and legislators from true democracies. Socio-economics is not yet a normative system of economics, but it may yet become one.

3 Socio-economics in the hands of its founder, Etzioni, has not yet laid the basis for a re-examination of morals in the economic system. Four types of inquiry are open for discussion: (1) The rules of personal behaviour, *vis-à-vis* one's self and *vis-à-vis* other people. (2) The rules of personal behaviour when one is part of the elite of a collectivity, or the team which runs a collectivity. (3) The rules of behaviour appropriate to polity – usually included under political philosophy. (4) The rules of personal and collective behaviour *vis-à-vis* the environment, both the bio-mass and the physical environment.

In my view, it is time to abandon the partition of human behaviour into social science disciplines of sociology, political science and economics, and deal with human behaviour in its interpersonal or social aspects as a single phenomenology. Behaviour is controlled by the central nervous system (CNS), which is one of the areas studied in the neurosciences; it follows that no social science can assign attributes to behaviour that violate the capabilities of the CNS, as established by the neurosciences. Behaviour occurs in response to stimuli, and the relationship between behaviour and stimuli lies in psychology, and a similar restriction holds there: social science cannot contradict psychology. Since the behaviour of interest to social science occurs in a social context, and is influenced by mind content, which, in turn, is influenced by the local culture, the formation and content of local cultures must necessarily form the major content of the study of behaviour. And it is to this subject that we now turn.

SOCIETY AND BEHAVIOUR

In primitive societies, whether ancient or contemporary, the function of provisioning to sustain life required a great deal of community time and effort. Provisioning was intimately related to governance, communal activities, ritual, play and warfare. Doubtless, the distribution of goods was conditioned on status, contribution to community, physical strength, wisdom and other factors. In periods of adversity, it is likely that virtually everyone in the community suffered.

In contrast to primitive societies, in contemporary developed societies, the potential productive capacity to sustain life is many times larger than requirements. The actual production of goods and services needed to sustain life is, however, considerably less than the potential production capacity because the social organization of production leaves much of the capacity under-utilized. Moreover, much of the actual production of goods, if not overtly devoted to collective or individual destructive purposes, serves only as a marker of social class or has largely ritualistic significance. The actual distribution of goods and services leaves substantial portions of the population ill-fed, ill-housed, under-educated and under-medicated, even in the best of times. To anticipate the argument somewhat, this situation is immoral according to a communitarian viewpoint.

In the light of this, it seems ill-advised to attempt to devise a science of economic activity on the basis of individual choice when, in fact, all interpersonal behaviour and the results of such behaviour are essentially social. It thus seems natural to attempt to understand individual man by starting with the planet earth, and then the species, *Homo sapiens sapiens*, proceeding then to the national/cultural societies into which the species is divided. Each of the national societies consists not only of individual members of the species, but of institutions, bound together in a culture.

The infant is born in a helpless condition into a family, and into the collectivities of which his family is a member, and even at birth he's in a particular relationship with other people and with institutions. The infant's brain, only partially developed at birth, acquires specific biologic capacities during maturation. Simultaneously, it acquires mind-content and the capacity to retrieve additional information from artefacts and the printed word. The basis for perception of events in the environment is established by what the child absorbs into mind-content from its biologic relatives, its peers, the collectivities of which he's a member, and from the culture. Its mental capacities then permit him to process incoming stimuli and to respond. As a matter of language usage, one can say that an individual responds to incoming stimuli by doing what seems appropriate to him for his own betterment, barring the possibility that he's psychopathically self-destructive. But it hardly follows from this language usage to say that human behaviour – even the human behaviour of individuals in a highly advanced country – is socially appropriate, demonstrates a high level of cognitive processing, is efficient, or rational in the sense of a mathematically demonstrable optimum. Behaviour remains highly individualistic, as the different genetic endowment of each person reacts to its own environment, beginning with the environment of the womb.

In the course of childhood and early adult development, each individual learns of community standards. It has become a cliché that each person is socialized to his environment, but this is an overstatement, as the process of socialization is a highly individual affair. Later in development, one may learn of the community standards of the neighbouring community, or of other communities. Moreover, by study and contemplation, one may formulate one's own standards of behaviour. The fact that there is such a thing as standards of behaviour does not imply that such standards are philosophically justifiable. Indeed, in contemporary America, the standards of conduct in some local cultures are destructive to an extreme; a male child may believe that his social status depends upon carrying a weapon and killing or maiming some other member of the community. From hindsight, one can see that the community standards of illustrious civilizations of the past were not justifiable. Thus adherence to community standards – even where these are regarded by contemporaries as enlightened – is no guarantee of moral worth.

Every interpersonal behavioural act of an individual involves a comparison by him of his contemplated action with community standards. It is he who makes a choice to accept or reject the community standard. The options open to an individual, however, may be severely limited: police, security devices, informers and other institutional aspects of the society may give an individual no option but to obey community standards. In contemporary developed societies, however, there may be many more options open to an individual, but this depends on his personal capacity to see his options and on the economic resources or power he enjoys in society. High-risk takers also have more options from which to choose.

I believe that a meaningful and usable theory of economics must examine all behaviour, of which behaviour related to provisioning, that is, economic affairs, is a part. As no behaviour is free of ethical import it is essential that an improved theory of human behaviour also includes an ethical component.

In our present Western culture, the ethical component of behaviour is contained by the word morality, which essentially deals with the rules of right conduct by an individual in his personal and interpersonal behaviour. As the field of ethics deals with this subject, there is no need to pursue that subject further here. Social science, however, is much more concerned with the action of collectivities, whether these be private or public ones, which together make up the community. In the role of decision maker in a collectivity, an agent of the collectivity, or a member, a person may conduct himself according to high moral rules, but the collectivity itself can do great damage, particularly if the collectivity holds itself to no moral standards. The subject of major interest to social science is not personal morality, but the morality of collectivities.

In the same manner that the highest rules of personal morality derive from the axiom of universality – contained in the Judaeo-Christian tradition and later stated more generally by Kant – so do the rules of collective morality. The test of every act of a collectivity is whether it advances the general welfare. Whose general welfare? It cannot be that of any one racial, language or national group or that of one class. It can only be the general welfare of *Homo sapiens sapiens* and the physical environment in which he lives.

As society precedes and shapes the individual born into it, it is society itself which can advance towards or retreat from the achievement of the general welfare. The general welfare is a process and not an end point; that is, it is the embodiment of the good society, containing robust institutions and systems leading to human progress. The opposite is the general diswelfare, the embodiment of the bad society: it contains failing institutions and systems which lead to the physical destruction of human lives and property, jails crammed with inmates, human derelicts walking the streets, and cramped and bruised lives. A good society dispenses justice to its residents and acts morally in its dealings with all, including all other societies. It is one capable of increasing the quality of life of all mankind, today and in the future; this implies that it acts also to preserve the environment. A bad society is characterized by governance on behalf of a special interests, a lack of justice and immoral personal behaviour on the part of government leaders, both in their domestic and their foreign dealings.

Since it is obvious enough that there are few, if any, good societies, in the sense defined above, goodness cannot be a product of any particular system, such as capitalism or democracy, or of any particular religion. It is certainly not located in the human genes, as the history of the human race to this point is filled with injustice and immorality.

Since humankind has generally moved in a positive direction towards justice and morality there must be social forces which are the sources of progress. Surely, among these must be increase in knowledge of all sorts, humanistic, philosophical, conceptual, natural sciences and social sciences. Another supposition, that evolutionary forces are at work bettering the race of man, is far-fetched on its face, since there is no evidence of this at all.

It would evidently help if national states could energize themselves into articulating concrete goals intended to advance the general welfare. It would seem self-evident that the general welfare requires that the biological and mental health needs of all persons be met, and that each individual has the fullest feasible opportunity to improve the quality of his own life without detriment to others and the planet and to make contributions to the quality of life of others.

The articulation of a practical and comprehensive set of national goals, covering such things as life expectancy, reduction in disease rates, educational attainment, nutritional levels, etc., is a simple and necessary step to informing people what is possible if everyone in a society acts in the interest of the community; the process of stating national goals can be understood as the process of establishing the moral rules of a particular collectivity, namely, the national government. Countries which use national planning devices regularly do this. It seems natural to leave such a task to experts in the respective fields of medicine, education, etc. There is also ample room for the participation of lawyers, political scientists, humanists and philosophers in this process, since most of the goals of society have to do with procedural and distributive justice. Clearly, the moral standards of countries will have different qualities, some low and some high, and probably all capable of improvement. It is the task of informed citizens and experts to debate these standards and to constantly advance them.

In the present social climate, in which taxes are regarded as robbery, and regulation an infringement on liberty, each citizen is led to believe that he is an island unto himself. The sacrifices he makes end with him, as there is no community to benefit from them. It is easy to come to such an opinion when the head of government proclaims that government is the problem and not the answer. It is the claim of communitarians that the present social climate is in part the result of an erroneous philosophic base, namely, utilitarianism.

The present state of knowledge makes it possible to outline programmes capable of improving nutrition, health, educational and other standards. The great and unfortunate impediment to this is neoclassical economics to the extent it proclaims the doctrine that the system it purportedly describes, namely, capitalism, is sufficiently robust to constitute governance; hence, that there is no need for governance other than to assure defence and law and order.

It thus should be clear that we who write these essays and we who read them are engaged in a great task: to point the way towards human progress. While the increase in potential productive capacity of all the economies can make a contribution to a good society, it is of little benefit if in fact social disorganization leaves the capacity under-utilized and if the national output is used wastefully and destructively. Thus, even if it were true that neoclassical economics theory points the way to increasing potential industrial production, there would be adequate grounds for lessening its status in our culture. The free market certainly has its place in an economy and society, but only in those situations which fit the perfectly competitive model.

Neither capitalism nor democracy are robust enough as systems to stand independent of culture. Indeed, it is only if the culture is rooted in justice and morality that these systems can function for the good of mankind. Experience has amply shown that each of these institutions alone installed into a society without the supporting culture are forces of evil; when both systems are installed without the supporting culture, as in the Philippines, the result can be havoc. The danger to present-day developed capitalist democratic countries is that the required cultural base is eroding, accentuating structural weaknesses in the systems. Unfortunately, the leading social science, economics, not only contributes to this cultural erosion by elevating acquisitiveness to a civic virtue, but is unable to provide science-based guidance to ameliorate the economic situation to remedy the social problems plaguing society. The unsatisfactory economic situation, if not the chief cause, is the chief contributing cause to prevailing social problems of crime in high and low places, deteriorating family situations, faulty educational standards and inadequate healthcare.

Contrary to the populist version of the American doctrine, a remedy cannot come from individuals acting within their view of their best interests. Nor can it come from local communities expelling crime from their streets, only to end up in neighbouring streets, nor from parental or community guidance of educational institutions, nor from the cities rebuilding themselves by enticing employment centres from other areas, nor from any one class or ethnic group proclaiming the superiority of its values over the values of others. It cannot come from *laissez-faire* economics and it cannot come from more people registering to vote and entering the political process, without any serious study of the nature of society. It cannot and has not come from a Thousand Points of Light. At least, it cannot come in this manner without a national programme dedicated to the national welfare to which people can adhere. In America, only the President has the standing to proclaim the general welfare and the desired direction of social progress.

The burden falls heavily on those institutions presumably dedicated to the general welfare, such as the learned professions and universities, to develop the sciences appropriate to the national programme. One ought to be honest on this matter too and state that both the learned professions and the universities are only too often not dedicated to the general welfare but represent special interests and, increasingly, class interests. While the professions develop and promulgate rules of professional ethics (which still constitutes best practice, but not prevailing practice), they have not yet developed professional policies serving the general interest and dedicated to justice. The universities continue, for the most part, their tradition of serving the elites.

While it might sound incredulous to some, if there is any professional group which is capable of making a difference in our society, it is philosophy, because it is by philosophy that we live, whether we acknowledge this or not. Unfortunately, the professional philosophical literature is unreadable to the layman, and popularizers, such as Mortimer J. Adler, are disdained by the profession.

Since this book of essays is aimed at a wide mix of thinkers, the message which I would like to leave with readers is the recommendation that they look carefully at their own psyche, recognize and evaluate the moral basis of their respective fields and dedicate their efforts to advancing the general welfare.

ACKNOWLEDGEMENTS AND BIBLIOGRAPHIC NOTES

This essay attempts to discredit the received neoclassical economics theory paradigm and substitute an alternative one. It is thus intended to be 'revolutionary' in the sense intended by:

Kuhn, Thomas (1970) *The Structure of Scientific Revolutions*, Chicago: University of Chicago Press.

One would think that the philosophy of science would offer the best basis for re-examining the fundamentals of social science theory. Actually, writers in the philosophy of science usually start out as physicists or mathematicians and have little to say about the social sciences. It is thus more profitable to read historians of social science; particularly recommended is:

Wallerstain, Immanuel (1991) *Unthinking Social Sciences*, Cambridge: Polity Press.

Referential notes

Successful 'revolutionary' paradigms in any one field usually are simultaneously proposed by a number of people who are not otherwise in contact with each other. The new paradigms usually arise because new ideas on a variety of subjects are in the air – ideas which may be thrown up by the course of history: new requirements of society, new technology, developments in literature or the arts, or scientific developments. It is the task of future historians to identify and date the onset of a revolution in ideas and to explain its genesis.

The compelling reason for new scientific paradigms in the field of economics is that there is virtually no consequential national state not now in crisis. Those academics who have reason to be critical of neoclassical economics on scientific grounds tend to believe that poor economics theory bears substantial responsibility for the state of the world. While this may appear laughable or a gross exaggeration to those who believe that theory has little to do with how the world actually functions, to those who believe that civilization lives principally on its stock of ideas, it is natural to attribute real-world failures to failures in scientific disciplines.

While each person is entitled to choose the base from which he can examine prevailing paradigms, this writer has chosen mathematics, ethics and the study of the mind (neuroscience, artificial intelligence), as his frame of reference.

Most economists and other social scientists know how to use mathematics as a tool, but may not conceive of mathematics as a method for examining reality critically. The non-professional mathematician might benefit from reading:

National Academy of Sciences (National Research Council) (ed.) (1969) *The Mathematical Sciences*, Cambridge, MA: MIT Press.
National Academy Press (1986) *State of the Art Reviews, Mathematical Sciences. A Unifying and Dynamic Resource* (35 pages).

These readings furnish a corrective to popularized treatments of chaos and complexity. For non-technical approaches, see:

Gleick, J. (1987) *Chaos*, New York: Viking.
Lewin, R. (1992) *Complexity*, New York: Macmillan.

These books can be roughly characterized as in non-linear dynamic mathematics. What is required, however, is a mathematics that can deal with history. For this, we require a concept from physics called hysteresis (see Lerner, R. G. and Trigg, G. L. (1991) *Encyclopedia of Physics* (2nd edn), New York: VCH Publishers). This topic, as well as the whole topic of modelling, is treated in:

Beltrami, E. (1993) *Mathematical Models in the Social and Biological Sciences*, Boston: Jones & Bartlett.
Casti, J. L. (1989) *Alternate Realities*, New York: Wiley.
Jackson, E. A. (1989) *Perspectives of Nonlinear Dynamics*, Cambridge: Cambridge University Press.
Morrison, F. (1991) *The Art of Modeling Dynamic Systems*, New York: Wiley.

An economist versed in econometrics and thus the treatment of stochastic events might well wonder whether these references are of any use to him. It is helpful to read:

Epstein, R. J. (1987) *A History of Econometrics*, Amsterdam: North-Holland

to obtain an appreciation of the foundation weaknesses in the econometric method. It has helped me understand the differences between randomness and chaos to read:

Charles, R. (1989) *The Physics of Chance*, original French edition, Oxford: Oxford University Press.

The application of complexity to economic theory can be examined in:

Barnett, W. A., Geweke, J. and Shell, K. (eds) (1989) *Economic Complexity*, New York: Cambridge University Press.

The reader should be alerted to the fact that the term in mathematics 'computational complexity' does not refer to the same concept as that discussed here; the topic, moreover, is not related to complex numbers.

It is a basic proposition of this essay, intended as a given, that all human behaviour – in contrast with the behaviour of other living things – can be evaluated from a moral perspective. This statement is not testable, and modern economists, whatever they believed in other areas, do not generally accept this as true. It was the signal contribution of:

Etzioni, A. (1988) *The Moral Dimension. Toward a New Economics*, New York: Free Press.

To bring this notion into modern economics as it had been in classical economics. Etzioni embedded this doctrine in his notion of communitarianism, but it is actually separable from it.

My own views of ethics were formed early in my life by a study of the Old Testament, and by the works of Mortimer J. Adler, who, in 1991, was still publishing: *Desires, Right and Wrong. The Ethics of Enough*, London: Macmillan. I was also influenced in my undergraduate years by the Frankfurt School and later by Jurgen Habermas. Recent works on ethics which I found rewarding are:

MacIntyre, A. (1990) *Three Rival Versions of Moral Enquiry*, Notre Dame, Indiana: University of Notre Dame Press.
Rorty, R. (1980) *Philosophy and the Mirror of Nature*, Oxford: Blackwell.
Stout, J. (1988) *Ethics after Babel*, Boston: Beacon Press.
Sullivan, R. J. (1989) *Immanuel Kant's Moral Theory*, Cambridge: Cambridge University Press.
Zwiebach, B. (1988) *The Common Life*, Philadelphia: Temple University Press.

Readings in ethics should be supplemented by those in political philosophy:

Degler, C. N. (1991) *In Search of Human Nature*, Oxford: Oxford University Press.
Macedo, S. (1990) *Liberal Virtues*, Oxford: Clarendon Press.
Sandel, M. J. (1982) *Liberals and the Limits of Justice*, Cambridge: Cambridge University Press.

The third basic field, pertinent to an adequate social science theory, deals with human behaviour. While there are some excellent popular books, such as:

Ritzak, R. M. (1988) *The Mind*, London: Bantam Books,

the busy reader could content himself with:

The Economist: The Human Mind, 'Touching the intangible', 26 December 1992, pp. 115–120.
Scientific American, September 1992 issue.

The relevancy of the study of the mind to social science theory will be illuminated by:

Donald, M. (1991) *Origins of the Modern Mind*, Cambridge, MA: Harvard University Press.
Edelman, G. M. (1992) 'Bright air, brilliant fire', *On the Matter of the Mind*, New York: Basic Books.
Ornstein, R. (1991) *The Evolution of Consciousness*, Englewood Cliffs, NJ: Prentice Hall.

With some knowledge of the newest scientific findings on the mind, one is in a better position to tackle the field of rationality in social science. One ought to be conscious of the fact that the concept of bounded rationality, introduced by Herbert Simon, was a semantic dodge, intended to overcome the affective resistance of those who held to a tenet of Christianity that man could freely choose to be as pure as Jesus or as evil as Satan. This religious concept is not compatible with the notion that the brain of *Homo sapiens* represents only a small advance in the area of language and consequently abstraction over the brain of the chimpanzee. The major issues as these pertain to economics are well discussed in:

Hogarth, R. M. and Reder, M. W. (eds) (1986/1987) *Rational Choice*, Chicago: University of Chicago Press.
Thaler, R. H. (1991) *Quasi-rational Economics*, New York: Russell Sage Foundation.

Much of the remainder of the essay deals with conventional topics in economic theory.

Exhibit 16.A Locus of selected serious problems of American society

I Individual Life Style

A. Use of harmful substance: drugs, tobacco.
B. Abuse of socially approved substances: alcohol.
C. Sexual practices with adverse consequences: Aids and other venereal diseases; teenage pregnancy; prostitution; abortion.
D. Nutritional practices: excessive caloric intake; excessive intake of saturated fats; poor infant- and child-feeding practices.
E. Criminality as choice of career.
F. Corruption as choice of life style.

II Interpersonal Relationships

A. Discrimination and harassment based on sex, race.
B. Child abuse.
C. Divorce, domestic violence, suicide.
D. Supervisor–employee relationships resulting in poor work, strikes, lockouts, class and social conflicts.

III Collectivities

A. Corporations: exploitation of company assets by managers, unethical company practices, e.g. in advertising dysfunctional management styles.
B. Labour unions: lack of democracy class conflict ideologies.
C. Government.
   1. Abuse of natural environment: global and local.
   2. International relations: reliance on war and terror; reliance on nuclear weapons; imperialism.
   3. Social: polarization of rich and poor culture or poverty; inadequate social infrastructure: education, health, housing.
   4. Economic.
      (*a*) Income distribution – unequal and deteriorating.
      (*b*) Structural – hollowing-out of corporation; excessive leveraging; frailty of banking structure.
      (c) Growth – slowdown of productivity growth.
      (d) Macro-inflation, excessive consumption and under-saving debtor–creditor status, excessive government debt, current account deficit.
      (e) Geographic distribution of population and capital: urban slums.
      (*f*) Micro problems – loss of competitiveness in various industries.

Chapter 17

Politics, public choice and ethical progress

Ralph E. Miner

The doors which had for so long been barred against the entry into economics of any (openly acknowledged) moral concepts have been blown open. All the supposed logical barriers to fruitful exchange between economic theory and moral philosophy, political philosophy and the philosophy of law are down, and the honest confrontation of the issues which properly concern the moral sciences can relieve economists from the shameful pretence of ethical neutrality.

> (Vivian Walsh (1987) 'Philosophy and economics', in John Eatwell, Murray Milgate and Peter Newman (eds), *New Palgrave Dictionary of Economics*, London: Macmillan, pp. 861–869)

INTRODUCTION

Most observers of American politics, including most political scientists, believe that 'special interests' as political actors and self-interest as a legitimating credo made significant gains in the conduct, discourse and evaluation of American politics in the 1960s, 1970s and particularly the 1980s (Berry, 1989; Etzioni, 1984; Fiorina, 1980). The intellectual and increasingly socio-ethical legitimation of individual self-interest in politics has come, in recent years, in part from one segment of American neoclassical political economy: public choice, the application of economic methods to the study of political phenomena. Political theorist Adam Przeworski (1985, p. 379) claims that 'the public choice approach reigns over political science', and Amitai Etzioni, while noting that the neoclassical economic paradigm 'plays a key role in contemporary political science (e.g., in the Public Choice School)' (1988, p. 2), concludes that 'there is likely to be a negative, anti-moral effect' (1988, p. 251) as a result of its teachings. More pointedly, Steven Kelman (1987b) of Harvard's Kennedy School of Government has portrayed public choice as a grand self-fulfilling prophecy of ethical decline. He describes its emphasis upon materialistic self-interest as a tragedy for public life and public spirit.

Noted public choice theorists Geoffrey Brennan and James Buchanan

(1988) have responded specifically and directly to Kelman's complaint[1] by calling attention to work in the subfield of 'constitutional economics' or 'constitutional political economy', the normative exploration of alternative contractarian conceptions. The aim of constitutional economics is the development of new or revised and mutually agreed-upon rules to constrain the use of government for the advancement of particularistic economic ends. While Brennan and Buchanan (1988, p. 188) agree with Kelman that there is 'danger' that public choice, if used in an empirical manner 'typical of "positive economics"', will breed undesirable moral consequences, they propose a remedy – a return to the constitutional drawing board to fashion new rules to govern the government's rule-making.

Before succumbing to the pathos of Kelman's tragedy, or committing to the 'radical reforms' (McKenzie, 1985) of constitutional economics, let us examine in more detail the intellectual positions of Kelman, on the one hand, and Brennan and Buchanan, on the other. It is suggested here that there is a more moderate perspective that can avoid the bleak prospects for the American political ethic predicted by Kelman and by Brennan and Buchanan with their respective views of this new American dilemma. This perspective is embodied in socio-economics, an aspiring paradigm-cum-movement fathered and led by Amitai Etzioni (1988). Socio-economics strives to focus upon the range and nature of the variance unexplained and, from Kelman's viewpoint, obscured by the assumptive character of many public choice analyses of contemporary politics.

First, back to basics: in order to illuminate the fundamental political nature of the public choice–public spirit question, we will review two early and important public choice contributions to our understanding of the intertwined problems of individual and collective interest representation: 'the C-R model', and the differential costs of information. Just who is 'the public' whose spirit is at risk? How is this public structured and how effectively are its segments represented?

THE C-R MODEL

In *The Calculus of Consent* (1962), Buchanan and Gordon Tullock present, in their discussion of representative government, the 'external costs' of a representative system (like the American single-member district system where one votes for individual candidates) measured against the norm of direct democracy. We shall see that these costs to those in the system who prefer that political outcomes be determined by the voters themselves are high indeed when, as a matter of efficiency, a system of representative government is decided upon.

Figure 17.1 presents constituent preferences and representatives' votes and is adapted from Buchanan and Tullock's (1962, p. 220) presentation of a model, which I term the 'C-R (constituent-representative) model'. If three

R_1	R_2	R_3	R_4	R_5
yes	yes	yes		
yes	yes	yes		
yes	yes	yes		

Figure 17.1 The C-R (constituent-representative) model

representatives vote as a majority of their constituents want them to, then nine persons in this community have determined the outcome for the total electorate of twenty-five.

Question: is this majority rule or minority rule? It is, of course, formal majority rule (i.e., three representatives outvote two representatives), the rule that counts when it comes to the adoption of public policy, but it is *de facto* minority rule when measured in terms of the number of constituents whose preferences are represented in the adopted legislation.

While Buchanan and Tullock discuss the C-R model within the context 'of the structure of control in representative democracy', their consideration at this point focuses principally on the implications of this minority rule for those related legislative behaviours known to Americans as 'pork-barrel' and 'log-rolling', and for other decisions concerning public sector programmes, and thus important to the size of governments, their budgets and their deficits. Their discussion does not focus on the implications for pure democratic norms of the discordance between public policies that might be adopted directly by voters and those adopted by representatives, even under the idealized conditions of perfectly responsive bivalent majority representation, perfect apportionment, perfect information and a perfectly equal distribution of political resources.[2]

Buchanan and Tullock demonstrate that representation of subsystem majorities can produce minority rule at the system level. However, minority log-rolling can be considered to be the ultimate technique of *district-*representation, and the system can be considered as the sum of the districts. In a 'representative democracy', ought not the representative log-roll benefits for his or her district on every possible occasion as long as he or she complies with the district's preferences? Are projects without merit simply because they are log-rolled? Is the representative to vote for what some out-of-district person terms 'the national interest' or 'the public interest' even when his or her constituents are unanimous in urging him or her to vote to the contrary?

These questions become crucially problematic for the system, of course, when any taxes levied to finance local projects will be borne by all constituents in the system, not just those in the district receiving the benefit. But if, as a solution to this dilemma, tax jurisdictions are congruent with the areas receiving the direct benefits of projects, we regress to a plethora of micro-governments. Thus, before considering multiple-minority pluralism, we must recall that the constitutional politics of representation is district-constituency-based, and therefore, usually minority-, not system-, based. The representative system responds to multiple, geographically bounded, minorities which may be, however, majorities or even unanimous at the subsystem level. A system-level constituent majority does not exist very often, except paradoxically, as we note below, when it comes to the limitation or reduction of system-wide taxes.[3]

The constituent minority of nine in the C-R model can also hold the majority in check by voting against their benefit measures, but, of course, this again violates the system-wide norm of majority rule. We thus confront what Buchanan and Tullock (1962) and other public choice theorists (Buchanan and Wagner, 1977; Buchanan et al., 1987) are especially concerned about: the legislative body responding to multiple minorities when it comes to expanding government and increasing its expenditures.[4] At the same time, we can note what is becoming an American national tradition: multiple system-wide majorities opposed to general taxes to finance those expenditures, effectively favouring continuing federal deficits and mounting national debt. The collective summation of public choice's individualistic rationality – 'maximize my benefits and minimize my costs' – on the part of voters and politicians heads the system towards bankruptcy.[5]

How can we reconcile Kelman's critique of public choice as an ethical tragedy with the conceptual insight, the logical coherence and the dynamic implications of Buchanan and Tullock's model? The following sections attempt to sort out and clarify some of this by examining (1) the relevance and usefulness of contributions of public choice to our understanding of the socio-political economy of information, (2) the neglect of the implications of some of those studies by public choice theorists themselves, as well as by those presumably interested in the reform of our political institutions to make them more reflective of and responsive to egalitarian norms, and (3) the neglect by Kelman of the implications for what he terms 'good public policy'[6] of consistently pro-benefit minorities and anti-tax majorities.

THE DIFFERENTIAL COSTS OF INFORMATION

In his classic, *An Economic Theory of Democracy* (1957),[7] Anthony Downs presents a careful review of the relationship between the division of labour and the socio-political distribution of information costs. It is unfortunate that the important structural implications of his analysis have been largely ignored, even by those, and perhaps especially by those, with the greatest concern for the asymmetric nature of American politics, a concern about the structure of 'lop-sided pluralism'. To rectify this, at least in part, and in an attempt to deal directly with and appreciate the importance of the politics of differential information costs, we will quote representative portions of Downs's exposition and then analytically superimpose the structural implications of that analysis on the egalitarian, yet flawed, structure of the C-R model.

Downs's explication of the structural implications of differential information costs could hardly be more specific and emphatic. Thirty-five years ago, he spelled out at some length and in strong language the importance of the socio-economic division of society for the relative costs of economic–political information, and thus for the distribution of political power in representative systems. The quotations which follow (and the additional ones in the appendix to this paper) from *An Economic Theory* give the thrust and the tenor of his reasoning:

> Inequality of political power is inevitable, in every large society marked by uncertainty and a division of labor, no matter what its constitution says or how equal its citizens are in every other respect [p. 239].

> Naturally, the men who stand most to gain from exerting influence in a policy area are the ones who can best afford the expense of becoming expert about it. Their potential returns from influence are high enough to justify a large investment of information. In almost every policy area, those who stand the most to gain are the men who earn their incomes there.

> . . . because of the very structure of society, each government decision cannot result from equal consideration of the wishes of men who are equally affected by the decision. When we add to this inherent disparity of influence the inequalities of power caused by the uneven distribution of income, we have moved a long way from political equality among citizens [p. 257].

> . . . our model does tend to verify the following assertion: even if a society's rules are specifically designed to distribute political power equally, such equality will never result in an uncertain world as long as men act rationally [p. 258].[8]

Thus, constitutional economics, from a Downsian perspective, can be regarded, even if not its founders' intention, as a movement that would embed in the constitution additional artefacts promoting the institutional conversion of differential economic power into complex, yet real, hegemonic political power, power wielded through the choices of natural and artificial, corporate persons.[9] It can be viewed as the installation of another locked-in structure to protect from predatory minorities and majorities, possessed by 'distributional envy' (Brennan and Buchanan, 1985, p. 140), what Charles Lindblom (1982) calls the 'privileged position of business'; i.e., the position of natural persons and corporate actors with high business incomes, great wealth and extensive property.

THE CONSTITUTION AND THE HEGEMONIC LOGIC

Some of those scholars concerned about corporate power and the operation of its 'hegemonic logic' in the American political economy find their inspiration in Antonio Gramsci's 1919–25 prison notebooks (Hoare and Smith, 1971). They can also find a clear explanation in Downs's theory of economic–political information, as excerpted above (and in the appendix), of the way in which the division of labour determines the distribution of political power, and the way in which conventional American economic theory legitimates for those in the superior *and* the inferior socio-economic strata the existing pattern of that distribution.[10]

Downs's language quoted above conveys a powerful image of the potent reinforcement of the structural *status quo* by a logic of information and, by extension, organization costs, a logic whose implications for political–economic structure are seemingly ignored by both the critics of markets referred to above, and by the critics of politics, particularly those critics from that segment of political economy with which we are concerned here, public choice.

According to Downs's theory of politically relevant economic information and its distribution and relative costs, the 'privileged position of business' which 'does not fit' democratic theory (Lindblom, 1977, p. 356) is secure under the existing American Constitution and law. It may well be, in fact, that any attempt to construct a new constitution embodying a flat-rate tax and equal per capita transfer payments, as proposed by Brennan and Buchanan, would suggest for some a re-evaluation of the bases of the corporate world's conversion of its economic power to (multinational?) political power, including the legal 'personhood' of corporations, the political ramifications of market competition and the legitimating logical power of economic theory. Corporate accumulation of political information as a by-product of daily operations makes well-financed political action committees and aggressive rent-seeking[11] possible, efficient and highly rational. However, contemporary public choice analyses rarely extend from the theory of rent-seeking to the real-life political behaviour of market actors, to the uneven-handedness of the market's distribution of political power.

'THE TRAGEDY OF "PUBLIC CHOICE"'

Kelman's article, '"Public choice" and public spirit' (1987b) takes public choice scholars to task for the negative implications of their studies for public spirit. His concluding paragraph, quoted almost in full at the head of Brennan and Buchanan's (1988) response, is as follows:

> Norms are crucial. They can also be fragile. Cynical descriptive conclusions about behavior in government threaten to undermine the norm prescribing public spirit. The cynicism of journalists – and even the writings of professors – can decrease public spirit simply by describing what they claim to be its absence. Cynics are therefore in the business of making prophecies that threaten to become self-fulfilling. If the norm of public spirit dies, our society would look bleaker and our lives as individuals would be more impoverished. That is the tragedy of 'public choice' [pp. 93–94].

The extension of public choice modes of thought into economics in general and its conversion of some political scientists represents for Kelman (1987b, p. 80) an 'inapposite and pernicious' development which threatens the norms of public service and public-spiritedness. However, this same criticism has been made on previous occasions of empirical political science, and by political scientists at that (Ricci, 1984). The problem involves not only public choice and its paradigmatic imperialism; it involves the more profound question of the implications for the democratic norm of a 'science of politics' in general.

We cannot consider this broad question here. We return instead to our specific concern: the increasingly hegemonic public choice logic that legitimates the spread of 'the market spirit' into areas of public spirit and moral sentiments.

In their response to Kelman, Brennan and Buchanan (1988, p. 187) assert that

> Public choice – the hard-headed, realistic, indeed cynical model of political behavior – can be properly defended on moral grounds if we adopt a 'constitutional' perspective – that is, if the purpose of the exercise is conceived to be institutional reform, improvements in the *rules* under which political processes operate. . . . The public choice theorist['s] task is that of advising all citizens on the working of alternative constitutional rules.

Towards the end of their paper, Brennan and Buchanan (1988, p. 188) come into a somewhat surprising agreement with Kelman, to wit:

> we agree that there is cause for some concern with public choice interpreted as a predictive model of behavior in political roles. Where public choice is used to develop a predictive theory of political processes in a manner typical of 'positive economics' – that is, with the focus solely

on developing an empirically supportable theory of choice *within* rules, and with the ultimate normative purpose of constitutional design swept away in footnotes or neglected altogether – then the danger is that it will indeed breed the moral consequences previously discussed.

Note that in proposing the normative project of constitutional design, Brennan and Buchanan 'sweep away' all social structure, presumably into individual utility functions, as does public choice generally (with the notable exception of Downs as considered above).[12] It is as if, in their view, there is a blank slate upon which public choice can draft a new constitution with two primary constraints: a flat tax rate and uniform individual transfer payments. Brennan and Buchanan do not present in this *Virginia Law Review* article the direction and shape of other constitutional changes they envisage as saving us from the consequences of positive economics. However, we do find an explicit and forceful agenda in *The Reason of Rules* (1985, p. 150), where, harking back to Schumpeter in a powerful conclusion, they maintain that,

> . . . democratic societies, as they now operate, will self-destruct, perhaps slowly but nonetheless surely, unless the rules of the political game are changed, and that there is increasing awareness that something other than ordinary politics will be required to generate *fiscal and monetary discipline*, that a regime is needed that will function in the acknowledged long-term *interests of all participants in the body politic*. The search for, and discussion of, alternative fiscal and monetary rules has begun.

Brennan and Buchanan have

> hope that a new 'civic religion' is on the way to being born, a civic religion that will return, in part, to the skepticism of the eighteenth century concerning politics and government and that, quite naturally, will concentrate our attention on the *rules that constrain governments* rather than innovations that justify ever expanding political intrusions into the lives of citizens. Our normative role, as social philosophers, is to shape this civic religion, surely a challenge sufficient to us all.

Etzioni calls for 'a new public civility' (1984, p. 282), Kelman for the resurrection of 'public spirit', Tullock and others (Koford and Collander, 1984; Rowley *et al.*, 1988) for the end of rent-seeking, and Brennan and Buchanan for a new 'civic religion' to avert democratic self-destruction.

CIVIC RELIGION, PUBLIC SPIRIT AND GOOD PUBLIC POLICY

These social evangelists agree, despite their widely disparate perspectives, that there is a palpable socio-normative entropy, a trend towards Hobbesian disorder, implicit in positive public choice. Focusing on the two extreme positions, we have seen that Kelman leaves us confronted with the tragedy for 'good public policy' of this downward spiral and disintegration, while Brennan and Buchanan call for a civic religion which will have as its chief mission the development of a new and improved constitution to constrain the expansion and intrusions of an overreaching government characterized by ever-increasing expenditures, taxes and deficits.

Economists model an apolitical economy; public choice theorists model an economic polity. Perhaps constitutional economists will succeed in modelling an apolitical polity. Political scientists recognize that there is a strong, albeit futile, yearning in America for 'good public policy' and an 'end of politics', but, unfortunately perhaps, the appropriate criteria for judging alternative public policies are what the argument is all about – e.g., under given conditions, how big should the national debt be? Elevating expenditure and tax questions to the constitutional level, as advocated by the constitutional economists, is a complex project. It is one that confronts not only the massive economic–political gains to important low-information-and-organization-cost-minorities from rent-seeking, but also the normative political strength of the time-honoured doctrine of majority rule which effectively legitimates the empirical prevalence of minority rule. Kelman's public spirit, Etzioni's (1984, p. 281) 'rolling back of interest groups' and the creation of a new public civility, the public choice theorists' reform of rent-seeking and the civic religion of Brennan and Buchanan are all up against the powerful implications of Downs's structural theory of political–economic information, its costs and its systematically uneven distribution.

The notion of a new American ethic that reconciles hegemonic self-interest and budget balance by way of revised constitutional 'rules of the game' assumes that politics can, in some sense, be transformed. But there is no incentive for successful rent-seekers or for rent-offerers, contemporary politicians, to support such a movement. Even if that movement somehow developed, however, those reciprocally empowered actors would be systemically compelled to kill it or at least control it in view of its essential and fundamental threat to their joint hegemony.

CONCLUSION

Socio-economics is a new transdisciplinary field and, in my view, its intellectual breadth complements the public choice perspective and its incisive rent-seeking analytic. Its recognition of the need for a constrained politics is based, not on the need to disable government, but on the impossibility, in the face of the hegemonic logic, of electing one that cannot be bought and sold. The likelihood that socio-economics can make major contributions to the ethical progress of the American socio-political economy through the 'encapsulation of competition' (Etzioni, 1988, ch. 12) will be increased if it meets head-on the normative challenges of public choice and constitutional economics. Needed are articulate studies of *intersectoral ethics* – studies which focus on those collective consequences of market incentives which, by their very power, give rise to the asymmetric, unrelenting political search for economic returns. This intersectoral profit search impedes progress along the moral dimension that leads to a new civility, and a refurbished democratic ethic. Many economists, political scientists, political economists, public choice theorists, constitutional economists and socio-economists can agree on this.

APPENDIX

Additional statements of Anthony Downs in *An Economic Theory of Democracy* regarding the socio-political economy of information:

Society's free information stream systematically provides some citizens with more politically useful information than it provides others.

Any concept of democracy based on an electorate of equally well-informed citizens is irrational; i.e., it presupposes that citizens behave irrationally [p. 221].

The foundations of differential political power in a democracy are rooted in the very nature of society.

Furthermore, to be at all realistic, we must add to [these] . . . differentiating forces the unequal distribution of income.

All information is costly; therefore, those with high incomes can better afford to procure it than those with low incomes [p. 236].

. . . the foundations for inequalities of power are inherent in democratic societies, even though political equality is their basic ethical premise [p. 237].

Furthermore, the cost of data purchased in order to influence government policy in an area of production can often be charged to a business firm or labor union. These corporate units can, in turn, deduct the cost from their taxable income [p. 254].

For all these reasons, producers are much more likely to become influencers than consumers. The former can better afford to invest in the specialized information needed for influencing [public policy] and to pay the cost of communicating their views to the government. This conclusion even applies to business firms, since their revenue nearly always comes from fewer policy areas than their cost inputs [p. 255].

For instance, legislators are notorious for writing tariff laws which favor a few producers in each field at the expense of thousands of consumers. . . . Each producer can afford to bring great influence to bear upon that section of the tariff law affecting his product. Conversely, few consumers can bring any influence to bear upon any parts of the law, since each consumer's interests are spread over so many products [p. 255].

NOTES

1 Etzioni's comment quoted above was published later than the Brennan and Buchanan article.

2 Buchanan and Tullock (1962, p. 222) point out that the result under a representative system 'is not precisely equivalent to that which would be expected under direct bargaining [between voters] . . .'. That seems like an understatement. However, they state that they chose not to consider the differences in *The Calculus*.

3 Public choice theorists (Buchanan and Wagner, 1977; Buchanan *et al.*, 1987) point to the increasing American national debt, and our collective inability to do anything about it, as overwhelming evidence of the structural conflict between multiple-minority interests and any assumed national or public interest.

4 Or, equivalently, creating tax deductions or exemptions.

5 If the nine minority voters were spread across the entire jurisdiction rather than concentrated in three districts, they would lose. However, Brennan and Buchanan (1985, pp. 126–127; pp. 149–150) maintain that the exploitation of majorities by numerical minorities recurs with a frequency sufficient to require new constitutions for the Western democracies, and for the United States in particular, constitutions that lock in a system-wide proportionate tax on income and equal per capita 'demogrants' to each man, woman and child.

6 Kelman (1987b) uses this phrase several times without defining it, but see Kelman (1987a). Empirically, one could cite the infrequency of significant Congressional public policy decisions that are passed unanimously. Obviously there are frequent and sharp differences as to what constitutes 'good public policy'. Kelman has substituted 'good public policy' for that well-known phantom, the public interest.

7 Volumes could be written about the epistemological status of Downs's statements, but they are invoked here in the heuristic spirit of Downs's argument in *An Economic Theory*.

8 See the Appendix to this paper for additional statements by Downs concerning the distribution of political information.

9 Two interesting articles concerning natural and corporate persons are Adelstein (1991) and Coleman (1991).

10 It is contended here that, as noted above, many of those scholars have, perhaps, in Downsian terms, let their thought, time- and energy-saving ideologies screen out the contributions of Downs's (1957) theory of ideology to a critical appraisal of contemporary American politics.

11 The seeking of market advantage through non-market means, particularly through lobbying of governments for tariffs, subsidies, tax advantages and regulation or deregulation as the case may be.

12 See Coleman (1984, 1987).

REFERENCES

Adelstein, R. A. (1991) 'The life and times of the corporate person' (with an alternate title of 'Deciding for bigness: constitutional choice and the growth of firms'), *Constitutional Political Economy*, vol. 2, no. 1 (Winter), 7–30.

Berry, J. M. (1989) *The Interest Group Society*, Glenview, IL: Scott, Foresman/Little, Brown.

Brennan, G. and Buchanan, J. M. (1985) *The Reason of Rules: Constitutional Political Economy*, Cambridge: Cambridge University Press.

Brennan, G. and Buchanan, J. M. (1988) 'Is public choice immoral? The case for the nobel lie', *Virginia Law Review*, 74: 2 (March) 179–189.

Buchanan, J. M. (1975) *The Limits of Liberty*, Chicago: University of Chicago Press.

Buchanan, J. M. and Tullock, G. (1962) *The Calculus of Consent: Logical Foundations of Constitutional Democracy*, Ann Arbor: University of Michigan Press.

Buchanan, J. M. and Wagner, R. E. (1977) *Democracy in Deficit: The Political Legacy of Lord Keynes*, New York: Academic Press.

Buchanan, J. M., Rowley, C. K. and Tollison, R. D. (eds) (1987) *Deficits*, London: Blackwell.

Coleman, J. S. (1984) 'Introducing social structure into economic analysis', *American Economic Review*, vol. 74, no. 2, 84–88.

Coleman, J. S. (1987) 'Norms as social capital', in G. Radnitzky and P. Bernholz (eds), *Economic Imperialism: The Economic Approach Applied Outside the Field of Economics*, New York: Paragon House, pp. 133–55.

Coleman, J. S. (1991) 'Natural persons, corporate actors, and constitutions', *Constitutional Political Economy*, vol. 2, no. 1 (Winter), 81–106.

Downs, A. (1957) *An Economic Theory of Democracy*, New York: Harper & Row.

Eatwell, J., Milgate, M. and Newman, P. (eds) (1987) *New Palgrave Dictionary of Economics*, London: Macmillan.

Etzioni, A. (1984) *Capital Corruption*, New York: Harcourt Brace Jovanovich.

Etzioni, A. (1988) *The Moral Dimension: Toward a New Economics*, New York: Free Press.

Fiorina, M. (1980) 'The decline of collective responsibility in American politics', *Daedalus*, 109: 3, 25–45.

Hoare, Q. and Smith, G. N. (eds) (1971) *Selections from the Prison Notebooks of Antonio Gramsci* [1919–25], New York: International Publishers.

Kelman, S. (1987a) *Making Public Policy*, New York: Basic Books.

Kelman, S. (1987b) '"Public choice" and public spirit', *The Public Interest*, 36 (Spring), 80–94.

King, R. F. (1983) 'From redistributive to hegemonic logic: the transformation of American tax politics, 1894–1963', *Politics and Society*, 12: 1, 1–52.

Koford, K. J. and Colander, D. C. (1984) 'Taming the rent-seeker', in D. C. Colander (ed.), *Neoclassical Political Economy: The Analysis of Rent-seeking and DUP Activities*, Cambridge, MA: Ballinger, pp. 205–216.

Lindblom, C. E. (1977) *Politics and Markets: The World's Political–Economic Systems*, New York: Basic Books.

Lindblom, C. (1982) 'The market as prison', *The Journal of Politics*, 44: 2 (May), 324–336.

McKenzie, R. B. (ed.) (1985) *Constitutional Economics*, Lexington, MA: Lexington Books.

Przeworski, A. (1985) 'Marxism and rational choice', *Politics and Society*, 14: 4, 379–409.

Ricci, D. M. (1984) *The Tragedy of Political Science: Politics, Scholarship and Democracy*, New Haven: Yale University Press.

Rowley, C. K., Tollison, R. D. and Tullock, G. (eds) (1988) *The Political Economy of Rent-seeking*, Boston: Kluwer.

Tullock, G. (1984) 'How to do well while doing good!', in D. C. Colander (ed.), *Neoclassical Political Economy: The Analysis of Rent-seeking and DUP Activities*, Cambridge, MA: Ballinger, pp. 229–240.

Walsh, V. (1987) 'Philosophy and economics', in J. Eatwell, M. Milgate and P. Newman (eds), *New Palgrave Dictionary of Economics*, London: Macmillan.

Wicksell, K. (1958) 'A new principle of just taxation (1896)', in R. A. Musgrave and A. T. Peacock (eds), *Classics in the Theory of Public Finance*, London: Macmillan, pp. 72–118.

Chapter 18

Economics and the Enlightenment
Then and now

Norman E. Bowie

Although the work of Albert O. Hirschman is well known by socio-economists, one of his papers has not received the attention it deserves. In a 1982 paper 'Rival interpretations of market society: civilizing, destructive, or feeble', Hirschman considered three competing interpretations of the effect of market capitalism on society. The three views are that the effects of markets are civilizing, destructive or feeble. The interpretation that markets are civilizing, Hirschman correctly attributes to thinkers of the eighteenth century. The eighteenth century is frequently referred to as the age of the Enlightenment.

In Hirschman's (1982) view, the civilizing function of the market is found in the market's ability to make relationships easier and more gentle. As representatives of this view, Hirschman quotes Montesquieu, Condorcet and Thomas Paine.

> It is almost a general rule that wherever manners are gentle (*moeurs douces*) there is commerce; and wherever there is commerce, manners are gentle. Commerce . . . polishes and softens [*adoucit*] barbaric ways as we can see every day [Montesquieu].

> Manners [*moeurs*] have become more gentle [*se sont adoucies*] . . . through the influence of the spirit of commerce and industry, those enemies of the violence and turmoil which cause wealth to flee . . .' [Condorcet].

> [Commerce] is a pacific system, operating to cordialize mankind, by rendering Nations as well as individuals, useful to each other. . . . The invention of commerce . . . is the greatest approach toward universal civilization that has yet been made by any means not immediately flowing from moral principles [Paine].

My favourite quotation in this regard is from David Hume's *Of Refinement in the Arts* (1752):

> The same age which produces great philosophers and politicians, renowned generals and poets usually abounds with skillful weavers and

ship carpenters. We cannot reasonably expect that a piece of woolen cloth will be wrought to perfection in a nation which is ignorant of astronomy or where ethics are neglected. Thus industry, knowledge and humanity are linked together by an indivisible chain, and are found, from experience as well as reason, to be peculiar to the more polished, and what are commonly denominated, the more luxurious ages.

(pp. 270–271)

Although Hirschman's analysis is suggestive, I think it is incomplete. The civilizing impact of the market is far more extensive than Hirschman describes. In this paper I will identify a number of Enlightenment ideals or values and then argue that market capitalism supports most of these ideals and values. I suggest that this more extensive civilizing feature of markets has not been noticed because markets have been primarily national rather than international. As commerce is becoming internationalized, these civilizing effects will become more apparent. Several specific hypotheses in this regard are advanced. Indeed the twenty-first century may be that point in history where a number of eighteenth-century ideals are realized.

In the current postmodern intellectual climate, the Enlightenment is the 'bête noire' in intellectual thought. Contemporary critics contend that the view that reason is the way to knowledge is the mistake that has dominated the conventional wisdom for nearly two centuries. What seems especially arrogant to postmodern critics is the notion that reason provides a privileged position beyond the contingencies of history, language and culture to reach an objective truth. Many trees have been felled to show that there is no such privileged position. In the face of such intellectual criticisms, why should we take Enlightenment values seriously?

Because the Enlightenment is the birthplace of classical economics; Adam Smith is an Enlightenment figure and the intellectual rationale for capitalism was developed during the Enlightenment period. Study of Enlightenment ideals and values will show the historical relationship between economics and these values and serve as a corrective to the neoclassical view of economics as value neutral. Moreover, even if the epistemological view that reason can provide a privileged position for objective knowledge is dead, capitalism is very much alive. Indeed, with the virtual collapse of Marxist economic systems and the trend towards decentralization and deregulation nearly world-wide in the 1980s, the legitimacy of the market model has never been higher. Although scorned by postmodern critics, other intellectuals and the conventional wisdom of the age have embraced the market model. Of all the various ideas of the Enlightenment, the free market model of classical economics is the most robust survivor. In what follows I will focus on how an understanding of capitalism enables us to make sense of other Enlightenment ideals.

In my introduction, I indicated that Hirschman's characterization of the market as civilizing is too tepid. I wish to argue a much bolder thesis. First, I wish to argue that market economies depend on the existence of a number of values for their survival. The market depends on the so-called contractual values – honesty, trust and fair dealing. To the extent that market economies become international, a universal morality – at least in business affairs – will develop. I will also argue that the market promotes certain values, specifically secular values at the expense of religious values, democratic values at the expense of authoritarian values and international values at the expense of nationalistic values. As markets become international societies will become more secular, democratic and cosmopolitan. Most importantly in this paper I argue that the growth of international capitalist organizations will contribute greatly to the realization of a fundamental Enlightenment ideal – world peace or perpetual peace as the German philosopher Immanuel Kant said in 1795.

A MARKET MORALITY

Central to a capitalist morality are such notions as freedom of voluntary exchange, the sanctity of contracts and the removal of impediments to trade. Consider the sanctity of contracts. Kant argued in the 'Foundation of the metaphysics of morals' that promise-keeping was a necessary requirement of morality since lying when you could get away with it could not be made universal without being self-defeating.

Kant's strategy is to show that if one contemplated breaking a promise, because keeping it was inconvenient or detrimental to oneself, such an action could not be consistently universalized. Consider this: if your reason for breaking a promise was that it was inconvenient for you, then your reason universalized would be, 'Everyone should break a promise when it was inconvenient for him or her'. But this is self-defeating, for if anyone consistently recommended that everyone should break promises when it worked to his or her advantage, the very practice of making promises would be undermined. Promises, after all, are made because sometimes people want the security that something will be done or not done even if it turns out that such an action or inaction would not work to the advantage of one of the promisers. If such a universal practice developed, one could never make promises because no one would trust others to keep promises, and without trust that promises will be kept, making promises becomes impossible.

Kant's point can be restated so that it applies specifically to business. There are many ways of making a promise. One of the more formal ways is by a contract. A contract is an agreement between two or more parties, usually enforceable by law, for the doing or not doing of some definite thing. The contract device is extremely useful in business. The hiring of employees, the use of credit, the ordering and supplying of goods and the notion of warranty, to name but a few, all make use of the contract device. Using a Kantian-type argument, I maintain that if contract breaking were universalized, then business practice would be impossible. If a participant in business were universally to advocate violating contracts, such advocacy would be self-defeating, just as the universal advocacy of lying was seen to be self-defeating. What is significant about Kant's argument is that it applies everywhere regardless of culture.

A similar analysis can be used against such practices as theft or fraud and all acts of deception. If universalized, such activities would undermine the practice of business for the same reasons that the universalizing of contract breaking and lying would. Theft and fraud involve the taking of property that belongs to someone else. If theft and fraud were universal, private property would cease to exist. Nothing could belong to someone because it was always subject to theft or fraud. Those committing theft or fraud must free-ride off those who do not. The only way to escape Kant's argument is to abandon the notion of private property. In capitalist societies such a move is not a viable option.

Business then requires moral behaviour such as trust and keeping promises. Kenneth Boulding makes this exact point in 'The basis of value judgments in economics' (1967) when he says that 'without an integrative framework, exchange itself cannot develop, because exchange, even in its most primitive form, involves trust and credibility' (p. 68). In business relations, trust and credibility are exhibited in promise keeping, especially in the honouring of contracts.

But the arguments for a capitalist morality are not merely logical. A number of 'immoral' practices are practices that increase transaction costs. Other things being equal, a firm with lower transaction costs will be more competitive than a firm with higher transaction costs. As a result competition will force business firms to adopt more moral practices. This argument is incredibly simple, but its importance has been lost on many managers – especially in the US. In the analyses to follow, I give several examples of moral practices that lower transaction costs. As competition becomes truly international, I hypothesize that the more moral practices (the ones that lower transaction costs) will tend to be adopted universally.

Consider employee theft. A firm with lower employee theft has less costs than firms with more. As such, other things being equal, firms with less employee theft will be more competitive and in the long run replace firms with greater employee theft. But suppose a firm with low employee theft achieves those results with a heavy investment in monitoring devices. That firm is at a competitive disadvantage with a firm that has employees who are not inclined to steal. Since the employees of these latter firms are not inclined to steal, these firms spend far less for monitoring costs. A firm with naturally or genuinely honest employees has the best competitive advantage – other things being equal. Hence, cultures with more employees who are naturally inclined to be honest will, other things being equal, have a competitive advantage. Then as a result of international competition, we would expect honesty to increase throughout the world. Thus we have the following hypothesis:

H1 – *As international business increases, employee honesty will tend to rise.*

Consider bribery and kick-backs. Both increase transaction costs and usually distort efficiency. First, consider a company offering a bribe. Suppose the company could have received the contract on the merits of its product without paying the bribe. If so, paying bribes adds to its costs and it will lose out to competitors that have equally good products but incur less costs since they do not bribe. Other things being equal, companies that do not bribe have a competitive advantage in such circumstances.

On the other hand, if the company would not have received the contract because another company has a superior product, then the competitive disadvantage would be shifted to the company that receives the bribe. That bribe-receiving company could be receiving a product of less quality than it would have received for the same expenditure. Hence, other things being equal, companies that insist on neither offering nor taking bribes will have a competitive advantage. Thus in a competitive economy, such companies will be more successful, other things being equal.

The above argument assumes that bribery is not a common practice in the country under discussion. If bribery were the norm, the argument breaks down. If everyone accepts and pays bribes in a given country, no single company can get a niche as a non-bribe giver or non-bribe taker since no one will do business with it. In that society such firms are unlikely to arise. However, that situation moves the argument to a higher level. A culture where bribery is the norm will be at a competitive disadvantage versus a non-bribing country – other things being equal. That country will not be engaged in efficient terms of trade. Hence, we can predict:

H2 – *As international business among countries increases, bribery will decrease.*

A firm that builds stakeholder relations on the basis of trust has a competitive advantage. Lawyers are expensive but are often needed to write unbreakable contracts or to replace handshakes with contracts. In a trusting environment, the handshake is sufficient and the transaction costs are low. The necessity of formal contracts and the accompanying expense of lawyers can be greatly diminished. Many have commented on the competitive advantage Japanese companies have over US companies because they are a non-litigious society and have so few lawyers per capita compared to the United States. (For example, see Robert Reich's *The Next American Frontier*, 1983.)

Trust provides a competitive advantage in other ways as well. Suppose a manufacturer is having a quality control problem in a component produced by a supplier. For example, suppose General Motors was having a quality control problem with its supplier of gaskets. As things now stand in the

United States, General Motors would be reluctant to invest time and money in a partnership with its gasket supplier for fear that the gasket supplier would sell its improved product to Ford and Chrysler. In that event Ford and Chrysler would benefit at GM's expense, so GM would not make the investment. In a trusting world, the supplier could promise not to sell the product to a competitor and the investment would be made. Quality control would improve.

Again it is argued that the Japanese *keiretsu* system, with its stable supplier relationships and its higher level of trust, gives the Japanese a competitive advantage. Hence, we can predict:

H3 – *As international business increases, we will see higher levels of trust with business firms and between business firms and their stakeholders.*

To illustrate this same analysis with respect to fair dealing, let us consider the troublesome issue of discrimination. Many argue that discrimination, particularly against women, is rampant in the international arena. The argument that discrimination is inefficient goes back to Milton Friedman's *Capitalism and Freedom* (1962).

> There is an economic incentive in a free market to separate economic efficiency from other characteristics of the individual. A businessman or an entrepreneur who expresses preferences in his business activities that are not related to productive efficiency is at a disadvantage compared to other individuals who do not. Such an individual is in effect imposing higher costs on himself than are other individuals who do not have such preferences. Hence, in a free market they will tend to drive him out. The man who objects to buying from or working alongside a Negro, for example, thereby limits his range of choice. He will generally have to pay a higher price for what he buys or receive a lower return for his work. Or, put the other way, those of us who regard color of skin or religion as irrelevant can buy some things more cheaply as a result [pp. 109–110].

If Friedman is right, the kind of discrimination against women characteristic of Middle East businesses, and to a lesser extent characteristic of Central and South America as well as Japan puts these countries at a competitive disadvantage with respect to countries that do not discriminate.

Although there is much that is right in Friedman's argument, it is too simple as it stands. It works fine against discrimination based on simple prejudice as in cases where an employer just will not consider a black or a woman. The discriminating employer makes no economic claim such as 'women produce less' that provides the rationale for the discrimination; the employer simply believes a woman's place is at home. Such employers really are at a competitive disadvantage.

However, Friedman's argument will not work if there is a factual statistical basis for the discrimination. Suppose it were true that a higher percentage of blue-eyed people were lazy. It would then pay not to hire blue-eyed people. Lester Thurow made the theoretical case in *Generating Inequality* (1975):

> Consider two individuals, one who belongs to a preferred group and another who does not. The first one belongs to a group in which the expected probability of being fired for unsatisfactory job performance is only 5 percent, whereas the second belongs to a group with a 15 percent probability of being unsatisfactory. Although 85 percent of the second group will prove to be satisfactory, the employer refuses to hire individuals from this group because he can avoid the costs of hiring and firing an additional 10 percent of his labor force. As a result, the acceptable 85 percent of the individuals in group two suffer from statistical discrimination. They are not hired because of the objective characteristics of the group to which they belong, although they, themselves, are satisfactory [p. 182].

For this argument to work, it does not matter whether the slightly higher probability of laziness is an inherent trait or socially caused by a history of discrimination against blue-eyed people in the society – by denying them adequate education for example. From a hiring standpoint it still would not pay to hire blue-eyed people. Discrimination based on valid statistical references would not disappear in an international capitalist morality.

Before we get too pessimistic here, discrimination based on false impressions would not survive either. There are all sorts of apocryphal information around about the undesirable traits of various races, religions and ethnic nationalities. Much of it is false. A firm that ignores such information will reap the advantages of a more skilled workforce and gain a competitive advantage. The Friedman argument applies as well in cases based on false impressions as it does in cases of overt discrimination.

Friedman's argument does not apply in another case – when the tensions of a diverse workforce cause productivity losses greater than the gains of a non-discrimination policy. What I have in mind here are societies characterized by a high degree of tension among nationalities, religious orientations or races. In these societies discrimination may be less costly than non-discrimination. The disruption caused by non-discrimination would negatively impact productivity even more than losing productive workers from the class discriminated against.

But even here there is reason for optimism. Countries that are more homogeneous and countries with pluralistic workforces that do not practise discrimination and have harmoniously functioning workforces have a competitive advantage over countries that discriminate and countries where a high degree of tension exists in a pluralistic workforce. The message of this analysis to countries with diverse populations is that it is economically important for such societies to eliminate tensions among various races, religions and ethnic nationalities. For example, sectarian strife in Northern Ireland hurts that country's economic development. Hence, we can predict:

H4 – *As international business increases, discrimination based on sex, race, religion or national origin will decrease when that discrimination is based on tastes or misinformation about those discriminated against. In addition one can expect countries with a high degree of tension among various races, religions and ethnic nationalities to seek to reduce that tension.*

The fact that markets in the interests of efficiency should help eliminate discrimination and ethnic, religious or racial tension indicates how markets can civilize and induce a more cosmopolitan atmosphere – just the kind of results Enlightenment thinkers desire.

What the logical arguments of Kant and these 'practical' arguments based on transaction cost economics are designed to show is that certain moral principles are necessary to the conduct of business. These principles may be referred to as the morality of the marketplace. The existence of such a morality of the marketplace is significant because as countries develop capitalist markets, these countries will develop the required morality as well. Systematic violation of marketplace norms would be self-defeating because that behaviour would put the company at a competitive disadvantage. Thus, whenever a multinational establishes businesses in a number of different countries, the multinational practises something approaching a universal morality – the morality of the marketplace itself. If Romans are to do business with the Japanese, then whether in Rome or Tokyo, there is a morality to which members of the business community in both Rome and Tokyo must subscribe – even if the Japanese and Romans differ on other issues of morality.

If this analysis is correct, an issue of some controversy in international business ethics will become less important. The so-called 'When in Rome do as the Romans do' problem will tend to take care of itself. If there is, as I have argued, a capitalist market morality and if following the norms of a market morality provides firms with a competitive advantage, the differences between business morality in Tokyo, New York and Rome will begin to disappear. Business persons will need to learn what constitutes proper behaviour (etiquette) in countries different from their own, but the ethical norms for doing business will become standard. There is already some indication that the universalization of norms is under way.

In a recent international study of codes of ethics entitled 'Do corporate codes of conduct reflect national character? Evidence from Europe and the United States' (1990), Professors Catherine Langlois and Bodo B. Schlegelmilch observed that corporate codes of conduct are increasingly being adopted by European companies. Although the authors certainly found many differences among codes, they none the less concluded:

Many ethical issues transcend national barriers. Fairness and honesty in a company's relations to the public are concepts found in corporate codes of ethics on both sides of the Atlantic. . . . Thus companies in Europe and the US ban the acceptance of gifts or bribes, promote the use of accurate records, and warn against conflicts of interest [p. 528].

In this section I have argued that the market rests on contractual values like honesty, trust and fair dealing. As a result I have made four predictions regarding the development of international norms of ethics as the result of a competitive international market. Interestingly enough as this paper was being written, a news report on NBC and a story in the *San Francisco Chronicle* described attempts in Japan and throughout the world to end discrimination against women. In the sections that follow I identify several Enlightenment values and argue that the development of an international market will result in their flourishing.

REASON AND OBJECTIVITY

The age of the Enlightenment is often called the age of reason. The way to the truth is through reason rather than faith – through science rather than religion. Let us accept the commitment to reason as the way of knowing as the primary ideal of the period. What can be said about this ideal?

Reason has several advantages over faith, intuition, emotion and imagination. The latter are all particularized by individual circumstances. None is common to all human beings. Reason is the only candidate for a universal way of knowing. Enlightenment thinkers believed that mathematical and scientific thinking were not culturally dependent. The Chinese and the French solve calculus problems in the same way. Later they would use the same scientific laws to put up rocket ships. Scientific thinking then became the model to which ethical thinking was to aspire.

If the error of the Enlightenment age was the hubris of reason to provide objective truth, the disease of the postmodern age is the nihilistic relativism that follows from its basic tenets. For the postmodernists, there is no truth, there are only vocabularies. In my view the philosopher Richard Rorty best articulates the postmodernist position. A few quotations from *Contingency, Irony, and Solidarity* (1989) may be instructive.

Interesting philosophy is rarely an examination of the pros and cons of a thesis. Usually it is implicitly or explicitly a contest between an entrenched vocabulary which has become a nuisance and a half-formed new vocabulary which vaguely promises great things [p. 9].

Truth cannot be out there – cannot exist independent of the human mind – because sentences cannot so exist or be out there. The world is out there, but descriptions of the world are not [p. 5].

Although many socio-economists, like Amitai Etzioni in *The Moral Dimension* (1988), are critical of reason, one need not go to the postmodernist extreme to show the limitations of reason. Neoclassical economists have an instrumental view of reason. For them reason is nothing more than choosing the most efficient means to a given end. For Enlightenment thinkers reason provided objectivity rather than just the most efficient means to a given end.

By focusing on an internationalized market economy, I think I can provide an account of objectivity that escapes both the hubris of Enlightenment reason and the relativism of much postmodernism. An internationalized market capitalism is (will be) historically contingent. Economic institutions are produced by historical and cultural forces and they may well pass away. Capitalism is neither a Utopian state nor does it necessarily represent the final stage in the development of economic institutions. In this respect, I think the postmoderns are nearer the mark than people like Francis Fukuyama who seem to think that capitalism and democracy mark the 'end of history'. In his book *The End of History and the Last Man* (1992), Fukuyama said: 'Today . . . we have trouble imagining a world that is radically better than our own, or a future that is not essentially democratic and capitalist' (p. 46).

But as an international market capitalism comes about, we can be sure that certain values will accompany it and reasonably certain that it will exist in the midst of a certain type of political and social order. Governments will be more democratic than authoritarian, the role of the Church will either start to decline or continue to decline. Moreover as capitalist market practices become international (all countries become capitalist trading partners), a universal morality will evolve. On this point the Enlightenment thinkers are nearer the mark.

Of course a capitalist morality is not a true morality in the sense that it can be objectively validated. Its objectivity is contingent upon the historical circumstances of international capitalism rather than upon being in harmony with the natural order of things. Indeed many postmodernists will find much to criticize in capitalist morality. So will those who believe in objective right and wrong. None the less such a capitalist market morality will have some good things to be said for it. The likelihood of war will decrease and the feeling of human solidarity will increase. Whatever its weakness, that will be its strength.

DEMOCRACY

Since reason is a faculty that is in each individual, human beings need only exercise their reason to know the truth. What keeps people from exercising the truth; the autocratic power of religion and the state? What people need is freedom.

Which restriction is an obstacle to enlightenment, and which is not an obstacle but a promoter of it? I answer: The public use of one's reason must always be free and it alone can bring about enlightenment among men.

(Kant, 'What is Enlightenment?', 1784, p. 5)

But what institutions are supportive of freedom? Many thinkers have argued that capitalist economic institutions are necessary, although not sufficient, for political freedom. In other words it is possible to have both capitalist economic institutions and totalitarian political institutions but it is not possible to have collectivist economic institutions and democratic political institutions.

The best contemporary arguments that capitalism supports freedom are found in Milton Friedman's *Capitalism and Freedom*:

Economic arrangements play a dual role in the promotion of a free society. On the one hand freedom in economic arrangements . . . is an end in itself. In the second place economic freedom is also an indispensable means toward the achievement of political freedom [p. 8].

No one who buys bread knows whether the wheat from which it is made was grown by a communist or a Republican, by a constitutionalist or a Fascist, or for that matter by a Negro or a white. This illustrates how an impersonal market separates economic activities from political views and protects men from being discriminated against in their economic activities for reasons that are irrelevant to their productivity – whether these reasons are associated with their views or their color [p. 21].

Friedman also points out that freedom of speech is more meaningful so long as alternative opportunities for employment exist. However, these alternatives are impossible if the government owns and operates the means of production. In a private diversified economic community someone has a better chance to publish views that are contrary to the views of a given editor, the government or even a majority of the public. Usually one can find some audience that is interested. Moreover, even publishers who disagree with an author might still publish her. Fear of competition and the opportunity for profit often overcome the distaste for certain ideas.

Capitalist economic institutions are supportive of democratic institutions in another way as well. Capitalist economic institutions are individual and voluntary. In principle no one enters an exchange one does not perceive to be a benefit to oneself. Political decisions, even in democracies, are coercively enforced on the minority. Persons who do not believe that the expenditures by government for national defence or education are correct must nevertheless submit to the majority. Whenever a decision that could be made in the market is made in the political arena, an unnecessary element of coercion is added. Collectivist economies make nearly all economic decisions politically and hence create much unnecessary coercive activity. As coercion is increased, the losers (minority) become more resentful. This increases social tension and creates strains in the social fabric that can lead to social instability. This eventuality threatens democratic institutions. The more decisions can be made in markets, the more secure democratic institutions are.

COSMOPOLITANISM

One of the great goals of the Enlightenment was to promote the notion of humankind. The spirit of the Enlightenment was cosmopolitan. Enlightenment thinkers were strongly critical of religious and nationalistic values. Enlightenment thinkers believed that local customs and religious doctrines got in the way of a cosmopolitan spirit. Commercial values and international markets supported cosmopolitan values. Commerce pulls in the opposite direction from nationalism and religious sectarianism. As it developed in the late eighteenth and early nineteenth centuries, the intellectual movement that went under the name of liberalism supported free trade abroad as a means of linking the nations of the world together peacefully and democratically. As John Stuart Mill said in *Principles of Political Economy* (1848):

> It is hardly possible to overrate the value, in the present low state of human improvement, of placing human beings in contact with persons dissimilar to themselves and with modes of thought and action unlike those with which they are familiar. Such communication has always been, and is peculiarly in the present age, one of the primary sources of progress [p. 270–271].

The cosmopolitan spirit of the eighteenth century rapidly gave way to the nationalism of the nineteenth. Many explanations can be given for the shift towards nationalism and the failure of the eighteenth century's international outlook. I believe the most important explanation is that the world did not have an international business system nor the technology to support it. Commercial transactions among countries were too slow and too uncertain. Most people had little contact with foreigners – indeed they seldom travelled far beyond their own villages.

Remember the Industrial Revolution was in its infancy in a select few countries in Europe. Elsewhere it had not even been born. At the end of the century in 1799 there was no electricity, no telephones, no automobiles. Water power was the basic source of power for industry that was making use of pulleys and chains, inclined planes and gears as the chief means for producing goods. Goods were transported by beasts of burden or by sailing craft. If one could make twenty-five miles a day on land, it was a good day. It is not easy for people living in the last decade of the twentieth century to imagine how primitive life was in the eighteenth century.

Technology has advanced so that a truly international marketplace is now possible. I contend that the development of this international market will make the cosmopolitan dream of the eighteenth century a reality in the twenty-first. Before arguing that case, let me remind you how the US has changed in thirty years.

In 1961, the US was still quite regional. The interstate highway system was well under way but still had a long way to go to completion. There were wide disparities in culture. Country and western music dominated the radio airwaves in the South; there were few listeners in the North-east. Restaurants and motels were primarily individually owned; there were few national chains and no golden arches. A person travelling US Route 1 in Maine and US Route 1 in Georgia would have no difficulty in telling the two states apart.

It is much different today. If you travel the vast interstate system in the US, geography and climate are the best determinants of where you are. Whether your taste runs to contemporary rock, golden oldies or country and western, you will find a station on your car radio; a rock station in Minneapolis sounds exactly like one in Mississippi. Taco Bell's, Hardees, McDonald's, Howard Johnson's, Sheraton and Holiday Inns are everywhere. A McDonald's hamburger in Denver tastes just like the one in Boston. As you drive by at 65 mph, one shopping mall looks just like the rest.

What about culture? Certainly different regions are proud of their local culture but two points must be taken into consideration. First, local culture has gone national. Bluegrass performers from West Virginia perform nationally as do Dixieland and Jazz groups from New Orleans. There is a national audience for regional culture.

What has happened here is happening world-wide and the trend will continue until it will be as routine to fly from Minneapolis to Tokyo as from Minneapolis to Miami, and I should add, for the Japanese to fly from Tokyo to Minneapolis as from Tokyo to Kumamuto. National chains are becoming international. CNN is a world-wide television station. American popular culture especially in popular music, film and television is everywhere. Twelve thousand people recently attended a lecture by the Dali Lama in relatively tiny Ithaca, New York and an exhibit of treasures from King Tutankhamun's burial pyramid drew record crowds in the US. The Italians are concerned that the English-language TV ads are corrupting the Italian language.

I realize these remarks are impressionistic but I believe my viewpoint is similar to modernization theorists like Talcott Parsons who flourished immediately after the Second World War. The growing international economy will decrease the differences and increase the similarities in ethical conduct among nations. More specifically as capitalism becomes a world-wide phenomenon, so will a capitalist culture. As David Hume put it in 'Of refinement in the arts' (1752): 'Where several neighboring nations have a very close communication together, either by policy, commerce, or traveling, they acquire a similitude of manners, proportioned to the communication.'

WORLD PEACE

It was a main contention of the Enlightenment that a cosmopolitan world-view supported by international commerce would support world peace. For the Enlightenment war was the greatest evil – an evil caused in part by an excessively fervent nationalism. Kant, for example, wrote a blueprint for world peace that is aptly titled 'Perpetual peace' (1795). Kant's belief in the inevitability of world peace is found in many of his works. The following quotation from 'Idea for a Universal History from a Cosmopolitan Point of View' is representative:

> In the end, war itself will be seen as not only so artificial, in outcome so uncertain for both sides, in after effects so painful in the form of an ever-growing war debt (a new invention) that cannot be met, that it will be regarded as a most dubious undertaking. The impact of any revolution on all states on our continent, so closely knit together through commerce will be so obvious that other states, driven by their own danger but without any legal basis, will offer themselves as arbiters, and thus they will prepare the way for a distant international government for which there is no precedent in world history [p. 23].

The notion that commerce might someday help end war and the unjust exploitation of weaker nations is also found in Adam Smith's *Wealth of Nations* (1776).

> At the particular time when these discoveries were made, the superiority of force happened to be so great on the side of the Europeans, that they were enabled to commit with impunity every sort of injustice in those remote countries. Hereafter, perhaps, the natives of those countries may grow stronger, or those of Europe may grow weaker, and the inhabitants of all the different quarters of the world may arrive at the equality of courage and force which, by inspiring mutual fear, can alone overawe the injustice of independent nations into some sort of respect for the rights of one another. But nothing seems more likely to establish this equality of force than that mutual communication of knowledge and of all sorts of improvements which an extensive commerce from all countries to all countries naturally, or rather necessarily, carries along with it . . . [p. 281].

During the 1970s and 1980s Americans defending the US trade agreement with the Soviet Union argued that trade would lessen the likelihood of war. Not only would trade increase physical contact which would show that neither Americans nor Russians were monsters, but trade would bring benefits that it would be irrational to destroy. A war between the US and the

Soviet Union would be in neither's economic interest. As it turned out, the collapse of communist economies has been a leading cause of the lessening of tensions between the superpowers and towards reconciliation in Europe. As the former Eastern bloc adopts capitalism and the former Soviet Union struggles towards it, the threat of armed conflict has diminished.

Even in the areas of the world where nationalism is strongest, business leaders are urging peace. *Business Week* (13 May 1991) reports on the efforts of Hyundai founder Chung-Ju-Yung to unite North and South Korea. He has already launched a joint venture with the Soviet Union and is negotiating with the Chinese. Even more astonishing is a *Fortune* article (20 May 1991) proclaiming a Middle Eastern common market as a cure for fighting in the Middle East. In that article, Israeli Steff Wertheimer who owns Ivcar Corporation, a $300-million-a-year producer of machine tools, says he has employed Arab workers for thirty years. 'In our plants and offices, Arabs and Jews work side by side to make products instead of mischief'. The crisis in Kuwait was in fact handled internationally through the UN and despite the barbed remarks directed towards George Bush his rhetoric of a 'new world order' is not without foundation. At long last, Kant may be right – war among the industrialized countries has become too destructive, too expensive and economically irrational. In the 1700s a truly international market was a dream. In the 2000s, it is not. That fact may do more than anything else to bring the Enlightenment's dream of an end to war to fulfilment.

OBJECTIONS AND REPLIES

Some may accuse me of the Enlightenment disease of optimism. Critics will contend I have underestimated the power of nationalism. Look at what is happening in the former Soviet Union, Yugoslavia and the Middle East. We may be world traders but we hardly think of ourselves as world citizens. Critics in political science are certain to remind me of Raymond Vernon's claim from *Sovereignty at Bay* (1971) that the nation-state is an anachronism and how events in the 1970s and 1980s have refuted it. Economics, they will argue, is rather helpless when faced with the passions of ethnic and national identity.

I certainly do recognize the power of nationalism. For me the question is this. Are the predominant forces in the world today likely to lead to a waxing or waning of nationalism? I argue that the forces will lead to a waning. First, nations are banding together to form regional economic trading blocs. Trading alliances among the US, Canada and Mexico are inevitable and the countries of South America might, some day, be included. Second, as Hume saw trade and mass communication will lead us to think more alike and to come to closer agreement on matters of right and wrong. Nor is such a view limited to eighteenth-century thinkers like Hume. In *Global Responsibilities* (1991) the theologian Hans Kung has issued a call for a New World Ethic. In

Japan, the followers of Chikuro Hiroike are propounding the study of Moralogy which seeks to clarify and puts into practice certain universal moral principles based on the writings of Christ, Buddha, Socrates and Confucius. The ideal of the Institute of Moralogy is strikingly reminiscent of the ideals of eighteenth-century philosophers and of the views expressed in this paper (*An Outline of Moralogy*, 1987):

> Supreme morality is the universal moral criterion for creating peace in the world for mankind. Given the present progress and direction of human society, the time has come when races of people who do not share the same language, thought and religion must nevertheless cooperate internationally. The present situation seems to demand, therefore, that we establish the necessary criteria for a universal morality. The moral criteria fit for an international age must be ones which can first of all integrate the cultures of the East and the West; they should be built on a spirit of respect for human beings and on rationality, transcending sectarian faiths, factionalism, and ideologies [p. 11].

Third, many of our social problems are no respecters of national boundaries. The most obvious problem is the degradation of the environment. To address the problems of the over-use of resources, the pollution of the oceans, global warming, and the depletion of the ozone layer will require international cooperation. The recent Rio conference, whatever its limitations, marks the first attempt at an international solution to environmental degradation. International problems are not limited to the environment. In a world of international travel, the outbreak of a disease in one part of the world can easily become a problem world-wide. Aids is now an international problem.

Fourth, as the similarities among people grow, it will be more possible to tolerate the differences. Tolerance has always been central in Enlightenment thought. However, to tolerate another person or group seems to presuppose some sympathetic understanding of that person or group. But if the person or group to be tolerated is seen as totally other – as totally different – how is such sympathetic understanding possible? The growth of international capitalism provides some of the requisite similarities.

Ethnic identity is important. Ethnic culture will thrive in a cosmopolitan world because human beings who see themselves as world citizens will find it easier to appreciate and tolerate the differences in cultures dissimilar from their own. In a truly cosmopolitan international marketplace nationalism is expressed aesthetically in Greek food, Greek art and Greek folk dances. When nationalism expresses itself politically, it is divisive and can lead to conflicts. When nationalism expresses itself culturally, it is easy for other nationalists to both tolerate and often appreciate and enjoy nationalistic expressions of others.

My thoughts on nationalism develop those of Fukuyama who said:

If nationalism is to fade away as a political force, it must be tolerant like religion before it. National groups can retain their separate languages and senses of identity, but that identity would be expressed primarily in the realm of culture rather than politics.

(Fukuyama, 1992, p. 271)

But how does nationalism become tolerant?

I would endorse Enlightenment ideas here. Commercial trade provides a reason for tolerance, the common norms of commercial morality provide an experience of sameness that makes it easier to experience and appreciate cultural differences. This experience and appreciation only reinforces the tolerance.

As it is with nationalism so it will be with religion. Religion will find its expression artistically rather than politically. The Enlightenment was even more critical of religion than it was of nationalism. Enlightenment thinkers were appalled by sectarian strife and religious toleration was a constant theme in Enlightenment philosophy. Although some Enlightenment figures were atheists or sceptics, and others were deists, many others belonged to traditional Christian sects. However, no Enlightenment figure supported a theocratic state or the establishment of a state religion. More importantly no Enlightenment thinker believed that their religion held the only key to salvation or even to truth. Given the proximity of the Enlightenment to the Middle Ages, it is not surprising that the Enlightenment viewed itself as a move away from religious persecution and intolerance towards rationalism and religious tolerance.

Again the spiritual traditions in which people grew up will have a great influence on how individuals grow spiritually. However, this aspect of their lives should again be viewed as analogous to artistic expression. Religion neither provides truth nor functions as a model for world citizenship. Let us view places of worship different from our own in the same spirit as we view forms of art, dance or cuisine different from our own. Different religions provide diversity just as different ethnic customs do. They are not worth fighting over. As markets become truly international, this Enlightenment ideal will gain new support.

ACHIEVING ENLIGHTENMENT VALUES

Let me conclude by reminding you what I am not saying. I am not saying that the global economy's influence on a common culture and a common morality are all to the good. There is much to praise in the Enlightenment set of values, but other values are either ignored or omitted. A secular materialist culture brings difficulties of its own. We have seen the dangers that come from extending the market into every corner of our lives. See, for example, Posner's discussion in *Economic Analysis of Law* (1977) on selling babies. There are other more noble reasons for non-discrimination and keeping one's promises than the fact that such behaviour improves efficiency or cuts transaction costs. The values of love, friendship and charity are more fully developed outside the commercial context (see Titmus's discussion from *The Gift Relationship* (1970) of the advantages of volunteering to give blood rather than having a market in blood).

None the less, if the rise of international business helps people see themselves as members of a world community, establishes minimum moral standards for commercial dealings, and diminishes the chances of war, a significant step towards a better world will have been taken. The Enlightenment had many of the right values but neither technology nor markets had reached a point where their achievement was possible. Perhaps in the twenty-first century, we will have the heavenly cities of the eighteenth-century philosophers.

REFERENCES

Boulding, K. E. (1967) 'The basis of value judgments in economics', in S. Hook (ed.), *Human Values and Economic Policy*, New York: New York University Press.

Etzioni, A. (1988) *The Moral Dimension: Toward a New Economics*, New York: Free Press.

Friedman, M. (1962) *Capitalism and Freedom*, Chicago: University of Chicago Press.

Fukuyama, F. (1992) *The End of History and the Last Man*, New York: Free Press.

Hirschman, A. (1982) 'Rival interpretations of market society: civilizing, destructive, or feeble?', *Journal of Economic Literature*, vol. XX (December), 1463–1484.

Hume, D. (1987) 'Of refinement in the arts', in E. Miller (ed.), *Essays: Moral, Political and Literary* (1752), Indianapolis: Liberty Classics.

Institute of Moralogy (1987) *An Outline of Moralogy*, Japan: Institute of Moralogy (English translation).

Kant, I. (1963) 'Idea for a universal history from a cosmopolitan point of view' (1784), in L. W. Beck (trans. and ed.), *On History*, Indianapolis: Bobbs Merrill.

Kant, I. (1963) 'What is enlightenment?' (1784), in L. W. Beck (trans. and ed.), *On History*, Indianapolis. Bobbs Merrill.

Kant, I. (1963) 'Perpetual peace' (1795), in L. W. Beck (trans. and ed.), *On History*, Indianapolis: Bobbs Merrill.

Kant, I. (1990) 'Foundation of the metaphysics of morals' (1785), in L. W. Beck (trans.), New York: Macmillan.

Kung, H. (1991) *Global Responsibilities: In Search of a New World Ethic*, New York: Crossroad Publishing.

Langlois, C. C. and Schlegelmilch, B. B. (1990) 'Do corporate codes of ethics reflect national character? Evidence from Europe and the United States', *Journal of International Business Studies*, vol. 21, no. 4, 519–539.

Mill, J. S. (1965) 'Principles of political economy' (1848), in *Collected Works*, vols II and III, Toronto: University of Toronto Press.

Parsons, T. (1964) 'Evolutionary universals in society', *American Sociological Review*, 29 (June), 339–357.

Posner, R. (1977) *Economic Analysis of Law*, 2nd edn, Boston: Little, Brown.

Reich, R. (1983) *The Next American Frontier*, New York: Times Books.

Rorty, R. (1989) *Contingency, Irony, and Solidarity*, New York: Cambridge University Press.

Smith, A. (1987) *Wealth of Nations*, in R. Heilbroner (ed.), *The Essential Adam Smith*, New York: Norton.

Thurow, L. (1975) *Generating Inequality*, New York: Basic Books.

Titmus, R. M. (1970) *The Gift Relationship*, London: Allen & Unwin.

Vernon, R. (1971) *Sovereignty at Bay*, New York: Basic Books.

Chapter 19

Endpiece

Alan Lewis and Karl-Erik Wärneryd

Many 'lay' people have their own theories to explain every malaise from increasing crime rates to global warming. Take the 'breakdown of law and order': any eavesdropper can hear that it is 'the fault of the parents' or 'schools are to blame'. And alongside the explanations are the remedies: 'What we need is a return to corporal punishment.' 'The police should have more backing from the courts.'

One must be wary not to demean such explanations, for in a democracy, these views, if commonly held (and consistent with voting preferences) can have a bearing on policy making. Who then are the 'experts' when it comes to ethics and economic affairs? If there is a moral decline where is it to be found? How can it be checked? The advice of the 'experts' is not so very different from the everyday; perhaps it is only the language which is changed: 'It's the socialization process'; 'It's the result of unbridled capitalism' or more popularly: 'It's due to the rise of the "me" society'. What are we to do about it? Reintroduce moral education in schools? Teach managers (and prospective managers) about ethics and fair trade? Strengthen laws: write a code of ethics?

It is summer and the academic year is reaching its conclusion in England. It is a time filled with examination, invigilation, adjudication. Across the land there is the ubiquitous committee whose job it is not only to decide who passes and who fails but the grade of pass: is it a first or a third; an upper or a lower second? But how are we to decide? In all these committees there are arguments and disagreements, especially about undergraduates on the borderline between classes: a disagreeable consequence for some committee members who as a response develop complex rules in order to divert such unpleasantness, rules and guidelines that become increasingly convoluted as more and more 'exceptional cases' have to be dealt with in the rules. Everyone feels that the examination board must do what is right, what is fair; the trouble is people do not agree about precisely what *is* fair and what is not. The rule book is the answer for some while for others there is agreement only that what is the correct course of action will be argued about and that, however well intentioned their construction, all these rules are mutable.

Thomas Donaldson in his book *The Ethics of International Business* (1989) describes himself as a 'practical philosopher'. Cultural relativism is too pessimistic, argues Donaldson. Instead Donaldson lists ten international rights which he feels should dictate international trade (cf. Stone and Rosansky, Chapters 2 and 3 of the current volume, respectively) namely freedom of physical movement, ownership of property, freedom from torture, access to a fair trial, freedom from discrimination, assurance of physical security, speech and association, access to minimal education, political participation, subsistence. But Donaldson is not bureaucratically rule-bound and realizes that there must be arbitration and a certain amount of pragmatism when weighing up home and host interests and conflicts. It appears that rules in themselves are not enough; you have to have the sense to know how to apply them. Yet for Donaldson rules are necessary and unlike Bowie (this volume, Chapter 18) he has little confidence that Adam Smith's 'invisible hand' can work wonders all on its own.

For those who feel that rules are the way forward, the ultimate rules are those of law. Is an 'ethical' law as Mr Bumble in *The Pickwick Papers* would have it 'a ass . . . a idiot'? In their excellent contribution, Kaufmann *et al.* (this volume, Chapter 7) put the reader in the position of judge. There are legal and ethical inconsistencies alluded to in the paper between the apparent acceptability of large variations in the prices of jewellery and unacceptable house price variations, not brought to the attention of purchasers. The law itself is influenced by values; it is as though house purchasing is qualitatively different from the flippancy of gems; in the first case it seems wrong to be 'cheated' when engaged in such an important purchase, the largest most people make in their lives, compared to the extravagance of diamonds, where the purchasers, if duped, may be seen as fair game. Not all goods are the same: not all purchases are the same.

An increase in litigation is an expensive and heavy-handed way to encourage better ethical practice, nevertheless this is the direction in which the current is flowing: many large companies now have lawyers among their directors. Protective measures are not the only ones being taken; producers have become aware and monitor carefully the effects of ethical and unethical practices on consumer demand (Menezes, 1991). The wider issues not only concern the best use of the law but whether successful marketing and ethical considerations need be in conflict (cf. Menezes, 1991; Smith and Quelch, 1993; and Lewis and Webley, this volume, Chapter 8). Taking marketing as an example: stores are now awash with 'environmentally friendly' products variously claiming to be free of CFCs, biodegradable and untested on animals. Perhaps all is well in the garden. Cynics/economists/realists (please delete as you feel appropriate) see it differently – for producers it is just another gimmick to differentiate their product from the others; it is a sales pitch. And here comes the law again, this time in the guise of consumer protection: what exactly is a 'natural' product, 'home-cooked' food, 'recycled' paper? Closer examination may reveal that our 'natural' food product is not entirely free from chemical additives, the 'home-cooked' food is cooked in no one's home, but in the 'home' country, and that 'recycled' paper is made from fibre trimmings at the paper mill.

Let us try the automobile showroom. Sex and speed are still high on the agenda, but fast climbing the popularity charts are fuel economy and safety. Are airbags and safety cages being provided out of the goodness of manufacturers' hearts? Of course not. But if manufacturers are responding to consumer demand, and the demand is for cleaner and safer cars, is this not a case where everyone wins?

If these various 'changes' for the better are consumer-led, led by a raising of environmental consciousness, perhaps there is no need for government intervention either through the legal system or via tax increases on scarce commodities like fossil fuels. This surely will only work if (1) consumer environmental consciousness continues and people are prepared to pay the extra cost of goods which are genuinely 'green' or otherwise 'ethical'; (2) failing this (and the evidence is not strong that many people are prepared, at the moment, to put their money where their morals are) a competitive market will encourage manufacturers to compete in 'ethicalness'; (3) a free market will produce what is needed to solve the global environmental problem *and in time*. The second point in this list may have some validity for the market in the 1990s, certainly Varta, the first company to market mercury-free batteries in the UK have shown an increased market share growing from 2 per cent to 13 per cent; several mercury-free batteries are now (of course) on the market.

Certainly companies have an incentive to put their own houses in order, so even if there is no persistent ethical consumer demand it is prudent to invest in the design and manufacture of safe and environmentally sensitive products before they are made to do so.

Economic factors, in the narrow sense, are far from the only factors that structure the business world. If economic actors were to express naked self-interest all the time the economic system would break down. An optimistic view is that the business world is far from unethical, people already have notions of fair play, know not to push too hard in negotiations, make a reasonable profit rather than an unreasonable one.[1] The policy implications based on this belief lead not to more laws or other forms of increased government intervention but to some way of engendering, nurturing, the goodwill that already exists. We are neither benevolent angels nor malevolent demons but some kind of amalgam of the two (cf. Gustafsson, in this volume, Chapter 5).

Ideas about self-interest and competition have become so widespread that there have even been claims, in for instance the field of socio-biology, that these motives form part of our biological make-up and the evolutionary process as a whole. Axelrod (1984) has no qualms associating motives with biology; the difference is he sees cooperation, not just competition, as universal. Social animals (including ourselves) have to have agreements with one another in order to achieve common goals, e.g. providing sufficient food. If the leap can be made across the biological ravine – a social economy, an organizational economy is a biological necessity – cooperation is the 'natural' state, not competition. This notion of cooperation need not be at odds with a more broadly based self-interest, we are not talking about giving and not counting the cost, but rather reciprocal cooperation. It does not imply collusion. Showing some generosity to other human beings usually produces a social bond requiring the recipient to reciprocate in kind or lose status (there is now an extensive literature on this in psychology and sociology and anthropology (Frith, 1978) and in experimental economic psychology (Webley and Wilson, 1989)). In fact it is naked self-interest which is often counterproductive. In the prisoner's dilemma game defection is the best strategy providing that the other player does not do the same, it then becomes the worst – in a recent experimental study with students as players, economic students defected 60 per cent of the time, non-economists, 39 per cent of the time (Frank *et al.*, 1993).

Frank (1988) also agrees that egoism has few rewards; marriages would not work, a player who hogs the ball will not make the team. Emotional predispositions are not unreasonable: in order to be trusted you must trust; if you want to be loved, love. This has to be real. This is not straightforward as we have meta-knowledge and meta-perspectives – we can know certain things about ourselves and social relationships. We can know that when a social bond is formed, even a superficial one between a salesperson and a potential client, this can make the client committed to a sale. Training a salesperson in this way may make many of us feel uncomfortable and sincerity is probably more effective . . . and if you can fake that . . . !

But surely like priests, doctors and teachers, business people have responsibilities towards society and in their turn mould it, they help create the social and moral climate of a nation. Or as Gui (this volume, Chapter 12) puts it: 'We have a moral obligation to treat other persons not as means, but rather as ends . . . a merely instrumental interpersonal behaviour is below the standard of human dignity'.

ETHICS AND ECONOMICS

It is our duty as editors to take another view on the theoretical relationship between ethics and economics. Wieland (in this volume, Chapter 13) relates the ethical problems connected with economic theory to problems in the economy: 'The emergence of ethical discussions is always an expression of the crisis in what has been taken for granted, of the fact that practices that have been viewed as unproblematic till now have themselves become problematic.' The essence of the problems is the overproduction of negative external effects which can be interpreted as environmental pollution, poverty, ill-effects of modern technology.

There are apparently three different stances with respect to the relations between economics and ethics:

1 Economics is value-free and has no relationship to ethics. The possible inclusion of ethical considerations into the theory does not improve its predictive power.
2 Economic theory can (in principle) very well handle ethical considerations within the frame of utility maximization, but it has so far not done so. 'Political economy merely expresses moral laws in its own way' (Marx, quoted by Wieland, this volume, Chapter 13).
3 Economic theory needs to be rewritten so as to accommodate ethical considerations.

It is productive to compare and contrast the contributions of Söderbaum, Bowie, Miner and Burk (Chapters 11, 18, 17, 16, respectively),[2] who variously consider a new economics which is more social (less reductionist), more realistic, more socially responsible, less positive, more holistic.

Among these four authors, the themes of Bowie are the most optimistic. Bowie who deals with ethics and the economy spends little time discussing economic theory *per se* and chooses instead to sing the praises of the free market economy and its liberating and enlightening effects. Far from markets appealing to base motives, markets for Bowie are civilizing places, where good behaviour pays dividends, where moral practices reduce transaction costs. Bowie steps back from the brink of quite saying that the free market cures all known ailments, but it *is* claimed to reduce racial and gender discrimination in the (perhaps very) long run. Furthermore, the free market goes hand in hand with democracy; it follows that the provision of too much collective goods threatens that democracy. A world free to trade will engender a universal moral code; there is no need to worry about 'nihilistic' cultural relativism any more. And we can sleep safely in our beds knowing that the market economy and its companion the science of economics will save us from the 'disease' of postmodernism.

All this is a long way from Söderbaum, Miner and especially Burk. We must be careful not to put words in Bowie's mouth (or anyone else's for that matter) or surmise too much, but there appear to be important differences in ideology: the kind of economics which excludes ethics or recommends that free market economics encourages ethical behaviour might be connected with right-wing politics; while the view that economics is too important to be the sole responsibility of economists, that a broader economics discipline is necessary, might be associated with a more left-wing orientation. Bowie favours science and appears to want to make a clear distinction between science and ideology; the others do not. The aim of positive economics, crudely put, is to remove from the discipline any normative or value-laden baggage and this decision to travel light is an ideologically neutral one based (among other things) on principles of parsimony.[3] Söderbaum, for one, believes that insistence on self-interest (narrowly defined) as the sole motivator of human behaviour, is far from ideologically neutral as ignoring our better side, our moral sense, actually encourages selfish behaviour in society:

> Assuming that individuals in all possible roles are motivated by self-interest may serve the purpose of making analysis more tractable and simple but will not do much to raise issues of ethics and social responsibility in society. Rather these assumptions serve the purpose of legitimizing thinking and behavioural patterns that themselves are essential components of the problems faced
>
> (Söderbaum, this volume, Chapter 11)

Miner seems to take a similar line, that self-interest assumptions are not neutral, influence the way we think about ourselves and others, reduce our 'public-spiritedness' – the 'market-spirit' should not dilute a sense of community, a sense of 'us' and not just 'me'. Burk is the most critical of all, turning the tables by accusing neoclassical economics of being unscientific, 'mere' ideology thus providing the wrong inputs for monitoring and modifying the economy.

Bowie and Burk, in their different ways, both proselytize – might there be some middle ground? Although he may not agree, Amitai Etzioni, in his persuasive and readable book *The Moral Dimension* (1988) seems to be reinventing a mild kind of socialism, more familiar and less feared in Europe than the USA. People are motivated both by utilitarian principles and moral commitment; motives which qualitatively feel different – a denial of our moral side may actually diminish its importance in everyday life with deleterious consequences.

In the end an atmosphere needs to be created whereby economists are prepared to take on what is best from the social sciences; they may have to do this for themselves as Samuelson has reputedly remarked, economics is more likely to be changed by its friends than by its critics. Finally in business as in theory we prefer not the metaphor of the 'invisible hand' but rather that of the 'invisible handshake', the spirit of cooperation *and* competition.

Politic.. commentators have dubbed the late 1980s and 1990s as the 'me' generation, the growing up of Reagan's and Thatcher's children. People need not feel guilty about being selfish goes the free-market philosophy, far from it, lay beliefs are that seeking to maximize personal profit, via the 'invisible' hand, benefits all (you cannot expect people to have a full critical understanding of the writings of Adam Smith, while some elements of political rhetoric will, however, stick). If as Etzioni (1988) has suggested we, as scholars and researchers, should grasp the nettle and take a normative stance, and if we consider selfishness narrowly defined when enacted in real life corrupting, how can we help improve ethical behaviour in business, politics and elsewhere?

The socio-economic position (apparently shared by Burk, Miner and Söderbaum) resembles a version of socialism not least because of its call for communitarianism rather than utilitarianism: a consideration for others, but also through the determined development of a 'we' culture rather than a 'me' culture. But how are these changes to be brought about, if indeed they are desirable? Education and bringing the existence of ethical dimensions into everyone's awareness come high on the agenda. The research in the current volume by Wärneryd *et al.* (Chapter 9) at the Stockholm School of Economics and by Etzioni during his stay at the Harvard Business School illustrates that research and courses in ethics and management, ethics and business are finding their way into universities, due in part initially to the efforts of an enthusiastic few (zealots of a kind).[4] Zealots (and whistle-blowers identifying corruption from within business enterprises) cannot do the job on their own, they have, sooner or later, to have a significant element of public opinion behind them. And now the timing might be right. Ethical and environmental issues are now more widely discussed in elite as well as in wider circles, marketers and manufacturers (for whatever reason) are more likely to take them into account. Surveys indicate a symmetrical growth of interest in environmental and ethical issues among the general public. The last indicator that the timing is right is that the 1960s (who knows for how long) are fashionable again, concern for the 'global village' is associated with a rekindling of post-materialist values, perhaps as a reaction to the *utilitarian status quo*. The circle game.

NOTES

1 Of course the idea of 'self-interest' broadly defined is all embracing, e.g. making a reasonable profit may not mean *per se* that actions are dictated by fairness, only that people choose to make a smaller profit in the hope of larger profits through repeat business in the future.

2 Wieland (Chapter 13) makes a rather different point that ethics needs economics and not just the other way around. Similarly, Bhide and Stevenson (1991) point out that trust and honesty would be worthless morally, if treachery did not pay.

3 The literature dealing with this and similar issues is vast; a good starting point is Marr and Raj (1983).

4 There are now over 500 courses on business ethics available in the USA alone (*The Economist*, 5 June 1993, p. 87).

REFERENCES

Axelrod, R. (1984) *The Evaluation of Cooperation*, New York: Basic Books.

Bhide, A. and Stevenson, H. (1991) 'Why be honest if honesty doesn't pay?', in *Ethics at Work*, Harvard Business Review Paperback, no. 90077, Harvard, Cambridge, MA.

Donaldson, T. (1989) *The Ethics of International Business*, New York: Oxford University Press.

Etzioni, A. (1988) *The Moral Dimension: Toward a New Economics*, New York: Free Press.

Frank, R. (1988) *Passions within Reason*. New York: Norton.

Frank, R., Gilovich, T. and Regan, D. (1993) 'Does studying economics inhibit cooperation?', *Journal of Economic Perspectives*, Spring.

Frith, R. (1978) *Themes in Economic Anthropology*, London: Tavistock.

Marr, W. and Raj, B. (eds) (1983) *How Economists Explain*, London: University Press of America.

Menezes, M. (1991) 'Ethical implications of product policy decisions', paper presented at the joint SASE and IAREP conference, Stockholm School of Economics.

Smith, N. C. and Quelch, J. (1993) *Ethics in Marketing*, Homewood, IL: Irwin.

Webley, P. and Wilson, R. (1989) 'Social relationships and the unacceptability of money as a gift', *Journal of Social Psychology*, 129, 85–91.

Index